United States Edition

2023 Year A

Workbook for **Lectors**, **Gospel Readers**, and **Proclaimers** of the **Word**®

Catherine Cory

Peter O'Leary

Stephen S. Wilbricht, CSC

LTP

LITURGY
TRAINING
PUBLICATIONS

CONTENTS

Ordinary Time

Excerpts from the English translation of the *Catechism of the Catholic Church* for use in the United States of America © 1994, United States Catholic Conference, Inc.—Libreria Editrice Vaticana. Used with permission. English translation of the *Catechism of the Catholic Church: Modifications from the Editio Typica* © 1997, United States Conference of Catholic Bishops—Libreria Editrice Vaticana.

Excerpts from *Nostra aetate* are taken from *Vatican Council II: Constitutions, Decrees, Declarations—The Basic Sixteen Documents*, edited by Austin Flannery, OP © 1996. Used with permission of Liturgical Press, Collegeville, Minnesota.

WORKBOOK FOR LECTORS, GOSPEL READERS, AND PROCLAIMERS OF THE WORD® 2023, United States Edition © 2022, Archdiocese of Chicago. All rights reserved.

Liturgy Training Publications, 3949 South Racine Avenue, Chicago, IL 60609, 800-933-1800, fax: 800-933-7094, orders@ltp.org, www.LTP.org.

Cover art: Barbara Simcoe

This book was edited by Christina N. Condyles. Christian Rocha was the production editor, Anna Manhart was the designer, and Kari Nicholls was the production artist.

Printed in the United States of America

ISBN: 978-1-61671-665-3
WL23

In accordance with c. 827, permission to publish was granted on May 4, 2022, by Most Rev. Robert G. Casey, Vicar General of the Archdiocese of Chicago. Permission to publish is an official declaration of ecclesiastical authority that the material is free from doctrinal and moral error. No legal responsibility is assumed by the grant of this permission.

MESSAGE AND PROCLAMATION

According to the *Catechism of the Catholic Church*, the liturgy is an "action" of the *whole Christ*, one that recapitulates the eternal drama in which "the Spirit and the Church enable us to participate whenever we celebrate the mystery of salvation in the sacraments" (1139). It is a celebration of the whole community: participative, connective, and joyful. Crucial to the celebration is the Liturgy of the Word, through which the Holy Spirit awakens faith, offering signs—in the lectionary and the book of the Gospels; in procession, incense, and candles; and in the place of proclamation at the ambo—and instruction—through the proclamation itself of the Word of God to the faithfully assembled. As the *Catechism* puts it, "The Spirit makes present and communicates the Father's work, fulfilled by the beloved Son" (1155).

To read the Word of God is an act of proclamation. What is being proclaimed? The faith itself. *Kerygma* is the Greek word for proclamation; it appears multiple times in the New Testament, in St. Paul's letters and in the Acts of the Apostles, for instance, to refer to both the act and the content of proclaiming the Good News. In Paul's First Letter to the Corinthians, he confesses, "When I came to you, brothers and sisters, *proclaiming* the mystery of God, I did not come with sublimity of words or of wisdom. For I resolved to know nothing while I was with you except Jesus Christ, and him crucified. I came to you in weakness and fear and much trembling, and my message and my *proclamation* were not with persuasive words of wisdom, but with a demonstration of spirit and power, so that your faith might rest not on human wisdom but on the power of God" (1 Corinthians 2:1–5; emphasis added). St. Paul doesn't want to be persuasive; rather, he wants his proclamation to reflect the spirit of God's power that fills him. When you proclaim, you reflect this spirit of the power of God.

In his apostolic exhortation *Evangelii gaudium*, Pope Francis insists that evangelization relies on a deeper understanding of proclamation. Francis refers to proclamation (he calls it *kerygma*, using the Greek term) as the "first announcement," whose essential confidence brings us deeper into the mystery of faith. (It is first because it is primary.) Francis is thinking of the importance of instruction when he writes that the formation of Christians is grounded upon the proclamation of the Good News and our ongoing immersion in it; this is the basis for catechesis at any level (165). But this catechesis, which means simply a ministry of the Word (*catechesis*, which means "instruction," comes from the Greek word *katechein*, which means "echo"), has an

---

The word of God constantly proclaimed in the Liturgy is always a living and effective word through the power of the Holy Spirit. It expresses the Father's love that never fails in its effectiveness toward us.

---

instructive social element you involve yourself in whenever you attend Mass and whenever you participate as a proclaimer of the Word. Francis insists that the Good News of Jesus Christ always calls us to be in community (177). Engagement with the community and deepening your life in that community are precisely what you accomplish as a lector, Gospel reader, and proclaimer of the Word.

Alpha and Omega

"I am the Alpha and the Omega." Thus says the Lord in the Revelation to John. Twice, in fact, in the opening chapter and in the twenty-second. It's one of the most potent and memorable phrases in all of the New Testament. Among its many interpretations and purposes, it might usefully serve as a motto for all proclaimers of the Word in the Church: lectors, deacons, and priests. One way to paraphrase this claim is that God is saying, "I am the alphabet."

Language, of course, is the medium you use as a lector, the instrument you play. Effective proclaiming is like effective piano playing. As every music teacher knows, some students are no good at playing the piano because they don't practice and don't have a good feel for the instrument. Other students are pretty good because they practice and have learned how to read music and to play the notes in the proper order. A few students are superb because they combine the discipline of practice with an intimate and immediately audible feel for the instrument, combining voicing, pauses, skill, and poise. Proclamation involves a similar skill set. Practice is important, but so is developing as good a feel for language—your instrument—as you can.

How do we develop a feel for language? One of the main ways that meaning is conveyed when modern English is spoken is through the interplay of syntax (the order of words in a sentence or phrase) and stress (the emphasis in speech that falls on one part of a word or phrase over another). Poetry is the literary form most attentive to syntax and stress. Poetry in English is qualitative, which means that it relies on the repetition of strong stresses in words to convey its patterns and meanings. This is called meter.

Scripture is organized by book, chapter, and verse. This system of organization is modern, coming into use when the *Geneva Bible* was published in 1560. Verses refer, in the main, to sentences, since most of Scripture is written in prose. Some verses are poetic verse, including especially the Psalms but also the prophetic books in the Old Testament. Nevertheless, because the use and study of verse in English involve descriptive terminology, it is helpful to think about proclaiming the Word as a lector, deacon, or priest in terms of reading poetry aloud.

There are five basic metrical units in English, the names for which are all borrowed from Greek. A metrical unit is a pattern of stressed (DA) and unstressed (da) syllables. The five basic units, with examples of words that follow each pattern, are

iamb—da-DA (Detroit);

trochee—DA-da (London);

anapest—da-da-DA (Tennessee);

dactyl—DA-da-da (Arkansas);

and spondee—DA-DA (New York).

There are other meters of course, but it's useful to have a sense of these five basic units when you are reading anything aloud, including Scripture, much of which, even in English translation, comes through as poetry.

You will note that the two longest of these metrical units have only three syllables. This means, practically speaking, that every two or three syllables, when you read something aloud, there should

> It is necessary that those who exercise the ministry of reader . . . be truly suited and carefully prepared, so that the faithful may develop a warm and living love for Sacred Scripture from listening to the sacred readings.

be a stress, an emphasis. Identifying these stresses does not exaggerate the sound of the phrase; instead, it enhances the phrase, highlighting its natural expressiveness.

Consider again, "I am the Alpha and the Omega." This statement, one of the boldest of all in the New Testament, doesn't require any exaggeration or intensification on your part beyond identifying where the stresses in this statement lie. First, in the personal pronoun. Second, in the first syllable of Alpha. And third, in the second syllable of Omega. You could write the statement out this way, using capital letters to emphasize the stresses:

I am the ALpha and the oMEGa.

That captures the stresses. However, it doesn't entirely capture the most effective pace for proclaiming this statement.

Thinking about metrical units in English, you can identify where the pauses in this statement might usefully lie. The pauses in your speaking set the pace. Every two or three syllables, when speaking aloud, there is an opportunity for a pause, even if it's only a slight hesitation that allows you to enhance the stresses. We can use this symbol | to indicate pauses, however slight, and rewrite the statement from Revelation this way:

I | am the ALpha | and | the oMEGa.

An alternative reading would eliminate the third pause:

I | am the ALpha | and the oMEGa.

In the first version, the line has four beats:

1) I; 2) am the ALpha; 3) and; 4) the oMEGa.

The second version has three beats:

1) I; 2) am the ALpha; 3) and the oMEGa.

The Sacred Scriptures, above all in their liturgical proclamation, are the source of life and strength.

In the first version, the third pause, after "and," allows you to emphasize the parallel being drawn between the beginning and the end in the Lord's statement. In the second version, you speed ever so noticeably quicker to Omega, which is the word in the verse imbuing it with ominous power.

Both versions are effective. Both, if you speak them aloud (as practice), can be suited to your speaking style. And both possible readings reinforce one of the most helpful strategies for effective proclaiming: read slowly enough that stresses and emphases can be heard by the congregation. A good rule of thumb, easy to remember, when reading anything aloud is:

Read twice as loud and at half the pace that you normally speak.

Most lectors will be reading into a microphone, which means you need not increase your volume in the way you would without a microphone. However, the rule of thumb above can serve as a reminder that you are reading in front of an audience, your congregation, and the more clearly you proclaim, the more likely it is that they will pay attention. Like a teacher coming into a classroom and raising their voice above the level of the din or a coach blowing a whistle to get the attention of the team, you can command the attention of your congregation by the pitch and volume of your voice. Don't be afraid to use it.

Likewise, read slowly. Depending on the architecture of your church, it's likely that your amplified voice will echo. Reading slowly allows your words to be heard and absorbed, rather than reflected and distorted.

Similarly, the more clearly you read, while paying attention to where the stresses lie in the passage from Scripture you are reading, the more intelligible and available your proclaiming will be. You do not need to act out any of the phrases by changing the pitch of your voice or feigning emotion. Scripture already contains all the drama and power required for its proper expression. You need merely to voice it.

"Less is more" might be a useful axiom for proclaiming, but you don't want to excuse yourself from the work of proclaiming, which requires your presence for maximum effect. Your presence includes your voice, which allows you to announce the Word of God, but also your attention, which shows you where the stresses and emphases in the passage you are proclaiming lie. Simone Weil, the twentieth-century activist and mystic, wrote, "Absolutely unmixed attention is prayer." The attention you bring to your proclaiming enables you then to pray the Word of God with your congregation.

Readings Old and New

The Liturgy of the Word typically consists of a reading from the Old Testament, a reading from the New Testament (often one of the letters of Paul), and a reading from the Gospels. In the case of Year A, which this workbook covers, almost all of the Gospel readings, with exceptions on some of the feasts, come from Matthew.

Gospel readings during Ordinary Time tend to go more or less in order. In Year A, they start from early in Matthew and work toward the Gospel's end. Readings on feast days, as well as during the seasons of Advent, Christmas, Lent, and Easter, are selected specifically for those Sundays and don't necessarily follow a sequential order. The first reading—again, typically from the Old Testament—is selected to harmonize with the Gospel reading.

The second reading—again, often from one of the letters of Paul, but not always—is more deliberately instructive. Usually, from week to week at Sunday Mass, you will notice that one Sunday's second reading picks up where the previous week's left off.

Each of these parts of Scripture can be proclaimed differently, with subtle but valuable effects. First readings tend to be more poetic than second readings. You can effectively infuse your first reading with forms of poetic attention, being mindful especially of pauses, but also of some of the other rhetorical features that make Scripture so rich. These include

anaphora, which is the use of the repetition of a word or phrase;

parallel structure, in which an entire phrase is repeated with slight variation;

the imperative voice, in which the speaker commands the audience to do something, usually to listen, to hear, and to heed; and

the power of questions, in which the speaker asks forceful questions not necessarily easy or comfortable to answer.

Each of these rhetorical features serves to enhance the power of the words and phrases in the reading.

Consider the first reading for the Twenty-Fourth Sunday in Ordinary Time, from the twenty-eighth chapter of Sirach. This reading is in the imperative voice, spoken directly to the listener, making stern but earnest pronouncements the speaker expects the listener to take to heart:

Forgive your neighbor's injustice;
then when you pray, your own sins
will be forgiven.
Could anyone nourish anger against another
and expect healing from the LORD?
Could anyone refuse mercy to another
like himself,
can he seek pardon for his own sins?
If one who is but flesh cherishes wrath,
who will forgive his sins?
(Sirach 28:2–5)

The whole reading relies on repeated parallel structures in which a claim or question is made in the first line and then advanced or fulfilled in the line immediately following. So "Forgive your neighbor's injustice" is followed by its completion, "then when you pray, your own sins will be forgiven." The three verses that are questions are similarly structured, with two of them making use of the anaphora of "Could anyone." And finally, as indicated above, the imperative voice is used, which augments the urgency of the advice being given. Recognizing these patterns can show you how best to proclaim these verses and where to lay the emphasis.

The Gospel for the Twenty-Fourth Sunday in Ordinary Time comes amid a series of Gospel readings from Matthew in which Jesus uses parables to instruct his listeners about discipleship and the kingdom of God. It connects to the reading from Sirach because it concerns forgiveness and the way we treat others. In response to Peter's question about how often he must forgive someone, Jesus shares a parable about forgiveness freely given and wrathfully taken back. A servant who owes his master a great sum of money is forgiven his debt, yet shortly after the servant refuses to show mercy to another servant who owes him money. The first servant is punished by the master for not extending the same mercy he was offered. Jesus concludes the parable by suggesting that this is how God in heaven will treat those who fail to be forgiving. Note how the mes-

---

God's word shows us what we should hope for with such a longing that in this changing world our hearts will be set on the place where our true joys lie.

---

sage of the first reading and the Gospel reinforce each other.

The second reading for the Twenty-Fourth Sunday in Ordinary Time offers a succinct and beautiful reading from the Letter to the Romans. It follows a long stretch of sequential (but not continuous) readings from Romans that begins on the Eleventh Sunday in Ordinary Time this year. With this reading, Paul's teachings from Romans are concluded for this liturgical cycle. The reading makes use of an especially vivid and pointed contrast between living and dying, and what it means to live and die for the Lord.

Where the first reading is often poetic, the second reading is typically instructive. It's also almost always a shorter reading. You should proclaim it as instruction. Read slowly, take your time presenting its argument, and emphasize its point, which will come in the last sentence or two of the reading.

First and second readings always conclude with the phrase "The Word of the Lord." Try to pause a moment before you read this conclusion. Likewise, don't rush through the phrase. It will blur, sounding like "Word Lord." Instead, break the phrase into two units, reading it like this: The WORD | of the LORD. It's effective to pause for two or three beats after you say this before stepping away from the ambo.

Preparation and Execution

It helps to practice. You should read through your assigned reading at least a few times, once silently to yourself to get its sense and two or three times aloud to get a feel for its rhythm and pace, as well as any unusual words, names, or place names. (The marginal pronunciation guides will help you with these.)

If you are assigned to proclaim the first reading, read the Gospel for that week as well. They will be connected in thematic ways. If you are assigned to proclaim the second reading, take a look at the previous week's second reading as well as the following week's to see where the second reading is coming from and where it is going. This will give you some context for the insights it contains.

For many of us, our main experience reading aloud comes from reading to children. Proclaiming Scripture is something different. When you practice reading aloud, it's better to read in as straightforward a way as possible than it is to try to dramatize your reading through inflection, pitch, or voicing in the way you might if you were reading something to a child. Scripture is unusually powerful in its expressiveness, symbolism, and language. If you read in a steady, evenly pitched, and articulate voice, its power will come through your reading. You will be during Mass the instrument of its power.

For many people, it can be a little intimidating to stand before a congregation and proclaim. You might find it helpful to place one of your index fingers in the margin of the lectionary to remind you of your place. You might also find it helpful to place your other hand on the ambo to steady yourself. This has the effect of giving you the appearance of an open posture.

As you read, try to look up from time to time and make eye contact. Choose faces in different places of the assembled congregation to focus on when you look up, sometimes close by, sometimes farther back, and sometimes from one side to the other. This simple gesture has an inclusive effect; you are not merely reading *to* the congregation; you are reading *for* it and *with* it. If you use your index finger to keep your place in the lectionary, you will not worry about getting lost whenever you look up.

That said, you are not performing. You don't need to smile unnecessarily, you don't need to emote beyond what the words themselves suggest, and you don't need somehow to exemplify the words in your comportment or your presentation. The words of Scripture are utterly endowed with power. You are the instrument to voice that power. A sincere and plainspoken proclamation will invariably convey that power to your fellow congregants.

In addition to the margin notes and pronunciation guides that accompany each reading, many words have been bolded to aid in your preparation for proclaiming the Word of God. In each reading, there are a handful of key terms that set the tone and characterize the instruction that the reading contains. Nevertheless, you will find that many more words are bolded than just these key terms. All of these bolded words are there as guides, or landmarks, for your proclamation. They give you a sense of where you are in the reading, and they serve to remind you how to measure your spoken expression while you are proclaiming. They are not meant to be overly stressed! Bolded words simply indicate the natural places where the stresses in a given phrase or sentence lie, as well as words and phrases that enhance the message of the reading. Sometimes this means that prepositions get some extra stress. (Consider: "**Through** him, **with** him, and **in** him . . .") At other times, it means that the proper names of prophets or the disciples or place names get emphasis. And at other times, it means otherwise ordinary words get stressed because the rhythm of the proclamation compels it. If you practice your reading and test your proclamation against these bolded words, you will have a clear guide for how to proceed through the reading in a way that enhances your natural powers of spoken expression without obliging you to exaggerate your vocal mannerisms as you proclaim. It is important to note, again, that Scripture is already full of power. Your ministry is in service of this Word of God. You don't need to add anything to that power for it to ring out to your assembly. Instead, pay attention to stresses and emphases, as indicated in the bolded texts, and remember to proclaim twice as loud and at half the pace that you normally speak.

Participation

For inspiration, consider these words by Pierre Teilhard de Chardin, from *The Divine Milieu*, his "essay on the interior life."

> We may, perhaps, imagine that the Creation was finished long ago. But that would be quite wrong. It continues still more magnificently, and in the highest zones of the world. *Omnis creatura adhuc ingemescit et parturit.* And we serve to complete it, even by the humblest work of our hands. That is, ultimately, the meaning and value of our acts. Owing to the inter-relation between matter, soul, and Christ, we lead part of the being which He desires back to God in whatever we do. With each one of our works, we labor—atomically, but no less really—to build the Pleroma; that is to say, to bring to Christ a little fulfillment. (Pierre Teilhard de Chardin, *The Divine Milieu*, ed. Bernard Wall [New York: Harper & Brothers, 1960], 31)

The Church is nourished spiritually at the twofold table of God's word and of the Eucharist: from the one it grows in wisdom and from the other in holiness.

For Teilhard, "Pleroma" means the mysterious fullness of creation. The Latin phrase, *omnis creatura adhuc ingemescit et parturit*, refers to Romans 8:22, "all creation is groaning in labor pains until now." We are still in the process of creation; whenever you participate in the Mass, you are adding to that work. And whenever you proclaim at Mass, you are helping, by the humblest work of your voice, to bring to Christ a little fulfillment.

Pull-out quotations throughout this article are from the introduction to the *Lectionary for Mass*.

Peter O'Leary

The Authors

Catherine Cory is professor emerita of theology at the University of St. Thomas in St. Paul, MN. She holds a doctorate in New Testament studies with subspecialties in Old Testament and early Church. Her research interests are in the Gospel of John and Revelation. She has edited and authored several books including *The Christian Theological Tradition, A Voyage through the New Testament*, and *The Book of Revelation* in the New Collegeville Bible Commentary series. In addition to her academic teaching at the undergraduate and graduate level, she enjoys doing adult education presentations at local parishes.

Peter O'Leary studied religion and literature at the Divinity School of the University of Chicago, where he received his doctorate. He has written several books of poetry, most recently, *Earth Is Best*, as well as two books of literary criticism, most recently, *Thick and Dazzling Darkness: Religious Poetry in a Secular Age*. He teaches at the School of the Art Institute of Chicago and lives with his family in Oak Park, IL.

Stephen S. Wilbricht, CSC, is associate professor in the Religious Studies and Theology Department at Stonehill College in Easton, MA. He holds a doctorate in sacred theology from the Catholic University of America in Washington, DC, and has served in two parishes in the Southwest. He is the author of several books, including *Baptismal Ecclesiology and the Order of Christian Funerals* (LTP, 2018), *The Role of the Priest in Christian Initiation* (LTP, 2017), and *Rehearsing God's Just Kingdom: The Eucharistic Vision of Mark Searle* (Liturgical Press, 2013). He is also a team member for LTP's Catechumeneon.

The authors' initials appear at the end of the Scripture commentaries.

An Option to Consider

The third edition of *The Roman Missal* encourages ministers of the Word to chant the introduction and conclusion to the readings ("A reading from . . . "; "The word of the Lord"). For those parishes wishing to use these chants, they are demonstrated in audio files that may be accessed either through the QR codes given here (with a smartphone) or through the URL indicated beneath the code. This URL is case sensitive, so be careful to distinguish between the letter l (lowercase L) and the numeral 1.

The first QR code contains the tones for the first reading in both a male and a female voice.

http://bit.ly/l2mjeG

The second QR code contains the tones for the second reading in both a male and a female voice.

http://bit.ly/krwEYy

The third QR code contains the simple tone for the Gospel.

http://bit.ly/iZZvSg

The fourth QR code contains the solemn tone for the Gospel.

http://bit.ly/lwf6Hh

A fuller explanation of this practice, along with musical notation for the chants, is provided in a downloadable PDF file found under the supplement tab on the product's webpage: http://www.ltp.org /products/details /WL23.

Pronunciation Key

bait = bayt	thin = thin
cat = kat	vision = VIZH*n
sang = sang	ship = ship
father = FAH-ther	sir = ser
care = kayr	gloat = gloht
paw = paw	cot = kot
jar = jahr	noise = noyz
easy = EE-zee	poison = POY-z*n
her = her	plow = plow
let = let	although = ahl-THOH
queen = kween	church = cherch
delude = deh-LOOD	fun = fuhn
when = hwen	fur = fer
ice = īs	flute = floot
if = if	foot = foot
finesse = fih-NES	

Shorter Readings

In the Scripture readings reproduced in this book, shorter readings are indicated by brackets and a citation given at the end of the reading.

FIRST SUNDAY OF ADVENT

LECTIONARY #1

READING I   Isaiah 2:1–5

A reading from the Book of the Prophet Isaiah

> **This** is what **Isaiah**, son of **Amoz**,
>   **saw** concerning **Judah** and **Jerusalem**.
>   In **days** to **come**,
> the **mountain** of the LORD's **house**
>   shall be **established** as the **highest mountain**
>   and **raised** above the **hills**.
> All **nations** shall stream **toward** it;
>   many **peoples** shall come and **say**:
> "**Come**, let us **climb** the LORD's **mountain**,
>   to the **house** of the **God** of **Jacob**,
> that he may **instruct** us in his **ways**,
>   and we may **walk** in his **paths**."
> For from **Zion** shall go forth **instruction**,
>   and the word of the **Lord** from **Jerusalem**.
> He shall **judge** between the **nations**,
>   and impose **terms** on many **peoples**.
> They shall beat their **swords** into **plowshares**
>   and their **spears** into **pruning hooks**;
> **one nation** shall not **raise** the **sword** against **another**,
>   nor shall they **train** for **war again**.
> O **house** of **Jacob**, come,
>   let us **walk** in the **light** of the LORD!

Isaiah = ī-ZAY-uh

Amoz = AY-muhz

A rhythmical, forceful, and poetic reading.

Judah = JOO-duh

At "Come," the forcefulness of the reading intensifies. Raise your voice ever so slightly.

Zion = zī-uhn or zī-ahn

Emphasis on "swords" and "plowshares"; "spears" and "pruning hooks."

READING I Isaiah's role as prophet is to be interpreted in light of the Babylonian Exile, which spanned roughly the years 586 BC to 539 BC. Many of the exiled Israelites who had witnessed the destruction of Jerusalem were still alive when Isaiah tried to call the people back to their land. This was an unenviable task, as many of the Israelites had come to discover peace and prosperity in Babylon. What within the rubble of a destroyed Jerusalem could possibly entice them to return?

Isaiah's prophecy responds to this dilemma by proclaiming that, "in days to come," Jerusalem will be raised higher than any other nation on earth. It will be the envy of every nation, as all peoples will "stream toward it." Although the timeframe suggested by the words "in days to come" points to an eschatological reality, there is an urgency about Isaiah's vision. A return to the remnants of Jerusalem will offer the Israelites an opportunity to be instructed in the way of the Lord.

The instruction that the Lord will provide is not simply for the comfort and security of Israel as a restored nation. Instead, it is meant to radiate outwards to all the nations. Israel will know its redemption not only by taking possession of the land once more but also by being an example of God's justice that will turn "swords into plowshares" and "spears into pruning hooks." Instead of focusing on war, the nations of this world will learn to walk in the Lord's light. Thus, the prophecy of Isaiah is designed to make the restored nation of Israel a prophet itself.

READING II In his correspondence with the Church in Rome, Paul uses a variety of images to communicate

For meditation and context:

RESPONSORIAL PSALM   Psalm 122:1–2, 3–4, 4–5, 6–7, 8–9

R. Let us go rejoicing to the house of the Lord.

I rejoiced because they said to me,
  "We will go up to the house of the LORD."
And now we have set foot
  within your gates, O Jerusalem.

Jerusalem, built as a city
  with compact unity.
To it the tribes go up,
  the tribes of the LORD.

According to the decree for Israel,
  to give thanks to the name of the LORD.
In it are set up judgment seats,
  seats for the house of David.

Pray for the peace of Jerusalem!
  May those who love you prosper!
May peace be within your walls,
  prosperity in your buildings.

Because of my brothers and friends
  I will say, "Peace be within you!"
Because of the house of the LORD, our God,
  I will pray for your good.

READING II   Romans 13:11–14

A reading from the Letter of Saint Paul to the Romans

This reading is in the form of a personal address. Familiarity is what makes it forceful.

Brothers and **sisters**:
You **know** the **time**;
  it is the **hour now** for you to **awake** from **sleep**.
For our **salvation** is nearer **now** than when we **first** believed;
  the **night** is **advanced**, the **day** is at **hand**.

Note the parallels: "off" and "darkness"; "on" and "light."

Let us then throw **off** the works of **darkness**
  and put **on** the armor of **light**;
  let us **conduct** ourselves **properly** as in the **day**,
  not in **orgies** and **drunkenness**,

Note the pairings. Give them emphasis.

  not in **promiscuity** and **lust**,
  not in **rivalry** and **jealousy**.
But put on the **Lord Jesus Christ**,
  and make **no** provision for the **desires** of the **flesh**.

the importance of making "watchfulness" a foundational attitude of Christianity. These images include awakening from sleep, the contrast between night and day, the "armor of light," and various immoral activities. Paul's challenge for Christians to live fully awaken in this world and not to involve themselves in lewd conduct stems from the belief that the parousia is near. Therefore, everyone is to live as though *this* is the hour of Christ's victorious return.

The images Paul uses to communicate the need for vigilance first suggest that such waiting is comparable to engaging in

battle with an enemy. The "armor of light" is necessary to keep believers awake and ready to defend themselves from the temptations of the world. Note that Paul addresses the community as a whole, saying "let us" cast off evil deeds, rather than directly challenging individuals (as in, "you" cast off sin). The work to remain alert and ready for the coming of the Lord is that of the Church as a whole.

After shocking his readers with the words chosen to illustrate the way of immorality—and therefore activities of the night ("works of darkness")—the reading

ends with Paul's command to recognize a Christian's union with Christ. The one who has been baptized has been clothed in the robe of salvation and already lives in the time of promised salvation. Nevertheless, the mandate to "put on the Lord Jesus Christ" entails a daily act of clothing oneself, of making the conscious decision to resist the temptations of this world. The way of following the Lord Jesus in this life requires a constant putting to death fleshly desires. For Paul, the desire is as sinful as the action itself.

Jesus uses an example from Scripture to speak about the present. This creates a vivid ambience.

Note the parallels and repetitions; "two men" to "two women" and "one will be taken" to "one will be left."

Emphasis on "awake," but don't overdo it.

Note the repetition, reinforcing the message.

GOSPEL　Matthew 24:37–44

A reading from the holy Gospel according to Matthew

Jesus said to his **disciples**:
"As it **was** in the days of **Noah**,
　　so it will **be** at the **coming** of the **Son** of **Man**.
In **those days** before the **flood**,
　　they were **eating** and **drinking**,
　　marrying and **giving** in **marriage**,
　　up to the **day** that **Noah** entered the **ark**.
They did not **know** until the **flood came** and **carried** them
　　all **away**.
So will it be **also** at the **coming** of the **Son** of **Man**.
Two men will be **out** in the **field**;
　　one will be **taken**, and **one** will be **left**.
Two women will be **grinding** at the **mill**;
　　one will be **taken**, and **one** will be **left**.
Therefore, stay **awake**!
For you do not **know** on which **day** your **Lord** will **come**.
Be **sure** of **this**: if the **master** of the **house**
　　had known the **hour** of **night** when the **thief** was **coming**,
　　he would have stayed **awake**
　　and not let his **house** be broken **into**.
So too, you also must be **prepared**,
　　for at an **hour** you do not **expect**, the **Son** of **Man** will **come**."

TO KEEP IN MIND
The words in bold are suggestions for ways to express the meaning of the reading. Consider using them as you practice the reading, then choose to stress them or to find your own way of proclaiming.

GOSPEL Today's Gospel passage opens with the kind of behaviors that Paul, in his letter to the Romans, noted distract Christians from focusing on the parousia. Matthew refers to the time of Noah, when people ignored the call to repentance and continued with their dissolute ways, being focused on eating and drinking and entering into marriage. As a result, they were caught off guard when the flood came and destroyed the face of the earth.

Matthew likens this scene from Noah's day to the present age, as they wait for "the coming of the Son of Man." Unlike the story of Noah, in which all creation was treated the same, Matthew's depiction of the day of the Lord's return suggests the imposition of a judgment. This judgment is one that cannot be foreknown: one out of two men will survive, one out of two women will survive. The only means of survival, implied by Matthew, is the posture of staying awake. The one who is prepared is the one judged fit for God's reign.

Putting this Gospel in context with today's second reading, the theme of staying awake for the Lord is a clear connecting strand. When we consider the Gospel reading in light of Isaiah's prophecy in the first reading, a different theme appears to be emphasized, namely that of vocation. Just as Israel's return to Jerusalem testifies to the world of God's mighty judgment that will impose peace on all the peoples of the earth, so does the Gospel suggest that vigilance for the Lord's return is a commitment undertaken by true disciples. Our responsibility as followers of Christ is not to know *how* the Lord will judge but rather to be ready for that judgment at any hour. S.W.

SECOND SUNDAY
OF ADVENT

LECTIONARY #4

READING I   Isaiah 11:1–10

A reading from the Book of the Prophet Isaiah

Isaiah = ī-ZAY-uh

Jesse = JES-ee
The tone of this potent reading is hopeful.

Though not emphasized rhythmically, note how often "shall" is used in this reading. Let this word—and the hopeful, future tense in which it is set—guide your proclamation.

> On **that** day, a **shoot** shall sprout from the **stump** of **Jesse**,
>   and from his **roots** a **bud** shall **blossom**.
> The **spirit** of the LORD shall rest **upon** him:
>   a spirit of **wisdom** and of **understanding**,
> a spirit of **counsel** and of **strength**,
>   a spirit of **knowledge** and of **fear** of the LORD,
>   and his **delight** shall be the **fear** of the LORD.
> Not by **appearance** shall he **judge**,
>   nor by **hearsay** shall he **decide**,
> but he shall **judge** the **poor** with **justice**,
>   and **decide aright** for the **land's afflicted**.
> He shall **strike** the **ruthless** with the **rod** of his **mouth**,
>   and with the **breath** of his **lips** he shall **slay** the **wicked**.
> **Justice** shall be the **band** around his **waist**,
>   and **faithfulness** a **belt** upon his **hips**.
> Then the **wolf** shall be a **guest** of the **lamb**,
>   and the **leopard** shall lie **down** with the **kid**;
> the **calf** and the young **lion** shall browse **together**,
>   with a little **child** to **guide** them.

The images of animals help to focus the reading, making it vivid.

READING I Ancient Israelite theology bases the coming of the messiah upon three events. First, the anointed one will come from the line of David. Second, this righteous king will establish justice in the land. Finally, all of creation will be restored to the peace found in the original garden of Eden. In essence, the messianic age will see the establishment of right relationship on earth: right relationship among humans, between humans and God, and within the entire sweep of living things. All creatures will live in the harmony God intended for

his creation when he spoke his word and brought life into being.

"The stump of Jesse" that Isaiah refers to in the opening line reveals the present state of the ruling institution in Israel. For too many generations, Israel has known corrupt and self-seeking kings who have proven themselves unfaithful. But God promises to renew this kingship by sending his Spirit, who will inspire right judgment (counsel, strength, knowledge) and will ensure the king's proper reverence of God (fear of the Lord).

Unlike the wicked and unfaithful kings of recent generations, the spirit-filled king will execute justice throughout the land. This leader will act swiftly to overturn past sins. The poor and the afflicted will receive special attention, while the ruthless and the wicked shall be struck down. This is a king who will not have to use the sword to punish the unjust; rather, his words alone will restore justice. His entire strength will come from his worldview of justice and faithfulness.

The **cow** and the **bear** shall be **neighbors**,
    together their **young** shall **rest**;
    the **lion** shall eat **hay** like the **ox**.
The **baby** shall **play** by the **cobra's den**,
    and the **child** lay his **hand** on the **adder's lair**.
There shall be **no harm** or **ruin** on **all** my holy **mountain**;
    for the **earth** shall be **filled** with **knowledge** of the Lord,
    as **water** covers the **sea**.
On t**hat day**, the root of **Jesse**,
    set **up** as a **signal** for the **nations**,
the **Gentiles** shall seek **out**,
    for his **dwelling** shall be **glorious**.

Emphasis on "no harm."

Gentiles = JEN-tĭls

Don't overdo the emphasis on "glorious."

For meditation and context:

TO KEEP IN MIND

Read the Scripture passage and its commentary in Workbook. Then read it from your Bible, including what comes before and after it, so that you understand the context.

RESPONSORIAL PSALM Psalm 72:1–2, 7–8, 12–13, 17 (7)

R. Justice shall flourish in his time, and fullness of peace forever.

O God, with your judgment endow the king,
    and with your justice, the king's son;
he shall govern your people with justice
    and your afflicted ones with judgment.

Justice shall flower in his days,
    and profound peace, till the moon
    be no more.
May he rule from sea to sea,
    and from the River to the ends
    of the earth.

For he shall rescue the poor when
    he cries out,
    and the afflicted when he has no one
    to help him.
He shall have pity for the lowly and the poor;
    the lives of the poor he shall save.

May his name be blessed forever;
    as long as the sun his name shall remain.
In him shall all the tribes of the earth
    be blessed;
    all the nations shall proclaim
    his happiness.

Finally, this chosen envoy of God will not only restore right relationship within Judea, but he will end wars and discord among every faction on earth. No more will the world be guided by fear of others and by predatory relationships. The curse brought about by the serpent's sin in the garden of Eden (Genesis 2:19) will come to an end as "the calf and the young lion shall browse together." The kingdom of God is founded upon a just order in which no creature competes with another for survival. Instead of functioning according to competition, God's kingdom manifests itself in selfless cooperation. The passage ends with the reminder that "the root of Jesse," this just king, will be a sign for all the nations; God's kingdom of right relationship is to extend through all the world.

READING II Chapter 15 of Paul's Letter to the Romans aims at replacing dissention within the community with an attitude of harmony. He speaks not merely of Christlike hospitality but of the way of mercy. The problem the Roman community faces is the divide between the circumcised and the uncircumcised and the debate as to whether or not circumcision is necessary to become a follower of Christ. This was a community composed of both Jewish and Gentile members. How were they to follow the Christian way with different ethnic practices?

For Paul, the answer lies in "endurance" and through "the encouragement of the Scriptures." The Word of God is filled with examples of divine patience, and it is only fitting that communities discover hope in this Word. Paul suggests that fidelity to the Word will yield a sense of true unity by which the community thinks in harmony

READING II   Romans 15:4–9

A reading from the Letter of Saint Paul to the Romans

Brothers and sisters:
Whatever was written previously was written
    for our instruction,
      that by endurance and by the encouragement of the Scriptures
      we might have hope.
May the God of endurance and encouragement
    grant you to think in harmony with one another,
    in keeping with Christ Jesus,
    that with one accord you may with one voice
    glorify the God and Father of our Lord Jesus Christ.

Welcome one another, then, as Christ welcomed you,
    for the glory of God.
For I say that Christ became a minister of the circumcised
    to show God's truthfulness,
    to confirm the promises of the patriarchs,
    but so that the Gentiles might glorify God for his mercy.
As it is written:
    Therefore, I will praise you among the Gentiles
      and sing praises to your name.

The tone of this reading is hopeful. "May" indicates that Paul is making a petition.

"Welcome" redirects the hope to Paul's audience.
circumcised = SER-kuhm-sīz*d

patriarchs = PAY-tree-ahrks
Gentiles = JEN-tīls
Scripture's authority emphasizes the hope.

GOSPEL   Matthew 3:1–12

A reading from the holy Gospel according to Matthew

John the Baptist appeared, preaching in the desert of Judea
    and saying, "Repent, for the kingdom of heaven is at hand!"
It was of him that the prophet Isaiah had spoken when he said:
    A voice of one crying out in the desert,
    Prepare *the way of the Lord,*
      make straight his paths.

Judea = joo-DEE-uh or joo-DAY-uh
A very vivid story is told in this Gospel reading.
Isaiah = ī-ZAY-uh

and speaks with one voice. It is this harmony that makes for true worship; God's name cannot be glorified if people's hearts are torn apart in discord.

The final portion of this passage alludes to the core problem that separates the community in Rome, namely the status of those members who have not been baptized. Paul suggests that a spirit of welcome is necessary in order to overcome such a division. Furthermore, he writes that Christ came to those who were already circumcised as a sign of God's fidelity to the people of the covenant, but he also has a plan to include the Gentiles according to his gift of mercy. What Paul is saying here is that the Romans, and in fact all of the Gentiles, are not an afterthought in God's mighty plan of salvation but are very much part of the reason for which God sent his Son into the world. Thus, Paul cites Psalm 18:50 as proof: "I will praise you among the Gentiles / and sing praises to your name."

GOSPEL In the layout of Matthew's Gospel, the figure of John the Baptist serves as a bridge between the infancy narrative and the inauguration of Jesus' public ministry. While it is clear that John's ministry was one of calling Israel to repentance and to a baptism that would mark their restored allegiance to God and the coming of the kingdom of heaven, at some point, John became acutely aware that his cousin, Jesus, would play a particularly important role in heralding God's plan of salvation. In other words, while John's preaching did not initially point to Jesus, he became convinced that Jesus is God's revelation.

No matter when John came to believe in the power of Jesus' ministry, it is clear

Slight pause between "belt" and "around."

Slight pause between "time" and "Jerusalem."

Pharisees = FAYR-uh-seez
Sadducees = SAD-yoo-seez
Emphasis on "brood" and "vipers."

Emphasis on the pronouns as this reading concludes, especially as John the Baptist switches from first to third person.

Slight pause between "up" and "children."

Emphasis on the pronouns as this reading concludes, especially as John the Baptist switches from first to third person.

John wore **clothing** made of **camel's hair**
    and had a **leather belt around** his **waist**.
His **food** was **locusts** and **wild honey**.
At **that time Jerusalem**, all **Judea**,
    and the **whole region** around the **Jordan**
    were going **out** to him
    and were being **baptized** by him in the **Jordan River**
    as they **acknowledged** their **sins**.

When he saw **many** of the **Pharisees** and **Sadducees**
    coming to his **baptism**, he said to them, "You **brood** of **vipers**!
Who **warned** you to **flee** from the **coming wrath**?
Produce **good fruit** as **evidence** of your **repentance**.
And do not **presume** to say to **yourselves**,
    'We have **Abraham** as our **father**.'
For I **tell you**,
    God can **raise up children** to **Abraham** from these **stones**.
Even now the **ax** lies at the **root** of the **trees**.
Therefore every **tree** that does not bear **good fruit**
    will be cut **down** and **thrown** into the **fire**.
I am baptizing you with **water**, for **repentance**,
    but the **one** who is coming **after** me is **mightier** than **I**.
I am not **worthy** to **carry** his **sandals**.
He will baptize you with the **Holy Spirit** and **fire**.
His **winnowing fan** is in his **hand**.
He will **clear** his **threshing** floor
    and **gather** his **wheat** into his **barn**,
    but the **chaff** he will **burn** with **unquenchable fire**."

that Matthew wishes to cast John in the role of a subordinate. It is likely that Matthew wants the reader to see John as a radical outlier—He wears camel hair clothing and eats wild locusts as his diet. Thus, while John the Baptist is the precursor of the Lord, there ought to be no mistake that John is to remain always in the shadow of Jesus.

Interestingly, John attacks two major power players that will later criticize the actions of Jesus, namely the Pharisees and the Sadducees. The Pharisees are best known as strict keepers of the Mosaic law, while the Sadducees represented the priestly class and thus the work of the Temple. Here, in the context of his summoning an attitude of repentance on the part of the people, John uses them as examples of hypocrisy that will surely not give way to the conversion he is calling for. John suggests that even if they are unable to be transformed by the authority of his preaching and ministry of baptism, then they ought to prepare for the power and authority they will face in the one who is to come after him. Thus, the role that John the Baptist plays of bridging the birth of Jesus with his ministry is not simply one of a polite introduction, but rather, his words leave no doubt that the words and work of Jesus will be nothing like the world has ever seen before. Jesus baptizing "with the Holy Spirit and fire" and his figurative clearing of the threshing floor will serve to transform all opposed to the coming of God's kingdom. S.W.

THE IMMACULATE CONCEPTION OF THE BLESSED VIRGIN MARY

LECTIONARY #689

READING I   Genesis 3:9–15, 20

A reading from the Book of Genesis

Genesis = JEN-uh-sihs

This reading contains some of the conclusions of one of the foundational narratives of our faith. Because it is a very familiar story, slow your recitation slightly to emphasize its richness.

After the man, **Adam**, had **eaten** of the **tree**,
  the Lord God **called** to the man and **asked** him,
    "Where are you?"
He answered, "I **heard** you in the **garden**;
  but I was **afraid**, because I was **naked**,
  so I **hid myself**."
Then he asked, "Who **told** you that you were **naked**?
You have **eaten**, then,
  from the **tree** of which I had **forbidden** you to **eat**!"
The man replied, "The **woman** whom you **put here** with me—
  she **gave me fruit** from the **tree**, and so I **ate** it."
The Lord God then asked the **woman**,
  "Why did you **do** such a **thing**?"
The woman answered, "The **serpent tricked me** into it,
    so I **ate** it."

The shifting of blame from Adam to Eve and then from Eve to the serpent is crucial to the reading's drama. You can locate this shift in the repetition of the word "woman."

Then the Lord God said to the **serpent**:
  "**Because** you have done this, you shall be **banned**
    from all the **animals**
    and from all the **wild creatures**;
  on your **belly** shall you **crawl**,
    and **dirt** shall you **eat**
    all the **days** of your **life**.

Here, the scorn is heaped on the serpent. The punishment God metes out is as cruel as it is deserved.

READING I | Today's reading from Genesis, which focuses on the primeval account of the origins of human sinfulness, opens with God strolling through his beautiful garden. Certainly, some time has passed since Adam and Eve committed their sin of disobedience, since Adam exhibits both fear and shame for being naked. When God begins to question Adam, it is important to notice how the blame is passed from Adam to the woman to the serpent. Thus, in addition to fear and shame the sin of denial of responsibility, or

the failure to own up to one's mistakes, is revealed in the passing of blame.

With the sins committed in Eden comes the introduction of judgment into the world. Now God must decide a punishment according to participation in the sin. The author of Genesis is very careful to pair the punishment with the life experience of each sinner. God begins by punishing the snake and separating it from all other animals by making it crawl on its belly; it is therefore cursed by a perpetual posture of humility, unable to stand aright. The serpent will no longer hold a persuasive influ-

ence over God's human creatures. Between the serpent and the human there will now be "enmity." This state of discord will continue throughout all subsequent generations of the woman's offspring, meaning that humans forever more will have to contend with the ugliness of sin in their lives.

Today's reading omits the verses in which God doles out punishments for both Adam and Eve (Genesis 3:16–19). God turns first to the woman and punishes her with intense pain in childbearing as well as having to toil with domination imposed by a husband (Genesis 3:16). Finally, God speaks

enmity = EN-mih-tee = mutual hatred

> I will put **enmity** between **you** and the **woman**,
>   and between your **offspring** and hers;
> he will **strike** at your **head**,
>   while you **strike** at his **heel**."
>
> The man called his wife **Eve**,
>   because she became the **mother** of **all** the **living**.

The reading ends with Eve being named. The shift from "woman" to "Eve" feels significant. Convey this in your reading.

For meditation and context:

RESPONSORIAL PSALM   Psalm 98:1, 2–3ab, 3cd–4 (1)

R. Sing to the Lord a new song, for he has done marvelous deeds.

Sing to the LORD a new song,
  for he has done wondrous deeds;
His right hand has won victory for him,
  his holy arm.

The LORD has made his salvation known:
  in the sight of the nations he has
    revealed his justice.
He has remembered his kindness and
  his faithfulness
  toward the house of Israel.

All the ends of the earth have seen
  the salvation by our God.
Sing joyfully to the LORD, all you lands;
  break into song; sing praise.

READING II   Ephesians 1:3–6, 11–12

A reading from the Letter of Saint Paul to the Ephesians

Ephesians = ee-FEE-zhuhnz

Blessed = BLES-uhd
blessed = blesd
An exhortatory reading. Notice the three divisions: "Blessed be the God and Father . . . ," "In love he destined us . . . ," and "In him we were also chosen." Use these divisions to organize your reading.

Slight emphasis on "praise," "glory," and "grace."

Brothers and sisters:
Blessed be the **God** and **Father** of our **Lord** Jesus Christ,
  who has **blessed** us in Christ
  with e**very spiritual blessing** in the **heavens**,
    as he chose us **in him**, before the **foundation** of the **world**,
    to be **holy** and without **blemish** before him.
In **love** he **destined us** for **adoption** to himself
    through **Jesus** Christ,
  in **accord** with the **favor** of his will,
  for the **praise** of the **glory** of his **grace**
  that he **granted** us in the **beloved**. »

to Adam and bestows upon him the punishment of having to struggle with the land in order to produce food to eat (Genesis 3:17–19). The story ends on a positive note, as punishment gives way to hope for new life. Adam names the woman Eve because she will be the "mother of all the living." Thus, even though sin has entered the world and has marred the beauty of perfection with the sins of disobedience, fear, shame, and denial, God will not abandon his creation —life will triumph over sin.

READING II   The Letter to the Ephesians is one of several documents that is said to have been written by Paul but most likely was penned by one of his disciples ten or so years after his death. Unlike many of the letters in which Paul writes to a Christian community to challenge their behavior, the Letter to the Ephesians is constructed to champion several important facets of Christian doctrine.

In this particular portion of Ephesians, the subject matter revolves around the topic of "predestination." The author states that God "chose us in him [Christ], before the foundation of the world." The intention of this choice is so that we may live lives of holiness. Furthermore, the author suggests that it is not simply a predetermined choice for us to stand before God without stain, but rather, in time God is able to exercise his love by uniting us with his Son. In other words, God's love for us is bestowed as an act of mercy, which we can acknowledge by giving him all praise and glory. Paul challenges the Ephesians to recognize the abundance of God's grace that has been bestowed upon them through their faith in Christ. While they have been chosen, they

This is Paul's point.

You are assuring the assembly of this first hope.

In **him** we were also **chosen**,
    destined in accord with the **purpose** of the One
    who **accomplishes** all things according to the **intention**
      of his **will**,
    so that we might **exist** for the **praise** of his **glory**,
    we who **first hoped** in Christ.

GOSPEL   Luke 1:26–38

A reading from the holy Gospel according to Luke

A narrative reading of one of the most solemn passages in the Gospels, which is also one of the most frequently depicted by artists through the centuries. It's very easy to visualize as a result. Treat it like a pageant.

Because these words are so familiar from prayer, they can have a new life in the context of this reading.

"Most High" and "no end" share a rhythmical and thematic echo.

The **angel Gabriel** was **sent** from God
    to a **town** of **Galilee** called **Nazareth**,
    to a **virgin betrothed** to a man named **Joseph**,
    of the **house** of David,
    and the **virgin's name** was Mary.
And coming to her, he said,
    "**Hail**, **full** of **grace**! The **Lord** is with **you**."
But she was **greatly troubled** at what was **said**
    and **pondered** what sort of **greeting** this might be.
Then the **angel** said to her,
    "**Do not** be **afraid**, Mary,
    for you have found **favor** with God.
Behold, you will **conceive** in your womb and **bear** a son,
    and you shall **name him** Jesus.
He will be **great** and will be called **Son** of the **Most High**,
    and the **Lord God** will give him the **throne**
      of David his **father**,
    and he will **rule over** the house of **Jacob forever**,
    and of his **Kingdom** there will be **no end**."
But **Mary** said to the **angel**,
    "How can this **be**,
    since I have **no relations** with a **man**?"

---

must respond with their gift of constant thanksgiving.

As we celebrate the solemnity of the Immaculate Conception, it is important to reflect upon the abundance of grace that God poured upon Mary, whom he predestined to be the mother of his Son. The Letter to the Ephesians suggests that those chosen in Christ are destined to keep God's will and thereby "exist for the praise of his glory." Our purpose as disciples is to radiate the goodness of God every moment of the day. We are invited to contemplate the mystery of Mary's Immaculate Conception

because in her we see the perfect example of one who exists for nothing other than the praise of God's glory. In the Gospel passage that follows, the angel Gabriel proclaims Mary to be "full of grace." Although we, unlike Mary, are born into this world with the stain of original sin and struggle to free ourselves of temptation and sin each day, we are also called to discover God's grace in every moment of our lives.

GOSPEL | Both the Gospel of Matthew and the Gospel of Luke contain an infancy narrative that begins

with signs of Jesus' conception. With that said, Matthew and Luke intend to use the signs of the Lord's birth for different purposes. Matthew emphasizes the role of Joseph and his righteousness in preparing for Jesus' birth, whereas in Luke, this role is transferred to Mary. She is the one who receives a message from the angel and then runs to her cousin Elizabeth to announce to her all of the wonders that God has done for her.

The Gospel passage we read today is Luke's account of the annunciation, when the angel Gabriel appears to Mary and

This is the good news that Gabriel delivers to Mary.

And the **angel** said to her in **reply**,
 "The **Holy Spirit** will **come upon** you,
 and the **power** of the **Most High** will over**shadow** you.
Therefore the **child** to be **born**
 will be called **holy**, the **Son** of **God**.
And **behold**, Elizabeth, your relative,
 has **also conceived** a son in her old age,
 and this is the **sixth month** for her who was called **barren**;
 for **nothing** will be **impossible** for God."
Mary said, "**Behold**, I am the **handmaid** of the **Lord**.
May it be **done** to **me** according to **your word**."
Then the **angel departed** from her.

Mary's declaration defines the role of all believers, including the Church.

TO KEEP IN MIND
Pause after you announce the book of the Bible at the beginning of the reading. Pause again after the reading, before you proclaim the concluding statement ("The Word of the Lord" or "The Gospel of the Lord").

reveals God's plan for her. We are led to ponder the grace of Mary's sinlessness by focusing on her humble response to the angel: "Behold, I am the handmaid of the Lord. May it be done to me according to your word." Mary is the new Eve who is given the fullness of God's grace. However, unlike Eve, Mary remains obedient to God's voice throughout her life. Mary deserved to be fearful at what the angel spoke to her, but she listened and obeyed.

While it is important to focus on Mary's obedience, this passage also invites us to reflect upon the nature of God. Why does God choose Mary to be the mother of his Son? God chooses a lowly virgin peasant girl to be the one who will bear the most precious gift of God's love, his very Son. If God had wanted, God could have been born among us in a very powerful and successful family. Or he could have manifested his divinity in a fully-grown human person. Instead, his grace rested fully upon one who had no standing within her community. As a faithful Jewish girl, Mary was attuned to the working of God within her life. She listened carefully to God's will. Mary spent her life discerning his move-

ment in her life and was well prepared to offer herself as the chosen ark for God's incarnation. Like Mary, we are invited to cooperate fully with God's will, giving our entire lives over in service of his kingdom. S.W.

THIRD SUNDAY
OF ADVENT

LECTIONARY #7

READING I   Isaiah 35:1–6a, 10

A reading from the Book of the Prophet Isaiah

Isaiah = ī-ZAY-uh

The tone of this reading is set by the early repetitions of "rejoice" and "bloom."

Lebanon = LEB-uh-nuhn
Carmel = KAHR-m*l
Sharon = SHAYR-uhn

Note the shift into imperatives: "strengthen," "make," and "say."

Slight pause between "lame" and "leap."

The **desert** and the **parched land** will **exult**;
  the **steppe** will **rejoice** and **bloom**.
They will **bloom** with abundant **flowers**,
  and **rejoice** with joyful **song**.
The **glory** of **Lebanon** will be **given** to them,
  the **splendor** of **Carmel** and **Sharon**;
they will **see** the **glory** of the **LORD**,
  the **splendor** of our **God**.
Strengthen the **hands** that are **feeble**,
  make **firm** the **knees** that are **weak**,
say to **those** whose **hearts** are **frightened**:
  Be **strong**, fear **not**!
Here is your **God**,
  he **comes** with **vindication**;
with **divine recompense**
  he **comes** to **save** you.
Then will the **eyes** of the **blind** be **opened**,
  the **ears** of the **deaf** be **cleared**;
then will the **lame leap** like a **stag**,
  then the **tongue** of the **mute** will **sing**.

READING I The thirty-fifth chapter of the Book of Isaiah serves as something of a bridge between First and Second Isaiah. (Scholars typically divide the Book of Isaiah into three main parts, First, Second, and Third Isaiah.) While it continues much of the deliverance material found in the first part of Isaiah, the chapter introduces a theme that will be significant throughout Second Isaiah, namely, the people's journey home after exile. What is portrayed here is a world transformed. Isaiah's prophecy presents a series of grand reversals, images that demonstrate God's power

to rejuvenate and fully restore his deflated people.

The desert, through which the people sojourn on their way back to Judea, has been made abundantly beautiful with foliage and the joyful song of the pilgrims. As the Israelites take possession of the land once again, the cities of Lebanon, Carmel, and Sharon radiate God's glory. This stands in stark contrast to Isaiah's earlier description, in which he referred to Lebanon as withering and Sharon as a wasteland (see Isaiah 33:9).

Such images of renewal will certainly make strong hands that are weak and hearts that are frightened. Isaiah calls out to the people as they make their way back home: "Be strong, fear not!" He continues by making clear that God is not blessing his people from a distance. Just as he guided his people through the desert after ratifying the covenant with Moses on Mount Sinai, so now God comes into their midst to save them. At his coming, blind eyes will see, deaf ears will hear, the lame will leap, and all those who return to Jerusalem will sing a song that will serve to overturn

Zion = Zī-uhn or Zī-ahn
Slight pause between "Zion" and "singing."

TO KEEP IN MIND
Smile when you share good news. Nonverbal cues like a smile help the assembly understand the reading.

For meditation and context:

Those whom the LORD has **ransomed** will **return**
and enter **Zion singing**,
crowned with everlasting **joy;**
they will **meet** with **joy** and **gladness**,
sorrow and **mourning** will **flee**.

RESPONSORIAL PSALM   Psalm 146:6–7, 8–9, 9–10 (Isaiah 35:4)

R. Lord, come and save us.
or
R. Alleluia.

The LORD God keeps faith forever,
 secures justice for the oppressed,
 gives food to the hungry.
The LORD sets captives free.

The LORD gives sight to the blind;
 the LORD raises up those who were
 bowed down.
The LORD loves the just;
 the LORD protects strangers.

The fatherless and the widow he sustains,
 but the way of the wicked he thwarts.
The LORD shall reign forever;
 your God, O Zion, through all generations.

The tone of this reading is gentle.

READING II   James 5:7–10

A reading from the Letter of Saint James

Be **patient**, **brothers** and **sisters**,
 until the **coming** of the **Lord**.
See how the farmer **waits** for the precious **fruit** of the **earth**,
 being **patient** with it
 until it **receives** the **early** and the **late rains**.
You too must be **patient**.
Make your **hearts firm**,
 because the **coming** of the **Lord** is at **hand**.
Do not **complain**, **brothers** and **sisters**, **about** one **another**,
 that you may **not** be **judged**.
Behold, the **Judge** is **standing** before the **gates**. »

Note the repetitions of "patient."

The tone becomes firmer in the second half of the reading; allow your proclamation to reflect this shift.

"sorrow and mourning" with "joy and gladness." Isaiah beautifully portrays the redeemed people successfully entering the gates of Jerusalem, and he proclaims the people "crowned with everlasting joy." Without directly saying so, how foolish it would be to resist God's call to return home!

READING II   Some scholars believe the Letter of St. James to have been written somewhere between the years AD 65 and 85, well after the letters written by the apostle Paul. Scholars liken the letter to wisdom literature as it con-

tains a variety of loosely connected moral exhortations. Much of the material bears a great similarity to the sayings of Jesus found in Matthew and Luke that are attributed to the Q source. The bulk of these exhortations are oriented to turning people away from the ways of the world to seeking the wisdom of heaven, where injustice and poverty have no home.

The word *patience* occurs three times in today's short excerpt from the letter. The author exhorts his audience to have the patience of a farmer who has great expectations for the sprouting and growth of the

seeds that he has planted. The patience James calls for is not mere waiting but is a sort of hopeful yearning. There is much hope that the wait will be worth all that is to come. James encourages those who wait patiently to make firm their hearts. Thus, they are not to be distracted by other alluring forces of this world that may draw their attention away from the Lord's return, which "is at hand."

In a state of expectant waiting, it is possible that someone could become impatient with and cast judgment upon those uninterested in waiting. James cautions

Take as an example of hardship and patience, **brothers**
    and **sisters**,
    the **prophets** who **spoke** in the **name** of the **Lord**.

GOSPEL   Matthew 11:2–11

A reading from the holy Gospel according to Matthew

When **John** the **Baptist** heard in **prison** of the works of
    the **Christ**,
    he sent his **disciples** to **Jesus** with this **question**,
    "Are **you** the **one** who is to **come**,
    or should we **look** for **another**?"
Jesus **said** to them in **reply**,
    "**Go** and tell **John** what you **hear** and **see**:
    the **blind** regain their **sight**,
    the l**ame walk**,
    lepers are **cleansed**,
    the **deaf hear**,
    the **dead** are **raised**,
    and the **poor** have the **good news proclaimed** to them.
And **blessed** is the **one** who takes no **offense** at me."

As they were going **off**,
    Jesus began to **speak** to the **crowds** about **John**,
    "**What** did you go **out** to the **desert** to **see**?
A **reed swayed** by the **wind**?
Then **what** did you go **out** to **see**?
Someone **dressed** in fine **clothing**?
Those who wear fine **clothing** are in royal **palaces**.

Sidebar notes (left margin):

The tone in this narrative reading is urgent.

Note the pairs: "blind" and "sight," "lame" and "walk," and so forth.

Slight pause between "good news" and "proclaimed."
blessed = BLES-uhd

Jesus offers a series of urgent questions by way of setting up his praise of John the Baptist.

Bottom commentary:

against the temptation to complain about others and suggests that it will reverse the judgment upon the one who complains. Instead, those who await the Lord's return should look to the example provided by the prophets. The suffering and the hardship of those who attend to the Lord will not be long lasting but will yield the "precious fruit of the earth," the state of a world redeemed and living in the justice of God.

GOSPEL The animated discussion between the disciples of John the Baptist and Jesus embodies the early Church's struggle to understand the nature of Jesus as the messiah. The disciples of John would have been committed men who were radically concerned with the dawning of God's kingdom and wanted to stir up a spirit of repentance among the people. Matthew chose these dedicated disciples to be the ones who prompt Jesus to reveal the nature and purpose of his mission. They serve the role of verifying the authority of Jesus at a crucial juncture in

Matthew's Gospel, for in the previous chapter Jesus commissions the twelve apostles to go out into the world in his name, and now in chapter 11, Jesus begins to face controversy, especially the challenge waged by the Pharisees.

When John's disciples ask Jesus point-blank whether or not he is "the one who is to come," Jesus does not answer with a straightforward yes or no. Instead, he points to the results of his ministry. This list is not to be taken lightly: the blind see, the crippled walk, the sick are healed, the deaf hear, and the dead are raised to new life.

Slight pause between "way" and "before."

Emphasis on "none greater."

Then **why** did you go **out**? To see a **prophet**?
Yes, I tell you, and **more** than a prophet.
This is the **one** about **whom** it is **written**:
    *Behold, I am sending my **messenger ahead** of you;*
      *he will **prepare** your **way before** you.*
Amen, I say to you,
    among those **born** of **women**
    there has been **none greater** than **John** the **Baptist**;
    yet the **least** in the kingdom of **heaven** is **greater** than he."

Jesus concludes the list with the statement: "And blessed is the one who takes no offense at me." This suggests that he knows how an influential segment of the population will soon reject his ministry. Jesus manifests a messiah who is compassionate and just; this is far different from the image of the messiah popularized by the religious establishment of that day. The type of messiah Jesus describes is also different from the one John predicted (Matthew 3:10), who was full of judgment and power.

As the disciples of John depart—seemingly satisfied by their encounter with Jesus—Jesus turns to the crowds and asks what they saw when they witnessed John's preaching in the desert. At first, he suggests that perhaps they went out to see someone dressed in fine clothes, a kingly figure. Yet they certainly did not encounter this quality in John. Perhaps his prophetic preaching intrigued them. If so, Jesus tells them that they encountered "more than a prophet" in John. Jesus calls John the greatest of "those born of women." Nevertheless, Jesus states that "the least in the kingdom of heaven" are even greater than John. Who are the least? They are the ones who have been touched by encounter with Jesus, they are his disciples, they are the ones who take no offense at what he does. They are the ones who have been born into the kingdom of heaven. S.W.

FOURTH SUNDAY
OF ADVENT

LECTIONARY #10

Isaiah = ī-ZAY-uh

Ahaz = AY-haz

The tone of this reading is prophetic. It has a solemn, imaginative quality.

Note the repetition of "weary," which you can emphasize, slightly.

The reading concludes with a prophecy. Proclaim it in a solemn and straightforward voice.

Emmanuel = ee-MAN-yoo-el

For meditation and context:

READING I   Isaiah 7:10–14

A reading from the Book of the Prophet Isaiah

The LORD spoke to **Ahaz**, saying:
    Ask for a **sign** from the LORD, your GOD;
    let it be **deep** as the **netherworld**, or **high** as the **sky**!
But **Ahaz** answered,
    "I will not **ask**! I will not **tempt** the LORD!"
Then **Isaiah** said:
    Listen, O **house** of **David**!
Is it not **enough** for you to **weary people**,
    must you also **weary** my **God**?
Therefore the **Lord himself** will give you this **sign**:
    the **virgin** shall **conceive**, and bear a **son**,
    and shall **name** him **Emmanuel**.

RESPONSORIAL PSALM   Psalm 24:1–2, 3–4, 5–6 (7c, 10b)

R. Let the Lord enter; he is king of glory.

The LORD's are the earth and its fullness;
    the world and those who dwell in it.
For he founded it upon the seas
    and established it upon the rivers.

Who can ascend the mountain of the LORD?
    or who may stand in his holy place?
One whose hands are sinless, whose heart
        is clean,
    who desires not what is vain.

He shall receive a blessing from the LORD,
    a reward from God his savior.
Such is the race that seeks for him,
    that seeks the face of the God of Jacob.

READING I   The story of Ahaz is situated in an eighth-century BC political conflict. As king of Judah, Ahaz needs to make a critical choice whether or not to submit to Assyria and be counted among one of its territories or to join an alliance with the northern tribe of Israel. With the help of Isaiah's prompting, Ahaz makes the decision to rely on the help of God and to act independently of Israel, since Isaiah prophesies that this will lead to destruction.

Isaiah is once again at work with Ahaz as we enter into today's reading. Ahaz has another difficult decision to make: to ask God for a sign of his providence or not. Isaiah suggests that if Ahaz asks for a sign that God is supporting him that it could come in the form of something truly spectacular; it could be something deep within the sea or something as lofty as the skies. Ahaz should not be hesitant to ask for such a sign. However, Ahaz has made up his mind that he will not ask God to provide a sign.

Nevertheless, despite the king's trust in God, Isaiah knows the heart of the people, who yearn for God to prove himself to be providential. Thus, he informs the kingdom of Judah that it will be given a sign, and the sign is to be a virgin giving birth to a son who is to be named "Emmanuel." This name itself, meaning "God-with-us," suggests that God will continue to be with his people. Because this prophecy has been made to the house of David, it takes on a messianic nature that is linked with the Davidic kingdom found in 2 Samuel 7:2–16.

READING II   Romans 1:1–7

A reading from the Letter of Saint Paul to the Romans

Paul, a **slave** of Christ **Jesus**,
   called to be an **apostle** and set **apart** for the **gospel** of **God**,
   which he promised **previously** through his **prophets** in the
     holy **Scriptures**,
   the **gospel** about his **Son**, descended from **David** according
     to the **flesh**,
   but established as Son of **God** in **power**
   according to the **Spirit** of **holiness**
   through **resurrection** from the **dead**, **Jesus Christ** our **LORD**.
Through him we have received the **grace** of **apostleship**,
   to bring about the **obedience** of **faith**,
   for the **sake** of his **name**, among **all** the Gentiles,
   among whom are you **also**, who are **called** to **belong**
     to Jesus **Christ**;
   to all the **beloved** of **God** in **Rome**, **called** to be **holy**.
Grace to **you** and **peace** from **God** our **Father**
   and the **Lord** Jesus **Christ**.

The tone of this reading, which begins Paul's letter to the Romans, is unusual. It's a list of qualifications, almost like a spiritual resume.

Emphasis on "Through him."

Even emphasis on "among whom are you also," with slight added emphasis to "also."

READING II Paul opens his letter to the Romans with a summary statement of the incarnation of the Son of God that proceeds through to his lordship as the resurrected Christ. In his greeting, Paul does not simply introduce himself by name, but he provides several indicators of his authority. First, Paul identifies himself as "a slave of Christ Jesus." This does not mean that Paul is held captive against his own will but rather that he has committed himself totally to Christ. Second, Paul refers to himself as an "apostle," an eyewitness to the Lord's resurrection. Finally, like the prophets of old, Paul has been "set apart" for the task of preaching the Gospel. Paul's audience would be foolish to reject his authority.

After Paul gives witness to the authority of Christ, namely that he was born of the flesh according to the line of David but is to be named the "Son of God," being born of the Spirit, Paul proceeds to extend his mission to those who are receiving his letter. Paul tells the Romans that they too "have received the grace of apostleship." Although they have never seen the resurrected Christ in bodily form, their authority comes from "the obedience of faith." It is this faith that allows the Romans to "belong to Jesus Christ" and to share in the mission "to be holy." In these few lines, Paul has clearly opened the way for his challenging word to be heard among the Christians at Rome. While he blesses them with the gifts of "grace" and "peace," he will likewise challenge the community to establish unity among Gentile and Jewish members. He writes to a community he calls "the beloved of God," the holy ones of Rome; surely they feel a summons to live up to their name.

GOSPEL   Matthew 1:18–24

A reading from the holy Gospel according to Matthew

The rich tone of this familiar story is mysterious. "This" is the word that initiates the mystery.

This is how the **birth** of Jesus **Christ** came **about**.
When his mother **Mary** was **betrothed** to **Joseph**,
    but **before** they **lived** together,
    she was **found** with **child** through the **Holy Spirit**.
Joseph her **husband**, since he was a **righteous man**,
    yet **unwilling** to **expose** her to **shame**,
    decided to **divorce** her **quietly**.

The word "behold" initiates the angelic vision of the reading.

Such was his **intention** when, **behold**,
    the **angel** of the **Lord appeared** to him in a **dream** and said,
    "**Joseph**, son of **David**,
    do not be **afraid** to take **Mary** your **wife** into your **home**.
For it is through the **Holy Spirit**
    that this **child** has been **conceived** in her.
She will bear a **son** and you are to name him **Jesus**,
    because he will save his **people** from their **sins**."
All this took **place** to **fulfill** what the **Lord** had **said** through
    the **prophet**:

Emphasis on "all this."

Here, "Behold" reinforces the scriptural vision of the events depicted.

Emmanuel = ee-MAN-yoo-el

*Behold, the virgin shall conceive and bear a son,
and they shall name him Emmanuel,*
    which means "**God** is **with** us."
When Joseph **awoke**,
    he did as the **angel** of the **Lord** had **commanded** him
    and took his **wife** into his **home**.

GOSPEL Matthew has just finishing detailing the lineage from which Jesus flows, the impressive genealogy that ends with the proclamation that Jesus is called the "Christ." Now Matthew continues his theological examination of the incarnation by demonstrating how Jesus is both Son of God and son of Mary.

At the outset of the reading is the conflict that originates from Mary both being betrothed to Joseph and found to be pregnant. However, unlike those who discovered Mary's pregnancy, we are told of its divine origins, namely that this pregnancy came about "through the Holy Spirit." Nevertheless, we are meant to struggle with the potential outcome of this serious charge. Although Joseph and Mary were betrothed, they were not married; therefore this offense could be punished by death. Joseph's decision to quietly divorce her demonstrates his concern to protect Mary from the law. However, his mind is changed when careful discernment of a dream leads him to take Mary as his wife and to bring her into the protection of his home. He must have recognized that God would keep them from all harm.

The passage ends with a bit of commentary from Matthew. He tells us that this encounter between the angel and Joseph was meant to allow for the fulfilment of Isaiah's prophecy that a virgin shall give birth to a son and that he will be named "Emmanuel." The beginning of Matthew's Gospel is clearly meant to impress upon his audience that through the bloodline of David and through the obedient listening of one of its own, Joseph, God would be with his people. S.W.

THE NATIVITY OF THE LORD (CHRISTMAS): VIGIL

LECTIONARY #13

READING I Isaiah 62:1–5

A reading from the Book of the Prophet Isaiah

For **Zion's** sake I will **not** be **silent**,
 for **Jerusalem's** sake I will **not** be **quiet**,
until her **vindication shines forth** like the **dawn**
 and her **victory** like a burning **torch**.

Nations shall **behold** your **vindication**,
 and all the **kings** your **glory**;
you shall be **called** by a new **name**
 pronounced by the **mouth** of the LORD.
You shall be a **glorious crown** in the **hand** of the LORD,
 a **royal diadem** held by your God.
No more shall people call you "**Forsaken**,"
 or your land "**Desolate**,"
but you shall be called "**My Delight**,"
 and your land "**Espoused**."
For the LORD **delights** in you
 and makes your land his **spouse**.
As a young man marries a **virgin**,
 your **Builder** shall **marry** you;
and as a **bridegroom rejoices** in his **bride**
 so shall your God rejoice in **you**.

Isaiah = ī-ZAY-uh

Notice the repetitions of the phrase "you shall." Pace your readings with each expression of "you shall" (or its variations) as a marker.

Notice the sound carried from "Zion's" to "silent" to "quiet."

Give extra emphasis to each of these four names.

Even emphasis on all the words in this last line, with extra added on "you."

There are options for today's readings. Contact your parish staff to learn which readings will be used.

READING I The four weeks of Advent serve as a time of preparation for the great feast of the Lord's Nativity, the Christian celebration of the mystery of the incarnation. While much of our preparation has been meant to be "eschatological," in that we are patiently awaiting for Christ's return at the end time, thereby ushering in the completion of God's kingdom, the final portion of Advent allows us to prepare with joy for the celebration of the birth of Jesus in history. The Masses that constitute Christmas Day, beginning with the Vigil on December 24 through the Mass at Night and continuing through the Mass at Dawn and the Mass during the Day, balance artfully the two themes of eschatological waiting and joyful celebration for God's manifestation in the baby Jesus.

The Vigil's first reading, from the latter part of Isaiah (often referred to as Third or Trito-Isaiah), opens with a sense of victory. The one who witnesses Jerusalem's renewal is incapable of being silent, but instead, must proclaim in speech and in deed that she has been vindicated. Those who shall see the success of the nation are not simply its own citizens but peoples around the world. This restored creation will be a prized possession for God—"a glorious crown" and "a royal diadem." Unlike the stance of waiting for a future glory to appear, the words of Isaiah represent a form of "realized eschatology," whereby salvation takes place now. The Israelites do not have to look forward to the future for God to prove his allegiance; they are able to see their chosen status in the present evidence.

For meditation and context:

RESPONSORIAL PSALM   Psalm 89:4–5, 16–17, 27, 29 (2a)

R. For ever I will sing the goodness of the Lord.

I have made a covenant with my chosen one,
  I have sworn to David my servant:
Forever will I confirm your posterity
  and establish your throne for
    all generations.

He shall say of me, "You are my father,
  my God, the rock, my savior."
Forever I will maintain my kindness
  toward him,
    and my covenant with him stands firm.

Blessed the people who know the
  joyful shout;
  in the light of your countenance, O LORD,
    they walk.
At your name they rejoice all the day,
  and through your justice they are exalted.

READING II   Acts of the Apostles 13:16–17, 22–25

A reading from the Acts of the Apostles

When **Paul** reached Antioch in Pisidia and entered
  the synagogue,
  he stood up, motioned with his hand, and said,
  "**Fellow Israelites** and you others who are **God-fearing, listen**.
The God of this people **Israel** chose our **ancestors**
  and exalted the people during their **sojourn** in
    the land of Egypt.
With **uplifted arm** he led them **out** of it.
Then he removed **Saul** and raised up **David** as king;
  of him he testified,
  'I have found **David**, son of **Jesse**, a man after my own **heart**;
  he will carry out my **every** wish.'
From this man's descendants **God**, according to his **promise**,
  has brought to Israel a **savior, Jesus**.

Antioch = AN-tee-ahk
Pisidia = pih-SID-ee-uhc

This reading sets up a prophetic succession, beginning with the Israelites in the desert and moving from David to John the Baptist, and finally to Jesus.

sojourn = SOH-jern (exile)

Though Paul is speaking in this reading, he is quoting the words of his predecessors. You can modulate your voice slightly to suggest this shift.

This is especially the case in the way in which the reading closes. Zion is portrayed as God's bride. Jerusalem is now to be called God's "Delight," for the land is his "Espoused." Such labels for Israel clearly express God's care and compassion for a people who have managed to stay faithful to him throughout the years of exile. The renewal of God's relationship with his people is so great that he approaches them "as a young man marries a virgin." In other words, Jerusalem is likened to a virginal state, without having been touched by another. Just as marriage is a sign of hope

for many years of blessing to come, so too is the return of the people a sign of great hope that manifests itself in festal joy.

Our awaiting the perfection of God's kingdom as well as our celebration of God's incarnation in history ought to manifest the same hope and joy to every corner of the earth. As the Christian community gathers in prayer and vigil this night, the proclamation of God's victory ought to be welling up in every heart, preparing every member of the Church to proclaim from every mountain peak and every roof top that our God has come to save us.

READING II   This reading opens with the continuing travels of Paul and Barnabas, who having just left Pamphylia have now arrived in the port of Antioch. As a major stop along a primary trade route, Antioch was a Roman colony with a significant population of Jewish citizens. Acts makes clear that Paul wastes no time, going immediately to the synagogue to share his message of Christ with the people.

Speaking to "fellow Israelites" and "God-fearing" Gentiles, Paul preaches with great poise and dexterity. His method is to trace the hand of God in significant histori-

John heralded his coming by proclaiming a **baptism** of **repentance**
   to **all** the people of Israel;
   and as John was completing his course, he would say,
   'What do you suppose that I **am**? I **am not he**.
Behold, one is coming **after** me;
   I am not **worthy** to unfasten the **sandals** of his **feet**.'"

GOSPEL Matthew 1:1–25

A reading from the holy Gospel according to Matthew

The book of the **genealogy** of **Jesus Christ**,
   the son of David, the son of Abraham.

Abraham became the father of **Isaac**,
   Isaac the father of **Jacob**,
   Jacob the father of **Judah** and his **brothers**.
Judah became the father of **Perez** and **Zerah**,
   whose mother was **Tamar**.
Perez became the father of **Hezron**,
   Hezron the father of **Ram**,
   Ram the father of **Amminadab**.
Amminadab became the father of **Nahshon**,
   Nahshon the father of **Salmon**,
   Salmon the father of **Boaz**,
   whose mother was **Rahab**.
Boaz became the father of **Obed**,
   whose mother was **Ruth**.
Obed became the father of **Jesse**,
   Jesse the father of **David** the **king**. »

Paul concludes with John the Baptist's memorable phrase about Jesus. A slight emphasis on "sandals" and "feet" will remind the assembly whose words these are.

A whopper of a reading. The first part of this reading is a performative, rhythmical incantation, one unusual name leading to the next. It goes from Abraham to David; from David to the Babylonian exile; from the Babylonian exile to Jesus. It's a folding screen with two hinges, each panel of the screen exactly the same size, and the image of Jesus' birth appears on its front.

Genealogy = jee-nee-OL-uh-jee
Abraham = AY-bruh-ham; Isaac = Ī-zik
Judah = JOO-duh
Perez = PAYR-ez; Zerah = ZEE-rah

Only five women are included in this list.
Tamar = TAY-mahr
Hezron = HEZ-ruhn
Ram = ram
Amminadab = uh-MIN-uh-dab
Nahshon = NAH-shon
Salmon = SAL-muhn
Boaz = BOH-az
Rahab = RAY-hab
Obed = OH-bed
Jesse = JES-ee

cal events, demonstrating how God consistently acted to support and nurture his people. First, Paul announces that God chose the people of Israel through "our ancestors," with the moment of the exodus from Egypt as a primary example of God's demonstration of preferring Israel to every other nation on earth. Second, God proved himself providential in providing the right king at the right time for the people of Israel as he replaced Saul by his anointing of David. Finally, God has provided a savior for the people named Jesus, who has come to them through the lineage of David. Paul

leaves no doubt that God has consistently proven his desire to protect and care for his people.

The passage ends with Paul referring to the testimony of John the Baptist. He portrays the Baptist as a trustworthy prophet who had attracted the attention of "all the people of Israel." His authority was so great that many mistook him for the messiah. However, Paul repeats the familiar saying of John that he claimed himself too unworthy to unlace the messiah's sandals. What Paul has done in this fairly short exhortation is to make credible the word

that he preaches. First, he has witnessed to the fidelity of God who journeyed with his people and protected them always, and secondly, God has seen fit to send the redeemer into the world through the bloodline of his chosen people. What God promised in his covenant with Israel has now been revealed in the one who has come to bring true and lasting freedom. The people of Antioch have every reason to listen to the message of salvation Paul brings to them.

Uriah = yoo-RI-uh

Rehoboam = ree-huh-BOH-uhm

Abijah = uh-BI-juh

Asaph = AY-saf

Jehoshaphat = jeh-HOH-shuh-fat

Joram = JOHR-uhm

Uzziah = yuh-ZI-uh

Jotham = JOH-thuhm

Ahaz = AY-haz

Hezekiah = hez-eh-KI-uh

Manasseh = muh-NAS-uh

Amos = AY-m*s

Josiah = joh-SI-uh

Jechoniah = jek-oh-NI-uh

Shealtiel = shee-AL-tee-uhl

Zerubbabel = zuh-ROOB-uh-b*l

Abiud = uh-BI-uhd

Eliakim = ee-LI-uh-kim

Azor = AY-sohr

Zadok = ZAD-uhk

Achim = AH-kim

Eliud = ee-LI-uhd

Eleazar = el-ee-AY-zer

Matthan = MATH-uhn

David became the father of **Solomon,**
   whose **mother** had been the wife of **Uriah.**
Solomon became the father of **Rehoboam,**
   Rehoboam the father of **Abijah,**
   Abijah the father of **Asaph.**
Asaph became the father of **Jehoshaphat,**
   Jehoshaphat the father of **Joram,**
   Joram the father of **Uzziah.**
Uzziah became the father of **Jotham,**
   Jotham the father of **Ahaz,**
   Ahaz the father of **Hezekiah.**
Hezekiah became the father of **Manasseh,**
   Manasseh the father of **Amos,**
   Amos the father of **Josiah.**
Josiah became the father of **Jechoniah** and his **brothers**
   at the time of the Babylonian **exile.**

After the Babylonian exile,
   Jechoniah became the father of **Shealtiel,**
   Shealtiel the father of **Zerubbabel,**
   Zerubbabel the father of **Abiud.**
Abiud became the father of **Eliakim,**
   Eliakim the father of **Azor,**
   Azor the father of **Zadok.**
Zadok became the father of **Achim,**
   Achim the father of **Eliud,**
   Eliud the father of **Eleazar.**
Eleazar became the father of **Matthan,**
   Matthan the father of **Jacob,**
   Jacob the father of **Joseph,** the husband of **Mary.**
Of her was born **Jesus** who is called the **Christ.**

Thus the total number of **generations**
   from **Abraham** to **David**
   is **fourteen** generations;

GOSPEL   Similar to Paul's preaching in Acts, which traced the critical events of salvation history that led to the coming of the messiah, the genealogy at the beginning of Matthew's Gospel serves the function of substantiating the credibility of Jesus. The word *genealogy* comes from the root word *genesis*, which means the origins of someone or something. For example, the Book of Genesis contains the story of the origins of the world's foundation. Matthew opens his Gospel with the family tree of Jesus because he wants he readers to have no doubt that Jesus is in keeping with God's plan of salvation. God acts within the established framework of history.

It is important to consider the context in which Matthew writes his Gospel. Biblical scholars tell us that the composition of this Gospel takes places shortly after the destruction of the Jerusalem Temple by the Romans in AD 70. Matthew writes to a very Jewish audience who were faced with a very significant decision: How are we meant to keep the covenant with God now that the Temple and sacrificial worship are no more? Matthew has an answer for them: Come to faith in Jesus, for he fulfills the covenant. No temple is required to follow after Jesus; instead, what is needed is faith in him through baptism and the keeping of his commands. Because Jesus fulfills the covenant, it is necessary that he be firmly positioned within Jewish history. For this reason, the story of Jesus' nativity is preceded by this lengthy genealogy.

Matthew 1:1–25 is not an easy reading to proclaim, and it is one that many presiders choose to replace with another of the Gospel passages from the other Christmas

from **David** to the Babylonian **exile**,
fourteen generations;
from the Babylonian **exile** to the **Christ**,
fourteen generations.

Now that Jesus' genealogy has been established, the story of his birth can be told. The focus is Joseph, the second-to-last name in the genealogy. Attune the dynamics of your reading to the figure of Joseph, with whom the assembly is meant to identify.

[Now **this** is how the **birth** of Jesus **Christ** came about.
When his mother **Mary** was betrothed to **Joseph**,
but before they **lived** together,
she was found with **child** through the Holy **Spirit**.
Joseph her **husband**, since he was a **righteous man**,
yet unwilling to expose her to **shame**,
decided to **divorce** her quietly.
Such was his intention when, **behold**,
the **angel** of the Lord appeared to him in a **dream** and said,
"**Joseph**, son of David,

When the angel says here Joseph's name, it is a summons. Read it that way.

do not be afraid to take Mary your wife into your **home**.
For it is **through** the Holy Spirit
that this child has been **conceived in her.**
She will bear a **son** and you are to name him **Jesus**,
because he will **save** his people from their **sins**."
All this took place to **fulfill**
what the Lord had said through the **prophet**:
Behold, the **virgin** *shall conceive and bear a* **son**,
and they shall name him **Emmanuel**,
which means "**God** is **with** us."

Joseph awaking is what happens to the assembly at this moment.

When Joseph **awoke**,
he **did** as the angel of the Lord had **commanded** him
and took his **wife** into his **home**.
He had no **relations** with her until she bore a **son**,
and he **named** him Jesus.]

[Shorter: Matthew 1:18–25 (see brackets)]

Masses. When the four Masses of the Nativity are taken as a whole, the choice to omit the genealogy is rather unfortunate. There is a natural progression that builds up our faith in the mystery of the incarnation, as we first hear of Jesus' family tree (Vigil), to his birth announced by the angels under the stars (Night), to the witness of the shepherds who encounter the infant lying in the manger (Dawn), to the theological synthesis of John who proclaims the coming of the Word into the world as pure light (Day). The story of Jesus' origins plays a crucial role in preparing us for the wonder

of his birth and pays honor and respect to all the many names that played a role in his coming into the world.

At the very end of the lengthy genealogy, we hear of Joseph's dream in which an angel tells him to fear not and to take Mary into his home. Joseph is of the household of David, and thus, having just heard of Joseph's family lineage, we are well prepared to trust in Joseph's righteousness. When the child is born to Mary, it is Joseph who provides him with the name "Jesus." This is the same child who will come to be named "Emmanuel," meaning "God-with-us."

Thus, the genealogy of Jesus provides for us not only his roots but also tells of the trust that Mary and Joseph have in the authority of God's plan. S.W.

DECEMBER 25, 2022

THE NATIVITY OF THE LORD (CHRISTMAS): NIGHT

LECTIONARY #14

READING I Isaiah 9:1–6

Isaiah = ī-ZAY-uh

A reading of great joy and mystery. Read with emphasis on the contrasts between light and gloom, battle and peace.

Take note here of the yoke, the pole, and the rod. These lines express parallel images in parallel constructions.

Midian = MID-ee-uhn

These names are the heart of this reading. Give them due emphasis.

A reading from the Book of the Prophet Isaiah

The people who walked in **darkness**
  have **seen** a great **light**;
upon those who dwelt in the **land of gloom**
  a **light** has **shone**.
You have **brought** them abundant **joy**
  and **great rejoicing**,
as they **rejoice** before you as at the **harvest**,
  as people make **merry** when dividing **spoils**.
For the **yoke** that burdened them,
  the **pole** on their shoulder,
and the **rod** of their taskmaster
  you have **smashed**, as on the day of **Midian**.
For every **boot** that **tramped** in **battle**,
  every **cloak rolled** in **blood**,
  will be **burned** as fuel for flames.
For a child is born to us, a **son** is given us;
  upon his shoulder **dominion** rests.
They name him **Wonder-Counselor**, **God-Hero**,
  Father-Forever, **Prince** of **Peace**.

There are options for today's readings. Contact your parish staff to learn which readings will be used.

READING I This installment of Isaiah's prophecy is part of the dialogue undertaken with King Ahaz of Judah, who has been promised the coming of a great and mighty king who would free the people from foreign rule and would establish a kingdom based upon justice (Isaiah 7–11). When isolated to the context of this eighth-century BC situation, the prophecy Isaiah utters speaks to the freedom of the northern tribes of Israel from Assyrian occupation. As they have managed to survive a period of oppression, they are now able to enjoy the new life of liberation. The people are described as journeying out of a time of "darkness" into "great light." This light is so bright that it can be likened to the joy of an abundant harvest, when people celebrate the ability to divide the profits. In the context mentioned above, Assyria is meant to be the "yoke," the "pole," and the "rod" that burdened the people with oppression. Now these and other military images, such as the "boot that tramped in battle" and the "cloak rolled in blood" will disappear as though burned up in flames. Israel's victory over the Assyrians is equivalent to the "day of Midian," when Gideon successfully defeated the pagan Midianites (see Judges 7:15–25).

After rehearsing the powerful victory of the Israelites, Isaiah turns his prophecy to the foretelling of the messiah. "For a child is born to us," the prophet announces. This child is to be given the name Emmanuel (Isaiah 7:14). Isaiah's words spoken in the time of Ahaz transcend this immediate context and become the vision

24

His dominion is **vast**
 and **forever** peaceful,
from David's **throne**, and over his **kingdom**,
 which he **confirms** and **sustains**
by **judgment** and **justice**,
 both **now** and **forever**.
The **zeal** of the Lord of **hosts** will **do** this!

Give each of the pairs in these three lines—confirms and sustains; judgment and justice; now and forever—equal emphasis.

For meditation and context:

RESPONSORIAL PSALM Psalm 96:1–2, 2–3, 11–12, 13 (Luke 2:11)

R. Today is born our Savior, Christ the Lord.

Sing to the Lord a new song;
 sing to the Lord, all you lands.
Sing to the Lord; bless his name.

Announce his salvation, day after day.
 Tell his glory among the nations;
 among all peoples, his wondrous deeds.

Let the heavens be glad and the earth rejoice;
 let the sea and what fills it resound;
 let the plains be joyful and all that is
 in them!
Then shall all the trees of the forest exult.

They shall exult before the Lord,
 for he comes;
 for he comes to rule the earth.
He shall rule the world with justice
 and the peoples with his constancy.

READING II Titus 2:11–14

Titus = TĪ-tuhs

A reading all in one long sentence, broken into three parts, beginning with "the grace of God," continuing with "the appearance of the glory," and concluding with "and who gave himself for us." Pace your reading accordingly.

Equal emphasis on these three adverbs.

A reading from the Letter of Saint Paul to Titus

Beloved:
The **grace** of God has appeared, saving **all**
 and training us to reject **godless ways** and **worldly desires**
 and to live **temperately**, **justly**, and **devoutly** in this age,
 as we await the blessed **hope**,
 the **appearance** of the **glory** of our great **God**
 and **savior** Jesus Christ,
 who gave himself for us to **deliver** us from all **lawlessness**
 and to **cleanse** for himself a **people** as his own,
 eager to do what is **good**.

Read the phrase "eager to do what is good" as a Christmas wish.

for a future child born in the line of King David. The authority of this just ruler is revealed by the names that Isaiah gives him: "Wonder-Counselor, God-Hero, Father-Forever, Prince of Peace." These titles suggest the qualities that will make up the messiah's character: he will be wise (Wonder-Counselor), strong (God-Hero), caring (Father-Forever), and just (Prince of Peace). This king will be revered for making his kingdom one of permanent peace and constant justice.

READING II This reading from the author's correspondence with Titus is proclaimed in the context of a Mass celebrated in the shadows of night, a time designated for vigilant and prayerful waiting for the dawning of a festival day. We are reminded here of the eschatological waiting that is necessary for the Lord's triumphant return at the end of days, but we too, in vigilant posture, await the joy that is to accompany our celebration of the Lord's nativity. Both the incarnation and the Lord's return are referred to in this passage: "the grace of God has appeared"

suggests the incarnation, while the "appearance of the glory of our great God and Savior Jesus Christ," refers to his coming at the end of time.

Paul's major concern in portraying the trajectory from the birth of Jesus until the parousia is to emphasize the importance for Christians to learn how "to reject godless ways and worldly desires." His plan for education on the Christian way involves training in how to live "temperately, justly, and devoutly." All three attitudes require discipline and focus. One must be carefully attuned to the difficult work of rejecting the

The reading is divided into two parts. The first part tells the story of the census, moving Joseph and Mary from Nazareth to Bethlehem where Jesus will be born. The second part shifts to the shepherds visited by the angel of the Lord. Two vivid Christian images come from this reading: the manger of the Nativity and the heavenly host with the angel proclaiming glory to God, witnessed by the shepherds watching over their flocks. Both images come alive in this reading.

Caesar Augustus = SEE-zer aw-GUHS-tuhs
Quirinius = kwih-RIN-ee-uhs
Judea = joo-DEE-uh

Place emphasis on these lines by slowing your pace just slightly to draw attention to the image.

In this line, each word should have almost equal emphasis.

TO KEEP IN MIND
Smile when you share good news. Nonverbal cues like a smile help the assembly understand the reading.

GOSPEL   Luke 2:1–14

A reading from the holy Gospel according to Luke

In those days a **decree** went out from Caesar Augustus
    that the **whole world** should be **enrolled**.
This was the **first** enrollment,
    when Quirinius was governor of Syria.
So **all went** to be **enrolled**, **each** to his own **town**.
And **Joseph too** went up from **Galilee** from the town of **Nazareth**
    to **Judea**, to the city of **David** that is called **Bethlehem**,
    because he was of the **house** and **family** of David,
    to be **enrolled** with **Mary**, his betrothed, who was with child.
While they were there,
    the time came for **her** to have her **child**,
    and she gave birth to her **firstborn son**.
She wrapped him in swaddling **clothes** and **laid** him in a **manger**,
    because there was **no room** for them in the inn.

Now there were **shepherds** in that region **living** in the fields
    and **keeping** the **night watch** over their flock.
The **angel** of the Lord appeared to them
    and the **glory** of the Lord **shone** around them,
    and they were **struck** with great **fear**.
The angel **said** to them,
    "**Do not be afraid**;
    for **behold**, I proclaim to you **good news** of **great joy**
    that will be for **all** the people.
For today in the city of **David**
    a **savior** has been **born** for you who is **Christ** and **Lord**.

ways of the flesh that can draw one's attention away from the life of the Spirit.
    The author suggests that the way to maintain this devotion is to focus keenly on the "blessed hope" that is the dawning of God's glory. Notice here that by the time this letter was written—one of the latter installments of the Pauline corpus—that "our great God" is not distinguished from the "savior Jesus Christ." Although the Father and Jesus are distinguished one from another, they are considered here as equal in authority. The passage concludes with a reference to deliverance that can be

likened to the Hebrew liberation from Egyptian slavery: Jesus gave himself to "deliver us" from the captivity of "lawlessness" in order to "cleanse" a people for himself. The reader might imagine the powerful effects of both the passage through the Red Sea and the saving relationship established in baptism.

GOSPEL   Luke's account of the Lord's birth opens with the portrayal of human authority attempting to keep control over the world. Caesar Augustus has pronounced that the population of "the

whole world" must be counted. The greater the numbers, the more powerful the Roman Empire could consider itself. However, it is the context of the census by which God is able to display a power that is much greater than any human authority could wield. To be counted, Joseph and Mary depart from the comfort of their home and go to Bethlehem in Judea. It is during their time in Bethlehem that Mary gives birth to her child.
    It is no mistake that Luke wants us to understand that the birth of God's Son takes place in the midst of a social context

Give emphasis again to the word "manger."

Give slight emphasis to "praising" as a way of characterizing the image arising from the familiar words to follow: pure praise.

And **this** will be a **sign** for you:
 you will find an **infant wrapped** in swaddling clothes
 and **lying** in a **manger**."
And **suddenly** there was a multitude of the heavenly host with
  the angel,
 praising God and saying:
  "**Glory** to God in the **highest**
    and on **earth peace** to those on whom his **favor** rests."

in which political officials are trying to manage the world. There is simply no preparing for the grace that God gives to the world. Even Joseph and Mary are caught off guard and away from home when the child is born. They were not able to plan accordingly for Jesus' birth and are forced to use a manger as the place of his delivery. The Holy Family is completely vulnerable when Jesus comes into his world, but God will work through this vulnerability to demonstrate the wonder of his authority.

Thus, while the Jewish people believed that the messiah would come amongst them as a king, full of power and might, with the ability to free them from the control of the Romans and all other nations, God choses to act in a way that astonishes all. God selects lowly shepherds to be his ambassadors to the world, bearing a message of "good news of great joy." And this is a message that goes out to all the world and not just to those awaiting the coming of the messiah.

Luke's theology in the story of the Lord's nativity is abundantly clear. God chooses the lowly to cast the mighty from their positions of power (Luke 1:52).

Through the message of the angels, the epiphany of God's love for the world is made manifest; this is a love that cannot be counted or measured by a human census. The child Jesus may be wrapped in swaddling clothes and lying in a manger, but our eyes of faith are able to behold the King of Kings and Lord of Lords. God enters this world in a way suspected by no one; all are astonished by his grace. S.W.

THE NATIVITY OF THE LORD (CHRISTMAS): DAWN

LECTIONARY #15

READING I   Isaiah 62:11–12

A reading from the Book of the Prophet Isaiah

See, the LORD **proclaims**
   to the **ends** of the earth:
say to daughter Zion,
   your **savior** comes!
Here is his reward with him,
   his **recompense before** him.
They shall be **called** the holy **people**,
   the **redeemed** of the LORD,
and you shall be called "**Frequented**,"
   a **city** that is **not forsaken**.

For meditation and context:

RESPONSORIAL PSALM   Psalm 97:1, 6, 11–12

R. A light will shine on us this day: the Lord is born for us.

The LORD is king; let the earth rejoice;
   let the many isles be glad.
The heavens proclaim his justice,
   and all peoples see his glory.

Light dawns for the just;
   and gladness, for the upright of heart.
Be glad in the LORD, you just,
   and give thanks to his holy name.

There are options for today's readings. Contact your parish staff to learn which readings will be used.

READING I A basic liturgical principle regarding the proclamation of God's Word in the gathered assembly is that when God speaks, something happens. God's Word is meant to be generative and fruitful; it is not meant to fall upon deaf ears with no corresponding action on the part of hearers. This is especially true when it comes to God's Word spoken by the prophets. The point of prophecy is to elicit a response from those to whom it is directed.

In this short reading from the prophet Isaiah, the prophecy begins with an active present, using the command to "see." The point of this command is very clear: those who hear this Word must be moved by it. And what is it that Isaiah's hearers are to do? They are to participate in the announcement of the Lord's coming. The evidence for his nearness is to be found in the change of name bestowed upon the people. They are to be called "the holy people," "the redeemed." Likewise, the name of the city of Zion is to be changed as well; from now on it will not be seen as desolate or forsaken but instead will bear the name "Frequented."

God has spoken, and a great transformation will take place. The Lord provides for the renewal of both people and the Land, and the most important achievement of all is the regeneration of the people's faith. Holiness and redemption are the fruit of the Lord speaking his Word and carrying out his plan to be faithful for all generations to come.

Titus = TĪ-tuhs

A reading in one long sentence. After the initial "Beloved," the lines of the reading form natural pairs. Read each pair of lines as a thought, proceeding from one to the next, offering advice, to conclude with a message of hope.

The rhythm of this line provides this reading with its reverberant note, so allow yourself to slow slightly as you come to this conclusion.

> **TO KEEP IN MIND**
> Pause to break up separate thoughts, set apart significant statements, or indicate major shifts. Never pause in the middle of a thought. Your primary guide for pauses is punctuation.

While the focus of this reading is on the infant Jesus lying in the manger, the eyes through which we see him are those of the shepherds. The shepherds modeled Christian devotion from the beginning of our faith.

manger = MAYN-jer

Amazement is the primary emotion of this story.

READING II   Titus 3:4–7

A reading from the Letter of Saint Paul to Titus

Beloved:
When the **kindness** and generous **love**
    of **God** our savior appeared,
not **because** of any righteous deeds we had done
    but because of his mercy,
He **saved us** through the **bath** of rebirth
    and **renewal** by the Holy **Spirit**,
whom he **richly poured out** on **us**
    through **Jesus** Christ our **savior**,
so that we might be **justified** by his **grace**
    and become **heirs** in **hope** of eternal **life**.

GOSPEL   Luke 2:15–20

A reading from the holy Gospel according to Luke

When the **angels** went away from them to **heaven**,
    the **shepherds** said to one another,
    "Let us **go**, then, to **Bethlehem**
    to **see this thing** that has taken place,
    which the **Lord** has made **known** to us."
So they went in **haste** and found **Mary** and **Joseph**,
    and the **infant lying** in the manger.
When they **saw** this,
    they made **known** the message
    that had been **told them** about this child.
All who heard it were **amazed**
    by what had been **told** them by the **shepherds**. »

READING II   The author of this pastoral letter writes to Christians in Crete. The major theme of the letter is to warn the community to be careful not to follow the instruction of false teachers (see Titus 1:9). The verses of today's excerpt from the letter come from its final chapter. And here the author provides several truths of Christian teaching, which he uses to substantiate why the community should follow his instruction and not that of other false teachers.

First, the author defines the nature of God's grace. It is a gift that is given according to God's kindness and generosity. It is not something we merit or accomplish through any deed of our own. Second, God's gift of a savior to the world is a sign of his great mercy. Thus, the mystery of the incarnation resides solely on the truth that God wishes to provide for his people; his coming into the world has nothing to do with our being deserving of such a gift.

A third truth of the Christian faith is found in his description of how salvation takes place. It begins with the kindness of God that is marked by the ritual of baptism and the "renewal" provided by the Holy Spirit, which proceeds from the Father through the Son. In turn, this regeneration brings the hope of eternal life. Because we have been brought into relationship with Christ through baptism, we are to be "justified" by God's grace.

GOSPEL   Recall that today's first reading from Isaiah opened with the command word "see." This Gospel passage from Luke is focused on the testimony of the shepherds who were commanded by the angels to go and see what God revealed in the city of Bethlehem. Such

The shepherds' glorifying and praising are to be our own.

And **Mary** kept all these things,
    reflecting on them in her **heart**.
Then the **shepherds** returned,
    glorifying and **praising** God
    for **all** they had **heard** and **seen**,
    just as it had been **told** to them.

a plan to seek out God's presence is important to Luke, who begins the mysterious circumstances of the incarnation with Mary running to her cousin Elizabeth who testifies to the truth she sees: "blessed are you among women, and blessed is the fruit of your womb" (Luke 1:42).

Luke wants the reader to see that God chooses the non-powerful and non-influential to make known the greatest gift the world has ever seen. Just like Mary ran to her cousin Elizabeth, so a pack of lowly shepherds goes "in haste" to find the infant. How it is that they were able to see such magnificence in an innocent and powerless child? What was it that spoke to them of God's grace present in the child? Whatever it was, Luke tells us that they do not delay in revealing what the angels had told them about this child, namely that a savior has been born into the world, the cause for this world's peace (Luke 2:11, 14). So great was the testimony of the shepherds that Luke makes sure to tell us that all who heard were "amazed."

As the shepherds leave the manger, it is important to notice that they go away "glorifying and praising God" for what they had seen. This is very much like the posture of the angels who approached them in the field and sang "Glory to God in the highest" (Luke 2:14). There should be no doubt that Luke wants us to "see" exactly what the shepherds saw; we who are as lowly as they have been chosen to testify to God's presence among us. "See, the Lord proclaims / to the ends of the earth: / . . . your savior comes" (see the first reading). S.W.

THE NATIVITY OF THE LORD (CHRISTMAS): DAY

LECTIONARY #16

READING I   Isaiah 52:7–10

A reading from the Book of the Prophet Isaiah

How **beautiful** upon the **mountains**
    are the **feet** of him who **brings glad tidings**,
announcing **peace**, bearing good **news**,
    announcing **salvation**, and saying to Zion,
    "Your **God** is **King!**"

Hark! Your sentinels **raise** a cry,
    together they **shout** for **joy**,
for they see **directly**, before their **eyes**,
    the LORD restoring Zion.
Break out together in song,
    O ruins of Jerusalem!
For the LORD comforts his **people**,
    he **redeems** Jerusalem.
The LORD has bared his holy arm
    in the **sight** of all the **nations**;
all the **ends** of the **earth** will **behold**
    the **salvation** of our **God**.

Isaiah = ī-ZAY-uh

A reading of great joy. In reading this, you are bringing glad tidings to the assembly.

"Hark" is a word with rich Christmas associations. Allow it to resonate in your reading.

Allow "salvation" to resonate here. This word is the key to the whole reading.

There are options for today's readings. Contact your parish staff to learn which readings will be used.

READING I Today's reading from the second part of the book of Isaiah provides a variety of vibrant images to express the joyful announcement of salvation to all the world. First, he suggests that the word goes out through the "beautiful" feet of a messenger who bounds throughout the mountain tops shouting the arrival of Zion's king. Next, Isaiah employs the image of sentinels who stand their guard at the city walls. They behold yet another vibrant image of God's victory, namely the reassembly of the city's ruins, which sing together a song of the Lord's gift of salvation. Finally, Isaiah uses the image of the Lord's mighty arm, which is shown for all the world to see.

Isaiah's prophecy is meant to call Israel to be a herald for the message that God has bestowed salvation upon a nation once destroyed and upon the world as a whole. Just as the messenger runs with his message upon the mountaintops, the Israelites are meant to hear and respond to Isaiah's prophecy with a great deal of urgency. There is no room for the people to hesitate; they must proceed with great courage.

And yet imagine how difficult a summons this would be. Those who returned to Jerusalem after the Babylonian Exile were surely overcome by fear for the future. If such destruction had taken place once, what was to keep it from happening again? Why would the people want to take such a risk to rebuild? The answer lies in the fact that they believed God was demanding great things of them to manifest his power. Their fidelity would result in others through-

For meditation and context:

RESPONSORIAL PSALM   Psalm 98:1, 2–3, 3–4, 5–6 (3c)

R. All the ends of the earth have seen the saving power of God.

Sing to the LORD a new song,
   for he has done wondrous deeds;
his right hand has won victory for him,
   his holy arm.

The LORD has made his salvation known:
   in the sight of the nations he has revealed
      his justice.
He has remembered his kindness and
   his faithfulness
   toward the house of Israel.

All the ends of the earth have seen
   the salvation by our God.
Sing joyfully to the LORD, all you lands;
   break into song; sing praise.

Sing praise to the LORD with the harp,
   with the harp and melodious song.
With trumpets and the sound of the horn
   sing joyfully before the King, the LORD.

A reading of poetic and argumentative power about the nature and glory of Christ. The reading consists of a long and poetic set-up that yields to an argumentative call-and-response. Allow the set up to gather tension in your reading that the call-and-response releases.

refulgence = ree-FUHL-j*nts = radiance or brilliance

"Universe," "refulgence," and "glory": This is celestial language to characterize the Son.

The call-and-response is like a small theater piece.

READING II   Hebrews 1:1–6

A reading from the Letter to the Hebrews

Brothers and sisters:
In times **past**, God **spoke** in **partial** and **various** ways
   to our **ancestors** through the **prophets**;
   in these **last days**, he has **spoken to us** through the **Son**,
   whom he **made heir** of all **things**
   and through **whom** he created the **universe**,
   who is the **refulgence** of his **glory**, the very **imprint**
      of his being,
   and who **sustains all things** by his **mighty** word.
   When he had **accomplished** purification from sins,
   he **took** his **seat** at the right **hand** of the **Majesty** on high,
   as **far superior** to the angels
   as the **name** he has **inherited** is more **excellent** than theirs.

For to **which** of the **angels** did **God** ever **say**:
   You are my son; this day I have begotten **you**?
Or **again**:
   *I will be a **father** to him, and he shall be a **son** to me?*
And **again**, when he leads the firstborn into the **world**, he says:
   *Let **all** the angels of God **worship** him.*

---

out the whole world coming to believe in God, as we see in the prophecy at the end of this reading.

After having endured the lot of forced slavery, it would have been quite natural for the Israelites to have turned in on themselves. However, this is not the plan of God's salvation. He does not carve out a people for himself simply for their own isolation. Instead, being the chosen people is a gift that comes with the responsibility of proclaiming the good news of salvation to all the earth. Such commissioning belongs to the followers of Christ as well. We are meant

to climb to the mountaintops and shout to all peoples that the Lord has come to save us! As Psalm 98, which responds to the first reading, proclaims: "All the ends of the earth have seen the saving power of God."

READING II The author of the Letter to the Hebrews begins his writing by speaking of the nature of God's revelation in the past and in the present age. First, he claims that in the past, God revealed himself in "partial" ways. Thus, the prophecy of Isaiah, which we just heard in today's first reading, would be an exam-

ple of revelation that was not quite complete. However, the author states that "in these last days" God's revelation has been fully bestowed by the giving of his word as it is spoken through his Son. Jesus is the fullness of God's revelation, and with him God's revelation cannot come nearer. The Word God has spoken in his Son is definitive; there can be nothing greater.

Part of these opening verses may have originally been sung as part of a liturgical hymn. They contain a marvelous soteriological portrait of God's working of salvation through the giving of his Son, who is

One of the pillars of Christian theology. The emphases in the opening verses are crucial to that theology.

Linger a little at the contrast between light and darkness.

This passage about John links his testimony with the light.

TO KEEP IN MIND
Be careful not to swallow your words. Articulate carefully, especially at the end of lines.

GOSPEL   John 1:1–18

A reading from the holy Gospel according to John

[In the **beginning** was the **Word**,
  and the **Word** was with **God**,
  and the Word **was** God.
He **was** in the beginning **with** God.
All things came to be **through** him,
  and **without him nothing** came to be.
What came to be **through him** was **life**,
  and **this life** was the **light** of the human **race**;
  the light **shines** in the **darkness**,
  and the **darkness** has not overcome it.]
A man named **John** was sent from God.
He came for **testimony**, to testify to the **light**,
  so that all might believe **through him**.
He was **not** the light,
  but came to **testify to** the light.
[The **true light**, which enlightens **everyone**,
    was **coming** into the world.
  He was **in** the world,
    and the **world** came to be **through** him,
    but the **world** did not **know** him.
  He **came** to what was his **own**,
    but his **own people** did not **accept** him.

But to those who **did** accept him
  he gave **power** to become **children** of God,
  to those who **believe** in his **name**,
  who were born **not** by natural generation
  nor by **human choice** nor by a man's **decision**
  but of **God**. »

---

his heir, his coworker in the project of creation, and is the "refulgence of his glory." After accomplishing God's mission by destroying the bonds of sin, the Son was seated at the Father's right hand.

Given the fact that the Letter to the Hebrews was written to people of Jewish background, these words which suggest that the post-resurrected Christ shares fully in God's majesty, being "far superior to the angels," would have seemed very radical indeed. For staunch Jews who continued to cling to God's covenant with Israel, these words would seem to substantiate a great

rupture—God has done something decidedly new and different "in these last days." But that is exactly the author's point, he wants to leave no doubt that former ways looked forward to what was to come, but the coming of the Lord into the world has made God's salvation abundantly clear and undeniable for those who honor the relationship between the Father and the Son.

GOSPEL Ponder for a moment the Gospel passages that have been proclaimed in the three Masses for the Lord's nativity, leading up to the final

celebration of Mass on Christmas day. The Vigil focused on the genealogy of Jesus from Matthew, the Mass at Night contained Luke's account of the visit by the angels to the shepherds in the field announcing the glory of God to be revealed to all the world, and finally, the Mass at Dawn continued Luke's infancy narrative with the shepherds' journey to the manger in Bethlehem. Throughout these Masses, there has been a progression in the theological dimension of God's plan of salvation: from a distinct bloodline in the course of history comes the fulfillment of God's promise of salvation, which

The Word becoming flesh is the heart of this reading.

And the **Word** became **flesh**
    and made his **dwelling among** us,
    and we **saw** his **glory**,
    the **glory** as of the **Father's only** Son,
    full of **grace** and **truth**.]
John **testified** to him and **cried out**, saying,
    "This was **he** of **whom** I **said**,
    'The one who is coming **after** me ranks **ahead** of me
    because he existed **before** me.'"
From his **fullness** we have **all** received,
    grace in place of **grace**,
    because while the **law** was given through **Moses**,
    grace and **truth** came through Jesus **Christ**.
No one has ever **seen** God.
The only **Son**, God, who is at the Father's side,
    has **revealed** him.

[Shorter: John 1:1–5, 9–14 (see brackets)]

And once again, John testifies. His testimony yields revelation. Give proper emphasis to the word "revealed" at the end of the reading.

is announced to the lowly of this world but is Good News to be shared with every creature on earth. God's Word is creative and enduring; it is meant for all to hear.

The Gospel passage from the Mass during the Day is taken from the prologue of John's Gospel. The last of the four Gospels to be written, the Gospel of John presents us with a very high Christology. This means that John wants to emphasize the divinity of Christ more than his humanity. For example, there is no infancy narrative in John nor is there any evidence of Jesus growing and maturing as a human;

instead, Jesus appears at the outset as the fully-grown anointed one of God.

For those who prefer the nativity story, complete with shepherds and angels, a manger and barnyard animals, these words from the opening of John's Gospel, may seem less than relatable. That is precisely John's method; he wants his hearers to contemplate the seriousness of a theology of the incarnation, the Word made flesh. The celebration of this Christian mystery presents us with the awesome wonder that God does not save the world from afar; instead, God chooses to experience all that

his human creation experiences, except the destructive forces of sin.

John's prologue places before us the symbol of Christ as the true Light of the World. In these days of winter darkness, the Church holds on to the hope that Christ's light will endure; there is no darkness that the light of Christ cannot dispel. Even though much of the world does not know the Son, and even though his own would reject him, his light reveals the totality of God's never-ending and always-abundant grace. S.W.

THE HOLY FAMILY OF JESUS, MARY, AND JOSEPH

LECTIONARY #17

READING I   Sirach 3:2–6, 12–14

A reading from the Book of Sirach

> God sets a father in **honor** over his children;
>   a mother's **authority** he **confirms** over her sons.
> Whoever **honors** his father **atones** for sins,
>   and **preserves** himself from them.
> When he **prays**, he is **heard**;
>   he stores up **riches** who reveres his **mother**.
> Whoever **honors** his father is **gladdened** by children, and,
>   when he **prays**, is **heard**.
> Whoever **reveres** his father will live a **long life**;
>   he who **obeys** his father brings **comfort** to his mother.
>
> My son, take **care** of your father when he is old;
>   grieve him **not** as **long** as he lives.
> Even if his **mind** fail, be **considerate** of him;
>   **revile** him not all the **days** of his **life**;
> **kindness** to a father will not be **forgotten**,
>   **firmly** planted against the **debt** of your sins
>   —a **house** raised in justice to **you**.

Sirach = SEER-ak; Sī-ruhk

Each set of phrases in this reading offers advice.

Note the parallels established by the repetition of the word "whoever." The word "and" serves a similar purpose. Each of these teachings is meant to be equal.

The advice in the second section, beginning here, is more familial, the words of a father to his son. You can proclaim it in this spirit.

There are options for today's readings. Contact your parish staff to learn which readings will be used.

READING I   The Book of Sirach, also known as Ecclesiasticus, is composed of fifty chapters of wisdom literature. Written between the years 200 and 175 BC by the Jewish scribe Ben Sira, the book contains ethical themes and poetic sayings that are similar to those found in the Book of Proverbs. Sirach's fundamental outlook on wisdom is that building up the quality of human relationships will result in the realization that the fear of God is a central dynamic of wise relationships. In other words, constructing right relationships between husband and wife, parents and children, the young and the old, the rich and the poor ultimately leads to better reverence of God.

Sirach's pursuit of right relationship is abundantly clear in these short verses that come near the beginning of the book. A father is to command the honor of his children, and a mother is to have authority over her sons. It is not simply that honoring one's parents allows for good order in the present, but it also "atones for sins" made in the past. Furthermore, not only are sins forgiven, but the honoring of one's parents also opens access for God to be able to hear the prayers that one utters. Thus, right relationship restores what has been broken in the past, strengthens bonds in the present moment, and prepares for the action of God in the future.

The wisdom of this reading that is imparted to us is of particular importance for today's families. Many families today are very fragile and are pushed and pulled by forces and commitments outside the

For meditation and context:

RESPONSORIAL PSALM   Psalm 128:1–2, 3, 4–5 (1)

R. Blessed are those who fear the Lord and walk in his ways.

Blessed is everyone who fears the LORD,
  who walks in his ways!
For you shall eat the fruit of your handiwork;
  blessed shall you be, and favored.

Your wife shall be like a fruitful vine
  in the recesses of your home;
your children like olive plants
  around your table.

Behold, thus is the man blessed
  who fears the LORD.
The LORD bless you from Zion:
  may you see the prosperity of Jerusalem
  all the days of your life.

Colossians = kuh-LOSH-uhnz

A reading that speaks of the virtues of building community.

Each of these qualities is worthwhile, deserving emphasis.

This passage concludes with a note of thanksgiving, a feeling to guide the community as it builds.

READING II   Colossians 3:12–21

A reading from the Letter of Saint Paul to the Colossians

[Brothers and sisters:
Put on, as God's chosen ones, **holy** and **beloved**,
  heartfelt **compassion**, **kindness**, **humility**, **gentleness**,
    and **patience**,
  bearing with one another and **forgiving** one another,
  if one has a **grievance** against another;
  as the **Lord** has forgiven **you**, so must you also do.
And over **all these** put on **love**,
  that is, the **bond** of perfection.
And let the **peace** of Christ control your **hearts**,
  the **peace** into which you were also **called** in one body.
And be **thankful**.
Let the word of Christ **dwell** in you richly,
  as in all wisdom you **teach** and **admonish** one another,
  singing **psalms**, **hymns**, and spiritual **songs**
  with **gratitude** in your hearts to God.
And whatever you **do**, in **word** or in **deed**,
  do **everything** in the name of the Lord **Jesus**,
  giving **thanks** to God the Father **through** him.]

---

household. These challenges often make honor and respect difficult to manifest at home. Yet Sirach calls each member of the household to manifest care and concern for familial relationships. The more we work to honor the relationships of our households, the more we will come to revere God—"a house raised in justice to you," God. The same could be said for the "holy family" that is the Church. The more we labor to care for one another and extend compassion, the greater force will our communal prayer have in praising God our Father.

READING II Paul writes to the infant church in Colossae, a city east of Ephesus. Although he had never visited Colossae, Paul has been provided information that this Christian community is struggling to follow the faith. Specifically, many Christians have resumed former pagan practices and are worshipping false gods. They were also wrestling with the teaching that Jesus is truly divine and not simply the greatest of all prophets sent by God. Thus, throughout his letter Paul underscores the divine nature of Jesus.

In today's reading from Colossians, Paul reminds them that those who have been baptized in Christ have a new life to live; all former ways of living must be put aside. The attitudes that belong to Christians are the markings of holiness: "heartfelt compassion, kindness, humility, gentleness, and patience," with forgiveness and love being the capstones that lead to perfection. Furthermore, the gifts of peace and thanksgiving belong to those who hold fast to their unity in Christ's body. These Christian attitudes simply cannot coexist with former outlooks on life.

A challenging passage to proclaim: it reinforces codes of conduct common to Greco-Roman society but which Paul typically disdains. (Most scholars of early Christianity regard these verses as added later by someone other than the original author, likely a scribe.) Probably best to read this in a neutral tone.

Wives, be **subordinate** to your husbands,
 as is proper in the Lord.
Husbands, love your **wives**,
 and avoid any **bitterness** toward them.
Children, obey your **parents** in everything,
 for this is **pleasing** to the Lord.
Fathers, do not **provoke** your children,
 so they may not become **discouraged**.

[Shorter: Colossians 3:12–17]

GOSPEL   Matthew 2:13–15, 19–23

A reading from the holy Gospel according to Matthew

The tone of this vivid and magical reading is nevertheless ominous—in that it is filled with omens.

Herod = HAYR-uhd

When the **magi** had **departed**, **behold**,
 the **angel** of the **Lord** appeared to **Joseph** in a **dream** and said,
 "**Rise**, take the **child** and his **mother**, flee to **Egypt**,
 and **stay** there until I **tell** you.
Herod is going to **search** for the **child** to **destroy** him."
Joseph rose and took the **child** and his **mother** by **night**
 and departed for **Egypt**.
He **stayed** there until the **death** of **Herod**,
 that what the **Lord** had **said** through the **prophet** might
  be **fulfilled**,
 Out of Egypt I called my son.

Slight pause between "Lord" and "appeared."

When **Herod** had **died**, **behold**,
 the **angel** of the **Lord appeared** in a **dream**
 to **Joseph** in **Egypt** and **said**,
 "**Rise**, take the **child** and his **mother** and go to the **land**
  of **Israel**,
 for **those** who sought the child's **life** are **dead**." »

Having established the general characteristics of what it means to pursue a Christian way of life that overflows in gratitude, as displayed in their response of praise and worship, Paul then turns to the relationships found within a family. If peaceful relations are to be found in the Church, then they must be found also in the Christian family. For this reason, Paul uses language such as wives being "subordinate" to their husbands, husbands avoiding all "bitterness" toward their wives, and children obeying parents in all things. Although we might find this language diffi-

cult to stomach in the twenty-first century, it is important to recognize that Paul is not interested in patriarchal power and control of wives and children, but rather, he believes that peace and harmony must reign in the domestic Church (the family) as well as in the worshipping assembly.

GOSPEL   Matthew's account of Jesus' nativity concludes with Joseph's dream that he should take Jesus and Mary to Egypt in order to escape the persecution of Herod. Inclusion of the journey of the Holy Family to and from Egypt

in Matthew's Gospel makes perfect sense considering his audience of Jewish Christians. He wants to place the story of Jesus into the framework of the Exodus experience of Israel sojourning in Egypt to avoid famine and returning to Canaan through the guidance of God's grace. Matthew makes it clear that such a story fulfills the prophecy of Hosea, quoting: "Out of Egypt I called my son" (see Hos 11:1). Joseph follows God's command to remain in Egypt until all is made safe for their return to Israel, information that is imparted by an angel to Joseph in yet another dream.

Archelaus = ahr-kuh-LAY-uhs

The omens in dreams guide this reading, leading toward its concluding prophecy.
Galilee = GAL-ih-lee

Nazorean = naz-uh-REE-uhn

> **TO KEEP IN MIND**
> Read the Scripture passage and its commentary in Workbook. Then read it from your Bible, including what comes before and after it, so that you understand the context.

He **rose**, took the **child** and his **mother**,
  and **went** to the land of **Israel**.
But when he **heard** that **Archelaus** was ruling over **Judea**
  in place of his father **Herod**,
  he was **afraid** to go **back** there.
And because he had been **warned** in a **dream**,
  he departed for the region of **Galilee**.
He **went** and **dwelt** in a town called **Nazareth**,
  so that what had been **spoken** through the **prophets** might be **fulfilled**,
  He shall be **called** *a* **Nazorean**.

Matthew does not provide many details regarding the journey to Egypt or the journey to return home. However, he is very clear that Joseph chooses to settle in the little town of Nazareth in order to avoid the danger waged by the new rule in Judea. In the village of Nazareth, located roughly 90 miles north of Jerusalem, Jesus will be able to grow in a quiet fashion until he is ready to begin his ministry.

Read in the context of the liturgical celebration of the Holy Family, we are invited to contemplate the righteousness of Joseph. He puts the care of his family above his own well-being, as he trusts God's intervention through the message of an angel. He is a beloved foster father who listens carefully to the will of God, forsaking his homeland and his work. We pray that our Christian families, bombarded by many voices in this world, may diligently discern the will of God for the good of their households. S.W.

MARY, THE HOLY MOTHER OF GOD

LECTIONARY #18

READING I   Numbers 6:22–27

A reading from the Book of Numbers

The LORD said to **Moses**:
  "**Speak** to Aaron and his sons and **tell** them:
  This is how you shall bless the Israelites.
Say to them:
  The LORD bless you and **keep** you!
  The LORD let his face **shine** upon you, and be **gracious** to you!
  The LORD look upon you **kindly** and give you **peace**!
So shall they **invoke** my name upon the **Israelites**,
  and I will **bless** them."

A reading built on advice that God gives to Moses. The verbs "speak," "say," and "invoke" are crucial, as are repetitions of "The Lord." Use these repetitions to guide your proclamation.

Note how the word "bless" is repeated.

Note how "bless" echoes in "peace."

For meditation and context:

RESPONSORIAL PSALM   Psalm 67:2–3, 5, 6, 8 (2a)

R. May God bless us in his mercy.

May God have pity on us and bless us;
  may he let his face shine upon us.
So may your way be known upon earth;
  among all nations, your salvation.

May the nations be glad and exult
  because you rule the peoples in equity;
  the nations on the earth you guide.

May the peoples praise you, O God;
  may all the peoples praise you!
May God bless us,
  and may all the ends of the earth fear him!

READING I As part of the instructions given by the Lord to Moses on the construction of the Tabernacle in the Book of Exodus, chapters 28 and 29 are devoted to the consecration of priests and the design of the vestments that are to identify their duty as "Sacred to the LORD" (Exodus 28:36). Levitical priests made daily burnt offerings as a sign of Israel's fidelity to the covenant. What is not made clear in Exodus is how priests are to relate to their fellow Israelites. Here in the Book of Numbers, which details Israel's beginnings in the Promised Land, we see a glimpse of

the role priests now play with the people. They are to bless the people.

Blessings had long been a part of the Israelite tradition, as the annual Passover, as well as the keeping of the Sabbath, called for God's name to be blessed. However, in this passage from Numbers, the role of blessing people is now reserved for priests, those who are the descendants of Aaron. Thus, we can see that the priesthood has expanded from the duty of performing daily sacrifice to strengthening the people's relationship with the Lord by reminding them of how he cares for them.

Thus, this blessing prayer invokes the name of the Lord over the people three times, as the people learn of his care: first, keeping them as his possession; second, experiencing the graciousness of God's face shining upon them; and third, receiving the gift of God's kindness and peace. The closeness of God to his people is suggested in all three of these invocations, but especially in the second, for Moses saw the face of God and was forever transfigured. The people are not to see the Lord's face, but they are certainly meant to radiate

A reading in which Paul connects the members of the early church in Galatia directly to Jesus. He does so in three sentences, introduced by "when," "as," and "so." In short order, he builds his argument and then concludes it.

The conclusion of Paul's argument, that we are no longer slaves but sons and heirs of God, is truly radical. It deserves some astonishment and emphasis.

A reading that concludes the Nativity story. While the focus is on the infant Jesus lying in the manger, the eyes through which we see him are those of the shepherds. The shepherds modeled Christian devotion from the beginning of our faith.

Amazement is the primary emotion of this story.

> **TO KEEP IN MIND**
> Recognize how important your proclamation of the Word of God is. Prepare well and take joy in your ministry.

READING II   Galatians 4:4–7

A reading from the Letter of Saint Paul to the Galatians

Brothers and sisters:
When the **fullness** of time had come, God sent his Son,
    born of a woman, **born** under the law,
    to ransom those **under** the law,
    so that we might **receive** adoption as sons.
As **proof** that you are **sons**,
    God sent the **Spirit** of his Son into our hearts,
    crying out, "**Abba**, Father!"
So you are **no longer** a slave but a **son**,
    and if a **son** then also an **heir**, **through** God.

GOSPEL   Luke 2:16–21

A reading from the holy Gospel according to Luke

The **shepherds** went in haste to **Bethlehem** and found **Mary**
    and **Joseph**,
    and the infant **lying** in the manger.
When they **saw** this,
    they made **known** the message
    that had been **told** them about this child.
All who heard it were **amazed**
    by what had been **told** them by the **shepherds**.
And **Mary** kept all these things,
    reflecting on them in her **heart**.

God's countenance. God's benefits will be given to all who call upon his name.

READING II In the fourth chapter of his letter to the Galatians, Paul discusses what it means to be an heir of God. He says that until a child matures and comes of age, he or she can be thought of as a slave, but when the proper age is reached, that person is free to inherit all that he or she has been promised. Paul then suggests that those who have been granted God's revelation of his Son through the power of the Spirit are no longer to be thought of as slaves, but instead, they are now free to inherit what God has promised them.

This passage from Galatians opens with Paul suggesting that the age of maturity arrived in the incarnation of Jesus, Son of God. This Son performs a twofold mission: first, he is to "ransom," or set free those who subscribe to the Law, and second, he is to provide "adoption" for those set free by his act of liberation. Furthermore, with adoption comes the movement of the Spirit into believers' hearts so that they might know God and be able to address him as "Father."

Thus, Paul's microscopic portrayal of salvation history suggests a basic change in relationships. Prior to the sending of the Son, people could only relate to God as a slave would to a master. Now, all who have the Spirit in their hearts have a different relationship with God; they are able to see themselves as children in relationship to a father. Because they are now adopted sons and daughters, they are able to inherit all that God promises, namely the fullness of salvation. God's power is ultimately revealed

The shepherds' glorifying and praising are to be our own.

Then the **shepherds** returned,
    glorifying and **praising** God
    for **all** they had **heard** and seen,
    just as it had been **told** to them.

When eight days were **completed** for his circumcision,
    he was named **Jesus**, the name **given** him by the **angel**
    before he was **conceived** in the **womb**.

in the relationships he forms with those who have been brought near by his Son by the working of the Spirit.

GOSPEL   Today we repeat the proclamation of the Gospel for the Mass of the Nativity at dawn, with the addition of the verse that announces the naming of Jesus at the time of his circumcision. In the context of today's feast, we are meant to focus particular attention on the figure of Mary. Luke reports that "Mary kept all these things" in her heart, as she receives the message of the angels through the ambassadorship of the shepherds. Thus, we see Mary, in a very real sense, as the first Christian contemplative. God has communicated with her in a special way, beginning with her own immaculate conception and continuing through the birth of Jesus. Certainly, pondering within her heart led her to marvel at what God might have in store for her next.

In addition to her contemplation of divine mystery, we are also meant to see Mary as the model of obedience. Throughout Luke's initial chapters, Mary listens completely to the message of the angel and gives herself over to God's will. In reporting that Jesus was circumcised and given the name spoken by the angel, we see that Mary is faithful not only to God but to her responsibilities as a Jewish mother. Jesus, like his cousin John before him (Luke 1:59), is to be raised in a thoroughly faithful Jewish household. As the *Theotokos* (an ancient Greek title for Mary, as Mother of God), Mary is the exemplar of contemplative obedience. S.W.

THE EPIPHANY OF THE LORD

LECTIONARY #20

READING I   Isaiah 60:1–6

Isaiah = ī-ZAY-uh

A reading filled with rich and poetic images and phrases. Radiance, light, gift giving, and praise guide this prophetic passage. Let these words guide your reading.

A reading from the Book of the Prophet Isaiah

Rise up in splendor, Jerusalem! Your **light** has **come**,
  the **glory** of the **Lord shines** upon you.
See, **darkness** covers the earth,
  and **thick clouds cover** the peoples;
but upon **you** the LORD **shines**,
  and **over** you appears his **glory**.
Nations shall walk by your **light**,
  and **kings** by your **shining radiance**.
Raise your eyes and **look** about;
  they all **gather** and **come** to you:
your **sons come** from **afar**,
  and your **daughters** in the **arms** of their **nurses**.

This passage is addressed to Jerusalem, but because it is written in the second person, it allows you to speak directly to the assembly. "Raise your eyes and look about. . . . "

Then you shall be **radiant** at what you **see**,
  your **heart** shall **throb** and **overflow**,
for the **riches** of the sea shall be **emptied** out before you,
  the **wealth** of nations shall be **brought** to you.
Caravans of **camels** shall **fill** you,
  dromedaries from **Midian** and **Ephah**;
all from **Sheba** shall come
  bearing **gold** and **frankincense**,
  and **proclaiming** the **praises** of the LORD.

dromedaries = DROM-eh-dayr-ees = single-humped camels

Midian= MID-ee-uhn

Ephah = EE-fuh

The camels and the gifts they carry prefigure the magi. Present this passage as a prelude to the Epiphany story.

READING I   Today's reading comes from the third part of Isaiah, which focuses on Israel's restoration after years of exile in Babylon. Rather than a prophecy of doom and gloom, Isaiah announces that the time has come for Jerusalem to reclaim its favored status: "Rise up in splendor, Jerusalem." It had to be an unenviable task to call the people to return to the land that had been ransacked, with its centerpiece—the Temple—in ruins. So many of the Israelites in their land of exile had to debate whether or not it would be worth the effort to return. But Isaiah tells the people that today is a new day in which the light of God's glory will shine upon a renewed nation and that this light will spread to other nations. In fact, Isaiah suggests that rulers from all over the world will have no trouble seeing the "shining radiance" that comes forth from the newly recreated land of the Israelites.

In an attempt to lure those who resist returning, Isaiah paints the picture of a great throng of people, young and old, journeying to behold the new Jerusalem. Just as the Egyptians gave their gold and silver to the Israelites when they were preparing to make their exodus from their state of slavery (Exodus 12:35–36), so does Isaiah suggest that visitors from foreign lands will pour out their wealth to the people when they see what God's glory has accomplished. Thus, it would be foolish for anyone to remain in Babylon when they are invited to be the recipients of such a great fortune. These foreigners will come not only with gifts of gold and frankincense, but they will also have the praise of God on their lips. A renewed Jerusalem benefits not only its inhabitants but also serves as a means of calling people to belief in God's

For meditation and context:

RESPONSORIAL PSALM   Psalm 72:1–2, 7–8, 10–11, 12–13 (11)

R. Lord, every nation on earth will adore you.

O God, with your judgment endow the king,
   and with your justice, the king's son;
he shall govern your people with justice
   and your afflicted ones with judgment.

Justice shall flower in his days,
   and profound peace, till the moon be
   no more.
May he rule from sea to sea,
   and from the River to the ends of
   the earth.

The kings of Tarshish and the Isles shall
   offer gifts;
   the kings of Arabia and Seba shall
   bring tribute.
All kings shall pay him homage,
   all nations shall serve him.

For he shall rescue the poor when he
   cries out,
   and the afflicted when he has no one to
   help him.
He shall have pity for the lowly and the poor;
   the lives of the poor he shall save.

Ephesians = ee-FEE-zhuhnz

A reading in which Paul emphatically includes the Gentile members of the early church in Ephesus into the community of believers. It's in two long sentences, emphasizing revelation and the Gospel respectively.

Emphasize "Gentiles," "coheirs," "members," and "copartners" as part of the "same body."

READING II   Ephesians 3:2–3a, 5–6

A reading from the Letter of Saint Paul to the Ephesians

Brothers and sisters:
You have **heard** of the **stewardship** of God's **grace**
   that was given to me for your **benefit**,
   namely, that the **mystery** was made known to me
     by **revelation**.
It was not made known to **people** in other **generations**
   as it has **now** been revealed
   to his **holy apostles** and **prophets** by the **Spirit**:
   that the **Gentiles** are **coheirs**, **members** of the **same** body,
   and **copartners** in the **promise** in Christ **Jesus** through
     the **gospel**.

wondrous care. Heard in the context of the celebration of Epiphany, this reading calls our attention to the way that God calls all the faithful to himself, not just those in a particular time or region.

READING II   The entirety of the Christmas season centers on the chief mystery of the incarnation, or the mystery of God-made-flesh. Christian faith in Jesus Christ holds fast to the belief that the depths of God's love is made manifest in the gift of his Son. The theology of Christianity's ancient Hebrew ancestors likewise believed

in God's desire to relate personally to his creation and to reveal his goodness to them. However, what is new with God's revelation in Christ is that God does not simply want believers who fall down in awe and worship before him, but he wants humanity to share in his divinity. This is the mystery we seek to contemplate during these days which mark the Lord's nativity.

The second reading chosen for the Epiphany comes from the Letter to the Ephesians, which is believed to have been authored by someone other than Paul. However, assuming the name of Paul, this

author declares himself to be a steward of God's grace. The mystery of God's providence has been revealed to him so that he might now reveal it to new generations of believers, precisely the Gentiles that dwell in regions far beyond the land upon which Jesus himself walked. Rather than being a gift that serves to carve out a particular people, the grace of God described here is that of a universal gift. The objective is to draw all peoples into Christ in order to unite them together into one body. In the very next chapter of Ephesians, the author will challenge the community to preserve

GOSPEL   Matthew 2:1–12

A reading from the holy Gospel according to Matthew

When **Jesus** was born in **Bethlehem** of **Judea**,
    in the **days** of King **Herod**,
    behold, **magi** from the **east** arrived in Jerusalem, saying,
    "**Where** is the newborn **king** of the **Jews?**
We saw his **star** at its **rising**
    and have **come** to do him **homage**."
When King Herod heard this,
    he was greatly **troubled**,
    and **all Jerusalem** with him.
Assembling all the chief priests and the scribes of the people,
    he **inquired** of them **where** the Christ was to be **born**.
They said to him, "In **Bethlehem** of **Judea**,
    for **thus** it has been **written** through the **prophet**:
       *And **you**, **Bethlehem**, land of **Judah**,*
          *are by **no means least** among the **rulers** of Judah;*
          *since from **you** shall **come** a **ruler**,*
            *who is to **shepherd** my people **Israel**."*
Then **Herod** called the magi **secretly**
    and ascertained from them the **time** of the star's **appearance**.
He sent them to Bethlehem and said,
    "**Go** and search **diligently** for the **child**.
When you have **found** him, bring me **word**,
    that **I too may go** and do him homage."
After their **audience** with the king they set out.
And **behold**, the **star** that they had seen at its rising
      preceded them,
    until it **came** and **stopped over** the place where the **child was**.

A reading that tells a rich and mysterious story, one that includes astrology and betrayal, providing a vivid context for the world into which Jesus was born.

The arrival of the magi sets the scene. Their desire to pay homage to the newborn king prepares the way for our own worship.

homage = HOM-ij

Herod's trouble represents doubt and deception, which the subsequent verses elaborate.

Pause slightly after "stopped."

---

the unity they have been given in Christ, for there is "one Lord, one faith" (Ephesians 4:5). All those who hear the Gospel and are called to be "copartners" must recognize that God's grace is revealed in striving for perfect unity.

 Chapter 1 of Matthew's Gospel, which focuses on the genealogy of Jesus as a means of situating his birth firmly within Jewish heritage, concludes with the briefest of mentions of his nativity and Joseph naming him Jesus (Matthew 1:25). Matthew is largely uncon-

cerned with how Jesus was born, but instead, he wants to underscore the infant's bloodline. Jesus is born in the line of David, and is thus thoroughly Jewish. This is an important detail for Matthew's Gospel because he is writing primarily for a community of Jewish Christians who recently witnessed the destruction of the Temple (AD 70). Thus, he wants his readers to understand Jesus as both fully Jewish and as the true "temple."

Keeping in mind this background information as we examine the story of the Magi's visit to Bethlehem, the encounter

opens with the foreigners' arrival in Jerusalem, as they inquire where they might find the "newborn king of the Jews." Notice the lack of dramatic details as well as the fact that the principle character here is really King Herod. Herod was king from 37 to 4 BC. While history portrays him as a powerful leader known for massive construction projects in Judea, Matthew records his cowardice as he calls for a sweeping massacre of all boys under the age of two (Matthew 2:13–18). Thus, the story of the wise men, who come from the ends of the earth, functions to show

prostrated = PROS-tray-t*d

Awe and wonder authenticate the magi and their prophetic visions. Their gifts are utterly precious. And their dream of warning is impossible to ignore. Don't sell their departure short. It's what makes this passage so vivid.

They were **overjoyed** at seeing the star,
   and on entering the house
   they saw the child with **Mary** his mother.
They **prostrated** themselves and did him **homage**.
Then they opened their treasures
   and **offered** him gifts of **gold**, **frankincense**, and **myrrh**.
And having been **warned** in a **dream** not to return to Herod,
   they **departed** for their country by **another** way.

how all of Herod's plotting is no match for God's designs.

Furthermore, this passage illustrates the universalism of God's revelation. It is not insiders from the Jewish establishment who recognize and pay homage to the newborn babe; instead foreigners come "from the east" to offer their gifts of gold, frankincense, and myrrh. Matthew records the Magi prostrating themselves before the child, a posture which we see elsewhere in the Gospel when the apostles encounter the risen Lord and he charges them to "make disciples of all nations" (Matthew 28:17–20). All the world is meant to recognize the saving power of Jesus.

At the end of this passage, we see that Herod's plan to find and destroy the infant Jesus is foiled, as the wise men are told in a dream not to give a report to Herod. We know from the remaining verses of chapter 2 that Herod will not relent in his search for the child king. Thus, Matthew demonstrates from the very outset of Jesus' birth that his mission upon earth will not be readily welcomed. In fact, Jesus' own people will pose one of the biggest threats to his ministry. We celebrate the Epiphany of the Lord to remember that God's message of salvation is not meant to be the sole possession of any one people; rather, God manifests himself to every nation so that the world will give him homage. S.W.

THE BAPTISM OF THE LORD

LECTIONARY #21

READING I   Isaiah 42:1–4, 6–7

A reading from the Book of the Prophet Isaiah

Thus says the LORD:
Here is my **servant** whom I uphold,
   my **chosen one** with whom I am **pleased**,
upon whom I have **put** my spirit;
   he shall bring forth **justice** to the **nations**,
not crying **out**, not **shouting**,
   not making his **voice heard** in the **street**.
A bruised reed he shall not break,
   and a **smoldering wick** he shall not **quench**,
until he establishes **justice** on the **earth**;
   the **coastlands** will wait for his **teaching**.

I, the LORD, have **called** you for the **victory** of justice,
   I have **grasped you** by the hand;
I **formed** you, and **set** you
   as a **covenant** of the people,
   a **light** for the nations,
to open the **eyes** of the **blind**,
   to bring out **prisoners** from **confinement**,
   and from the **dungeon**, those who live in **darkness**.

Isaiah = ī-ZAY-uh

A reading in which the Lord identifies his servant, characterizing his virtues in terms of his humility and preparedness, followed by a passage in which the Lord shifts from talking about his chosen servant in the third person ("he") to the second person ("you"), which allows you to direct your proclamation to the gathered assembly. Take advantage of this shift in pronouns.

Even stresses on the words in this line, which present a compelling image. A bruised reed is easy to break; why isn't the chosen servant breaking the reed?

Emphasize "grasped you" and "formed you."

The passage ends with images of dire things the Lord will use "you" to correct.

READING I The Book of Isaiah contains four poems that introduce the theme of God sending a "suffering servant," who will sacrifice his dignity and his entire self for the people's redemption. Chapter 42 begins the first of these poems. It opens by employing the Lord's voice to reveal this servant to Israel. The Lord deems this one as "chosen" because he has already pleased the Lord by all he has done. Empowered by God's spirit, the emissary has the task of bringing justice to the world. The Lord suggests that his servant's arrival will be highly anticipated, as even the far away regions of the earth await his teaching.

From a Christian perspective, we know that the teaching that Jesus brought to the earth was not what his own people wanted to hear. They were hoping for a political figure who would rid Judea of foreign control and would finally establish Israel's reign as supreme on earth. Instead, God has quite a different mission for his chosen servant. Verses 6 and 7 of chapter 42 describe the Lord providing instructions for the one he has chosen to establish God's justice. God calls his anointed one "a covenant of the people" and "a light for the nations." The law of the covenant that the faithful servant of God reveals to the people is one focused on mercy and compassion, as he will give sight to the blind, release to prisoners, and light to those trapped in darkness. The Suffering Servant will prove to be victorious not by his political might but by his loving justice.

READING II Chapter 10 of Acts witnesses Peter entering the house of Cornelius, a Roman centurion, and there experiencing a great change of heart.

For meditation and context:

RESPONSORIAL PSALM   Psalm 29:1–2, 3–4, 3, 9–10 (11b)

R. The Lord will bless his people with peace.

Give to the LORD, you sons of God,
    give to the LORD glory and praise,
Give to the LORD the glory due his name;
    adore the LORD in holy attire.

The voice of the LORD is over the waters,
    the LORD, over vast waters.
The voice of the LORD is mighty;
    the voice of the LORD is majestic.

The God of glory thunders,
    and in his temple all say, "Glory!"
The LORD is enthroned above the flood;
    the LORD is enthroned as king forever.

READING II   Acts of the Apostles 10:34–38

A reading from the Acts of the Apostles

This reading expresses ancient convictions of the earliest members of the faith.

Peter proceeded to speak to those gathered
    in the **house** of Cornelius, saying:
"In **truth**, I see that **God** shows no **partiality**.
Rather, in every nation whoever fears him and acts **uprightly**
    is **acceptable** to him.

"Peace," "Christ," and "Lord" express a unified vision of things.

Even emphasis on the words of this line.

You know the **word** that he sent to the **Israelites**
    as he proclaimed **peace** through Jesus **Christ**,
        who is **Lord** of all,
what has happened all over **Judea**,
    beginning in Galilee after the **baptism**
    that John preached,
    how God **anointed** Jesus of Nazareth
    with the **Holy Spirit** and **power**.

Even emphasis here as well, characterizing Jesus' powers.

He went about doing **good**
    and healing all those oppressed by the devil,
    for **God** was **with** him."

As a faithful Jew, entering the house of a Gentile would have caused Peter to stand apart from the Law. However, he listens to an angel in a vision and comes to have a new relationship with this foreign household.

Today's reading begins after Peter discerns the meaning of his vision. He discovers that "God shows no partiality" in bestowing his message of salvation upon all people. Instead of choosing people according to a particular nation, God finds acceptable the one who "fears him and acts uprightly." Furthermore, Peter deems those in Cornelius' household as "accept-able" to God precisely because they have heard the word intended for the Israelites but which is now extended to them. Thus, Peter names Jesus "Lord of all."

Our portion of Peter's discourse concludes with a summary statement of all that Jesus had accomplished in the land of Judea. We are right to suggest that Peter sees no partiality in the ministry of Jesus as his good deeds went out to all who were in need. In a similar way, Peter has come to know that those who have heard the word must also act with impartiality. Herein lies a primary gift of baptism; baptism in the Lord provides a unity that no human bias can divide.

GOSPEL   The entire liturgical season of Christmas might be thought of as a manifestation of divine theophany. A theophany occurs when God is made manifest to humankind. The manger scene, the celebration of Mary as the ark of God's coming into the world, the journey of the wise men to Bethlehem, and today, the baptism of Jesus in the Jordan are all grand theophanies which reveal the depth of God's love breaking into the world.

GOSPEL   Matthew 3:13–17

A reading from the holy Gospel according to Matthew

Jesus came from **Galilee** to **John** at the **Jordan**
    to be **baptized** by him.
John **tried** to **prevent** him, saying,
    "I need to be **baptized** by **you**,
    and yet **you** are coming to **me**?"
Jesus **said** to him in reply,
    "**Allow** it **now**, for **thus** it is **fitting** for us
    to **fulfill** all **righteousness**."
Then he **allowed** him.
After **Jesus** was **baptized**,
    he came **up** from the water and **behold**,
    the **heavens** were **opened** for him,
    and he saw the **Spirit** of **God descending** like a **dove**
    and **coming upon** him.
And a **voice** came from the **heavens**, saying,
    "**This** is my beloved **Son**, with **whom** I am well **pleased**."

Galilee = GAL-ih-lee
A reading that emphasizes the simple power of baptism.

Note the shift in the pronouns here, from "I" to "you," then from "you" to "me."

Slight pause between "God" and "descending."

Matthew's account of Jesus' baptism begins with John trying prevent Jesus from being baptized. Obviously, John does not believe that Jesus needs to undergo baptism as a means of repentance and conversion. Instead, he presents himself to Jesus as the one who needs to be baptized. Matthew's resolution to this dilemma is to put this event into the framework of "fulfillment," which he frequently employs throughout the Gospel as a whole. In this case, Jesus announces to John that he wishes to be baptized "to fulfill all righteousness," demonstrating total obedience to the will of God.

The theophany which seals the Lord's baptism is symbolized by the descent of a dove upon the head of Jesus. The Spirit provides a visible sign that accompanies the Father's voice in announcing the presence of his Son. Similar to the story of Noah sending the dove forth from the ark to testify to the dried earth (Genesis 8:6–12), so too is a dove associated with the regeneration of creation inaugurated at the Lord's Baptism. God chose Israel as his beloved possession, and now God's relationship with Jesus reveals him as the New Covenant; in Jesus God's promise is fulfilled, and the world begins anew. From the manger to the Jordan, God's in-breaking into the world manifests a new creation. S.W.

SECOND SUNDAY IN ORDINARY TIME

LECTIONARY #64

READING I   Isaiah 49:3, 5–6

A reading from the Book of the Prophet Isaiah

Isaiah = ī-ZAY-uh

The tone of this reading is encouraging. Slight pause between "Lord" and "said." Emphasis on "you."

Slight pause between "Israel" and "gathered."

The reading concludes with God's promise to Isaiah, which is God's promise to his people.

The LORD **said** to me: **You** are my **servant**,
    Israel, through **whom** I show my glory.
Now the LORD has **spoken**
    who **formed** me as his **servant** from the **womb**,
that **Jacob** may be brought **back** to him
    and **Israel gathered** to him;
and I am made **glorious** in the **sight** of the LORD,
    and my **God** is now my **strength**!
It is **too little**, the LORD says, for **you** to be my **servant**,
    to raise up the **tribes** of **Jacob**,
    and **restore** the **survivors** of **Israel**;
I will **make** you a **light** to the **nations**,
    that my **salvation** may **reach** to the **ends** of the **earth**.

READING I   This Sunday marks the end of the first week of the liturgical season called "Ordinary Time" and the beginning of its second week. Ordinary Time is the period of the church year that stands outside of the all-important Advent/Christmas and Lent/Easter seasons. However, to call this period "ordinary" is not to say that it is unimportant. Its name shares a root with the Latin term *ordinalis*, meaning "numbered." Thus, the thirty-four weeks of Ordinary Time mark the movement of time as the salvation story unfolds through the year. Green is the liturgical color for this season, which is appropriate because it represents a time of spiritual growth. The readings for this Second Sunday in Ordinary Time focus on the commissioning of God's servants to reveal God's plan of salvation for the world.

Today's first reading is taken from what is often called "the second servant song" of the Book of Isaiah. Altogether there are four. This servant song describes a commissioning of the servant as a prophet or spokesperson of God. Although the identity of the servant is sometimes unclear in the Book of Isaiah, here he is clearly identified with Israel. But which Israel? The setting for this commissioning is the period after the Babylonian Exile, when King Cyrus of Persia allowed the Judeans to return to their homeland and rebuild their temple. Although we cannot know for certain, it appears that this prophet is among a small group of Judeans who are persecuted because of their opposition to more powerful returnees who have a different view of life in Judea after the Exile. Thus, the prophet, who is personified Israel, is commissioned to effect a change of heart in the rest of Israel. God responds by saying that

For meditation and context:

RESPONSORIAL PSALM   Psalm 40:2, 4, 7–8, 8–9, 10 (8a, 9a)

R. Here am I, Lord; I come to do your will.

I have waited, waited for the LORD,
    and he stooped toward me and heard
        my cry.
And he put a new song into my mouth,
    a hymn to our God.

Sacrifice or offering you wished not,
    but ears open to obedience you gave me.
Holocausts or sin-offerings you sought not;
    then said I, "Behold I come."

"In the written scroll it is prescribed for me,
to do your will, O my God, is my delight,
    and your law is within my heart!"

I announced your justice in the vast assembly;
    I did not restrain my lips, as you,
        O LORD, know.

Corinthians = kohr-IN-thee-uhnz

The tone of this reading is introductory. It involves one long inclusive sentence followed by a much shorter blessing. Proclaim the first long part, up to "Grace to you . . . ," in the spirit of an introduction and the second, shorter sentence in the spirit of a blessing.

READING II   1 Corinthians 1:1–3

A reading from the first Letter of Saint Paul to the Corinthians

Paul, called to be an **apostle** of **Christ Jesus** by the **will** of **God**,
    and **Sosthenes** our **brother**,
    to the **church** of **God** that is in **Corinth**,
    to **you** who have been **sanctified** in Christ **Jesus**,
        called to be **holy**,
    with all those **everywhere** who call upon the **name** of our
        Lord Jesus Christ, their **Lord** and **ours**.
Grace to **you** and **peace** from **God** our **Father**
    and the **Lord Jesus Christ**.

this restored and true Israel will shine as a beacon, inviting everyone to share in its light.

READING II Our second reading is taken from the opening section of Paul's First Letter to the Corinthians. The mostly Gentile Christian church at Corinth was founded by Paul. Acts of the Apostles suggests that he spent a year and a half with this community before moving on to evangelize other locations in the Mediterranean (Acts 18:11), so he knew

them well, and the content of this first letter reveals as much. The opening follows the pattern of a first-century letter opening: sender, recipient, greeting. Paul, the sender, describes himself as an "apostle," that is, "one who is sent" by God's will. He describes the community as set apart for God and called to be "holy" in the fellowship of Christ. But Paul also wants to remind them that they belong to a much larger community of faith who serve the one God and the Lord Jesus Christ. What a good reminder for us, as well.

GOSPEL Today's Gospel reading is another version of the story of the baptism of Jesus that we heard last Sunday. This version from the Gospel of John is unique insofar as the author uses John the Baptist as the narrator of the baptism event, as he speaks to his own disciples, two of whom will soon shift their allegiance and become followers of Jesus. John the Baptist identifies Jesus as the Lamb of God and testifies that he is the Son of God.

GOSPEL John 1:29–34

A reading from the holy Gospel according to John

John the **Baptist** saw **Jesus** coming **toward** him and **said**,
  "**Behold**, the **Lamb** of **God**, who takes away the **sin**
    of the **world**.
He is the **one** of **whom** I **said**,
  'A **man** is coming **after** me who ranks **ahead** of me
  because he existed **before** me.'
I did not **know** him,
  but the **reason** why I came **baptizing** with **water**
  was that he might be made **known** to **Israel**."
John testified further, saying,
  "I saw the Spirit come **down** like a dove from **heaven**
  and **remain upon** him.
I did not **know** him,
  but the one who **sent** me to **baptize** with **water told** me,
  'On **whomever** you see the **Spirit** come **down** and **remain**,
  he is the one who will **baptize** with the Holy **Spirit**.'
Now I have **seen** and **testified** that he is the **Son** of **God**."

This reading begins with a very familiar phrase from the Eucharistic prayer we hear at Mass. Proclaim it with the same reverence you would hear during Mass.

The Baptist's words connect the Mass with the visionary reality he peered into. Speak the words "I saw" clearly.
Slight pause between "remain" and "upon."

Slight pause between "water" and "told."

Biblical scholars offer several possible scenarios for understanding the title "Lamb of God." Perhaps it is an allusion to a powerful and victorious lamb like the one depicted in the Book of Revelation, who stands before God's throne (Revelation 5:6–14) and who presides over an army of God's holy ones (Revelation 14:1–5). More likely, it is a reference to the Passover lamb, whose blood was placed on the lintels and door posts of the Israelites' homes in Egypt so that the angel of death would pass over their homes in the last plague of the Exodus story. Equally possible, "Lamb of God" might be an allusion to Yom Kippur, the Jewish day of atonement, when animal sacrifices were offered at the Jerusalem temple for the sins of the people.

Notice that this Gospel account does not include the tradition about Jesus and John the Baptist being related to one another (see Luke 1:26–38). Instead, the Baptist recognizes Jesus as Lamb of God and Son of God only because it was revealed to him through the work he was commissioned to do. The baptism which John was sent to perform is not a baptism of repentance like what we see in Matthew and Luke. Rather, its function was revelatory. John was called to reveal Jesus to all of Israel and to witness to the world that he is the Son of God. Finally, notice how the Baptizer knew Jesus' identity. It was because of the Spirit who descended on Jesus and remained on him. The verbs "to remain" and "to abide," in John's Gospel, are symbolic language used to describe discipleship and the special relationship of indwelling that Jesus enjoys with the Father. C.C.

THIRD SUNDAY IN ORDINARY TIME

LECTIONARY #67

READING I   Isaiah 8:23—9:3

Isaiah = ī-ZAY-uh

Zebulun = ZEB-yoo-luhn

The tone of this reading is triumphant and uplifting.

NAF-tuh-li

Gentiles = JEN-tīls

Emphasis on "no gloom."

"Abundant joy" and "great rejoicing" describe the message of this reading.

Emphasis on "yoke," "pole," and "rod."

Midian = MID-ee-uhn

A reading from the Book of the Prophet Isaiah

First the Lord **degraded** the land of **Zebulun**
and the land of **Naphtali**;
but in the **end** he has **glorified** the **seaward road**,
the land **west** of the **Jordan**,
the **District** of the **Gentiles**.

    Anguish has taken **wing**, **dispelled** is **darkness**:
        for there is **no gloom** where but **now** there was **distress**.
    The **people** who walked in **darkness**
        have **seen** a great **light**;
    upon **those** who dwelt in the **land** of **gloom**
        a **light** has **shone**.
    You have brought them **abundant joy**
        and **great rejoicing**,
    as they **rejoice** before you as at the **harvest**,
        as **people** make **merry** when **dividing spoils**.
    For the **yoke** that **burdened** them,
        the **pole** on their **shoulder**,
    and the **rod** of their **taskmaster**
        you have **smashed**, as on the **day** of **Midian**.

READING I On this Third Sunday in Ordinary Time, the theme of today's readings is the same as last Sunday: the commissioning of God's servants to reveal God's salvation to the world.

Our first reading is from the Book of Isaiah. When reading the prophets, it is important to know as much as we can about the historical context, because, regardless of the meanings we attach to their oracles today, the prophets were addressing real-life situations in their own time. We cannot be confident of the integrity of our contemporary interpretations of prophetic discourse unless we can connect the circumstances of the past with the present.

Isaiah served as God's prophet for approximately forty years, during which time he witnessed the Assyrian conquest of the northern kingdom of Israel, also known as Ephraim, beginning in 733 BC and Syria in 732 BC. When the oracle that comprises our first reading was delivered, Ahaz was king of Judah. He was facing considerable pressure from Syria and Israel to join a coalition against Assyria. When he refused, Syria and Israel invaded Judah with the intent of unseating Ahaz—an event known as the Syro-Ephraimite War. Eventually, the entire northern kingdom was decimated by the Assyrians and its people deported in 721 BC, while the southern kingdom of Judah became a vassal of Assyria.

This truly was a dark time in Judah's history. Isaiah attributes the destruction of Israel to God, according to the pattern of Deuteronomistic history: Israel sins; God punishes; Israel repents; God forgives. How does God show forgiveness? The Assyrian provinces of Dor, Gilead, and Megiddo, which were fashioned from land that once

For meditation and context:

RESPONSORIAL PSALM Psalm 27:1, 4, 13–14 (1a)

R. The Lord is my light and my salvation.

The LORD is my light and my salvation;
  whom should I fear?
The LORD is my life's refuge;
  of whom should I be afraid?

One thing I ask of the LORD;
  this I seek:
to dwell in the house of the LORD
  all the days of my life,
that I may gaze on the loveliness of the LORD
  and contemplate his temple.

I believe that I shall see the bounty
  of the LORD
  in the land of the living.
Wait for the LORD with courage;
  be stouthearted, and wait for the LORD.

Corinthians = kohr-IN-thee-uhnz

The tone of this reading is one of urgency and intensity.

Slight pause between "divisions" and "among."

Chloe = KLOH-ee

Apollos = uh-POL-uhs

Note the shifts in energy from the pronoun "I" to the proper nouns, "Paul," "Apollos," "Cephas," and "Christ."

Cephas = SEE-fuhs

These two questions shape Paul's argument to the Corinthians. Slight pause between "Paul" and "crucified."

READING II 1 Corinthians 1:10–13, 17

A reading from the first Letter of Saint Paul to the Corinthians

I **urge** you, **brothers** and **sisters**, in the **name** of our
  Lord Jesus **Christ**,
  that **all** of you **agree** in what you **say**,
  and that there be **no divisions among** you,
  but that you be **united** in the **same mind**
  and in the **same purpose**.
For it has been reported to **me about** you,
  my **brothers** and **sisters**,
  by **Chloe's** people, that there are **rivalries** among you.
I mean that **each** of you is **saying**,
  "I belong to **Paul**," or "I belong to **Apollos**,"
  or "I belong to **Cephas**," or "I belong to **Christ**."
Is **Christ divided**?
Was **Paul crucified** for **you**?
Or were you **baptized** in the name of **Paul**?
For **Christ** did not send me to **baptize** but to **preach** the **gospel**,
  and not with the wisdom of human **eloquence**,
  so that the cross of **Christ** might not be
  emptied of its **meaning**.

---

belonged to Israel, are allowed to prosper. Thus, as the prophet says, the gloom and darkness will be lifted, and light will shine on the land. The pronoun "you" in this passage refers to God; Isaiah is the speaker. Biblical scholars have described this part of today's reading as a hymn to accompany accession to the throne or a thanksgiving hymn directed to God. The "yoke," "pole," and "rod" are symbols of Assyrian oppression that will one day be thrown off in holy war, as in the day of Midian and as when God destroyed the Israelites' oppressors by the hand of Gideon, one of several judges

whose stories are told in the book of Judges (see Judges 6–8).

The remainder of this oracle, which is not part of today's first reading, is presumed to be about the son that would be born to Ahaz, whose name was Hezekiah and who would inherit Judah's throne after Ahaz. The Second Book of Kings and the Second Book of Chronicles portray him as a good and righteous king, in contrast to his father. However, the list of attributes of a good king, the verses that follow today's reading that describe the child to be born, might be intended to describe some future

and long-awaited king. Early Christians attributed this description to Jesus, the bringer of peace and the one who will usher in the fulness of God's kingdom.

READING II Today's second reading is the beginning of the body of Paul's First Letter to the Corinthians. Immediately following the thanksgiving (1 Corinthians 1:4–9), Paul exhorts the Corinthian community to unity, after hearing a report about divisions that have surfaced among them. The report came from "Chloe's people," who we can assume are

The tenuousness and excitement of Christ beginning his ministry pervade this reading. For the longer form of the reading, use the word "withdrew" to focus your proclamation.

Capernaum = kuh-PER-nee-*m or kuh-PER-nay-*m or kuh-PER-n*m

Zebulun = ZEB-yoo-luhn

Naphtali = NAF-tuh-lī

Slight pause between "death" and "light."

Use "fishers of men" to focus your proclamation for the second half of this reading.

Zebedee = ZEB-uh-dee

GOSPEL   Matthew 4:12–23

A reading from the holy Gospel according to Matthew

[When **Jesus** heard that **John** had been **arrested**,
    he **withdrew** to **Galilee**.
He left **Nazareth** and went to live in **Capernaum** by the **sea**,
    in the **region** of **Zebulun** and **Naphtali**,
    that what had been **said** through **Isaiah** the **prophet**
    might be fulfilled:
        Land of **Zebulun** and land of **Naphtali**,
            the **way** to the **sea**, beyond the **Jordan**,
            Galilee of the **Gentiles**,
        the **people** who sit in **darkness** have seen a **great light**,
        on those **dwelling** in a **land** over**shadowed** by **death**
            light has arisen.
From **that time on**, **Jesus** began to **preach** and **say**,
    "**Repent**, for the **kingdom** of **heaven** is at **hand**."]

As he was **walking** by the Sea of **Galilee**, he saw two **brothers**,
    Simon who is called **Peter**, and his brother **Andrew**,
    casting a net into the **sea**; they were **fishermen**.
He **said** to them,
    "**Come** after **me**, and I will make you **fishers** of **men**."
At **once** they left their **nets** and **followed** him.
He walked **along** from **there** and saw **two other brothers**,
    James, the son of **Zebedee**, and his brother **John**.
They were in a **boat**, with their father **Zebedee**, mending
        their **nets**.

employees or slaves of this otherwise unknown businesswoman. We can further assume that Chloe and her servants are followers of Jesus. The servants probably visited the community while on a business trip in or through Corinth and then reported to Paul what they had seen and heard.

Paul is understandably concerned about the divisions in the community, because of his understanding of church as *koinonia*, meaning "fellowship or partnership." This is why he urges them to "be united in the same mind and in the same purpose." Apparently, their divisions stem from allegiances that they formed around the person they claim as their spiritual leader. Apollos, who is mentioned here and elsewhere in this letter, is described in Acts of the Apostles as a Jewish rhetorician and scripture scholar from Alexandria in Egypt, who later became a Christian preacher (Acts 18:24–28). Most likely, the person whom Paul names as Cephas is Peter. Paul uses this same name in his Letter to the Galatians.

In context, the meaning of "I belong to Christ" is not clear, but Paul's response to the community was to fire off a set of rhetorical questions, in which the speaker is not looking for a response because the intended answer is imbedded in the question. This is much easier done in Greek than in English, but the three questions would read something like this: Then you are saying that Christ is divided, aren't you? And you are not saying that Paul was crucified for you, are you? And you cannot be saying that you were baptized in Paul's name, can you?

Paul's argument reaches its climax when he declares the primary purpose of his ministry: to preach the good news of

He **called** them, and immediately they left their **boat**
and their **father**
and **followed** him.
He went around **all** of **Galilee**,
teaching in their **synagogues**, proclaiming the **gospel**
of the **kingdom**,
and curing **every disease** and **illness among** the **people**.

[Shorter: Matthew 4:12–17 (see brackets)]

Jesus Christ, even if imperfectly, so that the power of Jesus' crucifixion can be made manifest in their hearts and minds.

 GOSPEL Perhaps you know that the lectionary is organized so that the themes of the first reading and the Gospel cohere in some way. Today's first reading and Gospel reading are a perfect example. Notice how the author of Matthew's Gospel situates Jesus' ministry in the region of Galilee and cites an abbreviated version of the prophecy we hear from Isaiah in the first reading. One might deduce from the way that the writer incorporated this quotation that he intends to suggest that Jesus is the light to the nations and the one who will initiate God's coming kingdom.

As an indication of the Gospel writer's Jewish background, he describes Jesus as calling for repentance and saying, "the kingdom of heaven is at hand" not "kingdom of God," as we see in the other Gospels. Out of respect for the name of God, our Jewish brothers and sisters do not speak the name aloud. Regardless of whether we use the phrase "kingdom of God" or "kingdom of heaven," it is important to recognize that Jesus is not talking about a place. Instead, we should think about the kingdom as the reign of God, when God's power is fully manifest for all to see and when there is no more hunger or violence, sickness or death in all the world. Such is the good news of Jesus Christ! C.C.

FOURTH SUNDAY IN ORDINARY TIME

LECTIONARY #70

READING I   Zephaniah 2:3; 3:12–13

A reading from the Book of the Prophet Zephaniah

Seek the LORD, all you **humble** of the **earth**,
  who have **observed** his **law**;
seek **justice**, seek **humility**;
  perhaps you may be **sheltered**
  on the **day** of the LORD's **anger**.

But I will **leave** as a **remnant** in your **midst**
  a **people humble** and **lowly**,
who shall take **refuge** in the **name** of the LORD:
  the **remnant** of Israel.
They shall **do no wrong**
  and **speak no lies**;
nor shall there be **found** in their **mouths**
  a **deceitful tongue**;
they shall **pasture** and **couch** their **flocks**
  with **none** to **disturb** them.

Zephaniah = zef-uh-NĪ-uh

The tone of this reading is urgent but also generous. Something ominous is on the horizon. But the prophet trusts in the decency of his audience, appealing to it. A note of care prevails through the reading.

remnant = REM-n*nt
Slight pause between "people" and "humble."

Note the emphatic parallel between "do no wrong" and "speak no lies."

 READING I Zephaniah prophesied in the land of Judah during the reign of King Josiah (640–609 BC). His writing is part of a group of texts known as the twelve minor prophets. His work is considered "minor" not because of any lack important content but because the Book of Zephaniah and the other eleven books of the minor prophets are much shorter in length than those of the prophets Isaiah, Jeremiah, Ezekiel, and Daniel.

The prophecy of Zephaniah takes place at a time when Babylon was soon to destroy Jerusalem and send the Israelites into exile. Zephaniah accuses the people of Judah of being far too prideful, and so he seeks to counter their arrogance with a message that calls them to reform and humility. The prophet speaks of a "remnant" who will successfully "take refuge" in the Lord on the day that he comes to seek vengeance for the nation's wrongdoing. Zephaniah hopes that, on that fateful day, the Lord will discover several contrite lowly ones, whose humility of heart will counter the pride of the people.

Throughout the Old Testament we can see the belief that the people held, that even after suffering a major disaster, such as a famine or a military collapse, some portion of God's chosen people would remain. Isaiah and Jeremiah likewise prophesied that some of the Israelites would be saved as a "remnant," who would one day be redeemed (for example, see Isaiah 6:13 and Jeremiah 31:7–14). It is also important to notice that Zephaniah suggests that salvation will take place by taking refuge in the Lord, not by standing up to warring invaders. Instead "they shall pasture and couch their flocks with none to disturb them." Thus, Zephaniah calls for a conver-

56

For meditation and context:

RESPONSORIAL PSALM Psalm 146:6–7, 8–9, 9–10 (Matthew 5:3)

R. Blessed are the poor in spirit; the kingdom of heaven is theirs! or Alleluia.

The LORD keeps faith forever,
  secures justice for the oppressed,
  gives food to the hungry.
The LORD sets captives free.

The LORD gives sight to the blind;
  the LORD raises up those who were
    bowed down.
The LORD loves the just;
  the LORD protects strangers.

The fatherless and the widow the
    LORD sustains,
  but the way of the wicked he thwarts.
The LORD shall reign forever;
  your God, O Zion, through all generations.

READING II 1 Corinthians 1:26–31

Corinthians = kohr-IN-thee-uhnz

The persuasion of this highly effective reading relies on a series of effective parallels and repetitions.

Note the repetition of "Not many."

Note the repetition of "God chose," as well as the parallels from "wise" to "strong" to "world," finishing with the inversion of "nothing" into "something."
despise = dih-SPĪZ

A reading from the first Letter of Saint Paul to the Corinthians

Consider your **own calling, brothers** and **sisters**.
Not many of you were **wise** by **human standards**,
  not many were **powerful**,
  not many were of **noble birth**.
Rather, **God chose** the **foolish** of the **world** to **shame** the **wise**,
  and **God chose** the **weak** of the **world** to **shame** the **strong**,
  and **God chose** the **lowly** and **despised** of the **world**,
  those who count for **nothing**,
  to **reduce** to **nothing those** who are **something**,
  so that **no human being** might **boast** before **God**.
It is **due** to **him** that you are in **Christ Jesus**,
  who **became** for us **wisdom** from **God**,
  as well as **righteousness**, **sanctification**, and **redemption**,
  so **that**, as it is **written**,
  "Whoever **boasts**, should **boast** in the **Lord**."

righteousness = RĪ-chuhs-nis
sanctification = sangk-tuh-fih-KAY-shuhn

Note the repetition of "boasts"/"boast."

---

sion of heart that replaces pride with humility, as the people place their complete dependence upon God.

 READING II This reading from 1 Corinthians serves as a perfect bridge between our first reading and the Gospel. In the first reading we heard how God protects those who are humble, and in the Gospel for today, we will hear how the Lord calls "blessed" those who are meek and humble of heart. The theme of this passage from 1 Corinthians is quite simply that God chooses those whom the world

considers to be fools in order to put to shame those who consider themselves to be wise. In all three readings, it is clear that God does not operate according to the standards of this world; belonging to God's kingdom requires selflessness rather than selfishness.

Paul has just finished telling the Corinthians that he preaches Christ crucified, which is considered folly according to the wisdom of the Greeks (1 Corinthians 1:18–25). Now he reminds them that they are considered chosen by God, not because of wisdom or nobility, but rather, because

of their faith in Christ, which the world sees as weakness. The mission of those chosen by God is to cling so tight to this faith that others will see that human boastfulness is empty and counts for nothing. What matters is being able to boast of one's faith. Paul employs the beautiful phrase, "Whoever boasts, should boast in the Lord," which he will repeat to the Corinthians in his second letter (2 Corinthians 10:17). With this strong faith, and not futile wisdom, the Corinthians may count themselves part of Christ. Relying solely on this wisdom, they know that God has saved them (redemp-

Emphasis on "teach." This reading includes some of Jesus' best-known instructions.

The power of this reading depends on the rhythm you establish between the words that anchor the phrases paired in each beatitude. Say "blest" rather than "blessed."

GOSPEL   Matthew 5:1–12a

A reading from the holy Gospel according to Matthew

When **Jesus** saw the crowds, he went **up** the **mountain**,
   and **after** he had sat **down**, his **disciples came** to him.
He began to **teach** them, saying:
   "**Blessed** are **the** poor in **spirit**,
      for **theirs** is the **kingdom** of **heaven**.
   Blessed are **they** who **mourn**,
      for **they** will be **comforted**.
   Blessed are the **meek**,
      for **they** will **inherit** the **land**.
   Blessed are **they** who **hunger** and **thirst** for **righteousness**,
      for **they** will be **satisfied**.
   Blessed are the **merciful**,
      for **they** will be shown **mercy**.
   Blessed are the **clean** of **heart**,
      for **they** will see **God**.
   Blessed are the **peacemakers**,
      for **they** will be called **children** of **God**.
   Blessed are **they** who are **persecuted**
         for the **sake** of **righteousness**,
      for **theirs** is the **kingdom** of **heaven**.
   Blessed are **you** when they **insult** you and **persecute** you
      and utter **every kind** of **evil against** you **falsely**
         because of me.
   Rejoice and be **glad**,
      for your **reward** will be **great** in **heaven**."

Emphasis on "reward" and "great."

TO KEEP IN MIND

When you proclaim of the Word you participate in catechizing the faithful and those coming to faith. Understand what you proclaim so those hearing you may also understand.

---

tion), freed them from the way of sin (sanctification), and called them to live upright before God (righteousness).

 GOSPEL Today's Gospel passage from the beginning of the fifth chapter of Matthew opens a reading of Jesus' Sermon on the Mount (chapters 5 to 7) that will continue for the next several Sundays in Ordinary Time. Jesus' inaugural preaching event takes place on a Galilean hillside to which crowds were coming from near and far (Matthew 4:25). When Jesus sees the crowd, he gathers his disciples closest to him and begins with the pronouncement of the beatitudes, telling them what it means to be counted among the "blessed" in God's kingdom.

While Luke portrays Jesus proclaiming four beatitudes (Luke 6:20–23), Matthew's version contains nine. A major difference between them is that Luke focuses on a preferential option in this life for the poor, the hungry, and those who mourn, while Matthew broadens these categories to make them more about a spirituality centered on the kingdom of heaven. For example, in Matthew, it is not simply the "poor" who are blessed, but the "poor in spirit." It is not simply the "hungry" who are blessed, but those who "hunger and thirst for righteousness." In all the beatitudes, those who are deemed "blessed" are those favored by God because their suffering in this world will be overturned under the reign of God. Keeping the attitudes of the kingdom in this life will lead to a reward in the heavenly kingdom. S.W.

FIFTH SUNDAY IN ORDINARY TIME

LECTIONARY #73

READING I   Isaiah 58:7–10

A reading from the Book of the Prophet Isaiah

Isaiah = ī-ZAY-uh

This highly poetic reading is in the imperative voice. God is speaking forcefully to the people through Isaiah. Use this to guide your proclamation.

Emphasis on "light."

Equal emphasis on all the things to be removed: "oppression," "false accusation," and "malicious speech."

Thus says the LORD:
    Share your **bread** with the **hungry**,
        shelter the **oppressed** and the **homeless**;
    clothe the **naked** when you **see** them,
        and **do not** turn your **back** on your own.
    Then your **light** shall break **forth** like the **dawn**,
        and your wound shall **quickly** be **healed**;
    your **vindication** shall go **before** you,
        and the **glory** of the LORD shall be your **rear guard**.
    Then you shall **call**, and the LORD will **answer**;
        you shall cry for **help**, and he will say: **Here** I am!
    If you **remove** from your **midst**
        oppression, **false accusation** and **malicious speech**;
    if you **bestow** your **bread** on the **hungry**
        and **satisfy** the **afflicted**;
    then **light** shall **rise** for you in the **darkness**,
        and the **gloom** shall **become** for you like **midday**.

READING I Today's reading comes from the third major section of the Book of Isaiah. This portion of Isaiah differs from the first two sections in that it is addressed to the Israelites who have returned from exile in Babylon and are now charged with the responsibility of building a new nation. Isaiah likens this restored generation to a light that will shine forth for other nations to behold.

While it is clear that political and military concerns will be on the minds of those attempting to rebuild their nation, Isaiah pays particular attention to their treatment of the poor. It is important to locate this reading within the larger framework of the chapter, which focuses on fasting and the need to avoid empty ritualism. Isaiah wants the people to understand that their fasting will be of little consequence if they do not feed the hungry, shelter the homeless, and clothe the naked. These and other acts of compassion will serve to scatter the darkness and reflect the light of God's love.

Moreover, not only will light emanate from Israel, but when their compassion is demonstrated and their underlying spirit of goodness is manifested, then God's glory will guard them. The prophet speaks of the people being vindicated. As we read these words, we call to mind how God has protected his people in the past. For example, consider how the ancient Israelites were vindicated at the Red Sea with God's angel leading the people in cloud by day and in fire by night. In today's reading, we hear Isaiah prophecy, "your vindication shall go before you, and the glory of the LORD shall be your rear guard." For Isaiah, attention to the poor and the oppressed will be like a key that opens the door to success for the former refugees. He envisions the return to

For meditation and context:

RESPONSORIAL PSALM   Psalm 112:4–5, 6–7, 8–9 (4a)

R. The just man is a light in darkness to the upright.
or
R. Alleluia.

Light shines through the darkness for
    the upright;
    he is gracious and merciful and just.
Well for the man who is gracious and lends,
    who conducts his affairs with justice.

He shall never be moved;
    the just one shall be in everlasting
        remembrance.
An evil report he shall not fear;
    his heart is firm, trusting in the LORD.

His heart is steadfast; he shall not fear.
    Lavishly he gives to the poor;
his justice shall endure forever;
    his horn shall be exalted in glory.

READING II   1 Corinthians 2:1–5

A reading from the first Letter of Saint Paul to the Corinthians

When I **came** to you, **brothers** and **sisters**,
    proclaiming the **mystery** of **God**,
    I did not **come** with **sublimity** of **words** or of **wisdom**.
For I **resolved** to know nothing while I was with you
    except **Jesus Christ**, and **him crucified**.
I came to you in **weakness** and **fear** and much **trembling**,
    and my **message** and my **proclamation**
    were **not** with persuasive **words** of **wisdom**,
    but with a **demonstration** of **Spirit** and **power**,
    so that your **faith** might rest **not** on **human wisdom**
but on the **power** of **God**.

Corinthians = kohr-IN-thee-uhnz

The energy of this reading relies on the accumulation of negatives—negative attributes as well as things Paul claims he did not do. And these accumulate right up to the concluding line of the reading, when the "power of God" bursts forth in a positive shower.

sublimity = suhb-LIM-ih-tee

TO KEEP IN MIND
Pause to break up separate thoughts, set apart significant statements, or indicate major shifts. Never pause in the middle of a thought. Your primary guide for pauses is punctuation.

---

the Promised Land as a renewal of the covenant that summons the people to act as God has acted toward them.

READING II One of Paul's major reasons for writing to the Corinthians was to combat the influence of those who considered themselves spiritually sophisticated. Within the Corinthian Church there were some who took on an air of elitism, believing that the way of Christ constituted the attainment of wisdom. Very similar to their gnostic counterparts among the pagans, these Christians believed that wisdom separated them from the cares and concerns of the world.

Thus, Paul wants to be perfectly clear near the beginning of his letter that he does not align himself with this group of elitists. His wisdom alone is that of Christ crucified, which he has just called a "stumbling block" and "foolishness" to the Jews and the Gentiles (1 Corinthians 1:23). Paul goes so far as to suggest that this message was all that he could offer the Corinthians during his time among them. Thus, they should not expect his message to be any different now. He admits to them that although he came to them "in weakness and fear and much trembling," his message proved to be powerful and true. It may not have been full of worldly wisdom, but it demonstrated the power and wisdom of God.

Paul's introduction of himself to the Corinthians in this passage is in keeping with a plan that appears in other letters written by him. In playing down his own power and authority, Paul seeks to win the listening ear of his audience for Christ alone. In speaking of himself as weak and fearful, his humility attracts the attention of the

GOSPEL Matthew 5:13–16

A reading from the holy Gospel according to Matthew

Jesus said to his **disciples**:
  "**You** are the **salt** of the **earth**.
But if **salt** loses its **taste**, with **what** can it be **seasoned**?
It is no longer **good** for **anything**
  but to be **thrown out** and **trampled** under**foot**.
You are the **light** of the **world**.
A city **set** on a **mountain cannot** be **hidden**.
Nor do they light a **lamp** and then **put** it under a **bushel basket**;
  it is **set** on a **lampstand**,
  where it gives **light** to **all** in the **house**.
Just so, your **light** must **shine** before **others**,
  that they may **see** your good **deeds**
  and **glorify** your heavenly **Father**."

This reading begins with a truly mysterious question. Slow your pace in these opening lines.

Express this characterization as sincerely as you can.

Give special emphasis to this line, with special emphasis on "light" and "shine."

Corinthians. Paul knows that it will not be an easy task to challenge the attitude of the spiritually elite in Corinth, and thus, he must make clear from the outset that God's grace prevails over human wisdom and action.

GOSPEL In hearing today's short Gospel reading, which continues Jesus' preaching that began last week in the Sermon on the Mount, we recall the theme of light which is present in today's first reading: when people act with justice for the oppressed, then their light shines in the darkness. In today's Gospel, Jesus refers to those who follow him as both salt and light.

While salt serves as a preservative and gives flavor to food, light illumines and allows clearer perception of the world. This passage immediately follows the beatitudes, in which Jesus calls "blessed" those who act with compassion and justice. Bringing these passages together forms a picture of discipleship: disciples of Jesus bring clarity into a darkened world by providing a vision revealed in selflessness. Furthermore, Jesus emphasizes that disciples will only be able to make a difference in the world if they use their gifts. Otherwise, they will be as useless as salt that has lost its taste and light that is hidden away.

The Gospel reading ends with Jesus cautioning his followers to avoid allowing their accomplishments to be a source of personal pride. Good deeds must always be done for the sake of others, and ultimately, all works of discipleship glorify God's name, not one's own. S.W.

SIXTH SUNDAY
IN ORDINARY TIME

LECTIONARY #76

READING I Sirach 15:15–20

Sirach = SEER-ak

A reading from the Book of Sirach

The tone of this reading is set by the "ifs" that begin it, placing it in the conditional. The claims it makes are somewhat harsh.

> If you **choose** you can keep the **commandments**, they will
>   **save** you;
>   if you trust in **God**, you **too** shall **live**;
> he has set **before** you **fire** and **water**;
>   to **whichever** you **choose**, stretch **forth** your **hand**.
> Before **man** are **life** and **death**, **good** and **evil**,
>   whichever he **chooses** shall be **given** him.
> **Immense** is the **wisdom** of the LORD;
>   he is **mighty** in **power**, and **all-seeing**.
> The eyes of **God** are on **those** who **fear** him;
>   he **understands** man's **every deed**.
> **No one** does he **command** to act **unjustly**,
>   to none does he give **license** to **sin**.

Emphasis on "no one" and "none."

For meditation and context:

RESPONSORIAL PSALM Psalm 119:1–2, 4–5, 17–18, 33–34 (1b)

R. Blessed are they who follow the law of the Lord!

Blessed are they whose way is blameless,
   who walk in the law of the LORD.
Blessed are they who observe his decrees,
   who seek him with all their heart.

You have commanded that your precepts
   be diligently kept.
Oh, that I might be firm in the ways
   of keeping your statutes!

Be good to your servant, that I may live
   and keep your words.
Open my eyes, that I may consider
   the wonders of your law.

Instruct me, O LORD, in the way of
   your statutes,
   that I may exactly observe them.
Give me discernment, that I may observe
   your law
   and keep it with all my heart.

TO KEEP IN MIND
The attention you bring to your proclaiming enables you to pray the Word of God with the assembly.

READING I The wisdom writing of Ben Sira comes from the early second century BC. This was a time of difficult choices for the descendants of Abraham. When the Babylonians destroyed the first Temple in 586 BC and forced the Israelites into exile, the chosen people wrestled with how to live the covenant with God without temple sacrifice. Their solution was to write down and to study the Torah, learning to inscribe the Law in their hearts. Upon their return to Jerusalem, with the second Temple reconstructed around the year 515 BC, the Israelites had to reconsider how

to worship. Did keeping the covenant demand animal sacrifice or study of the Torah?

The words in today's first reading can help illuminate what the life of the faithful should look like. Life is to be found in the choice to keep the commandments and to pursue understanding the Lord's wisdom. For generations, the Hebrew people learned to trust in the sacrifices they made as a means of assuring God's blessing. However, Sirach reminds them of the choice between truly trusting in God or relying upon them-

selves. Placing one's confidence and hope in God's wisdom will be the path to life.

This reading helps us to better understand the gift of free will. One who chooses the path of life does so freely. The same is true with the one who chooses to follow the way of death. God does not lead a person to choose one path over the other. God is not responsible for our sin; sin comes from human choice alone. Human freedom is a part of God's will, and God wills not to rid the world of sin, because to do so would be to remove the gift of freedom. Following the commandments prevents one from

READING II 1 Corinthians 2:6–10

A reading from the first Letter of Saint Paul to the Corinthians

Brothers and **sisters**:
We speak a **wisdom** to those who are **mature**,
    not a **wisdom** of this **age**,
    nor of the **rulers** of this **age** who are **passing away**.
Rather, we speak **God's wisdom**, **mysterious**, **hidden**,
    which **God predetermined** before the **ages** for our **glory**,
    and which **none** of the **rulers** of this age **knew**;
    or, if they had **known** it,
    they would not have **crucified** the **Lord** of **glory**.
But as it is **written**:
    *What **eye** has not seen, and **ear** has not **heard**,*
        *and what has not **entered** the human **heart**,*
    *what **God** has **prepared** for **those** who **love** him,*
        this God has **revealed** to us through the **Spirit**.

For the **Spirit** scrutinizes **everything**, even the **depths** of **God**.

GOSPEL Matthew 5:17–37

A reading from the holy Gospel according to Matthew

[Jesus said to his **disciples**:]
    "Do not **think** that I have come to abolish the **law**
        or the **prophets**.
I have come **not** to **abolish** but to **fulfill**.
Amen, I say to you, until **heaven** and **earth** pass **away**,
    not the **smallest letter** or the smallest **part** of a **letter**
    will **pass** from the **law**,
    until **all things** have taken **place**. »

Corinthians = kohr-IN-thee-uhnz

Paul deftly shifts the source of wisdom from the human to the divine, which is "mysterious" and "hidden." His tone is authoritative but also awed.

Emphasis on "Spirit" and "depths."

A lengthy reading extensively recording Jesus' instruction and advice to his disciples. Because of its legalistic quality, pacing yourself as you proclaim will be helpful, so its points can come through.
Emphasis on "not."

making the choice to sin; thus, how foolish one would be to choose sin over searching for the Lord's wisdom!

READING II It is not often in the Sunday lectionary that the first and second readings are closely connected thematically, but today's readings are a rare exception. Just as Ben Sira urges the pursuit of wisdom as a life-giving choice, so too does Paul call the Christians in Corinth to proclaim God's wisdom. Let us not forget that some within the Corinthian community believed themselves to be spiritually elite,

priding themselves over and above "weaker" members.

For Paul, wisdom is a gift provided by the Spirit that is meant to draw the community closer together. It is not to be a source of pride or a cause for division. Unlike the wisdom provided by this world, the wisdom of God is eternal and unknown by political forces or even those who claim to be religious (such as the type Paul suggests are responsible for the Lord's crucifixion). The wisdom of God is not something that human power can attain on its own, it belongs to those upon whom it is bestowed

by God. Thus, those who are wise ought to never be full of their own wisdom, since God is the source of this gift.

It is not by accident that wisdom, "mysterious, hidden," came into this world; rather, the revelation of wisdom is part of God's plan for salvation. If the "rulers of this age" (both the Jewish and Roman ones) had properly discerned this plan, they would not have put Jesus to death. According to God's plan, his wisdom rests on those who love him.

In establishing that the Spirit is the conduit through which God reveals himself,

This begins a long series of characterizations in which the word at the end of the line (for the most part) is emphasized. Let the emphasized words guide your proclamation.

Sanhedrin = san-HEE-druhn

Gehenna = geh-HEN-nah

Therefore, whoever breaks **one** of the **least** of these
    commandments
    and teaches others to **do** so
    will be called least in the **kingdom** of **heaven**.
But whoever **obeys** and **teaches** these **commandments**
    will be called **greatest** in the kingdom of **heaven**.
[I tell you, unless your **righteousness** surpasses
    that of the **scribes** and **Pharisees**,
    you will not **enter** the **kingdom** of **heaven**.

"You have **heard** that it was said to your **ancestors**,
    *You shall not **kill**; and whoever kills will be liable*
        *to **judgment**.*
But I **say** to you,
    whoever is **angry** with his **brother**
    will be **liable** to **judgment**;]
    and whoever says to his brother, '**Raqa**,'
    will be answerable to the **Sanhedrin**;
    and whoever says, 'You **fool**,'
    will be liable to **fiery Gehenna**.
Therefore, if you bring your **gift** to the **altar**,
    and there recall that your **brother**
    has anything **against** you,
    leave your **gift** there at the **altar**,
    go **first** and be **reconciled** with your **brother**,
    and then **come** and offer your **gift**.
Settle with your opponent **quickly** while on the **way** to **court**.
Otherwise your **opponent** will hand you **over** to the **judge**,
    and the **judge** will hand you **over** to the **guard**,
    and you will be **thrown** into **prison**.
Amen, I **say** to **you**,
    you will **not** be **released** until you have **paid** the last **penny**.

Paul loosely quotes Isaiah 64:3, writing: "What eye has not seen, and ear has not heard, and what has not entered the human heart, what God has prepared for those who love him." Love of God is necessary for the gift of wisdom. Paul suggests that one who does not love God, and therefore neighbor, is incapable of understanding God's ways. God's plan may have been kept secret for many ages, but now it is revealed to those who believe. The one who knows a Christian's belief is the Spirit alone; the spiritually wise are incapable of this discernment without the scrutiny of the Spirit.

GOSPEL   After first proclaiming the Beatitudes and then calling his disciples salt and light, Jesus now continues the Sermon on the Mount with teaching his disciples a new way of observing the commandments. His way of approaching the ancient law is not to throw it out but rather to fulfill it, which is fully in keeping with Matthew's presentation of Jesus' ministry in general. Even though the Gospel of Matthew highlights many of the confrontational interactions between Jesus and the Pharisees, Jesus consistently takes a positive approach to the Jewish law.

In this time of waiting for the eschatological conclusion of the world as we know it ("until heaven and earth pass away"), God's commands ought to continue to remain in force. With that said, Jesus probes the commandments deeper than most scribes and scholars of the law. He is interested not only in the overt actions which the law either permits or prohibits, but he also wants to scrutinize intentions and the movement of the heart. For example, the first topic from the law that Jesus addresses is murder. Jesus examines the law and suggests that this commandment also calls for the elimination of the anger which would

This volatile and problematic topic demands that you move slowly through this passage.

["You have **heard** that it was **said**,
  *You shall **not** commit **adultery**.*
But I **say** to **you**,
  everyone who looks at a **woman** with **lust**
  has already committed **adultery** with her in his heart.]
If your **right eye** causes you to **sin**,
  tear it **out** and throw it **away**.
It is **better** for you to lose **one** of your **members**
  than to have your **whole body** thrown into **Gehenna**.
And if your **right hand** causes you to **sin**,
  cut it **off** and throw it **away**.
It is better for you to lose one of your **members**
  than to have your **whole body go** into **Gehenna**.

Still slow.

"It was also said,
  *Whoever divorces his **wife** must give her a **bill** of **divorce**.*
But I **say** to **you**,
  whoever **divorces** his wife—unless the **marriage** is **unlawful**—
  causes **her** to commit **adultery**,
  and whoever marries a d**ivorced woman commits** adultery.

Slight pause between "Lord" and "all."

["**Again** you have **heard** that it was said to your ancestors,
  *Do **not** take a **false oath**,*
  *but make **good** to the **LORD all** that you vow.*
But **I** say to **you**, do not **swear** at all;
  not by **heaven**, for it is God's **throne**;
  nor by the **earth**, for it is his **footstool**;
  nor by **Jerusalem**, for it is the **city** of the great **King**.
Do not **swear** by your **head**,
  for you cannot make a **single hair white** or **black**.
Let your '**Yes**' mean '**Yes**,' and your '**No**' mean '**No**.'
Anything **more** is from the e**vil one**."]

[Shorter: Matthew 5:20–22a, 27–28, 33–34a, 37 (see brackets)]

eventually cause someone to kill another. Furthermore, anger within one's heart must not simply be overturned, it must also include proper reconciliation with the other. This teaching on the command "thou shall not kill" shows that Jesus demands a deeper sense of ethical responsibility whereby a person does not simply refrain from an evil action but must identify and correct the root causes for the evil action in the first place.

Jesus continues his teaching to his followers by addressing the thorny issues of adultery, divorce, and lying. Adultery is clearly forbidden by the law of Moses (see Exodus 20:14). However, Jesus wants his disciples to scrutinize the underlying reason for adultery, namely lust. As a means to avoid this temptation, Jesus figuratively suggests tearing one's eye out or cutting off one's sinful hand. The point is to underscore the importance of maintaining right virtue, as to lose virtue would be more detrimental than losing a valuable body part. One exception to the law here that Jesus does make is in regard to divorce. The Mosaic law permitted divorce in certain situations (see Deuteronomy 24:1–4). However, Jesus looks at divorce differently, suggesting that it leads the abandoned woman to commit adultery. Undoubtedly, Jesus understands the importance of the permanent nature of marriage, but also sees it as an institution that provides for the woman's needs. In the society of his day, a divorced woman would have been without any means of support or security. Finally, Jesus expands the command to refrain from taking the name of the Lord in vain (see Leviticus 19:12) to apply to oath-taking in general. Because God witnesses all false speech, it is necessary to be truthful in all things. S.W.

SEVENTH SUNDAY
IN ORDINARY TIME

LECTIONARY #79

READING I Leviticus 19:1–2, 17–18

Leviticus = lih-VIT-ih-kuhs

A short and potent reading that compresses into it the core of the Abrahamic faith.

A reading from the Book of Leviticus

The LORD said to **Moses**,
  "**Speak** to the whole **Israelite community** and **tell** them:
  Be **holy**, for **I**, the LORD, your **God**, am **holy**.

"You shall **not** bear **hatred** for your **brother** or **sister**
    in your **heart**.
Though you may have to **reprove** your fellow citizen,
    do **not** incur **sin because** of him.

Slight pause between "sin" and "because."

Take **no revenge** and cherish **no grudge** against
    any of your people.
You shall **love** your **neighbor** as **yourself**.
I am the LORD."

For meditation and context:

RESPONSORIAL PSALM Psalm 103:1–2, 3–4, 8, 10, 12–13 (8a)

R. The Lord is kind and merciful.

Bless the LORD, O my soul;
  and all my being, bless his holy name.
Bless the LORD, O my soul,
  and forget not all his benefits.

He pardons all your iniquities,
  heals all your ills.
He redeems your life from destruction,
  crowns you with kindness and
    compassion.

Merciful and gracious is the LORD,
  slow to anger and abounding in kindness.
Not according to our sins does he deal
    with us,
  nor does he requite us according to
    our crimes.

As far as the east is from the west,
  so far has he put our transgressions
    from us.
As a father has compassion on his children,
  so the LORD has compassion on those who
    fear him.

READING I The Book of Leviticus gives a legal framework for matters of ritual, society, and life. The law that undergirds the covenant between God and the people is based on an ethical understanding whereby the people are to act in a way that corresponds to God's actions. In today's passage from Leviticus, we hear of the call to holiness. Quite simply, because God is holy, all those bound to the covenant are called to be holy. The foundation of holiness for both God and the people is to give oneself for others. Such generative giving is demonstrated by God in Genesis in the very desire to create something out of nothing. Therefore, an attitude of "otherness" must always guide the outlook of God's people.

The law proceeds to provide examples of how an attitude toward "otherness" is to be lived. First, one is prohibited from harboring any anger toward another. This flows into a second manifestation of "otherness," namely fraternal correction. Rather than harboring a grudge against another (which is sinful), one must reach out to correct others who may have committed some wrongdoing. Third, vengeance is not to be tolerated, as it demonstrates a desire to hold a grudge against another. Finally, love is to be given to a neighbor according to the manner in which one wants to be loved. Besides the command to love God above all others, the instruction to love others is a capstone of the Israelite law. We can see this law of loving others as self as part of the foundation of the what is called the "golden rule" in Christianity and other religious and ethical traditions.

READING II   1 Corinthians 3:16–23

A reading from the first Letter of Saint Paul to the Corinthians

Brothers and **sisters**:
Do you not **know** that you are the **temple** of **God**,
    and that the **Spirit** of **God** dwells **in** you?
If **anyone** destroys God's **temple**, **God** will **destroy** that **person**;
    for the **temple** of **God**, which you **are**, is **holy**.

Let **no one deceive** himself.
If a**ny one among** you considers himself **wise** in this **age**,
    let him become a fool, so as to become **wise**.
For the **wisdom** of this **world** is **foolishness** in the eyes of **God**,
        for it is **written**:
            God **catches** the **wise** in their own **ruses**,
        and again:
            The **Lord** knows the **thoughts** of the wise,
                that they are **vain**.
So let **no** one **boast** about human **beings**, for **everything**
        belongs to **you**,
    Paul or **Apollos** or **Cephas**,
    or the **world** or **life** or **death**,
    or the **present** or the **future**:
    all belong to **you**, and **you** to **Christ**, and **Christ** to **God**.

Corinthians = kohr-IN-thee-uhns

Paul's focus in this reading is wisdom, specifically, its transcendent power. Take a forceful tone with this reading.

Slight pause between "one" and "deceive."

Apollos = uh-POL-uhs
Cephas = SEE-fuhs

The whole thrust of Paul's argument is felt in the shift from "you," to "Christ," to "God."

READING II Three Pauline themes can be detected in today's reading from 1 Corinthians. The first is that the Christian community may be likened to "the temple of God." The one who inhabits this temple is God's very Spirit, which is why this temple is to be called holy. Paul is not simply talking about a holiness that comes from participation in worship, but a holiness that characterizes the very nature of the Christian community. Similar to Paul's reference to the Church as the Body of Christ (1 Corinthians 6:15–20), this building imagery emphasizes unity. All members of the community have a responsibility to maintain the temple's holiness through their actions.

This leads to a second Pauline theme, namely that such holiness is not to be found in human wisdom. Paul writes that "the wisdom of this world is foolishness," as he suggests that human wisdom leads individuals to self-reliance and therefore away from dependence upon God, who is the source of all wisdom. Paul tells the Corinthians that God is able to see how foolish the way of their human wisdom is, as he quotes Job 5:13 and Psalm 94:11—God sees both their behavior and their thoughts.

Finally, a third Pauline theme appears at the end of today's pericope which provides for the proper ordering of the community, namely that all belong to Christ. Because all belong to Christ, every member of the community has personal responsibility for the other members. Belonging to Christ means that relationship with God is fortified and unbreakable. Proper order within the "temple of God" exhibits true "holiness": care and concern for all relationships from God right on down to the

A powerful reading filled with familiar but perennially challenging teachings to take to heart. Proclaim as though these things are being said for the first time.

GOSPEL   Matthew 5:38–48

A reading from the holy Gospel according to Matthew

Jesus said to his **disciples**:
  "You have **heard** that it was **said**,
  *An **eye** for an eye and a **tooth** for a **tooth**.*
But I **say** to **you**, offer **no resistance** to one who is **evil**.
When someone **strikes** you on your **right cheek**,
  turn the **other** one as **well**.
If anyone wants to go to **law** with you over your **tunic**,
  hand **over** your **cloak** as **well**.
Should anyone press you into **service** for one mile,
  go for **two** miles.
Give to the one who **asks** of you,
  and do **not** turn your **back** on one who wants to borrow.

At this point, Jesus intensifies his teachings. Proclaim sincerely, tingeing your voice with surprise.

"You have **heard** that it was **said**,
  *You shall **love** your **neighbor** and **hate** your **enemy**.*
But I say to you, **love** your **enemies**
  and **pray** for those who **persecute** you,
  that you may be **children** of your heavenly **Father**,
  for he makes his **sun rise** on the bad and the **good**,
  and causes **rain** to **fall** on the **just** and the **unjust**.
For if you **love** those who **love** you, what **recompense** will
    you **have**?
Do not the **tax** collectors do the **same**?
And if you greet your **brothers** only,
  what is **unusual** about **that**?
Do not the **pagans** do the **same**?
So be **perfect**, **just** as your heavenly **Father** is **perfect**."

The questions that conclude this reading are not merely rhetorical. Imagine posing these questions to the members of your assembly.

---

seemingly most insignificant member of the Church. Because all are one in Christ, thus, there is no cause for boasting of one's own merits.

 GOSPEL   This week we continue to hear from the Sermon on the Mount as Jesus focuses on two basic Christian attitudes: acting with selflessness and loving one's enemies. The taking of "an eye for an eye" is an often-quoted element of the Jewish law (for example, see Exodus 21:24), which was originally intended to keep the deliverance of retaliation in pro-

portion to the wrong committed. However, Jesus believes that a response in kind is not appropriate for the Christian disciple. Instead, the injured party must surrender pride and ego and take no retribution on the one who inflicts some sort of evil. This same selflessness is to guide Christian charity in general; one must go the extra mile in assisting those in need. By acting in such a way in all these circumstances, God's love prevails over sin.

The second teaching involves developing a love for one's enemies and not simply for one's neighbors. Once again, Jesus

instructs his disciples to grasp the spirit of the ancient law. Love is meant to break down barriers of every sort. Thus, extending love to one's neighbor ought to naturally lead a person to avoid the desire to judge others by turning them into enemies. In other words, friends and enemies must be treated alike. A disciple does not hold back love on account of human judgment, instead each follower is to strive for divine perfection, a perfection which bears no discrimination. S.W.

ASH WEDNESDAY

LECTIONARY #219

READING I   Joel 2:12–18

A reading from the Book of the Prophet Joel

Joel = JOH-*l
rend = tear

A reading in which Joel in his role as prophet becomes the mouthpiece for the Lord; it is as if God is addressing the people directly in this reading. Proclaim this reading like Joel himself, with a sure and steady voice and so that its vibrancy will come through.

Even **now**, says the LORD,
    return to me with your **whole heart**,
    with **fasting**, and **weeping**, and **mourning**;
Rend your **hearts**, not your **garments**,
    and **return** to the LORD, your **God**.
For **gracious** and **merciful** is **he**,
    slow to anger, **rich** in kindness,
    and **relenting** in punishment.
Perhaps he will **again** relent
    and leave **behind** him a **blessing**,
Offerings and **libations**
    for the LORD, your **God**.

This reading makes use of frequent parallels. Give the words in pairs emphasis: "hearts" and "garments"; "gracious" and "merciful"; "slow" and "rich"; "offerings" and "libations."

The energy picks up with a series of imperative verb forms. These words are highly charged—God is telling the assembly directly what to do. "Blow," "proclaim," "call," "gather," "notify," "assemble," "let."

Blow the trumpet in **Zion**!
    proclaim a fast,
    call an assembly;
Gather the people,
    notify the congregation;
Assemble the elders,
    gather the children
    and the **infants** at the breast;
Let the **bridegroom** quit his **room**
    and the **bride** her **chamber**. »

| READING I | The prophecy of Joel is directed toward a nation that is in the midst of a great crisis. Devastation of the land was brought on both by a drought as well as by a plague of locusts. The people believed that they had been abandoned by God because of a national sin. In today's reading from Joel, Joel has a message of repentance for the people: transformation of life will result in God's favor once more.

The reading that opens our Lenten season represents Joel's call to the people to assemble to hear God's redeeming Word. Joel's message is simple: "return to me [the Lord]." For the prophet, this return entails individual and communal transformation of heart. For him, it is not enough to fast, to weep, to mourn, and to perform outward gestures of penance such as tearing one's clothes. Instead, the people must seek the mercy of God together.

The communal importance of seeking the gift of this mercy is demonstrated by Joel's command to "blow the trumpet" and to summon the people to a public fast. People of every age are invited to seek the way of God's mercy together. God can eas-ily peer into the hearts of each individual, but the community needs the participation of all its members if it is to display its fidelity to strive to live anew for God.

In addition to the communal acts that make visible a real willingness to return to the Lord, Joel calls the priests to a particular responsibility. They are to weep for the sins of the people and are to intercede on their behalf, asking God to withhold his punishment upon the nation. Joel suggests that if God bestows mercy instead of punishment upon the people, then other nations will see God's blessing. Otherwise,

Between the **porch** and the **altar**
　　let the **priests**, the **ministers** of the LORD, **weep**,
And say, "**Spare**, O LORD, your **people**,
　　and make **not** your **heritage** a **reproach**,
　　with the **nations** ruling **over** them!
Why should they **say** among the **peoples**,
　　'**Where** is their **God**?' "

Then the LORD was stirred to **concern** for his **land**
　　and took **pity** on his **people**.

Allow for a slight pause between the question and the final expression in the reading.

For meditation and context:

RESPONSORIAL PSALM   Psalm 51:3–4, 5–6ab, 12–13, 14 and 17 (3a)

R. Be merciful, O Lord, for we have sinned.

Have mercy on me, O God, in your goodness;
　in the greatness of your compassion wipe
　　out my offense.
Thoroughly wash me from my guilt
　and of my sin cleanse me.

For I acknowledge my offense,
　and my sin is before me always:
"Against you only have I sinned,
　and done what is evil in your sight."

A clean heart create for me, O God,
　and a steadfast spirit renew within me.
Cast me not out from your presence,
　and your Holy Spirit take not from me.

Give me back the joy of your salvation,
　and a willing spirit sustain in me.
O Lord, open my lips,
　and my mouth shall proclaim your praise.

READING II   2 Corinthians 5:20—6:2

A reading from the second Letter of Saint Paul to the Corinthians

Brothers and **sisters**:
We are **ambassadors** for **Christ**,
　　as if **God** were appealing **through** us.
We **implore** you on behalf of **Christ**,
　　be **reconciled** to God.
For **our** sake he made him to **be** sin who did not **know** sin,
　　so that we might become the **righteousness** of **God** in **him**.

Corinthians = kohr-IN-thee-uhnz

A reading in which Paul seeks to impress upon the members of the early Church at Corinth the importance of reconciliation with God in preparation to receive God.

The phrasing in this statement, "he made him to be sin," is a little peculiar. Practice it a few times and sound it out. It's not an expression we commonly use in relation to sin. "Be" is paralleled with "know." Emphasize those two words to anchor your proclamation.

other nations might look at Israel and accuse God of being weak for not giving them aid. The passage ends with God's recognition of the people's contrition. Once again, God takes notice of the people and has "pity on his people." True repentance involves more than individuals striving to better themselves before God, it demands individuals work together to form a people that is just.

READING II Prior to the passage we read in today's second reading, Paul has been reminding the

Corinthians that they have been made a new creation by their membership in Christ. Furthermore, he explains that Christ is the way through which the world is reconciled with God. Being refashioned in Christ means that Christians have been called to take up Christ's ministry of reconciliation so that others may participate in this relationship between God and humanity (see 2 Corinthians 5:17–19). All of this leads him to the conclusion that Christians are called to be "ambassadors for Christ." An ambassador is not simply someone who represents another; he or she is someone

who has developed a relationship with the people to whom he or she has been sent. Because ambassadors know the life situation of the people with whom they live, they are better able to represent their needs.

Paul's point here is that Christians do not act alone in the mission of the Church. Instead, Christian ambassadors work together, satisfying the obligations of loving and serving God as well as creating a healthy community that is united in Christ. Notice Paul's use of the plural "we"—"we are ambassadors," "we implore you," and

Working **together**, then,
    we **appeal** to you not to **receive** the grace of God in **vain**.
For he **says**:

In an acceptable time I heard you,
    and on the day of salvation I helped you.

Behold, **now** is a **very acceptable time**;
    behold, **now** is the **day** of **salvation**.

GOSPEL   Matthew 6:1–6, 16–18

A reading from the holy Gospel according to Matthew

Jesus said to his disciples:
    "Take **care** not to **perform** righteous deeds
    in order that people may **see** them;
    otherwise, you will have **no** recompense from your
        heavenly Father.
When you give **alms**,
    do **not** blow a **trumpet** before you,
    as the **hypocrites** do in the **synagogues** and in the **streets**
    to win the **praise** of others.
Amen, I say to you,
    they have **received** their **reward**.
But when **you** give alms,
    do not let your left hand know what your **right** is doing,
    so that your **almsgiving** may be **secret**.
And your **Father** who sees in secret will **repay** you.

"When you **pray**,
    do **not** be like the **hypocrites**,
    who love to **stand** and **pray** in the **synagogues** and on
        street corners
    so that **others** may **see** them. »

The exhortation of the reading resolves in Paul's use of the word "acceptable." In its first appearance, you do not need to emphasize it. When it reappears, be sure to give it extra emphasis.

A reading in which Jesus provides advice for how to approach the practices of almsgiving, prayer, and fasting. Each section of advice is constructed very similarly, creating parallel expressions. Don't let them become formulaic in your proclamation. Each of these practices is important to Jesus for bringing us closer to God.

Almsgiving comes first.

TO KEEP IN MIND
Use the pitch and volume of your voice to gain the attention of the assembly.

Emphasis on "left," "right," "secret," "Father," and "repay."

Next comes prayer. The wording is very similar to that in the almsgiving section. Emphasis on "inner," "secret," "Father," "secret," and "repay."

"we appeal to you." As a spiritual leader in the community and an ambassador of Christ's Word, Paul does not stand above or apart from the people, but instead reminds all of their need to be open to the grace of God that reconciles people to himself.

In order to enact the ministry of reconciling the world to God, the Corinthians must make reconciliation among themselves a chief priority. To attain this "righteousness," the community must acknowledge the sacrifice of the cross and the grace that comes from it. The urgency for this reconciliation is great, as Paul contends that *"now"* is the

time for conversion of heart. Heard in our contemporary gathering today at the start of Lent, Paul challenges modern-day ambassadors of Christ to work together to discover the grace of God anew.

GOSPEL   Today's reading from Matthew is essentially taken from the midpoint of Jesus' inaugural sermon to his disciples, known as the Sermon on the Mount (Matthew 5:1—7:29). In the previous chapter, Jesus instructed his disciples on what it means to be blessed in the kingdom of heaven (the beatitudes) and

how to interpret the religious law in a new way. In this passage, Jesus teaches his disciples about the proper attitude of prayer and approaches to self-discipline.

When it comes to the personal disciplines of fasting, praying, and the giving of alms, Jesus tells his disciples that actions are to be performed in such a way as to avoid gaining recognition. How easy it is to misuse these core practices as a means of measuring spiritual achievement and personal righteousness. Gaining "recompense" from the Father takes place when the sacrifice of food, the attention to prayer, and the

Amen, **I** say to you,
      they have **received** their **reward**.
But when **you** pray, **go** to your inner **room**,
      close the door, and **pray** to your **Father** in **secret**.
And your **Father** who sees in **secret** will **repay** you.

"When you **fast**,
      do not look **gloomy** like the **hypocrites**.
They **neglect** their **appearance**,
      so that they may **appear** to others to be **fasting**.
Amen, I say to you, they have **received** their **reward**.
But when you **fast**,
      anoint your **head** and wash your **face**,
      so that you may not **appear** to be **fasting**,
      except to your **Father** who is **hidden**.
And your **Father** who sees what is **hidden** will **repay** you."

And finally comes fasting. Once again, similar wording. This time, emphasis on "head," "face," "appear," "Father," "hidden," and "repay."

gift of charity are all done from an inward attitude of selflessness. When almsgiving, fasting, and prayer are conducted in such a way as to lose the self for others, then they are rightly directed toward the fulfilment of God's kingdom. God knows the intentions of our hearts, and this is how we are to be repaid.

As we hear this Gospel passage proclaimed on the first day of Lent, it is important to return to the context of Joel's prophecy in the first reading. He calls the people to assemble. As a Christian assembly, we hear these cautionary words of Jesus to his disciples and are reminded that our Lenten journey is meant to help us grow together as a community. While fasting, prayer, and almsgiving are certainly prescribed in order for individuals to grow in the image of Christ, they are also in place that we might understand better our dependence upon one another as brothers and sisters in the Lord. Hopefully we are not like the hypocrites who simply want to be noticed, but rather like those Jesus calls "blessed" in the beatitudes, bearing poverty in spirit, acting with gentleness and compassion, striving for righteousness, showing mercy, exhibiting purity of heart, working for peace, and accepting persecution for the sake of justice. The season of Lent is all about our growth together in the Paschal Mystery of Christ—learning more and more how to die to self in order to live anew for others. S.W.

FIRST SUNDAY OF LENT

LECTIONARY #22

READING I   Genesis 2:7–9; 3:1–7

A reading from the Book of Genesis

The LORD God **formed man** out of the clay of the **ground**
and **blew** into his **nostrils** the **breath** of **life**,
and so **man** became a **living being**.

Then the LORD God planted a **garden** in **Eden**, in the **east**,
and **placed there** the **man** whom he had **formed**.
Out of the **ground** the LORD God made **various trees grow**
that were **delightful** to **look** at and **good** for **food**,
with the **tree** of **life** in the **middle** of the **garden**
and the **tree** of the **knowledge** of **good** and **evil**.

Now the **serpent** was the most **cunning** of **all** the **animals**
that the LORD God had **made**.
The **serpent** asked the **woman**,
"Did **God really tell** you not to **eat**
from **any** of the **trees** in the **garden**?"
The **woman answered** the **serpent**:
"We may **eat** of the **fruit** of the **trees** in the **garden**;
it is **only** about the **fruit** of the **tree**
in the **middle** of the **garden** that **God said**,
'You **shall not eat** it or even **touch** it, lest you **die**.'"
But the **serpent said** to the **woman**:
"You **certainly will not die!** »

Genesis = JEN-uh-sis

Slight pause between "God" and "formed." This is a very familiar reading of one of the foundational stories of the Abrahamic religions. Its tone is simultaneously austere, menacing, and playful.
Eden = EE-d*n

The serpent is the focal character in this narrative.

Slight pause between "serpent" and "said."
Slight pause between "certainly" and "will."

READING I   Lent is a time of repentance and renewal, which makes today's first reading from the Book of Genesis particularly fitting. It comes from the second of two creation stories. This one gives particular attention to the creation of the first parents and the sin that causes them to be removed from the garden in Eden.

This highly symbolic story begins with God forming a man (Hebrew, *ha adam*) "out of the clay of the ground" (Hebrew, *ha adamah*), and then he "blew into his nostrils the breath of life." Of course, this is the breath of God. Thus, the first human being is both of the earth and of God. Then God, as provider for his creatures, plants a garden with trees that are not just good for food but beautiful to look at and places the man (*adam*) in the garden to tend and care for it.

Two trees in the middle of the garden represent attributes that do not belong to humans—only to God—and from which humans must be protected for their welfare. One is the tree of life, which probably represents immortality. The other is the tree of the knowledge of good and evil. In Hebrew, "to know" is experiential. The phrase "good and evil" is an example of a literary technique called a merism, in which two contrasting elements represent those and everything in between. Thus, eating the fruit of the tree of the knowledge of good and evil signifies the experience of everything on the spectrum of good and evil, which is dangerous and life-threatening for humans who do not have the wisdom and mastery that God has.

With this background in mind, we can better understand what the author of this creation account sought to convey about

The serpent's argument that God knows what eating the fruit will be like for Eve is what persuades her to eat. Don't overdo this, but keep in mind that the serpent's cunning is persuasiveness.

The conclusion demonstrates the grim underside of the knowledge the serpent promised: self-awareness.

No, **God knows** well that the **moment** you **eat** of it
   your **eyes** will be **opened** and you will **be like gods**
   who **know** what is **good** and what is **evil**."
The **woman** saw that the **tree** was **good** for **food**,
   pleasing to the **eyes**, and **desirable** for gaining **wisdom**.
So she **took** some of its **fruit** and **ate** it;
   and she **also** gave some to her **husband**, who was **with** her,
   and **he ate** it.
Then the **eyes** of **both** of them were **opened**,
   and they **realized** that they were **naked**;
   so they sewed **fig** leaves **together**
   and made **loincloths** for **themselves**.

For meditation and context:

RESPONSORIAL PSALM   Psalm 51:3–4, 5–6, 12–13, 17 (3a)

R. **Be merciful, O Lord, for we have sinned.**

Have mercy on me, O God, in your goodness;
   in the greatness of your compassion wipe
      out my offense.
Thoroughly wash me from my guilt
   and of my sin cleanse me.

For I acknowledge my offense,
   and my sin is before me always:
"Against you only have I sinned,
   and done what is evil in your sight."

A clean heart create for me, O God,
   and a steadfast spirit renew within me.
Cast me not out from your presence,
   and your Holy Spirit take not from me.

Give me back the joy of your salvation,
   and a willing spirit sustain in me.
O Lord, open my lips,
   and my mouth shall proclaim your praise.

READING II   Romans 5:12–19

A reading from the Letter of Saint Paul to the Romans

[**Brothers** and **sisters**:
Through **one man sin entered** the **world**,
   and through **sin**, **death**,
   and thus **death came** to **all men**, inas**much** as all **sinned**]—
   for up to the **time** of the **law**, **sin** was in the **world**,
   though **sin** is not **accounted** when there **is** no **law**.

Slight pause between "man" and "sin"; slight pause between "sin" and "entered." Put another way, when you proclaim "sin," give it a little pause before and after.

The reading consists of Paul's discourse on sin, death, and redemption. Its tone is earnest.

human sin and its consequences. Adam and Eve are living in the garden in perfect harmony with God and God's creation. Then, into the garden appears a serpent. Many of us assume that this serpent is Satan or the devil, but, in fact, the narrator describes it as the most cunning of God's creatures. The serpent poses a question to the woman concerning what God told Adam about the tree of the knowledge of good and evil, and she responds with an imperfect facsimile of what God said. Finally, when the serpent assures her that they—Adam was with her—would not die if they ate

from the tree in the middle of the garden, but they would "be like gods who know what is good and what is evil," she ate of the tree and so did her partner. Like the word "knowing," eating is also a verb of experiencing. Why did they do it? The woman concluded, "the tree . . . was desirable for gaining wisdom." In other words, they wanted to be like God, despite God's warning that it would bring death to them. Immediately, the humans began to experience the consequences of their action—alienation, shame, and blame. What about us? How do we try to play god

with our lives and the lives of others, and what consequences come of it?

READING II   Today's second reading from Paul's Letter to the Romans adds another interpretive layer to the Genesis story of Adam and Eve and the introduction of sin into the world. Paul employs a literary feature called a type. Generally speaking, a type is a pattern or blueprint. When used as a tool for biblical interpretation, a type is a person or event from the Old Testament that is used as a

But **death reigned** from **Adam** to **Moses**,
  even over **those** who did not **sin**
  after the **pattern** of the **trespass** of **Adam**,
  who is the **type** of the **one** who was to **come**.

But the **gift** is not like the **transgression**.
For if by the **transgression** of the **one**, the **many died**,
  how much more did the **grace** of **God**
  and the **gracious gift** of the o**ne man Jesus Christ**
  over**flow** for the **many**.
And the **gift** is not like the **result** of the **one** who **sinned**.
For after **one sin** there was the **judgment** that brought
    condemnation;
  but the **gift**, after many **transgressions**, brought **acquittal**.
[For if, by the **transgression** of the **one**,
  death came to **reign** through **that** one,
  how much more will **those** who **receive** the **abundance**
    of **grace**
  and of the **gift** of **justification**
  come to **reign** in **life** through the **one Jesus Christ**.
In **conclusion**, just as through **one transgression**
  condemnation came upon **all**,
  so, through **one righteous act**,
  acquittal and **life** came to **all**.
For just as through the **disobedience** of the **one man**
  the **many** were made **sinners**,
  so, through the **obedience** of the **one**,
  the **many** will be made **righteous**.]

[Shorter: Romans 5:12, 17–19 (see brackets)]

Though unstressed, "But" signals an intensification of the earnest tone of the reading.

Slight pause between "man" and "Jesus."

The second half of the reading really focuses on the word "gift."

Note the inversion and repetition Paul uses here: disobedience and one man leading to many sinners; the obedience of the one, and many made righteous.

TO KEEP IN MIND
Make eye contact with the assembly. This helps keep the assembly engaged with the reading.

---

blueprint for a more perfect person or event in the New Testament.

In this reading, Paul uses the first human, Adam, as a type of the second human, Jesus Christ, but this type is a bit out of the ordinary, because it describes an inverse relationship between the two. Through the first human, Adam, sin and death entered into the world and all were affected by it. Paul then contrasts Adam's pitiful situation and the consequences that it had *for the many* with the overflowing abundance of grace that the second human, Jesus Christ, brought into the world *for the many*. He wants to make clear that the gift is not in proportion to the judgment and condemnation that one would expect from one man's sin, as if God's mercy covered over only this one sin.

And what is this gift? Paul describes it as justification, the process of being set right with God, or acquittal, as in a court of law. The defendant is sinful humanity from the time of Adam and Eve to the present. Through the sacrifice of atonement that Jesus effected in his crucifixion, God, the judge, declares that humanity is acquitted and the case against it is dismissed, so that humanity is restored to right relationship with God. This is Paul's teaching on justification by faith. But acquittal is not the same thing as innocence. Humanity did nothing to earn this gift of right relationship with God. Rather, it is given as a free gift to anyone who trusts in the graciousness of God as expressed through Jesus' sacrificial love.

Paul's Jewish background shines through when he writes about how sin was in the world even before the law was given to Moses and the Israelites. His logic is that people cannot be held responsible for

GOSPEL   Matthew 4:1–11

A reading from the holy Gospel according to Matthew

At that time Jesus was led by the **Spirit** into the **desert**
    to be **tempted** by the **devil**.
He fasted for **forty days** and **forty nights**,
    and **afterwards** he was **hungry**.
The **tempter approached** and **said** to him,
    "If **you** are the **Son** of **God**,
    command that these **stones** become **loaves** of **bread**."
He said in reply,
    "It is **written**:
    One does not live on bread alone,
        but on every word that comes forth
        from the mouth of God."

Then the **devil** took him to the **holy city**,
    and made him **stand** on the **parapet** of the **temple**,
    and **said** to him, "If **you** are the **Son** of **God**, **throw**
        yourself **down**.
For it is **written**:
    He will **command** *his* **angels concerning** *you*
        and with their **hands** *they will* **support** *you,*
    lest you **dash** *your* **foot** *against a* **stone**."
Jesus **answered** him,
    "**Again** it is **written**,
    You shall not put the Lord, your God, to the test."
Then the **devil** took him **up** to a **very high mountain**,
    and **showed** him all the **kingdoms** of the **world** in their
        magnificence,
    and he **said** to him, "**All these** I shall **give** to you,
    if you will **prostrate** yourself and **worship** me."

This reading relates a dramatic story in the life of Christ. Its tone is magical.
Slight pause between "time" and "Jesus."

A familiar statement. Proclaim as if it is being spoken for the first time.

parapet = PAYR-uh-puht

The exchange between Jesus and the devil has a rabbinical character, in which they argue by quoting Scripture to each other.

---

transgressing the law if it has not been given to them. Still, it is important to notice how Paul personifies sin as an evil force that is hostile to God and how he talks about death as not limited to physical death but as alienation from the relationship that God wishes for humanity.

 GOSPEL Today's Gospel reading is the story of Jesus' temptation in the wilderness as told by the author of Matthew's Gospel. This story is also included in Luke and Mark.

Mark's version of the story is very brief, indicating only that Jesus was driven into the desert by the Spirit and spent forty days there, before beginning his public ministry. Mark's reference to forty days might evoke in your memory the forty years that the Israelites wandered in the desert during the Exodus. But Matthew's "forty days and forty nights" further suggests the time that Moses spent on Mount Sinai, when the covenant between God and the Israelites was ratified (Exodus 24:18) and the forty days and nights that when he fasted on Mount Sinai in the presence of God and wrote the

words of the covenant on two stone tablets (Exodus 34:27–35). Forty is a symbolic number, representing transition from one state to another. In this case, it is a transition from Jesus' private life to his public ministry.

Mark's version of the story says that Jesus was tempted by Satan and ministered to by angels (Mark 1:12–13). Matthew's version has these same basic elements, but can you also imagine a second generation of Jesus followers wondering what Jesus was doing out in the desert for such a long time? Perhaps that is why Matthew's version includes an extended dialogue or

"Get away, Satan": As much an expression of exasperation as it is a command.

At this, Jesus **said** to him,
"Get **away**, **Satan**!
It is **written**:
*The **Lord**, your **God**, shall you **worship**
and **him alone** shall you serve."*

Then the devil **left** him and, **behold**,
angels came and **ministered** to him.

debate between Jesus and Satan, who is also identified as the tempter and the devil. Matthew tells us that Jesus was fasting during that time, and fasting has traditionally been understood to be a way of moving more deeply into prayer and preparing oneself for significant life transitions.

The enhancements that the author of Matthew's Gospel made to Mark's version of this story are significant because they flesh out what it meant when Jesus was declared Son of God at his baptism. In particular, pay attention to the three tests that are placed before Jesus: (1) "If you are the Son of God, command that these stones become loaves of bread," (2) "If you are the Son of God, throw yourself down" from the top of the Temple, and (3) "All these I shall give to you, if you will prostrate yourself and worship me." As a whole, these temptations are tests of Jesus' willingness, as Son of God, to rely on God alone for nourishment, protection, and safety. All three of Jesus' responses come from the Book of Deuteronomy, which consists mostly of a very long speech that Moses gives when recommitting the Israelites to the covenant that God made with them on Sinai, before they cross over to the Promised Land. More precisely, they come from Deuteronomy 6—8, a section of text devoted to what the Israelites must do to faithfully live out the covenant in the Promised Land. Moreover, there is cause for rejoicing, because, unlike the dialogue between Eve and the serpent, Jesus wins this debate! C.C.

SECOND SUNDAY OF LENT

LECTIONARY #25

READING I   Genesis 12:1–4a

A reading from the Book of Genesis

The LORD said to **Abram**:
   "Go **forth** from the **land** of your **kinsfolk**
   and from your **father's house** to a **land** that I will **show** you.

   "I will **make** of you a **great nation**,
      and I will **bless** you;
   I will make your **name great**,
      so that you will be a **blessing**.
   I will **bless** those who **bless** you
      and **curse** those who **curse** you.
   All the **communities** of the **earth**
      shall find **blessing** in **you**."

Abram went as the LORD **directed** him.

Genesis = JEN-uh-sihs

Abram = AY-br*m

The tone of this reading is commanding. God is speaking to Abram as if to all his people.

Though not emphasized, the repetition of "I will" guides this reading. These are promises God is making for the future of his people.

For meditation and context:

RESPONSORIAL PSALM   Psalm 33:4–5, 18–19, 20, 22 (22)

R. Lord, let your mercy be on us, as we place our trust in you.

Upright is the word of the LORD,
   and all his works are trustworthy.
He loves justice and right;
   of the kindness of the LORD the earth
     is full.

See, the eyes of the LORD are upon those who
     fear him,
   upon those who hope for his kindness,
to deliver them from death
   and preserve them in spite of famine.

Our soul waits for the LORD,
   who is our help and our shield.
May your kindness, O LORD, be upon us
   who have put our hope in you.

READING I The readings for this Second Sunday of Lent focus on God's invitation to enter into relationship with God and humans' response of trust in the covenant.

Today's first reading is one of three accounts of the covenant that God made with Abram. The other two accounts are Genesis 15 and Genesis 17:1–21. Each is interesting in its own right, but together they paint a rich and vibrant picture of Abram's relationship with God. It is in the last of these three accounts that God changes Abram's name to Abraham, mean-

ing "father of nations." But in this first account we hear today, we learn of God's invitation to Abram to leave his family and homeland to migrate to Shechem in the land of Canaan, which is in the central part of the West Bank today. Later he would migrate to the Negev in southern Israel.

Tradition tells us that he was living in Haran (in modern southeastern Turkey) at the time, but his original homeland was Ur of the Chaldees (in southern Iraq today). These are extremely long distances to travel on foot and with all their flocks and other belongings, especially when the com-

mand from a God that he does not yet know is so vague: "Go . . . to a land that I will show you."

This same God bestows a series of blessings on Abram. Some biblical scholars argue, based on the Hebrew text, that there are seven, but the English translation makes it hard to enumerate them exactly. Why seven? Seven is a perfect number representing wholeness or fullness. God also gives two promises: multitudes of descendants and possession of the land. Constructing altars to the God who appeared

READING II   2 Timothy 1:8b–10

A reading from the second Letter of Saint Paul to Timothy

Beloved:
Bear your **share** of **hardship** for the **gospel**
   with the **strength** that **comes** from **God**.

He **saved** us and **called** us to a **holy life**,
  not according to our **works**
  but **according** to his **own design**
  and the **grace bestowed** on us in **Christ Jesus** before
    time began,
  but **now** made **manifest**
  through the **appearance** of our **savior Christ Jesus**,
  who **destroyed death** and brought **life** and **immortality**
  to **light** through the **gospel**.

GOSPEL   Matthew 17:1–9

A reading from the holy Gospel according to Matthew

Jesus took **Peter**, **James**, and **John** his **brother**,
  and led them up a **high mountain** by **themselves**.
And he was **transfigured before** them;
  his **face** shone like the **sun**
  and his **clothes** became **white** as **light**.
And **behold**, **Moses** and **Elijah appeared** to them,
  conversing with him.
Then **Peter** said to **Jesus** in **reply**,
  "**Lord**, it is **good** that we are **here**.
If you **wish**, I will make **three tents** here,
  one for **you**, one for **Moses**, and one for **Elijah**." »

Side notes:

Beloved = bee-LUHV-uhd or buh-LUHV-uhd

The tone of this reading to Timothy, a personal addressee rather than the collective membership of one of the early Christian churches, is intimate and tender.

Slight pause between "grace" and "bestowed."

Slight pause between "savior" and "Christ Jesus."

"Transfigured" focuses this reading, sets its tone. This is a celestial event.

Moses = MOH-zihz or MOH-zihs
Elijah = ee-LĪ-juh

Initially, the appearance of Moses and Elijah intensifies the focus.

But then Peter humanizes things in his desire to set up a shrine.

---

to Abram indicates that he acknowledges God as having authority in that land.

READING II Our second reading is from the Second Letter to Timothy. Timothy is presented as a companion of Paul in his missionary activity and later the pastor of a Church in Ephesus. The letter is attributed to Paul, though biblical scholars mostly agree that it was written after Paul's death, perhaps as late as AD 100. While this might seem strange to us today, it was not unusual for disciples of a great teacher to write in the name of their honored one in order to extend his message to another generation.

This reading picks up a theme that we find in Paul's authentic letters, namely, enduring suffering for the sake of the Gospel. The sentence that immediately precedes today's reading is "So do not be ashamed of your testimony to our Lord, nor of me, a prisoner for his sake" (2 Timothy 1:8; see also Romans 1:16). Using the phrase "the strength that comes from God," the author of this letter goes on to give a rationale for not being ashamed of suffering for Christ and trusting in God's power to protect oneself.

GOSPEL In today's Gospel reading, we hear the magnificent story of Jesus' transfiguration. The narrator describes Jesus as taking his inner circle of disciples—Peter, James, and John—and going up a mountain. These same disciples will be with Jesus in the Garden of Gethsemane on the Mount of Olives before he is arrested (Matthew 26:36–46).

Mountains were thought to be places of divine revelation. In Matthew's Gospel,

At "behold," the focus shifts back to a heavenly perspective that overwhelms the earthly perspective.

Even emphasis on "very much afraid."

The mystery of this final command of Jesus is worth lingering over as you conclude your proclamation.

While he was **still speaking**, **behold**,
    a **bright cloud** cast a **shadow** over them,
    then from the **cloud** came a **voice** that said,
    "**This** is my beloved **Son**, with **whom** I am well **pleased**;
    listen to him."
When the **disciples heard** this, they fell **prostrate**
    and were **very much afraid**.
But **Jesus** came and **touched** them, saying,
    "**Rise**, and do **not** be **afraid**."
And when the disciples **raised** their **eyes**,
    they saw **no one else** but **Jesus** alone.

As they were **coming down** from the **mountain**,
    Jesus **charged** them,
    "Do not **tell** the **vision** to **anyone**
    until the **Son** of **Man** has been **raised** from the **dead**."

this mountain is unnamed. Most biblical scholars think it is a symbol of Mount Sinai, because of the two figures who appear with Jesus. When Moses ascended Mount Sinai to receive the words of God's covenant, Moses' face became radiant with light (Exodus 34:27–35). Here, too, Jesus' face shines like the sun and his clothes become brilliant white. Likewise, Elijah was given the privilege of experiencing God in "a light silent sound" when he was on Mount Sinai, and he hides his face (1 Kings 19:9–13). Here, too, Jesus' disciples hide their faces. Peter's offer to build tents for

Jesus, Elijah, and Moses suggests the Feast of Tabernacles, also called *Sukkot* or Booths, which is a reminder of the time that the Israelites spent dwelling in tents during the Exodus.

What a marvelous experience for these three disciples. Suddenly they see a shining cloud overhead. It is the *shekinah*, the glory of God's presence, which led the Israelites out of the wilderness in cloud and fire, and which fills the Holy of Holies in the Jerusalem Temple. And they hear a voice from the heavens, "This is my beloved Son, with whom I am well pleased; listen to

him." A voice from the heavens had a similar message at Jesus' baptism, when God's Spirit descended upon him like a dove (Matthew 3:13–17). They are so awestruck by the heavenly voice that they prostrate themselves in reverence. Suddenly, the vision passes, and they see only Jesus standing before them. Although some biblical scholars interpret this scene to be a preview of the resurrection, it is first and foremost a theophany, a manifestation of the divine Jesus, the Son of God. C.C.

THIRD SUNDAY OF LENT

LECTIONARY #28

READING I   Exodus 17:3–7

A reading from the Book of Exodus

In **those** days, in their **thirst** for **water**,
    the people **grumbled** against **Moses**,
    saying, "**Why** did you ever make us leave **Egypt**?
Was it just to have us **die** here of thirst
    with our **children** and our **livestock**?"
So **Moses** cried out to the LORD,
    "What shall I **do** with this **people**?
A little more and they will **stone** me!"
The LORD answered Moses,
    "Go over **there** in front of the **people**,
    along with some of the **elders** of **Israel**,
    holding in your **hand**, as you go,
    the **staff** with which you **struck** the river.
I will be **standing** there in front of you on the **rock** in Horeb.
Strike the **rock**, and the **water** will flow **from** it
    for the **people** to **drink**."
This Moses did, in the presence of the elders of Isracl.
The place was called **Massah** and **Meribah**,
    because the **Israelites** quarreled there
    and **tested** the LORD, saying,
    "Is the **LORD** in our **midst** or **not**?"

Exodus = EK-suh-duhs

A reading which is essentially a dialogue involving the Israelites, Moses, and the Lord. Its tone is dramatic; you need mainly emphasize when the different speakers begin to speak.

Moses is exasperated here.

The words of the Lord are meant to placate Moses' exasperation. But they are also instructions. Read them in this spirit.

Horeb = HOHR-eb

Massah = MAS-uh
Meribah = MAYR-ih-bah

The passage concludes with a naming of the place where this happened, but in the form of a question. The question does not shed the most generous light on the Israelites. Be sure to give emphasis to the word "not."

READING I The central image of this Sunday's lectionary readings is water. Depending on where we live, we might be tempted to take water for granted. But water is an essential element of life. Without water, plants dry up and forests burn. Without fresh water, animals and humans become sick and die. But when water is plentiful, all of creation flourishes. If we can say these things about water as an element of creation, how much more can we say about spiritual water, in all its forms, constantly flowing from God into our lives?

In today's first reading, we learn that the Israelites had escaped their slavery in Egypt and found themselves facing the harsh realities of life in the wilderness. These moments of challenge are described as tests that God imposed to see if their allegiance to God was strong and true. Two tests lead up to today's first reading. The first takes place at Marah in the wilderness of Shur. The people were thirsty, and there was water in that place, but they could not drink it, because it was too bitter. (*Marah* means "bitter" in Hebrew.) Moses cried out to God and God provided him with a stick,

which, when thrown into the water, turned the bitter water into fresh water (Exodus 15:22–27). The second test was similar. Now in the wilderness of Sin (or Zin) between Elim and Sinai, the people were hungry for food. Again, the people complained against Moses. Again, God did not rebuke the people. Instead, God sent manna from the heavens and quail for the people to eat (Exodus 16).

The third test, which is conveyed in today's first reading, also takes place in the wilderness of Sin at a place called Rephidim. Finding no water in this place,

For meditation and context:

RESPONSORIAL PSALM   Psalm 95:1–2, 6–7, 8–9 (8)

R. If today you hear his voice, harden not your hearts.

Come, let us sing joyfully to the LORD;
    let us acclaim the Rock of our salvation.
Let us come into his presence
        with thanksgiving;
    let us joyfully sing psalms to him.

Come, let us bow down in worship;
    let us kneel before the LORD who
        made us.
For he is our God,
    and we are the people he shepherds,
        the flock he guides.

Oh, that today you would hear his voice:
    "Harden not your hearts as at Meribah,
        as in the day of Massah in the desert,
    where your fathers tempted me;
        they tested me though they had seen
            my works."

READING II   Romans 5:1–2, 5–8

A reading from the Letter of Saint Paul to the Romans

A reading in which Paul provides a clear sense of how faith progresses from the proof of God's love evident in Christ's death. As is often true in Paul's letters, he gets right to the point. You should allow yourself to read this passage in the same spirit.

Brothers and sisters:
Since we have been **justified** by faith,
    we have **peace** with God through our **Lord** Jesus Christ,
    through whom we have gained **access** by faith
to this **grace** in which we **stand**,
    and we **boast** in hope of the **glory** of God.

The tone shifts slightly here, especially at "disappoint." Despite the difficulty of what Christ accomplished, his success means victory, giving us hope.

And **hope** does **not** disappoint,
    because the **love** of God has been **poured out** into our hearts
    through the **Holy Spirit** who has been **given** to us.
For **Christ**, while we were still **helpless**,
    died at the appointed time for the **ungodly**.
Indeed, only with **difficulty** does one **die** for a just **person**,
    though perhaps for a **good person** one might even find **courage**
        to die.

The words in this line should have almost equal emphasis, especially "proves," "love," and "us."

But **God proves** his **love** for us
    in that while we were **still sinners** Christ **died** for us.

the Israelites quarrel with Moses and grumble against him, but Moses challenges them in return, after making it clear in the preceding verse that their problem is not with him but with God: "Why do you put the LORD to the test?" Once again God does not rebuke the people but instead directs Moses to take the staff that he used in the execution of the ten plagues against the Egyptians and hit the rock in Horeb, making abundant water flow from the rock to quench the Israelites' thirst. The elders are there to witness God's work on behalf of the people.

The purpose of these three tests is now fully revealed in the closing sentence of this reading, "Is the LORD in our midst or not?" When we are angry with God and want to test whether God cares for us, can we also trust that God will not rebuke us and instead turn our hearts to witness God's benevolence on our behalf?

READING II   Our second reading comes from Paul's Letter to the Romans. In the preceding chapters of this letter, Paul gives an intensive but somewhat abstract teaching on justification by

faith. Here he focuses on the gifts that justification brings to believers who trust in the power of God on their behalf.

But first, what does Paul mean when he talks about justification by faith? The words *justification* and *righteousness* are synonyms for the same Greek word, *dikaiosuné*. In the broadest sense, it means "the condition that is acceptable to God." But Paul gives this word a somewhat more precise meaning. When he refers to the righteousness of God, he means something like "God behaving as God is in God's self," and when Paul refers to human righteousness,

GOSPEL John 4:5–42

A reading from the holy Gospel according to John

[Jesus came to a town of **Samaria** called Sychar,
     near the **plot** of land that **Jacob** had given to his son **Joseph**.
Jacob's well was **there**.
Jesus, tired from his **journey**, sat down there at the **well**.
It was about **noon**.

A woman of **Samaria** came to draw **water**.
Jesus said to her,
     "**Give me** a **drink**."
His disciples had gone into the **town** to buy **food**.
The Samaritan woman **said** to him,
     "How can you, a **Jew**, ask **me**, a **Samaritan woman**,
          for a **drink**?"
—For Jews use **nothing** in common with **Samaritans**.—
Jesus answered and said to her,
     "If you **knew** the gift of **God**
     and who is **saying** to you, 'Give me a drink,'
     you would have **asked** him
     and he would have **given** you living **water**."
The woman **said** to him,
     "**Sir**, you do not even have a **bucket** and the cistern is **deep**;
     where then can you **get** this **living** water?
Are you **greater** than our father **Jacob**,
     who **gave** us this cistern and **drank** from it **himself**
     with his **children** and his **flocks**?"
Jesus answered and said to her,
     "Everyone who **drinks** this water will be **thirsty** again;
     but whoever drinks the water **I** shall give will **never** thirst;
     the water I shall give will **become** in him
     a spring of water **welling up** to **eternal** life." ❯❯

Samaria = suh-MAYR-ee-uh
Sychar = Sī-kahr

A lengthy reading with a rich narrative progression. The focus of this reading is on the transformation of the Samaritan woman, who presents herself to Jesus as a skeptic but becomes a true believer by the end of the reading. Her conversion is presented in slight contrast to the work of Jesus' disciples, who themselves are skeptical of the Samaritan woman, mostly out of prejudice. Allow the rich social and spiritual realities of this passage to resonate in your proclamation.

At this point the dialogue between Jesus and the Samaritan woman begins. Distinguish between their words by slightly adjusting the pitch of your voice for each speaker. Samaritan = suh-MAYR-uh-tuhn

The rhythm of this line is emphatic. Notice the stresses.

cistern = SIS-tern

These words of Jesus are the core of his exchange with the Samaritan woman.

---

he means something like "having been put right with God." Why do humans need to be put right with God? Paul says it is because of the nature of the first sin that affected and continues to affect all humanity, namely, the refusal to acknowledge God as God and to worship God accordingly (see Romans 1:18–23). But justification is not something that humans can do for themselves. Rather, it is God's free gift effected through the atoning death and resurrection of Jesus to all who will receive it in trust. Such is the graciousness of God.

Thus, in today's second reading, Paul says that all of us who are justified by *faith* can enjoy peace (Greek, *eiréné* meaning, "tranquility, harmony, concord, security, or safety") with God as a free gift; we are acquitted of our sin and are no longer estranged but are now reconciled with God. This gift gives us assurance even in the face of difficulties, because these struggles develop our endurance, which in turn manifests as hope. And what is the source of this hope? It is not our doing, Paul says, but it is the outpouring of the superabundance of God's love through the Holy Spirit. It is

Christ who died for us; even when we did not deserve his sacrifice of love, he freely offered this gift so that we could be put in right relationship with God. How amazing is this gift!

| GOSPEL | This reading from the Gospel of John has as its central character an unnamed woman of Samaria, who appears nowhere else in the Gospels. Yet, when we dig deeply into her story, you will find this woman to be utterly unforgettable because of her journey of faith.

The woman **said** to him,
   "Sir, **give** me this **water**, so that I may **not** be thirsty
   or have to keep **coming** here to draw **water**."]

Jesus said to her,
   "Go **call** your husband and come **back**."
The woman answered and said to him,
   "I do not **have** a husband."
Jesus answered her,
   "You are **right** in saying, 'I **do not** have a **husband**.'
For you have had **five** husbands,
   and the one you have **now** is **not** your husband.
What you have **said** is **true**."
The woman said to him,
   "**Sir**, [I can see that you are a **prophet**.
Our **ancestors worshiped** on this mountain;
   but you people say that the place to worship is in **Jerusalem**."
Jesus said to her,
   "**Believe** me, woman, the **hour** is coming
   when you will **worship** the Father
   neither on this **mountain** nor in **Jerusalem**.
You people **worship** what you do not **understand**;
   we worship **what** we understand,
   because **salvation** is from the **Jews**.
But the hour is coming, and is **now** here,
   when **true worshipers** will worship the Father in **Spirit**
      and **truth**;
   and indeed the Father **seeks** such people to **worship** him.
God is **Spirit**, and those who **worship** him
   must **worship** in **Spirit** and **truth**."

With these words, the Samaritan woman's skepticism shifts into belief.

The setting for this story is Jacob's well in the city of Sychar. In biblical tradition, wells are described as places of first encounter between men and their soon-to-be spouses. Abraham's servant found a wife, Rebekah, for Isaac at a well (Genesis 24), Jacob met Rachel at a well (Genesis 29:1–20), and Moses met his wife Zipporah at a well (Exodus 2:15–22). But the well in today's Gospel is the setting for a different type of meeting.

The encounter between Jesus and the Samaritan woman is complicated. Both Jews and Samaritans tie their identity to Jacob, the son of Isaac, the ancestor of the twelve tribes of Israel. But Samaritans and Jews did not get along. In fact, they had been bitterly divided since after the Babylonian Exile in the sixth century BC. Things got so bad that the Samaritans built their own temple on Mount Gerizim in the fourth century BC, rather than participate in the Temple activities in Jerusalem. Sadly, this animosity continues even today.

The narrator of this story identifies the time of this encounter as noon, the brightest point of the day. The Gospel of John is highly symbolic, and here we see the author's use of dualism. He uses polar opposites like light and darkness, truth and falsehood, from above and from below to signal belief versus unbelief. In John's Gospel, belief is not a mental activity that results in assent to a set of doctrines; it is trusting in and allying oneself with Jesus and the Father. Thus, this encounter between Jesus and the Samaritan woman is not about clock-time but about coming into the full light of faith in Jesus Christ.

As this story unfolds, Jesus issues two commands to the woman: (1) "Give me a drink," and (2) "Go, call your husband and

And here, Jesus reveals himself as the messiah. Emphasize "he" and "speaking" to express the revelation.

The return of the disciples reinforces the "problem" of Jesus interacting with a Samaritan woman (something Jewish custom ordinarily forbad); it also marks a slight excursion, because the disciples want Jesus to eat while he has a lesson he wants to convey to them.

The woman said to him,
"I **know** that the Messiah is **coming**, the one called the **Christ**;
when he **comes**, he will tell us **everything**."
Jesus said to her,
"I am **he**, the one **speaking** with you."]

At that moment his **disciples** returned,
and were **amazed** that he was talking with a **woman**,
but still no one said, "What are you looking for?"
or "Why are you talking with her?"
The woman left her **water** jar
and went into the **town** and said to the **people**,
"Come see a **man** who told me **everything** I have **done**.
Could he possibly **be** the **Christ**?"
They went out of the town and **came** to him.
Meanwhile, the disciples urged him, "**Rabbi, eat**."
But he said to them,
"I have **food** to eat of which you do not **know**."
So the disciples said to one another,
"Could **someone** have brought him something to **eat**?"
Jesus said to them,
"My **food** is to do the **will** of the one who **sent** me
and to **finish** his **work**.
Do you not say, 'In **four** months the **harvest** will **be** here'?
I tell you, look **up** and see the fields **ripe** for the **harvest**.
The **reaper** is already **receiving** payment
and **gathering crops** for eternal **life**,
so that the **sower** and **reaper** can rejoice **together**.
For **here** the saying is **verified** that '**One sows** and
another **reaps**.' »

come back." After each command, Jesus and the Samaritan woman engage in dialog. Concerning the first command, the woman knows that Jews would not accept anything that had been in the possession of a Samaritan, and she is not subtle about pointing out their prejudice: "How can you, *a Jew*, ask me, *a Samaritan woman*, for a drink?" When Jesus offers to give her living water, she answers in retort: "Are you *greater than our father Jacob*?" But, of course, Jesus is greater than Jacob! She responds to his offer by saying, "*Sir,* give me this water, so that I may not be thirsty

or have to keep coming here to draw water." Notice how her tone and disposition toward Jesus is changing.

When Jesus delivers his second command, she responds that she has no husband, which Jesus confirms by detailing her history of having had five husbands and that the one she is currently with is not her husband. This bit of dialog has led some to conclude that this woman is a sinner, but the text does not support this view. Jesus does not condemn her or tell her to stop sinning, and later the townspeople immediately listen to her testimony about Jesus

and show no signs of her having been shunned by her neighbors. Was she the victim of many divorces? Was she widowed and married off again many times over? Or are the five husbands a symbol of her Samaritan beliefs that only the five books of the Torah are sacred scripture? Following this revelation of Jesus' knowledge, the woman's tone shifts again as she responds, "Sir, I can see that you are *a prophet.*"

This woman, who is not afraid to speak her mind, even when her culture forbade it, is also theologically literate. She takes advantage of this opportunity to ask

I sent you to **reap** what you have not **worked** for;
   others have done the **work**,
   and you are **sharing** the fruits of **their** work."

[Many of the **Samaritans** of that town began to **believe** in him]
   because of the **word** of the woman who **testified**,
   "He told me **everything** I have **done**."
[When the **Samaritans** came to him,
   they invited him to **stay** with them;
   and he **stayed** there two **days**.
Many more began to **believe** in him because of his **word**,
   and they **said** to the woman,
   "We no longer **believe** because of your **word**;
   for we have **heard** for **ourselves**,
   and we know that this is **truly** the savior of the **world**."]

[Shorter: John 4:5–15, 19b–26, 39a, 40–42 (see brackets)]

The conclusion returns us to the Samaritan woman; not only does she believe in Jesus, she is able to convert the other Samaritans because of her conviction. The words of the assembled Samaritans are spoken directly to the congregation's own faith.

---

about the right place to worship: the temple in Jerusalem or their temple on Mount Gerizim. When Jesus answers, saying that neither of these places of worship will matter in the end, because a time will come, "when true worshipers will worship the Father in Spirit and truth," she concludes that Jesus is talking about the messianic age. Her response is in the form of a statement, "I know that *the Messiah* is coming," but listen carefully and you can hear the question in her heart, "Is he the one?" Jesus answers by saying, "*I am.*" It is the same response that Moses received when he asked God to reveal his name: "I AM WHO I AM" (Exodus 3:14).

Almost immediately, the Samaritan woman leaves her water jar behind and goes into the village to tell the townspeople about her encounter with Jesus. When the villagers meet Jesus and hear his words, they proclaim him to be "*the savior of the world.*" Pay attention to the progression of titles given to Jesus, as we follow the trajectory of this woman's faith journey. She is transformed from a water carrier to a proclaimer of the Good News and shares the message of that " spring of water welling up to eternal life" Consider what this woman can teach us about our own journey of faith. C.C.

FOURTH SUNDAY OF LENT

LECTIONARY #31

READING I   1 Samuel 16:1b, 6–7, 10–13a

A reading from the first Book of Samuel

The LORD said to **Samuel**:
  "Fill your **horn** with **oil**, and **be** on your **way**.
I am **sending** you to **Jesse** of **Bethlehem**,
  for I have **chosen** my king from among his **sons**."

As Jesse and his sons **came** to the **sacrifice**,
  Samuel looked at **Eliab** and thought,
  "**Surely** the LORD's anointed is **here before** him."
But the LORD said to Samuel:
  "**Do not judge** from his **appearance** or from his **lofty** stature,
  because I have **rejected** him.
Not as **man sees** does **God see**,
  because **man** sees the **appearance**
  but the LORD looks into the **heart**."
In the same way **Jesse** presented seven **sons** before **Samuel**,
  but **Samuel** said to **Jesse**,
  "The LORD has not chosen any **one** of these."
Then Samuel asked Jesse,
  "Are **these** all the **sons** you **have**?"
Jesse replied,
  "There is still the **youngest**, who is **tending** the **sheep**." »

<hr>

Samuel = SAM-yoo-uhl
Jesse = JES-ee
A reading with a dramatic conclusion, in which Samuel, sent by the Lord and endowed with power, is sent among the sons of Jesse to find and anoint a new king. Samuel's power is the ability to recognize this king, whose appearance, when he sees him at last, thrills him. The words themselves convey the drama of this reading compellingly.

Eliab = ee-Lī-uhb

Emphasize the parallel: not as man sees does God see.

Samuel cannot see the chosen king among the sons. Subtle emphasis on "one."

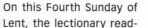 On this Fourth Sunday of Lent, the lectionary readings invite us to reflect on the nature of God's revelatory activity and our journey of faith.

The First Book of Samuel tells the story of Samuel's emergence as a prophet and spokesperson for God in the period leading up to Israel's transition to leadership under a king. Early on, Israel depended on charismatic leaders, called judges, whom God would raise up in times of trouble to rescue the people. Samuel is the last of these judges. When the people push him to give them a king like their neighbors had, Samuel delivers God's warning about what that could mean, and the picture is quite terrifying (see 1 Samuel 8:10–18). But on God's directive, Samuel relents and appoints Saul as the first king of Israel. However, almost immediately God rejects Saul, because he failed to obey God's word. Therefore, even as Saul continued to serve as king, God directs Samuel to anoint David as its second king, which he did secretly.

In today's first reading, we pick up with the story of David's anointing. God orders Samuel to fill his oil flask and ready himself for his journey to Bethlehem. Samuel purportedly comes to this town to offer sacrifice to God, and he asks both the elders and Jesse and his sons to come to the sacrifice. In actuality, he wanted God to point out the next king and have witnesses to testify to the selection. Saul examines seven of Jesse's sons, one by one, hoping for a sign. But God says no. Finally, Samuel asks, "Are these all the sons you have?" When Jesse produces David, his youngest and presumably least valued son, immediately Samuel knows that he is God's anointed. It is noteworthy that David came

Samuel said to Jesse,
"**Send** for him;
we will not **begin** the sacrificial **banquet** until he **arrives** here."
Jesse **sent** and had the young man **brought** to them.
He was **ruddy**, a youth **handsome** to behold
and making a **splendid** appearance.
The LORD said,
"**There**—anoint **him**, for **this** is the **one**!"
Then **Samuel**, with the **horn** of oil in hand,
anointed **David** in the presence of his **brothers**;
and from that day on, the **spirit** of the LORD **rushed**
upon David.

ruddy = RUHD-ee = having a reddish complexion

Samuel can see the chosen king at last. Equal emphases on "There," "anoint," "this," and "one."

For meditation and context:

TO KEEP IN MIND
On the Third, Fourth, and Fifth Sundays of Lent, these readings from Year A are connected with the celebration of the scrutinies— prayers for purification and strength—for the elect, those who will be baptized at the Easter Vigil.

RESPONSORIAL PSALM   Psalm 23:1–3a, 3b–4, 5, 6 (1)

R. The Lord is my shepherd; there is nothing I shall want.

The LORD is my shepherd; I shall not want.
In verdant pastures he gives me repose;
beside restful waters he leads me;
he refreshes my soul.

He guides me in right paths
for his name's sake.
Even though I walk in the dark valley
I fear no evil; for you are at my side
With your rod and your staff
that give me courage.

You spread the table before me
in the sight of my foes;
you anoint my head with oil;
my cup overflows.

Only goodness and kindness follow me
all the days of my life;
and I shall dwell in the house of the LORD
for years to come.

READING II   Ephesians 5:8–14

A reading from the Letter of Saint Paul to the Ephesians

Brothers and sisters:
You were **once darkness**,
but now you are **light** in the **Lord**.

Ephesians = ee-FEE-zhuhnz

A reading in which Paul tries to convince the Ephesians to live as children of the light.

from shepherding his father's sheep, because shepherding was also symbolic of a king's pastoral leadership toward his subjects. The narrator ends the story by saying, "and from that day on, the spirit of the LORD rushed upon David." The Hebrew word for "spirit" is *ruach*, which also means "breath or wind." Thus, in his anointing, the breath of God guided David's leadership.

READING II Our second reading comes from the Letter to the Ephesians and is attributed to Paul but was probably written by one of his disciples.

Most biblical scholars assign a date of composition of approximately AD 90–100. Today's reading is part of the paraenesis of this letter, that is, the section of the letter dedicated to advice about how the members of the Church at Ephesus ought to behave. In the verses immediately prior to this reading, the author is admonishing the community not to accept "empty arguments" nor to pay attention to people who promote them (Ephesians 5:6). We can assume that "empty arguments" refers to a way of life that is suggested by the catalog of vices found in Ephesians 5:3–5: behav-

iors like greed, various forms of idolatry, and "obscenity or silly or suggestive talk"— three words that are used nowhere else in the New Testament.

These are the unethical behaviors that the author of the Letter to the Ephesians is talking about, when he reminds his readers that they once lived in darkness, before they became followers of Jesus. The word *darkness* is used by this author to describe the personification of all that was evil in the world and of evil spirits that were always battling against the light, threatening to overcome it. Further, the letter writer

Take note of the parallels and shifts in these lines: from "everything" to "visible," and then "everything" to "light."

"Awake," "arise," and "light" are the focal points of these final lines. Don't rush through them.

Live as **children** of **light**,
    for **light** produces every kind of **goodness**
    and **righteousness** and **truth**.
Try to **learn** what is **pleasing** to the **Lord**.
Take no **part** in the fruitless works of **darkness**;
    rather **expose** them, for it is **shameful** even to **mention**
    the things done by them in **secret**;
    but **everything** exposed by the light becomes **visible**,
    for **everything** that becomes visible is **light**.
Therefore, it says:
    "**Awake**, O sleeper,
    and **arise** from the **dead**,
    and **Christ** will give you **light**."

GOSPEL   John 9:1–41

A reading from the holy Gospel according to John

Rabbi = RAB-ī

This is a complex reading with many characters, each with different motivations, as well as several scene changes. In this reading, Jesus upturns traditional rabbinic understanding of blindness as a punishment for immorality. It also relies on a defiant tone to make its point. Keep this in mind as you proclaim.

This line has an anticipatory, prophetic quality, characteristic of John's Gospel.

These details of Jesus' healing powers are interesting; don't rush through them.

Siloam = sih-LOH-uhm

[As Jesus passed by he saw a man **blind** from **birth**.]
His disciples asked him,
    "**Rabbi**, who **sinned**, this **man** or his **parents**,
    that he was **born blind**?"
Jesus answered,
    "Neither **he** nor his **parents** sinned;
    it is so that the **works** of God might be made **visible**
        through him.
We have to do the **works** of the one who sent me while it is **day**.
Night is coming when **no one** can **work**.
While I am in the **world**, I am the **light** of the **world**."
When he had **said** this, [he **spat** on the ground
    and made **clay** with the **saliva**,
    and **smeared** the clay on his **eyes**, and said to him,
    "**Go wash** in the **Pool** of **Siloam**"—which means **Sent**—.
So he **went** and **washed**, and came back **able** to see. »

---

encourages the community by saying "you are light in the Lord" and therefore they should "live as children of light." And what does the light of God produce? "Every kind of goodness and righteousness and truth." Clearly, this author is convinced that good will triumph over evil, because only good things come from God. Moreover, light has the ability to expose the darkness and has the potential even to transform it. This beautiful piece of poetic text that concludes today's second reading is most likely part of an early Christian hymn, perhaps

one that was used in the celebration of baptism.

GOSPEL   This reading from the Gospel of John has as its central character an unnamed blind man whom Jesus heals, even without the man asking to be healed. Although the other Gospels also include stories about Jesus healing a blind man or blind men, this is the only Gospel that includes a series of scenes in which the formerly blind man gives witness to Jesus when confronted by his neighbors and the scribes and Pharisees.

This reading consists of a miracle story and six follow-up scenes. The miracle story has the basic elements that we would expect of any New Testament miracle story: (1) a description of need, in this case, a man who was blind from birth; (2) the miracle worker's word or deed, in this case, Jesus making and putting clay on the man's eyes; and (3) evidence that the miracle took place, in this case, the man washing and being able to see. But the way in which the miracle story is framed is most important. When Jesus' disciples notice the blind man, they ask about who is at fault. Today, theo-

Any expression of "I am" in John's Gospel is freighted with authority.

The (formerly) blind man's tone here is somewhat exasperated.

Once again, the man who had been blind has to explain his story, this time to the Pharisees. His exasperation mounts to defiance when he proclaims Jesus a prophet.

His neighbors and those who had seen him **earlier**
    as a **beggar** said,
    "Isn't this the one who used to **sit** and **beg**?"
Some said, "It **is**,"
    but others said, "**No**, he just **looks** like him."
He said, "I **am**."]
So they said to him, "How were your **eyes** opened?"
He replied,
    "The man called **Jesus** made **clay** and anointed my **eyes**
    and told me, 'Go to **Siloam** and **wash**.'
So I **went** there and washed and was able to **see**."
And they said to him, "Where **is** he?"
He said, "I don't **know**."

[They brought the one who was once blind to the **Pharisees**.
Now Jesus had made **clay** and opened his eyes on a **sabbath**.
So then the **Pharisees** also asked him **how** he was able to **see**.
He **said** to them,
    "He put **clay** on my eyes, and I **washed**, and now I can **see**."
So some of the Pharisees said,
    "This man is **not** from God,
    because he **does not keep** the **sabbath**."
But others said,
    "How can a sinful man do such **signs**?"
And there was a **division** among them.
So they said to the blind man again,
    "What do you have to **say** about him,
    since he **opened** your **eyes**?"
He said, "He is a **prophet**."]

Now the Jews did not **believe**
    that he had been **blind** and gained his **sight**
    until they **summoned** the parents of the one who had **gained**
        his sight.
They asked them,
    "Is this your **son**, who you say was born **blind**?

logians would not espouse this view that physical ailments are caused by human sinfulness. Yet, we still hear people in crisis ask, "What did I do to deserve this?" Jesus makes clear that physical illness is not a platform for assigning blame but an opportunity to do the works of God. But there is an urgency to this work because, while Jesus is in the world, he tells us, he is the light of the world. When darkness comes, no one can work.

And what is the work of God? The man's blindness would have been viewed as an extremely serious condition. Ancients

believed that a person was able to see because of the light that was within them. If this person was blind from birth, it meant that he had no light in him, even from the moment that he was born. This is why the disciples ask about the parents' sin. At the end of the miracle story, we learn that the man did as Jesus directed; he went and washed in the pool of Siloam and was able to see. But in the symbolism of John's Gospel, seeing is believing, and believing is doing the work of God (John 6:26–29). Perhaps, then, the washing is an allusion to baptism, an action that Christ instituted as

the way of salvation and a way of commissioning us for our taking up of his mission.

The first scene to follow this miracle story describes the formerly blind man's neighbors who observe him being able to see and wonder whether the man they see is the one they knew when he was still blind or someone else. When the man confirms his identity and tells them how he was healed, he describes the healer as "the man called *Jesus*." In the second scene, we learn that the neighbors brought the man to the Pharisees, scholars of the Law, because the healing took place on the

Because the Pharisees don't believe the man who had been blind, they question his parents. Crucially, they repeat that he is of age and can speak for himself. Their tone is defiant. They believe their son.

How does he now **see**?"
His parents answered and said,
    "We **know** that this is our son and that he was born **blind**.
We do not **know** how he sees **now**,
    nor do we know who **opened** his eyes.
Ask him, he is of **age**;
    he can **speak** for **himself**."
His parents said this because they were **afraid** of the **Jews**,
        for the **Jews** had already **agreed**
    that if anyone **acknowledged** him as the **Christ**,
    he would be **expelled** from the **synagogue**.
For this **reason** his parents said,
    "He is of **age**; **question** him."

So a second time they **called the man** who had been blind
    and said to him, "**Give God** the praise!
We **know** that this man is a **sinner**."
He replied,
    "If he is a **sinner**, I do not **know**.
One thing I **do know** is that I was **blind** and now I **see**."
So they said to him,
    "What did he **do** to you?
    How did he open your **eyes**?"
He answered them,
    "I told you already and you did not **listen**.
Why do you want to hear it **again**?
Do you **want** to become his **disciples, too**?"
They **ridiculed** him and said,
    "**You** are that man's disciple;
    we are disciples of **Moses**!
We **know** that God **spoke** to **Moses**,
    but we do not **know** where this one is **from**."
The man answered and said to them,
    "This is what is so **amazing**,
    that you do not **know** where he is **from**, yet he **opened**
        my **eyes. »**

Exasperation and defiance.

The Pharisees cannot believe his temerity. This disbelief intensifies to the point where they throw him out because he has the gall to try to teach them. Ridiculous as they are, don't ridicule the Pharisees with your tone of voice.

sabbath. Sabbath observance was one of the most important obligations of the Law, which could only be broken in life-or-death situations. But a man born blind could certainly wait another day for healing, and now the Pharisees are divided about Jesus and whether he was from God. When questioned further, the formerly blind man says of Jesus, "He is a *prophet*."

In the third scene that follows this miracle story, the Pharisees summon the formerly blind man's parents to ask about their son's blindness. Sadly, the parents sacrifice their son to save themselves, because "the Jews" (i.e., religious authorities) had decided that anyone who recognized Jesus as *the Messiah* would be banned from the synagogue. Most likely, the parents are Jesus followers, though hidden ones, because they are not willing to endure the consequences of their belief.

In the fourth scene, the tone and direction of the story begins to change quite dramatically. The Jewish religious authorities call the man to stand before them again, as if in a court of law, and they announce their decision that Jesus is a sinner, presumably to get the man to denounce Jesus, as well. But the formerly blind man turns the tables on them. They treat him as the accused in earlier scenes of this story, but now he becomes the accuser, launching a fierce argument against them for their failure to recognize Jesus as coming *from God*. The consequence of the man's witness is immediate: "Then they threw him out."

In the fifth scene, Jesus seeks out the formerly blind man to ask him whether he believed in the *Son of Man*. In the other Gospel accounts, this title is used only by Jesus and only to speak of himself, and that

We know that **God** does **not** listen to sinners,
but if one is **devout** and does his **will**, he listens to **him**.
It is **unheard** of that **anyone** ever opened the eyes of a person
born **blind**.
If this man were **not** from God,
he would **not** be able to do **anything**."
[They **answered** and said to him,
"You were born **totally** in sin,
and are **you** trying to teach **us**?"
Then they **threw** him out.

When Jesus heard that they had **thrown him out**,
he found him and said, "Do you **believe** in the Son of **Man**?"
He answered and said,
"Who **is** he, sir, that I may believe in **him**?"
Jesus said to him,
"You have **seen** him,
and the one **speaking** with you is **he**."
He said,
"I **do believe**, Lord," and he **worshiped** him.]
Then Jesus said,
"I **came** into this world for **judgment**,
so that **those** who do not see might **see**,
and **those** who do **see** might become **blind**."

Some of the Pharisees who were with him **heard** this
and said to him, "**Surely** we are not also blind, **are** we?"
Jesus said to them,
"If you were **blind**, you would have no **sin**;
but now you are saying, 'We **see**,' so your **sin** remains."

[Shorter: John 9:1, 6–9, 13–17, 34–38 (see brackets)]

Jesus validates the belief of the man who had been blind.

The reading concludes with a crucial inversion: blindness to sight, sight to blindness. The sin tradition indicated in the blind man has been shifted to the Pharisees. When we believe something blindly, are we believing or are we blind?

appears to be the case here, as well. Earlier in the Gospel of John, when Jesus is calling his disciples, he uses the story of Jacob's ladder to speak about the "greater things" that Nathanael will see because of his belief, and he likens the Son of Man to the ladder that bridges earthly and heavenly realities (see John 1:4351).

In the final scene of this story, Jesus condemns the religious authorities for being blind, even as they have eyes to see. Recall the comments that Jesus made to the disciples in the first scene. As light of the world, Jesus' mission is one of judgment, not against people who are physically blind, but against those who are spiritually blind and who refuse to recognize Jesus' true identity. Moreover, Jesus has the authority to judge, because he is the agent of God, who bridges the earthly and heavenly realities by doing only what the Father tells him to do.

And what about us? With whom do you most identify? Let us approach Jesus, the light of the world, so that he can shed light on our blindness and enable us to do the works of God. C.C.

FIFTH SUNDAY OF LENT

LECTIONARY #34

Ezekiel = ee-ZEE-kee-uhl

A reading in which a small number of promises are repeated and varied a few times to impressive effect. Focus on the phrase "O my people," which includes all the feelings of care and connection that motivate this reading.

This line rephrases the opening lines. Slow down very slightly to signal the repetition.

Emphasize "promised" and "do" to conclude the exhortation.

For meditation and context:

TO KEEP IN MIND
On the Third, Fourth, and Fifth Sundays of Lent, these readings from Year A are connected with the celebration of the scrutinies—prayers for purification and strength—for the elect, those who will be baptized at the Easter Vigil.

READING I   Ezekiel 37:12–14

A reading from the Book of the Prophet Ezekiel

Thus says the Lord GOD:
O my people, I will **open** your **graves**
and have you **rise** from them,
and bring you **back** to the land of **Israel**.
Then you shall **know** that I am the LORD,
when I **open** your graves and have you **rise** from them,
O my people!
I will **put** my spirit **in** you that you may **live**,
and I will **settle** you upon your **land**;
thus you shall **know** that I am the LORD.
I have **promised**, and I will **do** it, says the LORD.

RESPONSORIAL PSALM   Psalm 130:1–2, 3–4, 5–6, 7–8 (7)

R. With the Lord there is mercy and fullness of redemption.

Out of the depths I cry to you, O LORD;
LORD, hear my voice!
Let your ears be attentive
to my voice in supplication.

If you, O LORD, mark iniquities,
LORD, who can stand?
But with you is forgiveness,
that you may be revered.

I trust in the LORD;
my soul trusts in his word.
More than sentinels wait for the dawn,
let Israel wait for the LORD.

For with the LORD is kindness
and with him is plenteous redemption;
and he will redeem Israel
from all their iniquities.

READING I   As we move into the final days of Lent, the readings for this Fifth Sunday of Lent invite us to reflect on the movement from death to life.

Today's first reading is from the Book of Ezekiel, which contains the visions and oracles of the prophet Ezekiel as he ministered to the exiles of Judah during the Babylonian Exile. The Babylonian empire had already taken control of Judah in 605 BC, but Johoiakim, who was retained as its vassal king, made a mistake in considering Babylon's weakened state, after a failed invasion of Egypt, and refused to pay tribute to King Nebuchadnezzar. Babylon's armies responded in 598/7 BC by sacking Jerusalem and exiling its leading citizens. Biblical scholars think that Ezekiel was taken to Babylon with this first round of exiles. Not long afterward, Johoiakim's brother, Zedekiah, was installed by Nebuchadnezzar to oversee Judah. He, too, attempted to rebel against the Babylonians, whose armies returned in 589 and by 586 BC had decimated much of Judah, destroyed the Jerusalem Temple, and taken more of Judah's population into exile in Babylon.

Needless to say, this was a terrible time for the people of Judah, whether they were in exile in Babylon or left behind in devastated Judah and Jerusalem. Like prophets before him, Ezekiel sees Judah's political troubles as God's punishment for their unfaithfulness to God's covenant, but he also holds out the possibility that the people will repent and that God would restore them, because God's covenant is eternal and because God will never abandon his people. This is the backdrop to the vision of the dry bones (Ezekiel 37:1–10) and the *interpretation* of the vision (Ezekiel

93

READING II   Romans 8:8–11

A reading from the Letter of Saint Paul to the Romans

Paul's reading contrasts the flesh and the spirit. In Paul's letters, the spirit is superior to the flesh, which desires, fades, and dies, while the spirit lives. This can make it challenging to read him to an assembly, each member of whom is in the flesh, in a body.

Brothers and sisters:
Those who are in the **flesh cannot** please **God**.
But you are **not** in the flesh;
    on the **contrary**, you are in the spirit,
    if only the **Spirit** of God dwells in you.
Whoever does not **have** the Spirit of **Christ** does not **belong**
      to him.
But if **Christ** is **in** you,
    although the **body** is dead because of **sin**,
    the **spirit** is alive because of **righteousness**.
If the **Spirit** of the one who raised **Jesus** from the **dead** dwells
     in you,
    the One who raised **Christ** from the dead
    will give **life** to your mortal bodies **also**,
    through his Spirit dwelling in **you**.

The sense of life is decidedly in the spirit, but it can enter the mortal body, too. Emphasize the phrase "give life."

37:11–14), which is our first reading for today.

First, a word about the vision: Ezekiel tells us that he was led out by the spirit of the Lord into a broad valley filled with dry bones in every direction. When asked whether the bones could come back to life, Ezekiel answers, "LORD GOD, you alone know that" (Ezekiel 37:3). God responds by telling Ezekiel to prophesy over the bones, with these words: "Listen! I will make breath enter you so you may come to life" (Ezekiel 37:5). The Hebrew word for "breath" is *ruach*, also meaning "wind or spirit," but

remember that this is God's breath! Soon Ezekiel hears a loud clattering noise and the bones come together, muscles and tendons grow on them and skin covers them. Then God tells Ezekiel to prophesy to the breath (Hebrew, *ruach*) with these words: "From the four winds come, O breath, and breathe into these slain that they may come to life" (Ezekiel 37:9). Finally, Ezekiel is told that the dry bones now-come-to-life are the people of Israel.

This is where our first reading begins. God tells Ezekiel to prophesy to the people in these words: "I will open your graves.

. . . I will put my spirit [Hebrew, *ruach*] in you that you may live, and I will settle you upon your land." Thus, to the exiles in Babylon, who feel as good as dead, the prophet is saying that God has not abandoned them and that God will one day restore them to their land. And why will God do this? It is not because the people have earned forgiveness. No, it is so that the people will know that God is all-sovereign and that God's word can be trusted, because it is in the nature of God to care for God's people.

Lazarus = LAZ-uh-ruhs
Bethany = BETH-uh-nee

A long and complex reading energized by the intense emotions of the figures in the story. The outcome of this story is well known. Its mysteries reside in the power over death that Jesus demonstrates, as well as his declarations about himself ("I am the resurrection and the life"). There are also the curious details that texture the imagination, such as the days Lazarus has been dead and the potential stench of his corpse. You can linger on these details in your proclamation.

These are the four main characters in the story.

Rabbi = RAB-ī

Emphasize the relationships between walking and day, walking and night, the light, and stumbling.

GOSPEL   John 11:1–45

A reading from the holy Gospel according to John

Now a man was **ill**, **Lazarus** from Bethany,
 the village of **Mary** and her sister **Martha**.
Mary was the one who had **anointed** the Lord with perfumed **oil**
 and **dried** his feet with her **hair**;
 it was her brother **Lazarus** who was **ill**.
So [the sisters sent word to Jesus saying,
 "**Master**, the one you **love** is **ill**."
When Jesus **heard** this he said,
 "This **illness** is not to **end** in death,
 but is for the **glory** of God,
 that the **Son** of God may be glorified **through** it."
Now Jesus loved **Martha** and her **sister** and **Lazarus**.
So when he **heard** that he was **ill**,
 he remained for **two days** in the place where he **was**.
Then **after** this he said to his disciples,
 "Let us go **back** to Judea."]
The disciples said to him,
 "**Rabbi**, the Jews were just trying to **stone** you,
 and you want to go **back** there?"
Jesus answered,
 "Are there not **twelve hours** in a day?
If one **walks** during the **day**, he does not **stumble**,
 because he **sees** the **light** of this **world**.
But if one **walks** at **night**, he **stumbles**,
 because the **light** is not in him."
He said this, and then told them,
 "Our friend **Lazarus** is **asleep**,
 but I am going to **awaken** him." »

READING II Our second reading is taken from Paul's Letter to the Romans. The section from which today's second reading is excerpted begins with these words: "Therefore, since we have been justified by faith, we have peace with God through our Lord Jesus Christ, through whom we have gained access [by faith] to this grace in which we stand" (Romans 5:1–2). With that introduction, Paul continues to talk about the life of the justified (i.e., the Christian believer) in today's reading. Although somewhat indirectly, Paul suggests that the goal of the Christian believer should be to please God, because the believer has done nothing to justify themselves, that is, to put themselves in right relationship with God. Only God can restore humanity to the relationship that it had with God before the fall, and God does so through the death and resurrection of Jesus Christ as a free gift to all who trust in God, because it is in the nature of God to be righteous. This reading can be somewhat confusing, because Paul uses the titles and phrases "Spirit of God," "Spirit of Christ," and "Christ" interchangeably, but what is important to notice is that Paul is describing the Christian believer's participation in the divine life: we are in Christ and Christ is in us. We have been invited to share in the life of God!

Paul also talks about those who are in the flesh and those who are in the spirit. Sometimes people are tempted to interpret these phrases as referring to the body and the soul, but, in fact, Paul is talking about the way his readers lived before they became Jesus followers and how they live now in the Spirit of Christ. Like the Hebrew word *ruach*, the Greek word *pneuma* means "spirit, wind, or breath." Paul suggests that

Didymus = DID-uh-muhs = twin

So the disciples said to him,
    "**Master**, if he is **asleep**, he will be **saved**."
But **Jesus** was talking about his **death**,
    while they **thought** that he meant **ordinary sleep**.
So then Jesus said to them clearly,
    "**Lazarus** has **died**.
And I am **glad** for you that I was not **there**,
    that you may **believe**.
Let us **go** to him."
So **Thomas**, called **Didymus**, said to his fellow disciples,
    "Let us **also** go to **die** with him."

[When Jesus **arrived**, he found that **Lazarus**
    had already been in the **tomb** for four days.]
Now Bethany was near **Jerusalem**, only about **two miles** away.
And many of the **Jews** had come to **Martha** and **Mary**
    to **comfort them** about their **brother**.
[When **Martha** heard that **Jesus** was coming,
    she went to **meet** him;
    but **Mary** sat at home.
Martha said to Jesus,
    "**Lord**, if you had **been** here,
    my **brother** would not have **died**.
But even **now** I know that what**ever** you ask of **God**,
    God will **give** you."
Jesus said to her,
    "Your **brother** will **rise**."
Martha said to him,
    "**I know** he will rise,
    in the **resurrection** on the last **day**."
Jesus told her,
    "**I** am the **resurrection** and the **life**;
    whoever **believes** in me, **even if he dies**, will **live**,
    and **everyone** who lives and **believes** in me will **never** die.

This exchange, concluding with "everyone who lives and believes in me will never die," expresses the core of this reading. Read it with care, allowing for Jesus' striking expression that he is the resurrection and the life to arise directly, even irrefutably, from this exchange.

there was a time when humanity was not capable of pleasing God, because its priorities were focused on turning upside down the relationship between creator and creature (see Romans 1:16–23). But that is no longer the case, Paul says, because now they are committed to living according to the Spirit. Yet, sin still has power over humanity; this is what Paul means when he says, "the body is dead because of sin." But the Spirit of God gives vitality to our dead bodies, as he did to Christ's dead body in the resurrection. What a tremendous mystery.

GOSPEL   Today's Gospel is the story of the resuscitation of Jesus' friend, Lazarus, which is strange and compelling in so many ways. We learn of this story only in John's Gospel, and, although there are two characters named Mary and Martha in Luke's Gospel (Luke 10:38–42), they are presented quite differently here, even if they are the same characters.

The story in full is very long, but, in its essence, it is a highly embellished miracle story, which would have at least three parts: the description of the problem, in this case, the report that Jesus' friend Lazarus is ill; the miracle worker's healing word or deed, in this case, Jesus' words to his dead friend, "Lazarus, come out!"; and evidence that the miracle took place, in this case, the characters in the story who see Lazarus come out of the tomb, still wrapped in his burial bands. This is the seventh and last sign—the term that John's Gospel uses to refer to Jesus' miracles—which clearly points to Jesus' own impending death. Seven is a number symbolizing fullness or completion.

Do **you** believe this?"
She said to him, "**Yes**, Lord.
I have **come** to **believe** that you are the **Christ**, the Son of God,
   the one who is **coming** into the world."]

When she had **said** this,
   she went and called her sister Mary **secretly**, saying,
   "The **teacher** is here and is **asking** for you."
As soon as she **heard** this,
   she rose **quickly** and **went** to him.
For Jesus had not yet come into the village,
   but was **still** where Martha had **met** him.
So when the **Jews** who were **with her** in the house **comforting** her
   saw Mary get up **quickly** and go **out**,
   they **followed** her,
   presuming that she was going to the **tomb** to **weep** there.
When Mary came to where Jesus was and saw him,
   she **fell** at his feet and **said** to him,
   "**Lord**, if you had **been** here,
   my **brother** would not have **died**."
When Jesus saw her **weeping** and the **Jews** who had come
    with her **weeping**,
   [he became **perturbed** and deeply **troubled**, and said,
   "**Where** have you **laid** him?"
They said to him, "Sir, **come** and **see**."
And Jesus wept.
So the Jews said, "See how he **loved** him."
But some of them said,
   "Could **not** the one who opened the **eyes** of the **blind** man
   have done **something** so that this man would not have **died**?"

So **Jesus**, perturbed again, **came** to the tomb.
It was a **cave**, and a **stone** lay across it.
Jesus said, "**Take away the stone**." »

Even emphasis on the words in this line.

Even emphasis here as well.

Mary repeats the same words as her sister Martha. Repeat them yourself plainly.
perturbed = per-TERBD = agitated and upset

From here to the conclusion of the reading, Jesus is in complete command. He has an audience, to whom he relates his miracle. Take note of the rhythm of the words, "Take away the stone."

Within the framework of this miracle story, the author of John's Gospel includes several other literary units. The first is a two-part dialogue between Jesus and his disciples. This is followed by two very similar units, which we will call the Martha cycle and the Mary cycle. Finally, when the miracle story is complete and in the verses that follow today's reading, the author of this Gospel includes a section that describes the people's reaction to Jesus and the high priest Caiaphas' prophecy about him (John 11:45–52). It concludes with a resolve on the part of the Pharisees and chief priests of Jerusalem to put Jesus to death (John 11:53).

These additional literary units are laden with emotion, confusion, and befuddlement, but they are essential to the rich fabric of this story. The two-part interaction that Jesus has with his disciples immediately after the problem is described is an example. Jesus tells his disciples that Lazarus' illness "is for the glory of God, that the Son of God may be glorified through it." What is he talking about? If you do a deep dive into John's Gospel, you will recognize that John uses "glorification" to refer to

Jesus' death and resurrection, his lifting up on the cross and his lifting up to God in glory. But then Jesus waits for two days to begin the trip to Bethany in Judea. Why?

The sections of this story that we are calling the Martha and Mary cycles are remarkably similar to one another. First, we learn that Jesus is coming or calling to the women. Next, the narrator tells us that mourners are present. Third, we hear that the sister goes to meet Jesus and says to him "Lord, if you had been here, my brother would not have died."

Even emphasis on this line with a slight additional emphasis on "believe."

Martha, the dead man's sister, said to him,
  "**Lord**, by now there will be a **stench**;
  he has been **dead** for **four days**."
Jesus said to her,
  "Did I not tell you that if you **believe**
  you will see the **glory** of God?"
So they **took away** the **stone**.
And Jesus raised his eyes and said,
  "**Father**, I thank you for **hearing** me.
I know that you **always** hear me;
  but because of the **crowd** here I have **said** this,
  that they may **believe** that you **sent** me."
And when he had **said** this,
  he cried out in a **loud voice**,
  "**Lazarus**, come **out**!"
The dead man came **out**,
  tied **hand** and **foot** with **burial** bands,
  and his **face** was wrapped in a **cloth**.
So Jesus said to them,
  "**Untie** him and let him go."

Now **many** of the Jews who had come to **Mary**
  and seen what he had **done** began to **believe** in him.]

[Shorter: John 11:3–7, 17, 20–27, 33b–45 (see brackets)]

Both cycles contain some dialog. In the Martha cycle, Jesus consoles her by reminding her that her brother will rise, and Martha assumes that he is referring to the end-time resurrection of the dead. But Jesus tells her, "I am the resurrection and the life," and she responds with a beautiful and powerful profession of faith of who Jesus is. These three attributes—"the Christ, the Son of God, and the one who is coming into the world"—are central to the way the Johannine community understood Jesus and his mission.

In the Mary cycle, Jesus dialogs with others, while Mary weeps in grief and pain. Jesus, likewise, is filled with emotion. The author describes him as "perturbed" in his spirit (i.e., emotionally) and "deeply troubled" in his body (i.e., agitated). Finally, shedding tears, Jesus went to Lazarus' tomb and ordered that it be opened. Why did Jesus wait so long to come to Bethany? He could have avoided this tragedy by coming as soon as Martha and Mary called for him! Or is that the point of the story: to show that Jesus could raise the dead, even

as the act of resuscitating Lazarus will lead directly to his own death? C.C.

PALM SUNDAY OF THE PASSION OF THE LORD

LECTIONARY #37

GOSPEL AT THE PROCESSION   Matthew 21:1–11

A reading from the holy Gospel according to Matthew

When **Jesus** and the **disciples** drew near **Jerusalem**
and came to **Bethphage** on the **Mount** of **Olives**,
Jesus sent **two disciples**, **saying** to them,
"**Go** into the village **opposite** you,
and **immediately** you will find an **ass tethered**,
and a **colt with** her.
Untie them and **bring** them **here** to **me**.
And if **anyone** should say **anything** to you, **reply**,
'The **master** has **need** of them.'
Then he will **send** them at **once**."
This **happened** so that what had been **spoken** through the **prophet**
might be **fulfilled**:
Say to daughter ***Zion***,
"***Behold***, your king ***comes*** to you,
meek and ***riding*** on an ***ass***,
and on a ***colt***, the ***foal*** of a ***beast*** of ***burden***."
The **disciples went** and did as **Jesus** had **ordered** them.
They brought the **ass** and the **colt** and **laid** their cloaks **over** them,
and he sat **upon** them. ❯❯

This Gospel reading is full of mysterious commands and a sense of destiny fulfilled.
Bethphage = BETH-fuh-jee

Slight pause between "colt" and "with."

Zion = ZĪ-uhn or ZĪ-ahn

foal = fohl
Note the repetition of words from the Scriptural quotation in the narrative itself.

GOSPEL | *Gospel at the procession.* The reading that accompanies the procession with palms on this Palm Sunday comes to us from the Gospel of Matthew. A version of this story is found in all four Gospels. However, Matthew's version more closely follows Mark's version than the others (cf. Mark 11:1–11; Luke 19:28–38; John 12:12–19). The story is designed to suggest a joyful procession into the holiest city of early Judaism, not unlike a great king coming to visit an important city in his kingdom. However, as the

story unfolds, one can discern in it a sense of dark times ahead.

The setting for this story is a small village called Bethphage. The village opposite it is probably Bethany. Both were on the eastern slope of the Mount of Olives and one to two miles from the gates of Jerusalem. Jesus tells two of his disciples to go into Bethany and locate a female donkey and her colt waiting for them. Donkeys were beasts of burden and symbols of domestic life, whereas horses were more often associate with the military and warrior kings. As Matthew tells the story, the

disciples appear to be unphased by the strangeness of this request, and they simply do as Jesus commanded them to do. This kind of foreknowledge might be surprising to us, but people likely saw this as a measure of Jesus' prophetic powers. At the conclusion of this reading, when people of Jerusalem ask, "Who is this?" who is able to shake up an entire city, the crowds respond, "This is Jesus the prophet, from Nazareth in Galilee."

If you read the text carefully, perhaps you wondered how Jesus could ride two donkeys at once. The author of Matthew's

The **very large crowd** spread their **cloaks** on the **road**,
  while **others** cut **branches** from the **trees**
  and **strewed** them on the **road**.
The **crowds preceding** him and those **following**
  kept crying **out** and **saying**:
    "**Hosanna** to the **Son** of **David**;
    blessed is **he** who **comes** in the **name** of the **Lord**;
    hosanna in the **highest**."
And when he entered **Jerusalem**
  the w**hole city** was **shaken** and **asked**, "Who **is** this?"
And the **crowds replied**,
  "This is **Jesus** the **prophet**, from **Nazareth** in **Galilee**."

strewed = strood (scattered or spread)

Words very familiar to the assembly from the Sanctus (Holy, Holy, Holy) in the Mass. Proclaim them as if they are being spoken for the first time.

READING I   Isaiah 50:4–7

A reading from the Book of the Prophet Isaiah

The **Lord GOD** has **given** me
  a **well-trained** tongue,
that I might **know** how to speak to the **weary**
  a **word** that will **rouse** them.
Morning after **morning**
  he opens my **ear** that I may **hear**;
and I have not **rebelled**,
  have not turned **back**.
I gave my back to **those** who **beat** me,
  my **cheeks** to those who **plucked** my beard;
my face I did not **shield**
  from **buffets** and **spitting**.

The Lord GOD is my **help**,
  therefore I am not **disgraced**;
I have set my **face** like **flint**,
  knowing that I shall **not** be put to **shame**.

Isaiah = ī-ZAY-uh

A short and powerful reading in which Isaiah asserts his trust in God.

Note the poetic rhythm that begins with the phrase "Morning after morning."

buffets = BUF-its = slaps

Give "not" and "shame" equal emphasis. These last lines can be read with conviction.

Gospel regularly uses quotations from the Old Testament to shed light on events in Jesus' life. Biblical scholars have engaged in much debate over the years about the sources of Matthew's quotations, whether from a Hebrew text or a Greek translation of the Old Testament, but a likely reason why the author of this Gospel describes Jesus as riding two donkeys at once is that he was reading from a Hebrew text that read "riding on a donkey, even on a colt" and he interpreted it to read "riding on a donkey, and on a colt" in Greek. These things happen, and they should not be a concern for us, except for us to recognize how important it was for Matthew to show that Jesus was exactly what the prophets of old said the messiah would be. Thus, he also presents the crowds as crying out in the words of Psalm 118:25–26, a psalm of thanksgiving and possibly a liturgical prayer of welcome as God's people entered into the Jerusalem Temple, though here it is applied to Jesus. "Hosanna!" can be translated as "Please save us!"

The words that Matthew quotes from the Old Testament add richness to his Gospel, and often the context from which these quotes were taken can add even more meaning to the text. For example, the words of the prophet Matthew quotes is actually a conflation or mashing together of a quotation from Isaiah and another from Zechariah. The line that Matthew borrows from Isaiah reads, "Say to daughter Zion, / 'See, your savior comes!'" (Isaiah 62:11) and is taken from the part of the book that is associated with the period after the Babylonian Exile, when those who returned from exile were trying to rebuild the temple and the city of Jerusalem. It is a message of hope in the midst of hard times. The quote

For meditation and context:

RESPONSORIAL PSALM   Psalm 22:8–9, 17–18, 19–20, 23–24 (2a)

R. My God, my God, why have you abandoned me?

All who see me scoff at me;
   they mock me with parted lips, they wag
     their heads:
"He relied on the Lord; let him deliver him,
   let him rescue him, if he loves him."

Indeed, many dogs surround me,
   a pack of evildoers closes in upon me;
they have pierced my hands and my feet;
   I can count all my bones.

They divide my garments among them,
   and for my vesture they cast lots.
But you, O Lord, be not far from me;
   O my help, hasten to aid me.

I will proclaim your name to my brethren;
   in the midst of the assembly I will
     praise you:
"You who fear the Lord, praise him;
   all you descendants of Jacob,
     give glory to him;
   revere him, all you descendants of Israel!"

Philippians = fih-LIP-ee-uhnz

An exhortation in which Paul seems to quote to the members of the Church at Philippi an early Christian hymn, whose focus is the *kenosis*, or emptying, mentioned in the fourth line of the reading. It's an utterly mysterious presentation of the power of Jesus' Incarnation. When you get to "emptied," give the word extra emphasis.

Give emphasis and rhythm to the words "human," "human," and "humbled."

READING II   Philippians 2:6–11

A reading from the Letter of Saint Paul to the Philippians

Christ **Jesus**, though he was in the **form** of God,
   did not regard **equality** with God
   something to be **grasped**.
Rather, he **emptied** himself,
   taking the form of a **slave**,
   coming in **human** likeness;
   and found **human** in appearance,
he **humbled** himself,
   becoming **obedient** to the point of **death**,
   even **death** on a **cross**.
Because of this, God **greatly** exalted him
   and **bestowed** on him the name
   which is above **every** name,
   that at the name of **Jesus**
   every **knee** should **bend**,
   of those in **heaven** and on **earth** and **under** the earth,
   and every **tongue** confess that
Jesus Christ is Lord,
   to the **glory** of God the **Father**.

Even emphasis on these four words: "Jesus Christ is Lord."

from Zechariah reads, "Exult greatly, O daughter Zion! / Shout for joy, O daughter Jerusalem! / Behold: your king is coming to you, / a just savior is he, / Humble, and riding on a donkey, / on a colt, the foal of a donkey" (Zechariah 9:9). The oracle from which this quotation is taken proclaims the arrival of an earthly king who would bring peace to the land.

READING I   Our first reading for the Eucharistic celebration is taken from the third of four "servant poems" found in the Book of Isaiah. The others are

Isaiah 42:1–7, Isaiah 49:1–7 and Isaiah 52:13—53:12. These four poems are similar insofar as they reflect messianic hopes of the time in which they were written. They differ in the clues they offer about the identity of the servant. He is variously described as God's chosen one, a king who will bring peace, a prophet like Jeremiah, or a representative of suffering Israel whom God will raise up. In today's reading, the servant is described as a disciple, part of an inner circle of learned ones, whose teacher is God and who is given the ability to speak to the weary and faint of heart. Remember that

this text was written in the time of the Babylonian Exile. Whether left behind or exiled abroad in Babylon, the people of Judah were in a very dark place.

The servant first describes how he was given the authority to speak this word. Every morning, day after day, God awakens him and opens his ears to hear God's word and teach him as a disciple is taught, without any resistance on his part. Implied in this statement is the strong conviction that, when the disciple speaks, it is God's word and not his own. Second, in order to speak God's word of consolation with

GOSPEL Matthew 26:14—27:66

The Passion of our Lord Jesus Christ according to Matthew

One of the **Twelve**, who was called **Judas Iscariot**,
     went to the **chief priests** and **said**,
     "**What** are you **willing** to **give** me
     if I **hand** him **over** to you?"
They paid him **thirty pieces** of **silver**,
     and from **that time on** he **looked** for an **opportunity** to hand
          him **over**.

On the **first day** of the **Feast** of **Unleavened Bread**,
     the **disciples** approached **Jesus** and **said**,
     "**Where** do you **want** us to **prepare**
     for you to **eat** the **Passover**?"
He said,
     "**Go** into the **city** to a **certain man** and **tell** him,
     'The **teacher says**, "My **appointed time** draws **near**;
     in your **house** I shall **celebrate** the **Passover** with
          my **disciples**."'"
The **disciples** then **did** as **Jesus** had **ordered**,
     and **prepared** the **Passover**.

When it was **evening**,
     he **reclined** at **table** with the **Twelve**.
And while they were **eating**, he said,
     "**Amen**, I **say** to you, **one** of you will **betray** me."
Deeply distressed at this,
     they began to **say** to him **one** after **another**,
     "**Surely** it is not **I**, **Lord**?"
He **said** in **reply**,
     "**He** who has **dipped** his **hand** into the **dish** with me
     is the **one** who will **betray** me.
The **Son** of **Man** indeed **goes**, as it is **written** of him,
     but **woe** to that **man** by whom the **Son** of **Man** is **betrayed**.

Iscariot = ih-SKAYR-ee-uht

An intensely powerful reading of the story at the core of our faith. This is also the longest reading that most congregants experience during the annual cycle. It is as dramatic as a novel, told with unusual economy and speed. But it also lingers on vivid scenes, vivid moments. Although the reading is dramatic, its drama is inherent in the language and the pacing of the story. Allow the language itself to dictate the drama. You will need to remain focused during this lengthy reading. It is commonplace for lectors to be involved in the proclamation of this Gospel. Whether passages in the Gospel are divided up among a group of readers, including the celebrant, the deacon, and some lectors, or it's portioned out in something more dramatic (where there is a narrator and then readers for each of the speakers), avoid theatricality. You may have an instinct to intensify the drama by "acting out" some of the voices and scenes but this can give the passion narrative a community theater vibe. It is better to avoid that in favor of proclaiming boldly, clearly, and slowly.

Note the mystery nested in words within words.

The early portion of this reading focuses on betrayal.

integrity, this disciple would have had to experience what the people were experiencing. Thus, the servant explains how he was beaten and humiliated, like prophets before him. For ancient peoples, to have one's beard torn away was the epitome of insult. Likewise, spitting on someone is considered very disrespectful in most cultures, even today, and a sign of extreme hatred. But the servant stands strong in his trust in God's power to save and to take away his shame. The phrase to "set my face like flint" is also associated with other prophets like Jeremiah and Ezekiel, as flint is a metaphor for something that is extremely hard or firm, as in a firm resolve.

But this servant poem prompts a question for us today. Will we also be like the servant, a steadfast disciple of God and one who will speak words of consolation, even in the face of our attackers?

READING II Our second reading comes from Paul's Letter to the Philippians. Paul established this Christian community in Philippi. Acts of the Apostles tells us that Paul was prompted in a vision to go to the region of Macedonia and to the city of Philippi, an important Roman city that was likely populated by retired Roman military personnel (Acts 16:6–40). It was also an important trade city, located on the Egnatian Way, which traversed the countries we now know as Albania, Macedonia, Greece, and Bulgaria to northern Turkey. Biblical scholars think that Paul might have visited Philippi as early as AD 50. Identified as one of Paul's prison letters, this letter might have been written approximately AD 54–56, while he was in prison in Ephesus, some four hundred miles from Philippi. This letter is a particularly tender one, because

Don't overplay Judas' words. He's conflicted about the betrayal he is committing.

It would be **better** for that **man** if he had **never** been **born**."
Then **Judas**, his **betrayer**, said in **reply**,
    "**Surely** it is not I, Rabbi?"
He answered, "**You** have **said** so."

The words of institution. Though extremely familiar, proclaim them as if they are being spoken for the first time.

While they were **eating**,
    Jesus **took bread**, said the **blessing**,
    broke it, and **giving** it to his **disciples** said,
    "**Take** and **eat; this** is my **body**."
Then he took a **cup**, gave **thanks**, and **gave** it to them, saying,
    "**Drink** from it, **all** of you,
    for **this** is my **blood** of the **covenant**,
    which will be **shed** on **behalf** of **many**
    for the **forgiveness** of **sins**.
I **tell** you, from **now on I shall not drink** this **fruit** of the **vine**
    until the **day** when I **drink** it with you **new**
    in the **kingdom** of my **Father**."
Then, after **singing a hymn**,
    they went **out** to the **Mount** of **Olives**.

Slight pause between "night" and "all."

Then **Jesus said** to them,
    "**This night all** of you will have your **faith** in me **shaken**,
    for it is **written**:
        I will **strike** the **shepherd**,
            and the **sheep** of the **flock** will be **dispersed**;
    but after I have been **raised** up,
    I shall go **before** you to **Galilee**."
Peter said to him in **reply**,
    "Though **all** may have their **faith** in you **shaken**,
    mine will **never** be."
Jesus said to him,
    "**Amen**, **I say** to you,
    this **very night** before the **cock crow**s,
    you will **deny** me **three times**." »

Emphasize "three times."

Paul sees the community as suffering for the faith just as he suffers for the faith.

Today's reading is perhaps the most well-known section of this Letter to the Philippians. Written in the form of a poem, theologians point to it as the clearest and most definitive statement of what Paul believed about Jesus as the Christ. But the situation is complicated. Biblical scholars believe that this poem was already in use as a liturgical hymn in Paul's day and that Paul adapted it for his purposes, but it is not clear how much he changed it—perhaps adding only "even death on a cross"

to the statement about Jesus being obedient to death—or how he interpreted the parts that he did not change. Did he understand Jesus to be a new Adam, who was made in the image and likeness of God, but, unlike the first Adam, "did not regard equality with God something to be grasped," and instead was humbly obedient to God even to death? Alternatively, did Paul understand Jesus to be a divine being, who was equal to God, but who chose not to exploit his divinity and instead humbled himself to become like us, even to the point of death?

Unfortunately, we may never know with full certainty what Paul intended to say about Jesus as the Christ. What we can say, however, is that Paul's Christology centers on the death and resurrection of Jesus. He seems to know very little about Jesus' teachings and nothing about his miracle working, but he knows deeply in his body the transformative power of Jesus' death and resurrection, as it relates to his own suffering and his hope for exaltation, and he wants this community at Philippi to experience it, too. Therefore, he exhorts them to "have among yourselves the same

Peter **said** to him,
"**Even though** I should have to **die** with you,
I **will not deny** you."
And **all** the **disciples** spoke **likewise**.

Gethsemane = gehth-SEM-uh-nee

Then **Jesus** came with them to a place called **Gethsemane**,
and he **said** to his **disciples**,
"**Sit here** while I **go** over **there** and **pray**."

Zebedee = ZEB-uh-dee

He took along **Peter** and the two sons of **Zebedee**,
and began to feel **sorrow** and **distress**.
Then he **said** to them,

These words of Christ are very sad; let the words themselves convey the sadness.

"My **soul** is **sorrowful even** to **death**.
Remain here and keep **watch** with me."
He **advanced** a **little** and fell **prostrate** in **prayer**, saying,

prostrate = PROS-trayt (face down)

Christ's prayer to his Father is filled with pathos. Again, let the words convey the deep feeling and sadness.

"My **Father**, if it is **possible**,
let this cup pass from me;
yet, **not** as I **will**, but as **you will**."
When he **returned** to his **disciples** he found them **asleep**.
He said to **Peter**,

Christ's tone is exasperated.

"So you **could not** keep **watch** with me for **one hour**?
Watch and **pray** that you may **not** undergo the **test**.
The **spirit** is **willing**, but the **flesh** is **weak**."
Withdrawing a **second time**, he prayed **again**,
"My **Father**, if it is **not possible** that this **cup pass**
without my **drinking** it, your **will** be **done**!"
Then he **returned** once **more** and found them **asleep**,
for they **could not** keep their **eyes open**.
He **left** them and **withdrew** again and prayed a **third** time,

Even emphasis on "same thing again."

saying the **same thing again**.
Then he **returned** to his **disciples** and **said** to them,
"Are you **still sleeping** and **taking** your **rest**?
Behold, the **hour** is at **hand**
when the **Son** of **Man** is to be handed **over** to **sinners**.

attitude that is also yours in Christ Jesus" (Philippians 2:5). What might this exhortation mean for the way we live our lives as Christians today?

GOSPEL Today's Gospel reading is the entire narrative of Jesus' arrest, suffering, and death as told in the Gospel of Matthew. Its length can be a bit overwhelming, but it is important for helping us to grasp the enormity of the events that we commemorate during this Holy Week, from the time of the triumphant entry into Jerusalem on Palm Sunday to the last meal that Jesus shares with his disciples to the terrible death that he endures on Golgotha to his internment in a tomb that was not his own and a plan by the religious leaders to cover up news of an empty tomb, should the problem arise. Next year, on Palm Sunday, we will hear Mark's version of the story, and the following year we will hear Luke's version of the passion narrative. These three stories are similar in many ways, but each contains details that make the story both unique and compelling

The passion narrative according to Matthew begins with a plot in which Judas, one of the twelve apostles, agrees to hand Jesus over to the chief priests of the Temple for thirty pieces of silver, which they pay immediately. Only Matthew provides this detail, which appears to be an allusion to Zechariah 11:12–13. The prophet is instructed to perform a symbolic action for which he is paid thirty pieces of silver. Coincidentally, this was the penalty imposed on someone who allowed his ox to gore another person's slave (see Exodus 21:32). Zechariah is then told to throw the money into the Temple treasury, perhaps as a judgment against the Temple priests.

The focus in this passage is on the kiss.

Get **up**, let us **go**.
Look, my **betrayer** is at **hand**."

While he was **still speaking**,
   Judas, one of the **Twelve**, **arrived**,
     accompanied by a **large crowd**, with **swords** and **clubs**,
     who had **come** from the **chief priests** and the **elders**
       of the **people**.
His **betrayer** had **arranged** a **sign** with them, saying,
   "The **man** I shall **kiss** is the **one**; **arrest him**."
Immediately he went **over** to **Jesus** and **said**,
   "**Hail**, **Rabbi**!" and he **kissed** him.
Jesus answered him,
   "**Friend**, **do** what you have **come** for."
Then **stepping forward** they laid **hands** on **Jesus** and **arrested** him.
And **behold**, **one** of those who **accompanied** Jesus
   put his **hand** to his **sword**, **drew** it,
   and **struck** the high priest's **servant**, **cutting off** his **ear**.
Then **Jesus said** to him,
   "Put your **sword back** into its **sheath**,
   for **all** who take the **sword** will **perish** by the **sword**.
Do you **think** that I cannot **call** upon my **Father**
   and he will **not provide** me at this **moment**
   with **more** than **twelve legions** of **angels**?
But then **how** would the **Scriptures** be **fulfilled**
   which **say** that it must **come** to **pass** in this **way**?"

Note the rhythm of this line: "AT THAT HOUR JESUS SAID to the CROWDS."

At that hour Jesus said to the **crowds**,
   "Have you come **out** as against a **robber**,
   with **swords** and **clubs** to **seize** me?
Day after **day** I sat **teaching** in the **temple** area,
   yet you did **not arrest** me.
But **all this** has **come** to **pass**
   that the **writings** of the **prophets** may be **fulfilled**."
Then all the **disciples left** him and **fled**. »

Thus, Matthew seems to suggest that Judas' betrayal of Jesus is part of God's plan.

Next, we hear about preparations for Passover, one of three great pilgrimage feasts of early Judaism. Matthew's version of the story follows Mark's Gospel quite closely, but he strips away many of the unnecessary details, making the story appear stark in its brevity. In Matthew's description of the Passover meal itself, we see how Jesus transforms the meaning of the Passover elements of bread and wine into the sacrifice of his own body and blood. Immediately before this intimate

sharing with his disciples, Jesus prophesies Judas' betrayal and points him out as "he who has dipped his hand into the dish with me," which suggests that Jesus' betrayer is reclining close enough to Jesus that they can eat from the same bowl. How disquieting! After singing a hymn to bring their Passover meal to a close and departing for the Mount of Olives, Jesus makes a general statement about the disciples abandoning him, this time citing Zechariah 13:7, followed by a more specific prophecy about Peter's denial of Jesus. Peter is fierce in his protest, even swearing that he would die

for Jesus, but later we see how quickly he gives in and denies him.

Matthew continues to follow Mark's version of the Gethsemane scene in which Jesus takes aside three of his disciples—Peter and the two sons of Zebedee, James and John—and tells them that he is filled with sorrow and grief, "even to death." Before he goes off to pray, he tells them that they should watch with him. He prays that "this cup," meaning his death, will pass him by, but only by God's will, not his. And each time Jesus returns, he finds the disciples asleep. Finally, he tells them that "the

Caiaphas = KAY-uh-fuhs or Kī-uh-fuhs

Those who had arrested **Jesus** led him **away**
　　to **Caiaphas** the **high priest**,
　　where the **scribes** and the **elders** were **assembled**.
Peter was **following** him at a **distance**
　　as far as the **high priest's courtyard**,
　　and going **inside** he sat **down** with the **servants** to see
　　　　the **outcome**.

Here the outrage of the priests is introduced; it will intensify.

The **chief priests** and the **entire Sanhedrin**
　　kept **trying** to obtain **false testimony** against **Jesus**
　　in **order** to **put** him to **death**,
　　but they **found none**,
　　though **many false witnesses** came **forward**.
Finally two came **forward** who **stated**,
　　"**This man said**, 'I can **destroy** the **temple** of God
　　and within **three days rebuild** it.'"
The **high priest rose** and **addressed** him,
　　"**Have** you no **answer**?
What are these men **testifying against** you?"
But **Jesus** was **silent**.
Then the **high priest said** to him,
　　"**I order** you to **tell** us under **oath** before the **living God**
　　whether you are the **Christ**, the **Son** of **God**."
Jesus said to him in **reply**,
　　"You have **said** so.
But I **tell** you:
　　From **now on** you will see the '**Son** of **Man**
　　　　seated at the **right hand** of the **Power**'
　　　　and '**coming** on the **clouds** of **heaven**.'"
Then the **high priest** tore his **robes** and said,
　　"He has **blasphemed**!
What further need have **we** of **witnesses**?
You have **now heard** the **blasphemy**;
　　what is your **opinion**?"

As Jesus replies to the high priest, he alludes to Scripture.

blasphemed = blas-FEEMD
"Blasphemed!" The spite of the high priest.

---

hour is at hand," meaning the time of his death, and he mentions his betrayer, which moves us into the next scene of the passion narrative, in which Judas betrays Jesus to the crowd who come to arrest him.

The scene of Judas' betrayal is thick with irony and emotional distress. The kiss was understood as a sign of friendship among men in the first-century world, but Judas betrays Jesus with a kiss, turning him over to those who want to destroy him! And then he greets Jesus with the words, "Hail, rabbi!" Judas is feigning respect, but his words and action are disparaging in

every way. Jesus responds by calling Judas "friend" and he tells him to do what he came to do. Can you feel the tension?

Suddenly, someone from Jesus' company takes a sword and cuts off the ear of the high priest's servant. This is no ordinary servant and no accident; an assistant to the high priest who has a deformity such as this would not be allowed to serve in the Temple (see Leviticus 21:17–22). Thus, this act is an attack on the high priest and his Temple ministry. Only Matthew's Gospel has the saying "all who take the sword will perish by the sword" and the saying about

the Father's ability to protect Jesus with twelve legions of angels, if he chose to ask. Although the number of foot soldiers in a legion differed at different periods of history, biblical scholars think it numbered about 6,100 at this time. If so, twelve legions would amount to 73,200 angels. What an army of heavenly beings!

All three synoptic Gospels have this accusatory question addressed to the crowd: "Have you come out as against a robber, with swords and clubs to seize me?" The Greek word "robber" or "bandit" might be better translated as "plunderer."

prophesy (verb) = PROF-uh-sī

Here the focus shifts to Peter and his denial.

Galilean = gal-ih-LEE-uhn

"Do not know": These words will be repeated with the same emphasis two more times.

Nazorean = naz-uh-REE-uhn

They **said** in **reply**,
   "He **deserves** to **die**!"
Then they **spat** in his **face** and **struck** him,
   while some **slapped** him, **saying**,
   "**Prophesy** for us, **Christ**: who is it that **struck** you?"

Now **Peter** was sitting **outside** in the **courtyard**.
One of the **maids** came **over** to him and **said**,
   "**You too** were with **Jesus** the **Galilean**."
But he **denied** it in front of **everyone**, saying,
   "I **do not know** what you are **talking** about!"
As he went **out** to the **gate**, **another girl saw** him
   and **said** to those who were **there**,
   "**This man** was with **Jesus** the **Nazorean**."
Again he **denied** it with an **oath**,
   "I **do not know the man**!"
A little **later** the **bystanders** came **over** and said to **Peter**,
   "**Surely** you **too** are **one** of them;
   even your **speech** gives you **away**."
At that he began to **curse** and to **swear**,
   "I **do not know** the **man**."
And **immediately** a cock **crowed**.
Then **Peter remembered** the **words** that **Jesus** had **spoken**:
   "Before the **cock crows** you will **deny** me **three times**."
He went **out** and began to **weep bitterly**.

When it was **morning**,
   all the **chief priests** and the **elders** of the **people**
   took **counsel** against **Jesus** to **put** him to **death**.
They **bound** him, led him **away**,
   and handed him **over** to **Pilate**, the **governor**.

Then **Judas**, his **betrayer**, seeing that **Jesus** had
      been **condemned**,
   deeply regretted what he had **done**. »

Pilate = PĪ-luht
Here the focus shifts to Pilate.

Today, we might think of rioters or violent protesters. Thus, the synoptic Gospels present Jesus' arrest as a further sign of disrespect. The saying about the Scriptures being fulfilled is the Gospel writers' way of asserting that Jesus' crucifixion is part of God's plan, but the next statement is the most devastating of all: "Then all the disciples left him and fled." A literal translation of this sentence might read like this: "Then the disciples, all of them, went away from that place and ran for safety." Thus, Jesus is left utterly alone to face the crowd that wants him dead.

The next scene in the narrative is Jesus' appearance before the high priest and the Sanhedrin. The Sanhedrin consisted of an assembly of Jewish elders which might have functioned somewhat like a grand jury today. Although all four Gospels have a similar account of this scene, Matthew and John's Gospels are the only ones that name Caiaphas as the high priest at that time (see John 18:13). Matthew again follows Mark's version of the story more or less, but with a few exceptions. For example, Matthew describes Peter as coming into the high priest's

courtyard "to see the outcome," suggesting a formal trial, whereas Mark describes Peter as warming himself by the fire (Mark 14:54). Both Gospels describe the high priest and the Sanhedrin as seeking witnesses against Jesus without much success, until Jesus breaks his silence and says, "You will see 'the Son of Man seated at the right hand of the Power' and 'coming on the clouds of heaven'." Thus, Jesus is charged with blasphemy, a crime punishable by death. But we can expect that the initial readers of this account caught the irony of the situation: Jesus' statement is

Slow your pace slightly at this point to allow the grim fate of Judas to register with your assembly.

Slight pause between "field" and "even."

Jeremiah = jayr-uh-MĪ-uh

The word "Now" signals another shift in focus, this time back to Pilate.

He **returned** the thirty pieces of **silver**
   to the **chief priests** and **elders**, saying,
   "I have **sinned** in betraying **innocent blood**."
They said,
   "What is **that** to **us**?
   Look to it **yourself**."
Flinging the **money** into the **temple**,
   he **departed** and went **off** and **hanged** himself.
The **chief priests gathered** up the **money**, but said,
   "It **is not lawful** to **deposit** this in the **temple treasury**,
   for it is the **price** of **blood**."
After **consultation**, they used it to buy the **potter's field**
   as a **burial** place for **foreigners**.
That is **why** that **field even today** is called the **Field** of **Blood**.
Then was **fulfilled** what had been **said** through **Jeremiah**
    the **prophet**,
   *And they **took** the t**hirty pieces** of **silver**,*
   *the **value** of a **man** with a **price** on his **head**,*
   *a **price set** by some of the **Israelites**,*
   *and they **paid** it out for the **potter's field***
   *just as the **Lord** had **commanded** me.*

[Now **Jesus** stood before the **governor**, and he **questioned** him,
   "**Are** you the **king** of the **Jews**?"
Jesus said, "You **say** so."
And when he was **accused** by the **chief priests** and **elders**,
   he made **no** answer.
Then Pilate **said** to him,
   "Do you not **hear** how many **things** they are
    testifying against you?"
But he **did not answer** him **one word**,
so that the **governor** was greatly **amazed**.

---

not blasphemy, but rather the truth about his identity!

The next two scenes in this passion narrative share a similar structure and some common themes. In terms of structure, the story of Peter's denial of Jesus is so closely intertwined with the story of Jesus' hearing before the Sanhedrin that they appear to be happening at the same time. Likewise, the story of Judas' suicide is intertwined with the story of Jesus appearance before Pontius Pilate, the governor of the region including Jerusalem, as if they are happening at the same time. The themes that hold these two sets of stories together are judgment and the ancient Mediterranean values of honor and shame. The theme of judgment is easy to see. In the first set of stories, Jesus is forced to appear before the high priest and charges are made. In the second, he is brought before Pontius Pilate for judgment and execution.

The significance of an honor-shame culture is much harder for those of us who have been raised in the western world to appreciate. Honor has to do with one's status in the community and the public recognition of that person's status. Losing honor is a very serious thing, which requires a response designed to restore one's honor. The story of Peter's denial of Jesus is an example of honor lost. Notice how quickly the tension escalates as Peter is confronted three times about his association with Jesus. The first confrontation is from a female servant who speaks to Peter alone, though he responds to everyone, "I do not know what you are talking about!" Notice how he is being evasive so as not to lose honor. The second is from another woman who says to those around her that Peter had been seen with Jesus, and he swears

Another "Now," another shift, this time to the negotiation between Pilate and the people for Christ's possible release.

Barabbas = buh-RAB-uhs

Now on the **occasion** of the **feast**
the **governor** was accustomed to **release** to the **crowd**
one **prisoner** whom they **wished**.
And **at that time** they had a notorious prisoner called **Barabbas**.
So when they had **assembled**, Pilate **said** to them,
"**Which one** do you **want** me to **release** to you,
Barabbas, or **Jesus** called **Christ**?"
For he **knew** that it was out of **envy**
that they had **handed** him **over**.
While he was **still seated** on the **bench**,
his **wife** sent him a **message**,
"Have **nothing** to do with that **righteous** man.
I suffered **much** in a **dream** today **because** of him."
The **chief priests** and the **elders** persuaded the **crowds**
to ask for **Barabbas** but to **destroy Jesus**.
The governor **said** to them in **reply**,
"**Which** of the **two** do you **want** me to **release** to you?"
They answered, "**Barabbas!**"
Pilate **said** to them,
"Then **what** shall I **do** with **Jesus** called **Christ**?"
They all said,
"**Let** him be **crucified!**"
But he said,
"**Why**? What **evil** has he **done**?"
They only **shouted** the **louder**,
"Let him be **crucified!**"
When **Pilate saw** that he was not **succeeding** at **all**,
but that a **riot** was breaking **out** instead,
he took **water** and washed his **hands** in the **sight** of the **crowd**,
saying, "I am **innocent** of this man's **blood**.
Look to it **yourselves**."
And the w**hole people** said in **reply**,
"His **blood** be **upon** us and **upon** our **children**." »

Don't overplay these words. They are already powerful enough.

with an oath, "I do not know the man!" The third encounter is with a group of bystanders who insist that Peter had been with Jesus. Now he curses and swears, "I do not know the man!" It was only a few hours earlier that evening, when Jesus prophesied that Peter would deny him three times before the cock crow, the name given to the period just before dawn. Remember how Peter vowed that he would die for Jesus, before he would deny him? Peter clearly recognizes his failure to retain honor, as we are told that "he went out and began to weep bitterly." Peter's weeping is a sign of pain and grief. Leaving the scene and going out into the darkness is another sign of Peter's loss of honor. This is the last time that Peter is mentioned by name in this Gospel.

By contrast, the story of Judas' suicide is an example of an attempt to restore honor. This story is told only in Matthew's Gospel, though there is a reference to the violence of his death in Acts 1:18–19. Here we learn that Judas responds with regret or self-repentance, when he realizes that Jesus is condemned to death because of his action, and he does what he can to restore honor. He returns the thirty pieces of silver to the chief priests and elders, but they refuse to take back the money, thereby not allowing Judas to undo the terrible thing he had done. This is when he decides to end his life, not so much out of despair, but as a way of restoring honor in a situation that is about to result in the death of another. A word of caution is needed concerning this story; suicide is never a solution to remedy a bad situation—all life is precious, regardless of our moral failures—but this story is an example of the depth of Judas' remorse,

scourged = skerjd

Another grim word, "scourged." Allow its menace to linger.

Another shift in focus, this time to the soldiers crucifying Jesus.

praetorium = prih-TOHR-ee-uhm

The tone of this passage is mocking. But don't overdo the mockery. It will come through by way of a forceful proclamation focused on the words themselves.

Cyrenian = sī-REE-nee-uhn

Golgotha = GAWL-guh-thuh

gall = gawl
Slight pause between "drink" and "mixed."

Then he **released Barabbas** to them,
 but **after** he had Jesus **scourged**,
 he handed him **over** to be **crucified**.

Then the **soldiers** of the **governor** took **Jesus**
 inside the **praetorium**
 and gathered the **whole cohort around** him.
They **stripped** off his **clothes**
 and threw a **scarlet military cloak** about him.
Weaving a **crown** out of **thorns**, they **placed** it on his **head**,
 and a **reed** in his **right hand**.
And **kneeling before** him, they **mocked** him, saying,
 "**Hail**, **King** of the **Jews!**"
They **spat** upon him and took the **reed**
 and kept **striking** him on the **head**.
And when they had **mocked** him,
 they **stripped** him of the **cloak**,
 dressed him in his **own clothes**,
 and led him **off** to **crucify** him.

As they were going **out**, they met a **Cyrenian** named **Simon**;
 this man they **pressed** into **service**
 to **carry** his **cross**.

And when they **came** to a place called **Golgotha**
 —which means **Place** of the **Skull**—,
 they gave **Jesus wine** to **drink mixed** with **gall**.
But when he had **tasted** it, he **refused** to **drink**.
After they had **crucified** him,
 they **divided** his **garments** by casting **lots**;
 then they **sat down** and kept **watch** over him there.
And they **placed** over his **head** the **written charge against** him:
 This is **Jesus**, the **King** of the **Jews**.
Two revolutionaries were **crucified with** him,
 one on his **right** and the **other** on his **left**.

making forgiveness possible, if he had chosen another path in this moment.

Next, we hear the story of Jesus' appearance before Pontius Pilate. Again, Matthew makes a few changes to Mark's version of the story. For example, when Pilate is about to sentence Jesus to death, his wife sends a message to him, urging him not to be involved in this case, because of what she had suffered in a dream. This addition provides a fitting transition to the next scene where Pilate attempts to release Jesus by offering a prisoner release in celebration of the Passover feast. He offers the crowd two choices: Jesus or Barabbas, whose name ironically means "son of the father." Luke's Gospel describes the latter as an insurrectionist and a murderer (Luke 23:19). The author of Matthew's Gospel changes the title given to Jesus from "king of the Jews" to "the Christ," further suggesting that Jesus is not guilty of a crime deserving death. Matthew reinforces this point by adding the scene in which Pilate publicly washes his hands and declares himself innocent in the anticipated execution of Jesus. The narrator tells us that Pilate finally released Jesus to the crowd, because he feared a riot would break out, but we should not assume that he is an innocent victim in all this. Pontius Pilate was a very complex historical character, and even today historians are divided about how we should view him.

But we cannot leave this scene without commenting on Matthew's addition of the famous or infamous quotation that he attributes to the chief priests, the elders and the crowd: "His blood be upon us and upon our children." Regrettably, the historical context for this quotation was quickly lost—Matthew's community of

Once again, mockery dominates the tone.

Those passing by reviled him, **shaking** their **heads** and saying,
  "**You** who would **destroy** the **temple** and **rebuild** it in
    three days,
  save yourself, if **you are** the **Son** of **God**,
  and come **down** from the **cross!**"
Likewise the **chief priests** with the **scribes** and **elders mocked**
    him and said,
  "He s**aved others**; he **cannot** save **himself**.
So he **is** the king of **Israel!**
Let him **come down** from the cross **now**,
  and we will **believe** in him.
He **trusted** in **God**;
  let him **deliver** him now if he **wants** him.
For he **said**, 'I am the **Son** of **God.**'"
The **revolutionaries** who were **crucified** with him
  also kept **abusing** him in the **same way**.

From **noon onward**, darkness came over the **whole land**
  until **three** in the **afternoon**.
And about **three o'clock** Jesus **cried out** in a **loud voice**,
  "Eli, Eli, lema sabachthani?"
  which **means**, "My **God**, my **God**, **why** have you **forsaken** me?"
Some of the **bystanders** who **heard** it said,
  "**This** one is calling for **Elijah**."
Immediately one of them ran to get a **sponge**;
  he **soaked** it in **wine**, and **putting** it on a **reed**,
  gave it to him to **drink**.
But the rest said,
  "**Wait**, let us see if **Elijah** comes to **save** him."
But **Jesus cried out again** in a **loud voice**,
  and **gave** up his **spirit**.

[Here all kneel and pause for a short time.] »

Eli, Eli, lema sabachthani = ay-LEE, ay-LEE, luh-MAH sah-bahk-TAH-nee
These authentic words of Christ are as wrenching as they are solemn.

Elijah = ee-LĪ-juh

Jews together with some Gentiles who believed in Jesus as the Christ were battling with other Jews who refused to recognize Jesus as the Christ—but it soon became a rallying cry for fear and hatred of the Jewish people. They were seen as Christ-killers, who must pay the price for their crime of deicide! While antisemitism continues to persist even in our time, it is not representative of Catholic theology nor is it supported by the Gospels, which indicate clearly that Jesus' death was part of God's plan of salvation for the whole human race. The Second Vatican Council asserts that "neither all Jews indiscriminately at that time, nor Jews today, can be charged with the crimes committed during his [Christ's] passion" and that the Church "deplores all hatreds, persecutions, displays of antisemitism levelled at any time or from any source against the Jews" (*Nostra aetate*, 4).

Following Mark's Gospel, Matthew goes on to tell the story of the Roman soldiers mocking Jesus in the praetorium, Pilate's residence in Jerusalem. However, he changes the color of the robe that the soldiers placed on Jesus from purple in Mark's Gospel, a color of royalty, to red, the color that the soldiers wore, and he describes the soldiers as placing a reed scepter in Jesus' right hand, the hand of power. This act, along with stripping Jesus of his clothing and spitting on him, should be seen as efforts to destroy Jesus' honor status as messiah and Son of God. Likewise, the inscription placed on the cross, "This is Jesus, the King of the Jews" and the passersby who were hurling abuse at Jesus were attempts to strip Jesus of his honor. Yet, when all seems lost and Jesus gives up his spirit in death, the Gospel writer adds that the barrier that separated the Holy of

At "behold," another shift in tone, this time to wonder mixed with awe—it's even a little frightening.

And **behold**, the **veil** of the **sanctuary**
  was **torn** in **two** from **top** to **bottom**.
The **earth quaked**, **rocks** were **split**, **tombs** were **opened**,
  and the **bodies** of **many saints** who had fallen **asleep**
    were **raised**.
And coming **forth** from their **tombs** after his **resurrection**,
  they **entered** the holy **city** and appeared to **many**.

centurion = sen-TOOR-ee-uhn

The **centurion** and the **men** with **him** who were keeping **watch**
    over **Jesus**
  feared **greatly** when they saw the **earthquake**
  and **all** that was **happening**, and they **said**,
  "**Truly**, **this** was the **Son** of **God!**"]
There were **many women there**, looking **on** from a **distance**,
  who had followed **Jesus** from **Galilee**, **ministering** to him.

Magdalene = MAG-duh-luhn or MAG-duh-leen

Zebedee = ZEB-uh-dee

Among them were **Mary Magdalene** and **Mary** the mother of
    James and **Joseph**,
  and the **mother** of the **sons** of **Zebedee**.

Arimathea = ayr-ih-muh-THEE-uh

When it was **evening**,
  there came a **rich man** from **Arimathea** named **Joseph**,
  who was **himself** a disciple of **Jesus**.
He went to **Pilate** and asked for the **body** of **Jesus**;
  then Pilate **ordered** it to be handed **over**.
Taking the **body**, Joseph **wrapped** it in **clean linen**

hewn = hyoon

  and laid it in his **new tomb** that he had **hewn** in the **rock**.
Then he rolled a **huge stone** across the **entrance** to the **tomb**
    and **departed**.
But **Mary Magdalene** and the other **Mary**
  remained **sitting** there, **facing** the **tomb**.

Pharisees = FAYR-uh-seez

The **next day**, the one following the **day** of **preparation**,
  the **chief priests** and the **Pharisees**
  gathered before **Pilate** and **said**,
  "**Sir**, we **remember** that this **impostor** while **still alive** said,
  'After **three days** I will be raised **up**.'

Holies from the rest of the Temple was torn open—remember that the Holy of Holies was where God would reside when visiting God's people—the earth was trembling from earthquakes, and dead people were walking around. These signs prompt the centurion and some of his soldiers to proclaim, "Truly, this was the Son of God!" and thus Jesus' honor is restored.

Matthew's passion narrative ends rather quickly with an abbreviated version of Mark's story of Jesus' burial. Joseph of Arimathea is now described as a rich disciple of Jesus, though there is no mention of him being a member of the Sanhedrin. Further, Matthew describes the shroud, in which Jesus' body is wrapped, as clean and the tomb, in which he was laid, as new. Thus, Matthew portrays Joseph as attempting to give Jesus a burial that restores his honor in the world. Finally, the Gospel writer adds a scene in which the chief priests and the Pharisees request and are granted guards to secure the tomb so that Jesus' disciples cannot commit fraud by stealing the body and claiming that Jesus had risen from the dead. By suggesting that Jesus is a deceiver and arguing that Jesus' disciples might create an even greater deception, these religious leaders make one final effort to attack Jesus' honor. What they do not know is that God's efforts to restore Jesus' honor will win out in the end. All we need to do now is wait. C.C.

It's worth noting the anxious conclusion of this reading.

Give **orders**, then, that the **grave** be **secured** until the **third day**,
    lest his **disciples** come and **steal** him and **say** to the **people**,
    'He has been **raised** from the **dead**.'
This **last imposture** would be **worse** than the **first**."
Pilate **said** to them,
    "The **guard** is **yours**;
    go, **secure** it as **best** you can."
So they **went** and secured the **tomb**
    by **fixing** a **seal** to the **stone** and **setting** the **guard**.

[Shorter: Matthew 27:11–54 (see brackets)]

EVENING MASS OF THE LORD'S SUPPER (HOLY THURSDAY)

LECTIONARY #39

READING I   Exodus 12:1–8, 11–14

A reading from the Book of Exodus

The **LORD** said to **Moses** and **Aaron** in the land of **Egypt**,
  "This month shall **stand** at the head of your **calendar**;
  you shall **reckon** it the first month of the **year**.
Tell the **whole** community of **Israel**:
  On the **tenth** of this month every one of your families
  must **procure** for itself a **lamb**, one apiece for each **household**.
If a family is too **small** for a **whole lamb**,
  it shall **join** the nearest household in **procuring** one
  and shall **share** in the **lamb**
  in **proportion** to the number of **persons** who **partake** of it.
The lamb must be a **year-old male** and without **blemish**.
You may **take** it from either the **sheep** or the **goats**.
You shall **keep it** until the fourteenth day of this **month**,
  and **then**, with the whole assembly of Israel present,
  it shall be **slaughtered** during the evening **twilight**.
They shall take **some** of its blood
  and apply it to the **two doorposts** and the **lintel**
  of **every house** in which they **partake** of the **lamb**.
That **same night** they shall **eat** its roasted **flesh**
with **unleavened bread** and bitter **herbs**.

Exodus = EK-suh-duhs

A reading that includes detailed instructions from God to Moses and Aaron to convey to the Israelites so that they will be prepared for the events now commemorated as Passover. The instructions have ritual power anticipating one of the most spectacular narratives in the Old Testament. Read these instructions with some reverence.

These details are part of the appeal of this reading. Don't rush through them.

Emphasis on "slaughtered."

READING I Holy Thursday, also called Maundy Thursday, is a commemoration of the synoptic Gospels' story of the Passover meal that Jesus shared with his disciples before his death and a celebration of the institution of the Eucharist. Today's readings speak well to the robust, multilayered meanings attached to this feast.

In the first reading, we hear an account of the Passover ritual as explained in the Book of Exodus. It appears immediately after the announcement of the tenth plague, the death of the firstborn of Egypt (Exodus 11), and immediately before the execution of this tenth plague (Exodus 12:29–30). However, the ritual itself probably reflects a later period of development —in this case, a time when two separate rituals had been joined into one. The first is the ritual of the Passover lamb (Exodus 12:1–13) and the second is the ritual of the unleavened bread (Exodus 12:14–20). Here God is speaking to Moses, who will later describe the rituals to the Israelite peoples (see Exodus 12:21–27).

The ritual of the Passover lamb always occurred in the springtime and was con- nected to the tenth plague by the directive to the Israelites to put the blood of the lamb on the door posts and lintels of the homes where they were eating the sacrificial meal, so that God would know to pass over those places and protect them from the destruction that would come upon Egypt, when God killed all of the firstborn. Although it is troubling for us to think about God doing such a terrible thing, we need to remember that the plagues were God's "weapons" in the battle with the hard-hearted pharaoh, who claimed divinity but was not really a god. Thus, Passover is a

girt = gert = belted

This line announces the purpose of this reading; it is followed by the grim details of God's judgment. Give them the emphasis they deserve.

"This is how you are to **eat** it:
with your loins **girt**, **sandals** on your **feet** and your **staff**
in hand,
you shall **eat** like those who are in **flight**.
It is the **Passover** of the LORD.
For on this **same night** I will go through **Egypt**,
striking down **every firstborn** of the land, both **man** and **beast**,
and **executing judgment** on all the **gods** of Egypt—I, the LORD!
But the **blood** will mark the **houses** where you **are**.
Seeing the blood, I will **pass over** you;
thus, when I strike the land of **Egypt**,
no destructive blow will come **upon** you.

"This **day** shall be a **memorial feast** for **you**,
which **all** your generations shall **celebrate**
with **pilgrimage** to the LORD, as a **perpetual** institution."

For meditation and context:

RESPONSORIAL PSALM   Psalm 116:12–13, 15–16bc, 17–18
(1 Corinthians 10:16)

R. Our blessing-cup is a communion with the Blood of Christ.

How shall I make a return to the LORD
for all the good he has done for me?
The cup of salvation I will take up,
and I will call upon the name of the LORD.

Precious in the eyes of the LORD
is the death of his faithful ones.
I am your servant, the son of your handmaid;
you have loosed my bonds.

To you will I offer sacrifice of thanksgiving,
and I will call upon the name of the LORD.
My vows to the LORD I will pay
in the presence of all his people.

joyous, anticipatory celebration of freedom from slavery, which God will surely and immediately win for the Israelites.

READING II   Our second reading, from Paul's First Letter to the Corinthians, is part of a longer teaching on how to share the Eucharist with integrity and attention to the welfare of the entire community. In the early centuries of Christianity, the Eucharist took place as part of a common meal in the homes of wealthy patrons. But someone, perhaps Chloe's people (see 1 Corinthians 1:11), told Paul

about the community's bad behavior when they gathered to eat the Lord's supper. Apparently, the wealthy arrived early and were eating and drinking to excess, so that, when the poor arrived, the food was gone. Not only were the lower-class members of the community hungry, but they were shamed by the fact that the wealthy had no regard for their need.

Paul is being extremely radical here. When the Christian community gathered for Eucharist, they were doing exactly what everyone else was doing at banquets, in keeping with cultural practices in the first-

century Mediterranean world. But Paul is fierce in his condemnation of the community's behavior, arguing that, "anyone who eats and drinks without discerning the body, eats and drinks judgment on himself" (1 Corinthians 11:29). Why? Paul recites the words of the institution of the Eucharist that was already in use in Christian communities, tracing them back to the authority of Jesus. Biblical scholars think that Paul might have altered the original wording by adding "Do this, as often as you drink it, in remembrance of me" to the statement, "This cup is the new covenant in my blood,"

Corinthians = kohr-IN-thee-uhnz

A commemoration of the words at the heart of the Mass. These words of Paul's to the Corinthians are a Scriptural echo of the words in the reading from Exodus.

Here begin the words of institution, always spoken by a priest, but here, most likely, spoken by a lector. These words can take on a freshness in your proclamation.

In a slow, commemorative rhythm.

A reading that provides the basis for one of the most powerful of Christian rituals, the washing of feet. Its power resides in the directness of its depiction of the ritual itself but also the ways the act anticipates Christ's passion.

Iscariot = ih-SKAYR-ee-uht

READING II   1 Corinthians 11:23–26

A reading from the first Letter of Saint Paul to the Corinthians

Brothers and sisters:
I **received** from the Lord what I also **handed** on to you,
　that the **Lord** Jesus, on the **night** he was handed over,
　took **bread**, and, after he had given **thanks**,
　broke it and said, "**This** is my **body** that is for **you**.
Do this in remembrance of **me**."
In the **same way** also the **cup**, after **supper**, saying,
　"**This cup** is the **new covenant** in my **blood**.
Do this, as **often** as you **drink it**, in **remembrance** of me."
For as **often** as you eat this **bread** and drink the **cup**,
　you **proclaim** the **death** of the **Lord** until he **comes**.

GOSPEL   John 13:1–15

A reading from the holy Gospel according to John

Before the feast of **Passover**, Jesus **knew** that his **hour** had **come**
　to **pass** from this **world** to the **Father**.
He **loved** his own in the **world** and he **loved** them to the **end**.
The **devil** had already induced **Judas**, son of **Simon** the **Iscariot**,
　to hand him over.
So, during supper,
　fully aware that the **Father** had put **everything** into his **power**
　and that he had **come** from God and was **returning** to God,
　he **rose** from supper and took **off** his outer **garments**.
He took a **towel** and tied it around his **waist**.

thereby highlighting the Eucharist as a commemoration of a supreme act of love, Jesus' death on a cross. The community should do likewise, no matter how radical it might seem. They should love even those who were different from themselves.

GOSPEL   At first glance, today's reading from the Gospel of John might seem like a strange choice for Holy Thursday. John's story of Jesus' last meal with his disciples is not a Passover meal. Rather, it takes place several days before Passover, because, in John's Gospel,

Jesus is sentenced to death and crucified on the preparation day for Passover, when the Passover lambs were being sacrificed in the Temple. Also, the story begins on an ominous note, by explaining that Jesus' "hour," that is, the time of his death and return to the Father, had come and that he had loved his own to the end or to the fullest. These verbs are aorist tense, which denotes a past action completed. The narrator also notes that Judas had already plotted to hand Jesus over to his enemies.

Today's reading describes a ritual of hospitality, the washing of feet, that would

have preceded any banquet in the first-century Mediterranean world. This was a fitting way to indicate to your guests a sense of welcome. However, this work would have been done not by the master of the household or the host of a dinner but by the master's slaves. Hence, we can sense Peter's horror as he watches Jesus remove his outer garment in preparation for work and engage in a slave's task to provide hospitality to his guests.

But this foot washing is so much more than an act of hospitality. When Peter protests that he wants no part in Jesus' self-

The details here are important.

The details here are important.

Then he **poured water** into a **basin**
and **began** to wash the disciples' **feet**
and **dry them** with the **towel** around his **waist**.
He **came** to Simon **Peter**, who **said** to him,
"**Master**, are you going to **wash** my **feet**?"
Jesus answered and said to him,
"What I am **doing**, you **do not** understand **now**,
but you will **understand later**."
Peter said to him, "You will **never** wash my **feet**."
Jesus answered him,
"Unless I **wash** you, you will have no **inheritance** with **me**."
Simon Peter said to him,
"**Master**, then not only my **feet**, but my **hands** and **head**
as well."
Jesus said to him,
"**Whoever** has bathed has no **need** except to have his
feet washed, for he is **clean** all over;
so you are **clean**, but not all**.**"
For he **knew** who would **betray** him;
for this **reason**, he said, "Not **all** of you are **clean**."

So when he had **washed** their feet
and put his **garments** back on and **reclined** at table again,
he said to them, "Do you **realize** what I have **done** for you?
You call me '**teacher**' and '**master**,' and rightly so, for **indeed**
I **am**.
If I, therefore, the **master** and **teacher**, have **washed** your feet,
you ought to wash one another's feet.
I have **given** you a model to **follow**,
so that as I have done for **you**, **you** should also **do**."

Peter's inability to understand what Jesus is doing reflects the congregation's. Though Peter is a bit thick, Jesus is gentle but authoritative in his responses.

Emphasis on "feet washed."

These lines to the end of the reading are firm and mysterious.

TO KEEP IN MIND
Recognize how important your proclamation of the Word of God is. Prepare well and take joy in your ministry.

---

shaming act, Jesus tells Peter that, if he refuses, he can have no part in what Jesus has in store for the disciples. Peter's response is somewhat humorous, because he takes Jesus' words literally and requests a full bath! John frequently uses this literary technique of having characters understand only the plain meaning of Jesus' words so that Jesus can go on to explain the deeper meaning. Thus, Jesus responds, "Whoever has bathed has no need except to have his feet washed, for he is clean all over; so you are clean, but not all." The phrase "but not all" refers to Judas.

Biblical scholars have debated whether bathing is a reference to baptism. The Greek word is *louó*, meaning "to bathe or to wash," which can be applied in a variety of settings, but, at the very least, we can say that bathing is a symbol of abiding or remaining with Jesus. Abiding is the way this Gospel refers to discipleship. Now only the feet need to be washed. Why? The foot washing is an action and symbol of the extent to which the disciples must go to be servants of one another. They must follow Jesus' example of servanthood in loving others to the end.

And what about us? Are we willing to follow Jesus' example? For the author of John's Gospel, responding to the call of discipleship is more than pious thoughts. It requires that we be humble servants of all God's children. C.C.

FRIDAY OF THE PASSION OF THE LORD (GOOD FRIDAY)

LECTIONARY #40

READING I   Isaiah 52:13—53:12

Isaiah = ī-ZAY-uh

A reading whose power arises from bold claims and compelling rhythms. Allow these elements to ring out in your proclamation. Isaiah's prophecy speaks directly to the congregation and the mystery into which it is immersed.

Even emphasis on the words in this line.

A reading from the Book of the Prophet Isaiah

> **See**, my servant shall **prosper**,
>   he shall be **raised high** and greatly **exalted**.
> Even as **many** were **amazed** at him—
>   so **marred** was his look beyond **human semblance**
>   and his **appearance** beyond that of the **sons of man**—
> so shall he startle many nations,
>   because of **him kings** shall stand **speechless**;
> for **those** who have not been **told** shall see,
>   those who have not **heard** shall **ponder** it.

The questions Isaiah asks set the tone for the lines to follow.

> **Who** would **believe** what we have **heard**?
>   To **whom** has the **arm** of the LORD been **revealed**?
> He grew **up** like a sapling **before** him,
>   like a **shoot** from the parched **earth**;
> there was **in him** no stately bearing to make us **look** at him,
>   nor **appearance** that would **attract** us to him.
> He was **spurned** and **avoided** by **people**,
>   a man of **suffering**, accustomed to **infirmity**,
> one of **those** from whom people hide their **faces**,
>   **spurned**, and we **held him** in no **esteem**.

READING I | The first reading for today's liturgy is commonly known as the Suffering Servant Song. The tone is mournful at times—some have compared it to a dirge—but hopeful, too. Altogether, there are four servant songs, all of which are found in Second Isaiah (Isaiah 40–55). The time and place of this writing is the sixth century BC, while the Jews were in exile in Babylon.

In the opening sentence of this reading, God is the speaker, and God refers to the subject of this oracle as "my servant," but the text gives us few clues about the servant's identity. The Hebrew word translated here as "many" has the connotation of a number too big to count, and the word translated as "amazed" also means "appalled, stunned, or desolated," like a desert is desolate. The servant is presented as so disfigured that he could hardly be recognized as human. Further, we are told that the kings and nations were startled by him. The word translated as "to startle" is most often understood to mean "to spurt or splatter." The connection here might be that the servant's disfigurement is so terrible that it causes the observers to spurt,

metaphorically, or leap into a response of horror at what they see.

Suddenly and without transition, God is no longer speaking. Instead, a group identified only as "we" speaks. Their message is one of amazement at what is happening before their eyes. The "arm of the Lord" is a phrase designed to evoke the idea of God's intervention in history, usually in victory, though not always in a military sense. The servant is compared to a tender plant or a shoot emerging out of the dry desert soil, evoking the wonder that we experience on an early spring day in a

Note the rhythms in the lines in this section, many of which place an emphasis on two of the words in the line, "infirmities" and "bore"; "sufferings" and "endured"; and so forth. Let these rhythms carry your proclamation.

The story of the Suffering Servant is of course anticipatory of the Passion in John's Gospel.

The rhythms that prevail in the previous section continue in this one, often with an emphasis on two words in the line. Once again, let these rhythms carry your proclamation.

Words like "slaughter," "condemned," "wicked," and "evildoers" are loaded with significance. Recite them clearly and that significance will be evident to the assembly. No need to over-dramatize the words when you proclaim them.

Yet it was our **infirmities** that he **bore**,
    our **sufferings** that he **endured**,
while we **thought** of him as **stricken**,
    as one **smitten** by God and **afflicted**.
But he was **pierced** for our offenses,
    crushed for our sins;
upon him was the **chastisement** that makes us **whole**,
    by his **stripes** we were **healed**.
We had all gone **astray** like **sheep**,
    each following his **own** way;
but the LORD laid upon him
    the **guilt** of us **all**.

Though he was **harshly treated**, he **submitted**
    and **opened not** his mouth;
like a **lamb** led to the **slaughter**
    or a **sheep** before the **shearers**,
he was **silent** and opened not his **mouth**.
Oppressed and **condemned**, he was taken **away**,
    and who would have thought any **more** of his **destiny**?
When he was cut **off** from the land of the **living**,
    and **smitten** for the sin of his **people**,
a **grave** was **assigned** him among the **wicked**
    and a **burial** place with **evildoers**,
though he had **done** no **wrong**
    nor **spoken** any **falsehood**.
But the LORD was pleased
    to **crush him** in infirmity.

If he **gives** his life as an **offering** for sin,
    he shall **see** his descendants in a **long life**,
    and the **will** of the LORD shall be **accomplished**
        through him. »

climate that is somewhat hostile to new life (see also Isaiah 11:1), but the group notes that the servant, at his arrival, is nothing much to look at and is even rejected or forsaken by those around him. Notice also the use of the phrase "one of those from whom people hide their faces," which was used to describe a person's response to seeing a leper in the ancient world.

This same unidentified group goes on to talk about the suffering that the servant endured, not because of his own wrongdoing but on behalf of those who rejected him, because they thought his sorry state was due to his own misdeeds. The language used to describe the servant's suffering is extremely weighty and graphic. The word translated here as "pierced" is also translated as "thrust through," and the word translated here as "crushed" can mean "broken into pieces" or "shattered." Similarly, the word translated here as "stripes" can be translated as "scourging or beatings." Thus, although the group's amazement is proportional to the horror that they are witnessing, it is even more striking because they say, "the LORD laid upon him the guilt of us all." This kind of suffering for the sake of another is unheard of and is almost too much for our small minds to comprehend. How could God love humanity this much?

This Suffering Servant Song uses the sheep metaphor in two separate instances. First, the group identifies itself as sheep "each following his own way." Second, the sheep metaphor is applied to the servant who belongs to the flock and now is chosen to be a sacrificial offering for the rest. The onlookers mistakenly think that he is a lamb made ready for slaughter and cut off from life. But the prophet reminds us that

As the reading concludes, the mood lifts. There is a sense of promise and redemption. Don't, however, overdo it. The hope will come through when you proclaim these words straightforwardly.

Because of his **affliction**
    he shall **see** the light in **fullness** of days;
through his **suffering**, my servant shall **justify many**,
    and their **guilt** he shall **bear**.
Therefore I will give him his **portion** among the **great**,
    and he shall **divide** the spoils with the **mighty**,
because he **surrendered** himself to **death**
    and was **counted** among the **wicked**;
and he shall **take away** the sins of **many**,
    and win **pardon** for their **offenses**.

For meditation and context:

RESPONSORIAL PSALM   Psalm 31:2, 6, 12–13, 15–16, 17, 25 (Luke 23:46)

R. Father, into your hands I commend my spirit.

In you, O LORD, I take refuge;
    let me never be put to shame.
In your justice rescue me.
Into your hands I commend my spirit;
    you will redeem me, O LORD,
      O faithful God.

For all my foes I am an object of reproach,
    a laughingstock to my neighbors,
      and a dread to my friends;
    they who see me abroad flee from me.
I am forgotten like the unremembered dead;
    I am like a dish that is broken.

But my trust is in you, O LORD;
    I say, "You are my God.
In your hands is my destiny; rescue me
    from the clutches of my enemies
      and my persecutors."

Let your face shine upon your servant;
    save me in your kindness.
Take courage and be stouthearted,
    all you who hope in the LORD.

READING II   Hebrews 4:14–16; 5:7–9

A reading from the Letter to the Hebrews

Brothers and sisters:
Since we have a **great high priest** who has passed **through**
    the heavens,
    Jesus, the Son of **God**,
    let us **hold fast** to our **confession**.

A reading that prepares the assembly to understand the sacrifice of Jesus portrayed in the passion to follow. The theology suggested in this reading is as mysterious as it is natural. Christ is our model, our exemplar. As a man, he felt things just as we feel them. And yet his suffering, as God, is inconceivable.

this is not the end of the story. He tells us that God willed for the servant to be a reparation or guilt offering to seek purification from sin or to repair an offense. Thus, the servant, being one with the people of Israel, suffers for the sins of the people in fulfillment of God's plan of salvation.

You might recall that this oracle began with a declaration of the servant's eventual exaltation. Now, finally, the details of his victory are described. Having fulfilled God's will to give himself over and shed his blood as a guilt offering for a sinful people, he will see the light and have length of days.

Further, God says, "my servant shall justify the many." To justify means to be put in right relationship with God. Although the author of the Suffering Servant Song could not have anticipated the crucifixion and exaltation of Jesus some 550 years later, it is easy to see how early Christians would latch on to this oracle to make sense of their experience of the living Christ who now stands before the throne of God.

READING II   Like the servant in Isaiah's Suffering Servant Song, who is both one with the sheep and set

apart to be the sacrificial lamb in the guilt offering made on behalf of the people of God, the Letter to the Hebrews portrays Jesus as the great high priest who is without sin but who is one with God's people, even insofar as he could experience temptation and suffer pain. The Greek verb *sumpatheo*, translated here as "to sympathize," can also mean "to feel for or have compassion on another." Therefore, the author says, we can approach Jesus freely and with great confidence to receive mercy and grace in troubled times.

Though framed in a negative construction ("We do not have . . ."), this statement expresses the crucial sympathy Christ has for us and that we should have for him. Proclaim this sentence with care.

For we do not have a **high priest**
who is unable to **sympathize** with our **weaknesses**,
but one who has similarly been tested in **every** way,
yet **without** sin.
So let us **confidently** approach the **throne** of **grace**
to receive **mercy** and to find **grace** for timely **help**.

To intensify the sympathy, "In the days when Christ was in the flesh. . ."

In the **days** when Christ was in the **flesh**,
he offered **prayers** and **supplications** with loud **cries** and **tears**
to the **one** who was able to **save** him from **death**,
and he was **heard** because of his **reverence**.
Son though he was, he learned **obedience** from what he **suffered**;
and when he was made **perfect**,
he became the **source** of eternal **salvation** for all who
obey him.

Even stresses on "source," "salvation," and "obey."

GOSPEL John 18:1—19:42

Kidron = KID-ruhn

The passion narrative in John's Gospel depicts Jesus foreknowing all that will happen to him, giving him an appearance of calm in a storm. John's passion, like those in the synoptic gospels, is full of drama, with scenes as vivid as those in any novel or film, but whose focus, Jesus, is defined by quiet intensity. Let that guide your recitation and let the drama inherent in the narrative express itself through you.

It is not uncommon, because of the length of this reading, for it to be shared among a group of lectors as well as a deacon and priest. While there are several characters in this narrative, including different speakers, avoid the tendency to do voices or to add drama by raising your voice unnecessarily. Let this narrative speak for itself through you.

Don't overdo these expressions of "I AM."

The Passion of our Lord Jesus Christ according to John

Jesus went out with his **disciples** across the Kidron **valley**
to where there was a **garden**,
into which he and his disciples **entered**.
Judas his betrayer also **knew** the place,
because **Jesus** had often met there with his **disciples**.
So **Judas** got a band of **soldiers** and guards
from the **chief priests** and the **Pharisees**
and **went** there with **lanterns**, **torches**, and **weapons**.
Jesus, knowing **everything** that was going to **happen** to him,
went out and said to them, "**Whom** are you **looking** for?"
They answered him, "**Jesus** the **Nazorean**."
He said to them, "I **AM**."
Judas his betrayer was also **with** them. »

When the author refers to the days when Jesus "was in the flesh," he might have had in mind Jesus' forty days in the wilderness, when he was tempted by Satan, or the agony in the garden of Gethsemane before his arrest, or he might have been referring, more generally, to the human experience of fear in the face of suffering and death. Notice also that the author describes God as having heard Jesus' pleas "because of his reverence." This word can also be translated as "Godly fear or piety." Jesus is further described as having learned obedience from what he suffered. The Greek word for obedience also means "compliance or submission." In other words, although Jesus was Son of God, he perfected his humanity in filial piety, perfectly honoring his Father by freely submitting to the will of God even unto death, whereby he was consecrated as the eternal high priest, who could convey salvation to the rest of humanity.

GOSPEL John's story of the passion, death, and burial of Jesus, which is read every Good Friday, follows the general storyline of the synoptic Gospels, but it differs in several important ways, because John understood Jesus' death not as a discrete moment of despair, but simply as a necessary part of his "lifting up" or his "glorification." Thus, John's version of the story of Jesus' suffering and death is part of a larger story of victory over the world's hate. In John's Gospel, the world is a symbol for all that is opposed to Jesus.

This passion narrative begins and ends in a garden. Because the garden is unnamed, some scholars of John's Gospel have suggested that the garden symbolizes the primeval garden of Eden in the Book of

When he said to them, "I **AM**,"
    they turned **away** and fell to the **ground**.
So he again **asked** them,
    "**Whom** are you looking for?"
They said, "**Jesus** the **Nazorean**."
Jesus **answered**,
    "I **told** you that I **AM**.
So if you are **looking** for me, **let these men go**."
This was to fulfill what he had **said**,
    "I have not **lost** any of those you **gave** me."
Then Simon **Peter**, who had a **sword**, **drew it**,
    struck the high priest's slave, and cut off his right **ear**.
The slave's name was **Malchus**.
Jesus said to Peter,
    "Put your **sword** into its **scabbard**.
Shall I not **drink** the **cup** that the **Father** gave me?"

So the band of **soldiers**, the **tribune**, and the Jewish **guards**
        seized **Jesus**,
    bound him, and brought him to **Annas** first.
He was the **father-in-law** of Caiaphas,
    who was **high priest** that year.
It was **Caiaphas** who had counseled the **Jews**
    that it was **better** that one man should die rather than
        the **people**.

Simon **Peter** and another disciple followed **Jesus**.
Now the **other** disciple was known to the high **priest**,
    and he **entered** the courtyard of the high priest with **Jesus**.
But **Peter** stood at the gate **outside**.
So the **other disciple**, the **acquaintance** of the high priest,
    went out and **spoke** to the gatekeeper and brought Peter in.
Then the maid who was the gatekeeper said to Peter,
    "You are **not** one of this man's **disciples**, **are you**?"

Even stresses on "let these men go."

Even stresses on "struck the high priest's slave."
Malchus = MAL-kuhs

Annas = AN-uhs

Caiaphas = Kī-uh fuhs

John's Gospel tends to heap scorn upon the Jews, which has contributed to an ugly tendency toward anti-Semitism in Christianity. Mindfulness of this history can empower your proclamation.

The story of Peter's denial provides a sympathetic note in an often harsh narrative. Peter's weakness is the assembly's; his denials ("I am not") speak directly to our spiritual struggles.

Even emphasis on the words in this line.

Genesis. Much of what we see in this Gospel is overlaid with symbolism, so this connection with the garden of Eden is certainly possible, though of course, we cannot know fully what was in John's mind.

Almost immediately, the narrator tells us that Judas knew this place where Jesus and the other disciples were gathered. We have also been told repeatedly that Judas is the one who will betray Jesus, so the reader knows what will happen in this garden scene. And now Judas appears with a large contingency of Roman soldiers and Jewish temple guards. They come with lanterns and torches, indicating that this is the hour of darkness, which represents the absence of belief in John's Gospel (see John 8:12; 9:4). Likewise, Judas' betrayal of Jesus with a kiss is extremely dishonoring.

When Judas and the crowd of soldiers and temple guards arrive on the scene, Jesus initiates a dialog by saying "Whom are you looking for?" Elsewhere in John's Gospel, this question is an invitation to discipleship (see John 1:35–51 and John 20:11–18). But those who come to arrest Jesus understand only the plain meaning of his words. Thus, the crowd answers, "Jesus the Nazarene," clearly missing the irony of his call to discipleship. In response, Jesus says, "I AM," which is reminiscent of Moses' encounter with God in the burning bush, when he asks God to reveal the divine name and God says, "I AM" (Exodus 3:14). Three times in this brief scene, Jesus is identified as "I AM." In Greek, it is *ego eime*.

Peter, likewise, does not understand the significance of this moment, because, with a single sword, he attempts to defend Jesus from the well-armed crowd that seeks to arrest him. But the crowd of soldiers quickly grab Jesus and take him,

He said, "I am **not**."
Now the **slaves** and the **guards** were standing around
    a **charcoal** fire
      that they had **made**, because it was **cold**,
      and were **warming** themselves.
Peter was also **standing** there keeping **warm**.

The **high priest** questioned **Jesus**
    about his **disciples** and about his **doctrine**.
Jesus **answered** him,
    "I have spoken **publicly** to the **world**.
I have **always taught** in a **synagogue**
    or in the **temple** area where all the **Jews** gather,
    and in **secret** I have said **nothing**. Why **ask** me?
Ask **those** who **heard me** what I said to **them**.
They **know** what I **said**."
When he had **said** this,
    one of the temple guards standing there struck Jesus and said,
    "Is **this** the way you **answer** the high **priest**?"
Jesus **answered** him,
    "If I have spoken **wrongly**, **testify** to the wrong;
    but if I have spoken **rightly**, why do you strike **me**?"
Then **Annas** sent him bound to **Caiaphas** the high **priest**.

Now **Simon Peter** was standing there keeping **warm**.
And they **said** to him,
    "You are not one of his **disciples**, **are you**?"
He **denied** it and said,
    "I am **not**."
One of the **slaves** of the high **priest**,
    a **relative** of the one whose **ear Peter** had cut **off**, said,
    "Didn't I **see** you in the **garden** with him?"
Again Peter **denied** it.
And **immediately** the cock **crowed**. ≫

Even emphasis on the words in this line.

Jesus' response suggests the core of his resolve to face the suffering to come.

Again, a return to the story of Peter. Don't overly dramatize the denial. Peter's shame will come through clearly when you proclaim this passage deliberately and clearly.

bound, to Annas, the father-in-law of the high priest Caiaphas, who questions Jesus about his disciples and his teaching. The narrator reminds the reader that Caiaphas was the one who prophesied about Jesus' death after the Jewish religious authorities became fearful about the tumult that would arise when people started to learn about the raising of Lazarus (John 11:45–53).

Meanwhile, interspersed among the presentation of Jesus before Caiaphas and the trial before Pontius Pilate, we learn that Peter and another disciple, possibly the Beloved Disciple, who is first mentioned in the story of Jesus' last supper with his disciples (John 13:21–30), follow Jesus to the gate of the high priest's courtyard. The other disciple is allowed into the courtyard, but Peter was made to stay outside, until the other disciple summoned for him to be allowed inside. This detail is significant because, while Peter is in the high priest's courtyard and Jesus is inside of the high priest's home, Peter is confronted three times: first by a maid servant, next by the slaves and guards gathered around the fire, and finally by a slave who was related to the person whose ear was cut off by Peter.

Each time they ask whether he is one of Jesus' disciples, he denies it. Twice he says *ouk eimi*, that is, "*not* I am!" The sentence in Greek places the emphasis on "not," which calls our attention to the "I am" sayings attributed to Jesus earlier in the Gospel. It also signals to the reader the irony of Peter's denial of Jesus. Is the Gospel writer trying to present Peter as one who *should* be able to speak openly or publicly on Jesus' behalf but who cannot muster the courage to do so?

Next, John tells the story of Jesus' trial before Pontius Pilate, and he does it in

praetorium = prih-TOHR-ee-uhm
Here begins a long passage of exceptional vividness and power. It contrasts the conversation between Pilate and Jesus in the praetorium with the more aggressive exchanges between Pilate and the crowd. It is told from Pilate's point of view, which allows us to sympathize with Pilate. It's a truly remarkable passage whose drama need not be exaggerated. Pace your reading to allow its potent drama to come through on its own.

Pilate is dismissive here, but don't exaggerate his dismissiveness.

The crucial question. Again, don't exaggerate it. Pilate, a government official, is asking an earnest question.

Even emphasis on the words in this question.

Jesus' answer is completely mysterious but supercharged with confidence. Read these words clearly and plainly.

Then they **brought Jesus** from Caiaphas to the **praetorium**.
It was **morning**.
And they themselves did not enter the praetorium,
    in order not to be **defiled** so that they could **eat** the **Passover**.
So **Pilate** came out to them and said,
    "**What charge** do you bring **against** this **man**?"
They **answered** and **said** to him,
    "If he were **not** a criminal,
    we would not have handed him **over** to you."
At this, Pilate said to them,
    "**Take him yourselves**, and **judge** him according to your **law**."
The Jews answered him,
    "We do **not** have the right to execute **anyone**,"
    in **order** that the word of **Jesus** might be **fulfilled**
    that he said **indicating** the kind of **death** he would **die**.
So Pilate went back into the **praetorium**
    and **summoned Jesus** and **said** to him,
    "**Are you** the **King** of the **Jews**?"
Jesus answered,
    "Do you **say this** on your **own**
    or have others **told** you **about** me?"
Pilate answered,
    "I am not a **Jew**, am I?
Your own **nation** and the chief **priests** handed you **over** to me.
What have you done?"
Jesus answered,
    "My kingdom does not belong to this **world**.
If my kingdom **did** belong to this world,
    my **attendants** would be **fighting**
    to **keep** me from being handed **over** to the **Jews**.
But as it **is**, my **kingdom** is not **here**."
So Pilate said to him,
    "Then you **are** a king?"

seven scenes. In the first scene, we learn that it is early in the morning shortly before dawn, on the preparation day for Passover. Jesus had already been brought to the praetorium, the Roman governor's residence in Jerusalem. Those who came from Caiaphas' stayed outside. The narrator of the story says that it is to avoid being made ritually unclean and unable to celebrate the Passover meal, though we do not know whether there was such a rule in place at the time. But their action prompted Pilate to come *outside* into the predawn darkness to ask about the formal charges being

brought against Jesus. Because of their ambiguous response, Pilate first chooses not to get involved. But the exchange between the crowd and Pilate reveals that they want Jesus executed. The narrator adds that this scene is a fulfillment of Jesus' words that he would die by being "lifted up" in crucifixion (John 12:32–33).

The crowd is now identified as the *judaioi*, which is here translated as "the Jews." However, many scholars of John's Gospel would caution against the use of this term, because it can be misinterpreted as an antisemitic trope. To better under-

stand this term, it is helpful to know that the community for whom John is writing is also Jewish. Thus, these negative statements about the *judaioi* are more likely the effects of an intra-family fight: a minority community of Jewish Christians struggling against a larger community of Jews who refuse to believe that Jesus is the Christ. To avoid this problem, biblical scholars suggest that we translate *judaioi* as "Judeans" or that we substitute "Jewish religious authorities" in place of "the Jews."

In the second scene of this trial, Pilate goes *inside* the praetorium to question

Jesus answered,
"You **say** I am a king.
For **this** I was born and for **this** I came into the world,
to **testify** to the **truth**.
Everyone who **belongs** to the truth **listens** to my **voice**."
Pilate said to him, "What is **truth**?"

When he had **said** this,
he **again** went out to the Jews and **said** to them,
"I find no **guilt** in him.
But you have a **custom** that I release one **prisoner** to you
at **Passover**.
Do you want me to **release** to you the **King** of the **Jews**?"
They cried out again,
"Not **this** one but **Barabbas**!"
Now **Barabbas** was a **revolutionary**.

Then **Pilate** took Jesus and had him **scourged**.
And the **soldiers** wove a **crown** out of **thorns** and **placed** it
on his **head**,
and **clothed him** in a purple **cloak**,
and they **came** to him and said,
"**Hail**, **King** of the **Jews**!"
And they **struck** him **repeatedly**.
Once more Pilate went out and said to them,
"**Look**, I am **bringing** him out to you,
so that you may **know** that I find no **guilt** in him."
So **Jesus** came out,
wearing the **crown** of **thorns** and the **purple cloak**.
And he **said** to them, "**Behold**, the **man**!"
When the **chief priests** and the **guards** saw him they cried **out**,
"**Crucify** him, **crucify** him!"
Pilate **said** to them,
"**Take** him **yourselves** and crucify him.
I **find** no **guilt** in him." »

Again, mysterious and confident.

Almost even emphasis on the words in this line, with extra added to "guilt."

Barabbas = buh-RAB-uhs
Avoid the tendency to shout this line.

"Scourged" is a wicked word. Read it slowly, one elongated syllable.

No need to shout this line. It's all too clear what is happening.
Even stresses on the words in this line.

Pilate is at a loss, but he's also a dutiful Roman bureaucrat.

Lower your voice here. Don't exclaim.

Don't shout.

Jesus. He asks, "Are you King of the Jews?" Perhaps he had heard rumors about Jesus being called the messiah, meaning "anointed one." But Jesus refuses to answer Pilate's question about whether he is a king. Instead, he talks about a kingdom that is not of this world, which prompts Pilate to ask his question again. Jesus continues with statements about how he "came into the world, to testify to the truth" and how those who believe respond to the truth. The truth is the revelation of God, and Jesus is God's revealer (John 1:17–18). But Pilate remains totally clueless about Jesus and his identity. Hence, his sardonic question, "What is truth?"

In the third scene, Pilate again goes *outside*, this time to tell the crowd that he does not find Jesus guilty and that he wanted to make a deal. He would release Jesus whom he calls "King of the Jews" as a Passover prison release. But the crowd refuses and wants Barabbas, instead. The narrator tells us that Barabbas was a robber and revolutionary, but we should not miss the irony. His name means "son of the father."

In the fourth scene, Pilate goes back *inside* to have Jesus scourged. His soldiers mock Jesus by dressing him in a purple robe and placing a crown of thorns on his head. As they strike him repeatedly and shout "Hail, King of the Jews," the irony of their actions weighs heavily on the scene. Jesus really is the king of the Jews.

In the fifth scene, once again Pilate goes *outside*. He attempts to demonstrate to the crowd that he views Jesus as innocent of any crime. As Jesus stands before the crowd, beaten and bloodied but still wearing the regalia of a bemocked king,

This question has a note of astonishment.

Jesus' answer to Pilate's question once again is mysterious and confident.

Gabbatha = GAB-uh-thuh

Don't shout.

This line of the chief priests is dismissive; don't overdo the dismissiveness.

The Jews answered,
  "We have a **law**, and according to that **law** he ought to **die**,
  because he **made** himself the Son of **God**."
Now when Pilate **heard** this statement,
  he became even more **afraid**,
  and went **back** into the **praetorium** and said to Jesus,
  "**Where** are you **from**?"
Jesus did not **answer** him.
So Pilate **said** to him,
  "Do you not **speak** to me?
Do you not **know** that I have **power** to **release** you
  and I have **power** to **crucify** you?"
Jesus **answered** him,
  "You would have **no power** over **me**
  if it had not been **given** to you from **above**.
For this **reason** the one who handed me over to you
  has the greater **sin**."
Consequently, Pilate tried to **release** him;
    but the Jews cried out,
  "If you **release** him, you are not a **Friend** of **Caesar**.
Everyone who makes himself a **king** opposes **Caesar**."

When Pilate **heard these words** he brought Jesus **out**
  and **seated** him on the judge's **bench**
  in the **place** called Stone **Pavement**, in Hebrew, **Gabbatha**.
It was **preparation** day for **Passover**, and it was about **noon**.
And he **said** to the Jews,
  "**Behold**, your **king**!"
They cried out,
  "**Take him away, take him away! Crucify** him!"
Pilate **said** to them,
  "Shall I **crucify** your **king**?"
The chief priests answered,
  "We have no **king** but **Caesar**."
Then he handed him **over** to them to be **crucified**.

Pilate announces, "Behold the man!" Is this yet another insult hurled at Jesus, so as to say, "Look at this puny and powerless creature!" or is Pilate unwittingly setting the stage for the crowd to reveal the real reason for wanting Jesus to be put to death? They explain, Jesus "made himself the Son of God."

In the sixth scene, Pilate goes *inside* to question Jesus once more. He asks Jesus, "Where are you from?" Jesus refuses to answer, but the Christian community for whom this Gospel was written can quickly say, "Jesus is from God. He is the Son of God!" Pilate persists, even threatening Jesus with his power to put someone to death, but Jesus responds, saying "You would have no power over me if it had not been given to you from above." But Pilate knows that he is quickly losing control of the situation, as the crowd's spokespeople charge him with acting against the emperor if he fails to put Jesus to death.

In the final scene, Pilate goes *outside* again, bringing Jesus before the crowd. Taking his place on the judgment seat, Pilate makes one last attempt to release Jesus as he declares, "Behold your king!" but again here is the irony; Jesus really is the king of the Jews. The crowd screams for Jesus to be crucified. However, rather than issue the order, Pilate turns Jesus over to the crowd for sentencing. The narrator notes that this scene takes place at noon on the preparation day for Passover. Why is this detail important? Jesus, the Lamb of God (John 1:29, 36), is sentenced to death at the same time that the Passover lambs were being sacrificed in the Temple not far away.

These seven scenes of Jesus' trial before Pilate are organized to create a chi-

Golgotha = GAWL-guh-thuh

In two short lines the act of Jesus' crucifixion, to which this whole Passion has been building, is expressed. Read these lines plainly and slowly.

So they took **Jesus**, and, carrying the **cross** himself,
　he went out to what is called the **Place** of the **Skull**,
　in Hebrew, **Golgotha**.
There they **crucified** him, and **with** him two **others**,
　one on either **side**, with **Jesus** in the **middle**.
Pilate also had an **inscription** written and put on the **cross**.
It read,
　"**Jesus** the **Nazorean**, the **King** of the **Jews**."
Now **many** of the Jews **read** this inscription,
　because the **place** where Jesus was crucified was near the **city**;
　and it was **written** in **Hebrew**, **Latin**, and **Greek**.
So the **chief priests** of the Jews said to **Pilate**,
　"Do not write 'The **King** of the **Jews**,'
　but that he said, 'I **am** the King of the **Jews**.'"
Pilate answered,
　"What I have **written**, I have **written**."

Pilate's are his final, ominous words in this Passion. Pause slightly after proclaiming them.

When the **soldiers** had crucified **Jesus**,
　they took his **clothes** and divided them into **four shares**,
　a **share** for each **soldier**.
They also took his **tunic**, but the tunic was **seamless**,
　woven in one piece from the **top down**.
So they said to one **another**,
　"Let's not **tear** it, but cast **lots** for it to see whose it will **be**,"
　in order that the passage of Scripture might be fulfilled
　　that says:
　　　*They **divided** my garments among them,*
　　　　*and for my **vesture** they cast **lots**.*
This is what the soldiers **did**.
Standing by the cross of **Jesus** were his **mother**
　and his mother's **sister**, **Mary** the wife of **Clopas**,
　and Mary of **Magdala**.
When Jesus saw his **mother** and the disciple there whom
　　he **loved**
　he said to his **mother**, "**Woman**, **behold**, your **son**." »

Be sure to read the names of these women clearly.

Almost even stresses on the words in this line.

asm. In a chiasm, the first scene of this story matches the last scene, the second matches the second-to-last scene and so on. Since this chiasm has an odd number of scenes, the main theme and focus of the chiasm can be found in scene four, in which the soldiers mock Jesus as a king, but Jesus is not a victim. He truly is the king of the Jews.

Turning now to the crucifixion scene, the Gospel writer continues this theme of Jesus as the victor. The narrator tells us that Pilate placed an inscription at the head of Jesus' cross. The chief priests of the Temple expressed their opposition, saying,

"Do not write 'The King of the Jews,' but that he said, 'I am the King of the Jews.'" The difference is significant, since the first is a proclamation of faith, whereas the chief priests' attempted rewording is a statement of the charges made against Jesus. But Pilate insisted on his own wording, and the inscription was posted in three languages—Latin, Greek, and Hebrew—for the whole world to see. The Latin reads *Iesus Nazarenus Rex Iudaeorum*, which produces the acronym INRI, which we often see on crucifixes or in artistic renditions of the crucifixion.

Also noteworthy is the detail about Jesus' seamless garment, which is not found in the synoptic Gospels. Some have speculated that this is an allusion to Jesus' priestly role, because the first-century Jewish historian Josephus writes about the high priest wearing a seamless garment under his outer robes. Others have suggested that it is a symbol of unity, a theme that Jesus addresses in his lengthy farewell discourse before his arrest. The Gospel writer tells us only that it was to fulfill Scripture, namely Psalm 22:19: "They divide

"I thirst," concentrates the agony of the crucifixion. Say it simply and clearly.

hyssop = HIS-uhp

These words, "It is finished," culminate the drama of the Passion. Give each word even stress, pausing ever so slightly between them, almost: "It. Is. Finished."

The details in the passage that concludes John's Passion are of interest because they speak to the awful economy of torture and execution (on the part of the Roman soldiers) as well as the requirements of the burial of a corpse according to Jewish custom. It's effective to read these words with scrutiny and openness.

John is speaking directly to his audience in these words; through you, directly to the assembly.

Then he said to the disciple,
  "**Behold**, your **mother**."
And from **that hour** the **disciple** took her into his **home**.

After **this**, aware that everything was now **finished**,
  in order that the **Scripture** might be **fulfilled**,
  Jesus said, "**I thirst**."
There was a **vessel** filled with **common wine**.
So they put a **sponge** soaked in wine on a sprig of **hyssop**
  and put it up to his **mouth**.
When **Jesus** had taken the wine, he said,
  "**It is finished**."
And **bowing** his head, he **handed** over the **spirit**.

[Here all kneel and pause for a short time.]

Now since it was **preparation** day,
  in **order** that the bodies might not remain
  on the **cross** on the **sabbath**,
  for the **sabbath** day of that **week** was a **solemn** one,
  the **Jews** asked Pilate that their **legs** be broken
  and that they be taken **down**.
So the **soldiers** came and broke the **legs** of the first
  and then of the other one who was **crucified** with **Jesus**.
But when they came to **Jesus** and saw that he was already **dead**,
  they did **not** break his **legs**,
  but one **soldier** thrust his **lance** into his **side**,
  and immediately blood and **water** flowed **out**.
An **eyewitness** has testified, and his **testimony** is true;
  he **knows** that he is speaking the **truth**,
  so that **you also** may come to **believe**.
For this **happened** so that the **Scripture** passage might be
    fulfilled:
  *Not a **bone** of it will be **broken**.*
And again another passage says:
  *They will look **upon him** whom they have **pierced**.*

my garments among them; / for my clothing they cast lots."

Another detail that is only in John's Gospel is the scene in which we see Mary Magdalene, Mary, the mother of Jesus, her sister, and the Beloved Disciple at the cross. Jesus asks his mother to take the Beloved Disciple as her son, and likewise, the Beloved Disciple is asked to take Mary as his mother. The narrator tells us that the Beloved Disciple took Mary into his home "from that hour." Although the Gospel writer is not explicit about this connection, one can surmise that this scene reflects the notion that the Johannine community understood the Beloved Disciple to be their leader and spiritual guide.

Finally, Jesus is offered wine from a sponge that is attached to a branch of hyssop. Hyssop is associated with the first Passover (Exodus 12:22–23) and the narrator also notes Jesus' unbroken legs, which alludes to the unblemished lambs offered in sacrifice. This is in keeping with John the Baptist's introduction of Jesus as the Lamb of God (John 1:29, 36). We also have the detail about the piercing of Jesus' side and the blood and water pouring out. This detail might simply indicate that Jesus was dead. However, in John's Gospel, water is associated with baptism and new life, and blood reminds us of Jesus' statements about drinking the cup that the Father gave him to drink (John 18:11) and about consuming his blood in the "Bread of Life" discourse (John 6:53–56), which Johannine scholars associate with the Eucharist.

John's story of the burial of Jesus also has some unique details. We learn that Joseph of Arimathea was a disciple of Jesus, but a secret one for fear of being ostracized by his Jewish comrades for

Arimathea = ayr-ih-muh-THEE-uh

Nicodemus = nik-uh-DEE-muhs
Don't hurry over these details.
myrrh = mer
aloes = AL-ohz

Read this concluding phrase, "for the tomb was close by," slowly.

believing that Jesus was the messiah. And then there is Nicodemus, whom we hear about earlier in John (see John 3:1–21) and who never seems to make the leap to full faith in Jesus. As they lay Jesus' body to rest, do they believe he will be raised from the dead? What is the purpose of this closing scene of the passion narrative? What does it mean to you? C.C.

After **this**, Joseph of **Arimathea**,
   secretly a disciple of **Jesus** for **fear** of the **Jews**,
   asked **Pilate** if he could **remove** the body of **Jesus**.
And Pilate **permitted** it.
So he came and took his **body**.
Nicodemus, the one who had **first come** to him at **night**,
   also came bringing a mixture of **myrrh** and **aloes**
   weighing about one **hundred** pounds.
They took the body of **Jesus**
   and bound it with **burial cloths** along with the **spices**,
   according to the **Jewish burial custom**.
Now in the **place** where he had been **crucified** there was
      a **garden**,
   and in the **garden** a new **tomb**, in which **no one** had yet
      been **buried**.
So they laid **Jesus** there because of the Jewish **preparation** day;
   for the **tomb** was close **by**.

EASTER VIGIL
(HOLY SATURDAY)

LECTIONARY #41

READING I   Genesis 1:1—2:2

A reading from the Book of Genesis

[In the **beginning**, when God created the **heavens** and the **earth**,]
   the **earth** was a formless **wasteland**, and **darkness** covered
      the **abyss**,
   while a **mighty wind** swept **over** the **waters**.

Then God said,
   "Let there be **light**," and there was **light**.
God saw how **good** the light was.
God then **separated** the **light** from the **darkness**.
God called the light "**day**," and the darkness he called "**night**."
   Thus **evening** came, and **morning** followed—the **first** day.

Then God said,
   "Let there be a **dome** in the **middle** of the **waters**,
   to separate one **body** of water from the **other**."
And so it **happened**:
   God **made** the dome,
   and it separated the water **above** the dome from the water
      below it.
God called the dome "the **sky**."
Evening came, and **morning** followed—the **second** day.

Then God said,
   "Let the **water** under the **sky** be gathered into a **single basin**,
   so that the **dry land** may appear."

Genesis = JEN-uh-sihs

A reading of one of the most familiar passages in all of Scripture. Because the language in this reading is so grand, you will be tempted perhaps to dramatize your proclamation. No need: the language is so finely wrought, if you read at a measured pace, its glories will come through in your recitation.

The word "and" appears repeatedly in this reading. It's one of the main sources of its power. It functions almost like a verb. Let the word do the work for you as you proclaim.

Pause ever so slightly after "first day." You will repeat this slight pause five more times.

Pause slightly after "second day."

There are options for today's readings. Contact your parish staff to learn which readings will be used.

The vigil of Easter Sunday is a time for us to meditate on God's gracious deeds on behalf of humanity and the rest of the created order throughout the story of salvation from the beginning of time to the death and resurrection of Jesus, who is the Christ. Seven readings are taken from the Old Testament books of the law and the prophets.

Seven is a perfect number representing fullness or wholeness. The eighth reading is taken from Paul's Letter to the Romans and the Gospel is taken from Matthew's story of the resurrection of Jesus.

READING I The first reading, taken from the Book of Genesis, is not intended to be a science or history lesson about the creation of the world. Rather, it is a theological narrative about the nature of God and God's relationship to humans. In contrast to the origin stories of the Israelites' neighbors, which were often violent and chaotic, this story celebrates the sovereignty of God almighty, who creates everything by the power of his Word and declares all God's creation to be good. As the scene opens, we are told that the earth was uninhabitable—"a formless wasteland" is the translation of the Hebrew *tohu wabohu*—covered in water and enveloped in darkness. Ancients might have thought of this as a frightening and chaotic

Almost even stresses on the words in this line, with "good" receiving a little extra emphasis.

Pause slightly after "third day."

The passage that follows, describing the fourth day of creation, includes a series of oppositions to emphasize the separation of night from day. Stress the words that indicate these oppositions.

Pause slightly after "fourth day."

And so it **happened**:
    the **water** under the **sky** was gathered into its **basin**,
    and the **dry land** appeared.
God called the dry land "the **earth**,"
    and the basin of the water he called "the **sea**."
God saw how **good** it was.
Then God said,
    "Let the **earth** bring **forth** vegetation:
every **kind** of plant that bears **seed**
and every **kind** of fruit tree on **earth**
that bears **fruit** with its seed **in** it."
And so it **happened**:
    the **earth** brought forth every **kind** of plant that bears **seed**
    and every **kind** of fruit tree on **earth**
    that bears **fruit** with its **seed** in it.
God saw how **good** it was.
Evening came, and **morning** followed—the **third** day.

Then God said:
    "Let there be **lights** in the **dome** of the **sky**,
    to separate **day** from **night**.
Let them mark the **fixed times**, the **days** and the **years**,
    and serve as **luminaries** in the **dome** of the **sky**,
    to shed **light** upon the **earth**."
And so it **happened**:
    God **made** the two great **lights**,
    the **greater** one to govern the **day**,
    and the **lesser** one to govern the **night**;
    and he made the **stars**.
God set them in the **dome** of the **sky**,
    to shed **light** upon the **earth**,
    to govern the **day** and the **night**,
    and to separate the **light** from the **darkness**.
God saw how **good** it was.
Evening came, and **morning** followed—the **fourth** day. »

scene, except for the next phrase, which some translate as "a mighty wind" but which also can be translated as "the spirit of God," hovering over the water. Even from the very beginning, God is in charge!

The dramatic imagery of this opening sentence, along with its poetic word play, should alert us to the literary quality of the rest of the account. The narrator marks out each day of creation with the phrase "evening came, and morning followed," and each day follows the structure of "Then God said. . ." and "God saw how good it was." This is the power of God's word; it is a power only for good. Notice also that God names the various elements of creation. In the ancient world, to name something was to have authority over it.

The first three days of creation are focused on separation: On the first day, God separated light from darkness. On the second day, God separated the waters above from the waters below. On the third day, God separated the waters below from the earth.

The latter three days of creation are focused on populating creation: On the fourth day, God created the sun, moon, and stars to illuminate the earth. Notice the parallel with day one. On the fifth day, God populated the water below, the seas, with sea creatures and the dome that held up the water above, the sky, with birds. These God blessed and told them to be fertile and multiply. Notice the parallel with day two.

Then God said,
   "Let the **water teem** with an abundance of **living creatures**,
   and on the **earth** let birds fly **beneath** the dome of the sky."
And so it **happened**:
   God created the great **sea monsters**
   and all kinds of **swimming creatures** with which the
      water **teems**,
   and all kinds of **winged birds**.
God saw how **good** it was, and God **blessed** them, saying,
   "Be **fertile**, **multiply**, and **fill** the water of the **seas**;
   and let the **birds** multiply on the **earth**."
Evening came, and **morning** followed—the **fifth** day.

Then God said,
   "Let the **earth** bring **forth** all kinds of **living creatures**:
   cattle, **creeping things**, and wild **animals** of all **kinds**."
And so it **happened**:
   God made **all kinds** of wild **animals**, all **kinds** of **cattle**,
   and all **kinds** of **creeping things** of the earth.
God saw how **good** it was.

Then [God said:
   "Let us make **man** in our image, **after** our **likeness**.
Let them have **dominion** over the **fish** of the **sea**,
   the **birds** of the **air**, and the **cattle**,
   and over **all** the wild **animals**
   and **all** the creatures that **crawl** on the **ground**."
God created **man** in his **image**;
   in the **image** of **God** he created **him**;
   male and **female** he created **them**.
God **blessed** them, saying:
      "Be **fertile** and **multiply**;
      fill the earth and **subdue** it.
Have **dominion** over the **fish** of the **sea**, the **birds** of the **air**,
   and **all** the living things that **move** on the earth."

Pause slightly after "fifth day."

Keep an even pace through this line.

This passage repeats the word "kinds" four times. These "kinds" anticipate the image of "humankind" shortly to come.

Don't treat the appearance of humankind at this point as a break, as something separate; rather, treat it as part of a continuum. The tone and pitch of your proclamation does not need to change here.

On the sixth day, God populated the earth with every kind of creature, wild and tame, big and small. Also on the sixth day, God created human beings in God's image (Hebrew, *tselem*, also meaning "likeness or resemblance") and told them to be fruitful and multiply and have dominion over the rest of the created world. Notice the parallel with day three.

Thus, human beings are depicted as the crowning event of God's creation. But what does it mean to be created in God's likeness? Perhaps it lies in the phrase "have dominion over or master." This is God's role in creation—to bring everything out of chaos and make it ordered and fruitful—and now this role is extended to humans to maintain into the future. Notice that God makes no allowance for killing, even for

food. Then God rested on the seventh day, creating the foundation for the Jewish practice of Sabbath rest.

READING II The second reading in this series of seven Old Testament readings focuses on Abraham, often called the father of Judaism, and God's request that he sacrifice his only son. Knowing some background to the story will

God also said:
"**See**, I give you every **seed-bearing** plant all over the **earth**
and every **tree** that has seed-bearing **fruit** on it to be your **food**;
and to all the **animals** of the land, all the **birds** of the air,
and all the **living creatures** that crawl on the **ground**,
I give all the green plants for **food**."
And so it **happened**.
God looked at **everything** he had made, and he found it
very good.]
Evening came, and **morning** followed—the **sixth** day.

Thus the **heavens** and the **earth** and all their **array**
were **completed**.
Since on the **seventh** day God was **finished**
with the **work** he had been **doing**,
he rested on the seventh day from all the work he
had undertaken.

[Shorter: Genesis 1:1, 26–31a (see brackets)]

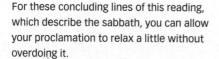

RESPONSORIAL PSALM   Psalm 104:1–2, 5–6, 10, 12, 13–14, 24, 35 (30)

R. Lord, send out your Spirit, and renew the face of the earth.

Bless the LORD, O my soul!
  O LORD, my God, you are great indeed!
You are clothed with majesty and glory,
  robed in light as with a cloak.

You fixed the earth upon its foundation,
  not to be moved forever;
with the ocean, as with a garment, you
    covered it;
  above the mountains the waters stood.

You send forth springs into the watercourses
  that wind among the mountains.
Beside them the birds of heaven dwell;
  from among the branches they send forth
    their song.

You water the mountains from your palace;
  the earth is replete with the fruit
    of your works.
You raise grass for the cattle,
  and vegetation for man's use,
producing bread from the earth.

How manifold are your works, O LORD!
  In wisdom you have wrought them all—
the earth is full of your creatures.
  Bless the LORD, O my soul!

Or:

help us to understand how significant it is for both Jews and Christians. The account of the interaction between God and Abraham, then called Abram, begins in Genesis 12, where he is told by this God whom he does not yet know to go to the land that God would show him. He is also told that God would make him a great

nation and a blessing and that in him "all the families of the earth will find blessing" (Genesis 12:2–3). This promise is reiterated two more times, at least in part, first in Genesis 15:2–7 and again in Genesis 17:3–10, even as Abraham faces numerous challenges and setbacks along the way, many of his own making.

At the beginning of Genesis 22, the phrase "Some time afterward" (Genesis 22:1a) is used to transition to the story we hear in this second reading. It is referring to the period of time after Abraham had settled a dispute over a well that he dug at Beer-sheba and after he made a covenant of mutual support with the Philistine King

---

Pause slightly after "sixth day."

For these concluding lines of this reading, which describe the sabbath, you can allow your proclamation to relax a little without overdoing it.

For meditation and context:

For meditation and context:

RESPONSORIAL PSALM   Psalm 33:4–5, 6–7, 12–13, 20, and 22 (5b)

R. The earth is full of the goodness of the Lord.

Upright is the word of the LORD,
  and all his works are trustworthy.
He loves justice and right;
  of the kindness of the LORD the earth
    is full.

By the word of the LORD the heavens
  were made;
  by the breath of his mouth all their host.
He gathers the waters of the sea as in a flask;
  in cellars he confines the deep.

Blessed the nation whose God is the LORD,
  the people he has chosen for his
    own inheritance.
From heaven the LORD looks down;
  he sees all mankind.

Our soul waits for the LORD,
  who is our help and our shield.
May your kindness, O LORD, be upon us
  who have put our hope in you.

READING II   Genesis 22:1–18

A reading from the Book of Genesis

[God put **Abraham** to the **test**.
He called to him, "**Abraham**!"
"**Here** I am," he replied.
Then God said:
  "Take your son **Isaac**, your **only** one, whom you **love**,
  and **go** to the land of **Moriah**.
There you shall offer him up as a **holocaust**
  on a **height** that I will point **out** to you."]
Early the next morning Abraham saddled his **donkey**,
  took with him his son **Isaac** and two of his **servants** as well,
  and with the **wood** that he had cut for the **holocaust**,
  set **out** for the place of which **God** had told him.

On the third day **Abraham** got sight of the place from **afar**.
Then he **said** to his servants:
  "**Both** of you stay here with the **donkey**,
  while the **boy** and I go on over **yonder**.
We will **worship** and then come **back** to you."

Genesis = JEN-uh-sihs

Moriah = moh-RĪ-uh

A reading of another very familiar story from Scripture. Its elements, including its conclusion, are universally known, something that in no way diminishes its power. A passage such as this one is already so inherently dramatic, your task is to proclaim as clearly as you can. Even though there are several exclamations in this passage, you will not need to raise your voice any more than you normally do when proclaiming.

Case in point: the first exclamation. There is an aura of otherworldly silence around Abraham's name. No need to shout.

The great literary critic Erich Auerbach describes this passage as "fraught with background." a delicious phrase. He means that while the action is spare, the scene itself is filling with tension. When you proclaim "On the third day," you are skipping over two full days of traveling.

Abimelech (Genesis 21:25–32). This is the beginning of Abraham's claim on the promised land. The story that precedes this reading, the birth of Isaac, is the beginning of the fulfillment of the promise that Abraham would have "descendants as countless as the stars of the sky and the sands of the seashore." Therefore, as we enter this second reading, Abraham and Sarah are safe and secure and are settled in the land. But this is where the story gets very complicated, and we see a true threat to the fulfillment of the promise that God made to Abraham that he would have numerous descendants. To make matters worse, it was not Abraham who was interfering with the fulfillment of the promise, as he had done so many times before, but now it appeared that God himself is standing in the way!

The narrator of this story describes the sacrifice of Isaac as a test instigated by God, who tells Abraham to take his son, Isaac, and go to Moriah and sacrifice him on the mountain. Pay careful attention to how Abraham is portrayed in this scene. Clearly, he understands what God is asking

Second exclamation: Don't shout.

"Continued": This word is "fraught with background."

Take note of the details. Abraham is preparing an altar for sacrifice.

Third exclamation: Don't shout.

Yahweh-yireh – YAH-way-YEER-ay

Thereupon Abraham took the **wood** for the **holocaust**
    and laid it on his son Isaac's **shoulders**,
    while he himself carried the **fire** and the **knife**.
As the two walked on together, Isaac **spoke** to his father Abraham:
    "**Father!**" Isaac said.
"Yes, son," he replied.
Isaac continued, "**Here** are the **fire** and the **wood**,
    but **where** is the **sheep** for the **holocaust**?"
"Son," Abraham answered,
    "God **himself** will provide the **sheep** for the **holocaust**."
Then the two **continued** going forward.

[When they **came** to the place of which **God** had told him,
    Abraham built an **altar** there and arranged the **wood** on it.]
Next he tied up his son **Isaac**,
    and put him on top of the wood on the altar.
[Then he **reached out** and took the **knife** to **slaughter** his son.
But the Lord's messenger **called** to him from **heaven**,
    "**Abraham, Abraham!**"
"**Here** I am," he answered.
"Do **not** lay your **hand** on the **boy**," said the messenger.
"Do **not** do the **least thing** to him.
I know **now** how devoted you are to **God**,
    since you did not **withhold** from me your o**wn beloved** son."
As Abraham looked about,
    he spied a **ram** caught by its **horns** in the **thicket**.
So he **went** and took the **ram**
    and offered it up as a **holocaust** in place of his **son**.]
Abraham named the site **Yahweh-yireh**;
    hence people now say, "On the **mountain** the Lord
        will **see**." »

him to do, and the narrator is keen to tell us about Abraham's affection for Isaac, but Abraham is unflinching in his resolve to obey God's word. Even as he and his son climb the mountain together and Isaac asks about the animal to be sacrificed, the only thing he says is "God himself will provide." Notice also the several times in which Abraham is described as saying, "Here I am." This is a phrase indicating openness and availability to respond to the speaker. Having arrived at the mountain, Abraham goes so far as to bind Isaac, place him on the wood that was set upon the altar, and raise his knife to slaughter him, before God's messenger intervenes and tells him not to harm his son, adding, "I know now how devoted you are to God." The Hebrew word translated here as "devoted" has the connotation of reverence or respect for God's authority. Abraham's devotion to God is confirmed, and God's angel appears again to renew the promises of land, descendants, and a blessing, because Abraham obeyed God's command.

    One of the ways that early Christians made sense of stories like this one was to

Though an angel of God is relaying these words, it's God himself who speaks here. Set off the phrase "declares the Lord" in such a way to make it clear that God is speaking.

[Again the LORD's **messenger** called to Abraham from **heaven**
     and said:
"I **swear** by myself, **declares** the LORD,
that **because** you acted as you **did**
in not **withholding** from me your beloved **son**,
I will **bless you** abundantly
and make your **descendants** as **countless**
as the **stars** of the **sky** and the **sands** of the **seashore**;
your **descendants** shall take **possession**
of the **gates** of their **enemies**,
and in your **descendants** all the **nations** of the earth shall
     find **blessing**—
all **this** because you **obeyed** my command."]

[Shorter: Genesis 22:1–2, 9a, 10–13, 15–18 (see brackets)]

For meditation and context:

RESPONSORIAL PSALM   Psalm 16:5, 8, 9–10, 11 (1)

R. You are my inheritance, O Lord.

O LORD, my allotted portion and my cup,
     you it is who hold fast my lot.
I set the LORD ever before me;
     with him at my right hand I shall not
     be disturbed.

Therefore my heart is glad and my
     soul rejoices,
     my body, too, abides in confidence;
because you will not abandon my soul to
     the netherworld,
     nor will you suffer your faithful one to
     undergo corruption.

You will show me the path to life,
     fullness of joys in your presence,
     the delights at your right hand forever.

see them as a *type* or pattern or example of something greater to come. Abraham's willingness and resolve to sacrifice his son, who is described as his only one and the one whom he loves, is a type of God who offers up his beloved son, Jesus, for the salvation of humanity. Similarly, the ram caught in the thicket, a dense group of bushes or trees, is a type of Jesus on the wood of the cross. Finally, this story contains an etiology, which in this case is a story that explains why the place of sacri-

fice was called "Yahweh-yireh" in some translations. It means "It will be provided of God" or "God will see to it." This is what Abraham said to Isaac, when Isaac asked about the animal to be sacrificed. Some biblical scholars suggest that Moriah is not a historical place name but another reference to the idea that God will provide, because it contains the same Hebrew root *ra'ah*, which means "to provide." In other words, this is a story of total and steadfast trust in a God who provides.

READING III | Tonight's third reading is the story of Moses parting the Red Sea and the Israelites' exodus into the wilderness. This, too, is a story about trust in a God who provides. The chapters of Exodus that precede this story recount the ten plagues, an extended contest between the God of Abraham, Isaac, and Jacob and the Egyptian pharaoh, who thought himself to be a god on earth, but clearly was not, because he lost every single bout of the contest and ended up with

Exodus = EK-suh-duhs

Another very familiar story, this reading is full of action, with occasional instruction by God himself. But mostly action. Its drama will come through your proclamation if you allow the details of the action to be voiced. Let the words of the reading speak for themselves.

Here, God instructs Moses on how to perform a miraculous act. He's a little impatient, but he's also providing the details of a carefully considered plan.

The passage that follows includes many vivid details.

READING III   Exodus 14:15—15:1

A reading from the Book of Exodus

The LORD said to Moses, "**Why** are you crying **out** to me?
Tell the **Israelites** to go **forward**.
And **you**, lift up your **staff** and, with **hand** outstretched
    over the **sea**,
  split the sea in **two**,
  that the **Israelites** may pass through it on **dry land**.
But I will make the **Egyptians** so **obstinate**
  that they will go in **after** them.
Then I will **receive glory** through **Pharaoh** and all his **army**,
  his **chariots** and **charioteers**.
The **Egyptians** shall know that I am the LORD,
  when I receive **glory** through **Pharaoh**
  and his **chariots** and **charioteers**."

The **angel** of God, who had been leading Israel's **camp**,
  now **moved** and went around **behind** them.
The column of cloud **also**, leaving the front,
  took up its place **behind** them,
  so that it came **between** the camp of the **Egyptians**
  and that of **Israel**.
But the cloud now became **dark**, and thus the night **passed**
  without the rival camps coming any **closer together** all
    night long.
Then **Moses** stretched out his **hand** over the **sea**,
  and the LORD swept the **sea**
  with a **strong east wind** throughout the night
  and so **turned** it into **dry** land.
When the **water** was thus **divided**,
  the Israelites **marched** into the **midst** of the sea on dry **land**,
  with the **water** like a **wall** to their **right** and to their **left**. »

nothing but a hardened heart (Exodus 7:8—11:10).

    After celebrating what came to be known as the first Passover, and after the pharaoh finally let Moses and the Israelites leave Egypt, they wandered in the wilderness for a bit until God directed them toward the Red Sea by means of a column of cloud during the day and a column of fire at night, but they were fearful, because they could see the Egyptian armies coming after them. These terrified refugees com-

plained to Moses about being brought out into the desert to die. What a disaster! But, to paraphrase God's word in today's vernacular, God tells Moses to stop whining and get his act together. This is where today's reading begins. Moses is told to ready the people to move out, and God tells Moses to lift his staff and raise his hand to divide the sea.

    About now, people of a certain generation might be imagining Charlton Heston's portrayal of Moses parting the sea in the

1956 movie *The Ten Commandments*. Tall and handsome, almost god-like in appearance, he commands everyone's attention and makes the water do his bidding. But in the Book of Exodus, God is clearly the hero. Moses does what he is told, but God controls the sea and even the hearts of the pharaoh and his armies, eventually drowning every one of the Egyptians. Why? "The Egyptians shall know that I am the Lord, when I receive glory through Pharaoh his chariots and charioteers." In other words,

Again, vivid details. Give your voice to them.

The **Egyptians** followed in **pursuit**;
all Pharaoh's **horses** and **chariots** and **charioteers** went
after them
right into the **midst** of the **sea**.
In the **night watch** just before **dawn**
the LORD cast through the **column** of the fiery **cloud**
upon the Egyptian force a **glance** that **threw** it into a **panic**;
and he so **clogged** their chariot wheels
that they could hardly **drive**.
With that the **Egyptians** sounded the **retreat** before **Israel**,
because the LORD was fighting for them against the **Egyptians**.

God speaks, once again instructing Moses on how to perform another miraculous act, one that parallels the earlier act.

Then the LORD told Moses, "**Stretch** out your hand over the **sea**,
that the **water** may flow **back** upon the **Egyptians**,
upon their **chariots** and their **charioteers**."
So Moses stretched **out** his hand over the **sea**,
and at dawn the **sea** flowed **back** to its normal **depth**.
The Egyptians were fleeing head **on** toward the **sea**,
when the LORD **hurled** them into its **midst**.
As the **water** flowed back,
it covered the **chariots** and the **charioteers** of Pharaoh's
whole army
which had followed the **Israelites** into the **sea**.
Not a single **one** of them **escaped**.

Don't overly dramatize the doom that comes to Pharaoh and his army. Let the grim details speak for themselves.

But the **Israelites** had marched on **dry land**
through the **midst** of the **sea**,
with the **water** like a **wall** to their right and to their **left**.
Thus the LORD saved **Israel** on that day
from the **power** of the **Egyptians**.

---

this God of Abraham, Isaac, and Jacob establishes with full certainty that he is sovereign and that no forces of evil will defeat him. It also reveals that God is the faithful and steadfast benefactor and protector of God's people. In concluding the story, the narrator expresses how the people now viewed God, that they revered God and trusted in the one who provides. After such a dramatic scene, an acknowledgement of God's graciousness is warranted and, thus, we hear how all the Israelites began to sing an ancient song of thanks-giving with these words: "I will sing to the LORD, for he is gloriously triumphant; / horse and chariot he has cast into the sea" (see the following responsorial psalm).

As you reflect on this reading and try to follow the plot of the story, you might find yourself a bit confused. For example, how exactly was the Egyptian army destroyed? Did they get scared when their chariots got stuck in the bottom of the sea and run away, or did the walls of water crash down on them, swamp their chariots, and drown the soldiers? We see these odd-ities in the text elsewhere in the Old Testament, but this example is worth noting. Biblical scholars have determined that bits and pieces of several versions of this story have been woven together to create the version that we are reading today. While the final result might appear somewhat choppy, it speaks to how pivotal this event was in Israel's identity formation that communities in different locations and time periods had their own versions of the story and that the final redactor decided that none of the details should be lost.

When Israel saw the **Egyptians** lying dead on the **seashore**
and beheld the great **power** that the LORD
had **shown** against the **Egyptians**,
they **feared** the LORD and **believed** in him and in his
servant **Moses**.

Then **Moses** and the Israelites sang this song to the LORD:
I will **sing** to the LORD, for he is **gloriously** triumphant;
horse and **chariot** he has **cast** into the **sea**.

RESPONSORIAL PSALM   Exodus 15:1–2, 3–4, 5–6, 17–18 (1b)

R. Let us sing to the Lord; he has covered himself in glory.

I will sing to the LORD, for he is
gloriously triumphant;
horse and chariot he has cast into the sea.
My strength and my courage is the LORD,
and he has been my savior.
He is my God, I praise him;
the God of my father, I extol him.

The LORD is a warrior,
LORD is his name!
Pharaoh's chariots and army he hurled into
the sea;
the elite of his officers were submerged
in the Red Sea.

The flood waters covered them,
they sank into the depths like a stone.
Your right hand, O LORD, magnificent
in power,
your right hand, O LORD, has shattered
the enemy.

You brought in the people you redeemed
and planted them on the mountain of your
inheritance—
the place where you made your seat, O LORD,
the sanctuary, LORD, which your
hands established.
The LORD shall reign forever and ever.

READING IV   Isaiah 54:5–14

A reading from the Book of the Prophet Isaiah

The **One** who has become your **husband** is your **Maker**;
his **name** is the LORD of hosts;
your **redeemer** is the **Holy One** of Israel,
called **God** of all the **earth**.
The LORD calls you **back**,
like a **wife** forsaken and **grieved** in spirit,
a wife **married** in youth and then **cast off**,
says your God. »

Side notes:

"Power": Its manifestation defines this reading.

The reading concludes with the words of a song. The song is triumphant, but its contents are a little grim. The entire song is sung as the responsorial psalm.

For meditation and context:

Isaiah = ī-ZAY-uh
A reading in which the prophet speaks on behalf of God to the people, seeking to intensify the intimacy between them.

The core of the reading is this simile comparing the people ("you") to a forsaken wife whom God, as the husband, wants back. The conflict described and the strife implied in this passage should be familiar to many in the assembly. Don't get too dramatic with your proclamation, but don't shy away from its implications.

READING IV Our fourth reading is part of an oracle from Second Isaiah (chapters 40–55) that dates to the period of the Babylonian Exile, when Judea and the Jerusalem Temple were destroyed and the people taken away to exile in Babylon. In the verses preceding this passage, we hear the prophet is telling the people that they will be able to sing a joyous song, because Zion or Jerusalem will once again be filled with her children. Jerusalem is personified as God's wife through much of this oracle, but this is not to be taken literally. Rather, it is a metaphor for the quality of God's covenant love for the people of Israel.

The reading begins with an intimate and tender statement about God's relationship to Jerusalem: "The One who has become your husband is your Maker." Notice how God—metaphorically, the husband of Jerusalem—is given four additional attributes or titles: the Lord of hosts, Zion's redeemer, the Holy One of Israel, and God of all the earth. The fact that this God chose battered and insignificant Israel to be his bride is amazing! Also remarkable is the hint of regret that the prophet attributes to God, after seeing how grief-stricken Jerusalem and the exiled people of Judea are in their current state of abandonment. The prophet asserts that God had a right to be angry with his chosen people, who, like an adulterous wife, broke covenant with God, but he also acknowledges that God's love is so steadfast and that the tenderness God feels for his beloved is so great that God quickly overcomes his "outburst of wrath" and calls Israel back into covenant relationship in mercy and without rebuke.

The prophet utilizes a second metaphor to describe God's change of heart

God promises peace, despite previously turbulent times.

Many jewels. The names of jewels are appealing to say and hear.

carnelians = kahr-NEEL-yuhnz = red semiprecious stones

carbuncles = KAHR-bung-k*lz = bright red gems

The peace God promises is like the jewels: enduring, precious, and consoling.

For a **brief moment** I **abandoned** you,
    but with **great tenderness** I will take you **back**.
In an **outburst** of wrath, for a **moment**
    I hid my **face** from you;
but with enduring **love** I take **pity** on you,
    says the LORD, your **redeemer**.
This is for me like the **days** of Noah,
    when I **swore** that the waters of Noah
    should **never again** deluge the **earth**;
so I have **sworn** not to be **angry** with you,
    or to **rebuke** you.
Though the **mountains** leave their **place**
    and the **hills** be shaken,
my **love** shall never **leave** you
    nor my **covenant** of peace be **shaken**,
    says the LORD, who has **mercy** on you.
O **afflicted** one, storm-battered and **unconsoled**,
    I lay your **pavements** in **carnelians**,
    and your **foundations** in **sapphires**;
I will make your **battlements** of **rubies**,
    your **gates** of **carbuncles**,
    and all your **walls** of precious **stones**.
All your **children** shall be **taught** by the LORD,
    and **great** shall be the **peace** of your **children**.
In **justice** shall you be **established**,
    far from the **fear** of **oppression**,
    where **destruction** cannot come **near** you.

toward Zion, namely, the story of Noah and the flood, which opens with the narrator telling us that God observed all of the evil in the world that was brought upon by humans, and "the LORD regretted making human beings on the earth, and his heart was grieved" (Genesis 6:6). This is the reason given for the flood that was intended to wipe away all evil from the earth and return everything to the way it was before creation, without form or shape, and covered with water (Genesis 1:1). "But Noah found favor with the LORD" (Genesis 6:8). Thus, when the rains stopped and the waters

receded, Noah and his family were permitted to leave the ark, along with the other creatures Noah had rescued. When God received Noah's offering he made this vow that we hear about in this passage from Isaiah: "Never again will I curse the ground because of human beings, since the desires of the human heart are evil from youth; nor will I ever again strike down every living being, as I have done" (Genesis 8:21). Thus, despite knowing what God knows about the failings of the human heart, he recreates the world as an act of love.

The final metaphor that the prophet brings into this oracle of salvation is that of a beautifully adorned and securely walled city, the new Jerusalem. The prophet does not tell us the significance of the various jewels that adorn the city, its streets, and its gates, but we can say, at least, that they signify a place that is worthy of God's presence (see also Revelation 4:1–6 and 21:9–21). The learning that takes place in this city will be divinely inspired, and the city will be established in God's justice (Hebrew, *tsedaqah*, meaning "righteousness"). When applied to God, "justice" describes how God

For meditation and context:

RESPONSORIAL PSALM　Psalm 30:2, 4, 5–6, 11–12, 13 (2a)

R. I will praise you, Lord, for you have rescued me.

I will extol you, O LORD, for you drew
　me clear
　　and did not let my enemies rejoice
　　over me.
O LORD, you brought me up from
　the netherworld;
　you preserved me from among those going
　down into the pit.

Sing praise to the LORD, you his
　faithful ones,
　and give thanks to his holy name.
For his anger lasts but a moment;
　a lifetime, his good will.
At nightfall, weeping enters in,
　but with the dawn, rejoicing.

Hear, O LORD, and have pity on me;
　O LORD, be my helper.
You changed my mourning into dancing;
　O LORD, my God, forever will I give
　you thanks.

Isaiah = ī-ZAY-uh

A reading in which God through the voice of the prophet Isaiah promises forgiveness. The message of this reading is direct and should be relatable to many in your assembly.

"You who have no money": Even in affluent parishes, there are people who have felt this pinch. God is speaking directly to these people.

READING V　Isaiah 55:1–11

A reading from the Book of the Prophet Isaiah

Thus says the **LORD**:
All **you** who are **thirsty**,
　come to the **water**!
You who have no **money**,
　come, receive **grain** and **eat**;
come, without **paying** and without **cost**,
　drink **wine** and **milk**!
Why spend your **money** for what is not **bread**,
　your **wages** for what fails to **satisfy**?
Heed me, and you shall **eat** well,
　you shall **delight** in rich **fare**.
Come to me **heedfully**,
　listen, that you may have **life**.
I will **renew** with you the everlasting **covenant**,
　the **benefits** assured to **David**. »

---

acts in keeping with God's nature as goodness itself and as being in eternal covenant with God's people. Thus, Israel has no need to fear for its well-being.

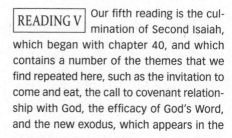 Our fifth reading is the culmination of Second Isaiah, which began with chapter 40, and which contains a number of the themes that we find repeated here, such as the invitation to come and eat, the call to covenant relationship with God, the efficacy of God's Word, and the new exodus, which appears in the

section immediately following this reading. Second Isaiah was written during the Babylonian Exile in the sixth century BC. Thus, many of its oracles are oracles of consolation.

This reading begins with a number of imperatives directed at the poor and needy, inviting them to attend God's banquet, which is a theme commonly used in the Bible's wisdom literature to describe God's desire to care for humanity. For example, the language is very similar to Proverbs 9:1–5 and Sirach 24:18–24, in which Lady

Wisdom invites those who wish to be wise to come to her banquet. Wisdom is not a deity separate from God but rather a power or attribute of God. Notice that there are no social or ethical restrictions on who can come to the banquet. One needs only to be thirsty for God and willing to listen to God's voice. Notice also that the covenant agreement made with David has now been extended to this wider audience: to be "a witness to peoples, a leader and commander of nations." This is an everlasting covenant, meaning that it extends back-

As I made him a **witness** to the **peoples**,
    a **leader** and commander of **nations**,
so shall you **summon** a nation you knew **not**,
    and **nations** that knew you not shall **run** to you,
because of the LORD, your **God**,
    the **Holy One** of Israel, who has **glorified** you.

Seek the LORD while he may be **found**,
    call him while he is **near**.
Let the **scoundrel** forsake his **way**,
    and the **wicked man** his **thoughts**;
let him **turn** to the LORD for **mercy**;
    to our **God**, who is generous in **forgiving**.
For my **thoughts** are not **your** thoughts,
    nor are your ways **my** ways, says the LORD.
As **high** as the heavens are above the **earth**,
    so high are my ways above your ways
    and my thoughts above your thoughts.

For **just** as from the **heavens**
    the rain and snow come **down**
and do not **return** there
    till they have **watered** the earth,
    making it **fertile** and **fruitful**,
giving **seed** to the one who **sows**
    and **bread** to the one who **eats**,
so shall my word be
    that goes **forth** from my **mouth**;
my word shall not **return** to me **void**,
    but shall do my **will**,
    achieving the **end** for which I **sent** it.

"Seek the Lord while he may be found": This command speaks to the hope inherent in this reading. We hope it's true, that God may be found, especially when we call him.

Forgiveness. This is the heart of this reading.

Even stresses on the words in this line.

ward and forward in time without end. Moreover, God's steadfast loyalty promised to David now encompasses all peoples. The "nation you knew not, and nations that knew you not" is most likely the Persian empire under King Cyrus the Great (reigned 559–530 BC). He is the one who released the Judeans from their exile (see Isaiah 45:1, 13–14). Here, it is generalized to emphasize Israel's leadership role in the world.

The second half of this reading issues a similar imperative to the people of Israel using a type of Hebrew poetry called synonymous parallelism, in which the second line of text repeats, but in different words, the content of the first line. The imperative is to "Seek the LORD . . . call him" to find mercy and forgiveness, which is followed by two arguments for why God's people should act on this command. The first argument is an assertion that God is utterly transcendent such that God's thoughts are not our thoughts, but yet God is so near to us as to be touched by our sinfulness and wants to heal us. The second argument is about the efficacy of God's Word. It comes upon us like a gentle rain or unexpected snow to water the thirsty soil and make it produce fruit for those who have need. God's Word does not dissipate in the wind, but rather it accomplishes everything that God wants it to accomplish. We can count on this because God is ever faithful.

READING VI The sixth reading of this Easter Vigil celebration is part of a longer poem in praise of personified Wisdom taken from the Book of Baruch. According to the first-century AD Jewish historian Josephus, Baruch was a scribe for the prophet Jeremiah from the sixth century BC (see Josephus' *Antiquities*

For meditation and context:

RESPONSORIAL PSALM Isaiah 12:2–3, 4, 5–6 (3)

R. You will draw water joyfully from the springs of salvation.

God indeed is my savior;
  I am confident and unafraid.
My strength and my courage is the LORD,
  and he has been my savior.
With joy you will draw water
  at the fountain of salvation.

Give thanks to the LORD, acclaim his name;
  among the nations make known his deeds,
  proclaim how exalted is his name.

Sing praise to the LORD for his
  glorious achievement;
  let this be known throughout all the
  earth.
Shout with exultation, O city of Zion,
  for great in your midst
  is the Holy One of Israel!

READING VI   Baruch 3:9–15, 32—4:4

Baruch = buh-ROOK

An exhortation on wisdom, personified in this reading in her ancient feminine principle. A powerful reminder.

The reading makes use of rhetorical questions. Use these questions—this first one stretches over several lines—to organize the pace of your proclamation.

Take note of the questions here.

A reading from the Book of the Prophet Baruch

Hear, O Israel, the **commandments** of life:
  listen, and know **prudence**!
How **is** it, Israel,
  that you are in the **land** of your **foes**,
  grown **old** in a foreign **land**,
defiled with the **dead**,
  accounted with those **destined** for the **netherworld**?
You have **forsaken** the fountain of **wisdom**!
  Had you **walked** in the way of **God**,
  you would have **dwelt** in enduring **peace**.
Learn where prudence is,
  where **strength**, where **understanding**;
that you may know **also**
  where are length of **days**, and **life**,
  where **light** of the eyes, and **peace**.
Who has found the place of **wisdom**,
  who has entered into her **treasuries**? »

---

of the Jews 10.9.1). However, this book that bears his name is generally thought to be an edited collection of smaller works by various unknown authors written in the style of the prophets and dating to the second century BC. After a brief introduction from the narrator of this book (Baruch 1:1–14), we find a confession of sin attributed to the exiles in Babylon and addressed to those who were left behind in Jerusalem and Judah (Baruch 1:15—2:10), in which they attribute their sorry situation to their refusal to listen to God and their failure to follow God's precepts (Baruch 1:18, 2:10).

This confession is followed by a prayer to God that Israel might have a change of heart during the time of its exile and return to a life lived in obedience to God's law (Baruch 2:11—3:8).

This reading, a poem in praise of Wisdom, is addressed to Israel and it continues the theme of obedience to God's law. It begins with a call to heed the commandments of life and know prudence. The Greek *phronesis*, translated here as "prudence" has a range of meanings, including intelligence, good judgment, and practical advice or action. Thus, wisdom is equated

with the law. This invitation is followed by a rhetorical question, which could be restated like this: "How did you get into such a mess?" The poet's answer: "You have forsaken the fountain of wisdom!" If Jewish law is equated with wisdom, then the fount of wisdom is God. The exiles in Babylon were "defiled with the dead" insofar as they lived in the diaspora, among Gentiles who were destined for death because they did not follow Jewish law. Had Israel not abandoned the fountain of wisdom, the nation would be experiencing long life, peace, and "light of the eyes" (per-

"Her" refers to Wisdom, *Hokhmah* in Hebrew, *Sophia* in Greek, always personified in feminine form in the ancient imagination.

Wisdom's divinity—the part she plays in God's creative imagination—is implied in this closing passage.

The One who knows all things **knows** her;
  he has **probed** her by his **knowledge**—
the One who established the **earth** for all time,
  and **filled** it with four-footed **beasts**;
he who **dismisses** the light, and it **departs**,
  calls it, and it obeys him **trembling**;
before whom the **stars** at their posts
  shine and **rejoice**;
when he **calls** them, they **answer**, "Here we are!"
  shining with joy for their **Maker**.
Such is our **GOD**;
  no **other** is to be **compared** to him:
he has **traced out** the whole way of understanding,
  and has **given** her to Jacob, his **servant**,
  to **Israel**, his beloved **son**.
Since then she has **appeared** on **earth**,
  and **moved** among people.
She is the **book** of the precepts of **GOD**,
  the **law** that endures **forever**;
all who **cling** to her will **live**,
  but those will **die** who **forsake** her.
Turn, O Jacob, and **receive** her:
  walk by her light toward **splendor**.
Give not your **glory** to another,
  your **privileges** to an alien **race**.
Blessed are **we**, O Israel;
  for what **pleases** God is **known** to us!

haps meaning insight; ancients believed that people could see because of the light that dwelt within them).

The next section of this poem (see Baruch 3:15–23), which is not fully included in the lectionary reading, begins with another rhetorical question: "Who has found the place of wisdom?" The answer is clear. No human can find wisdom through their own abilities. The poet notes that not even kings with great powers over the created world can find wisdom, nor can those who amass great wealth or scheme to acquire it. And later generations are no better off.

Whatever else they achieve in their lifetimes, they have not discerned the path to wisdom or found her. The poet notes that even the ancient seats of human knowledge —Phoenicia (here called Canaan) and Edom (including Teman)—did not know wisdom. Likewise, the descendants of Hagar—the tribes that trace themselves back to Ishmael, son of Abraham—did not find wisdom.

Why can no human find wisdom? The poet expounds on this question next, beginning with a statement about vastness of God's dwelling and the scope of God's authority. Only the one who knows all things

(i.e., God) knows wisdom, because "she is the book of the precepts of God," and "the law that endures forever." The poem concludes with an admonition to walk by wisdom's light and a somewhat veiled threat that God will give Israel's glory and privilege to another nation, if it refuses. Finally, at the end, there is a blessing! Although no one can secure wisdom on their own, God is pleased to make her known to God's people through the giving of the law.

READING VII The last in the series of seven readings for medi-

For meditation and context:

RESPONSORIAL PSALM Psalm 19:8, 9, 10, 11 (John 6:68c)

R. Lord, you have the words of everlasting life.

The law of the Lord is perfect,
   refreshing the soul;
the decree of the Lord is trustworthy,
   giving wisdom to the simple.

The precepts of the Lord are right,
   rejoicing the heart;
the command of the Lord is clear,
   enlightening the eye.

The fear of the Lord is pure,
   enduring forever;
the ordinances of the Lord are true,
   all of them just.

They are more precious than gold,
   than a heap of purest gold;
sweeter also than syrup
   or honey from the comb.

READING VII Ezekiel 36:16–17a, 18–28

A reading from the Book of the Prophet Ezekiel

The **word** of the Lord **came** to me, saying:
   Son of man, when the **house** of Israel lived in their **land**,
   they **defiled** it by their **conduct** and **deeds**.
Therefore I poured **out** my fury **upon** them
   because of the **blood** that they poured **out** on the **ground**,
   and because they **defiled** it with idols.
I **scattered** them among the **nations**,
   dispersing them over foreign **lands**;
   according to their **conduct** and **deeds** I **judged** them.
But when they **came** among the nations wherever they **came**,
   they served to **profane** my holy **name**,
   because it was **said** of them: "**These** are the **people** of the Lord,
   yet they had to leave their land."
So I have **relented** because of my holy **name**
   which the **house** of Israel **profaned**
   among the **nations** where they **came**. »

Ezekiel = ee-ZEE-kee-uhl

A challenging reading. Challenging because the tone of this passage is largely wrathful and accusatory. The language in this reading is so charged, the wrath will come through. It consists almost entirely of the words of God spoken to Ezekiel.

Here the tone is clear: the words "fury," "defiled," and "profane" set that tone.

tation on this Easter vigil comes from the Book of Ezekiel. Ezekiel was a prophet of the sixth century BC, who ministered to the exiled Judeans in Babylon. In this section of the prophet's writing, Ezekiel uses the Babylonian Exile as the historical reference for his theology of God's plan of salvation. It is written in the form of an oracle delivered to Ezekiel, who is addressed as "son of man," meaning "a human being," most likely to contrast with the utter transcendence of God. God is the speaker.

The oracle opens with a condemnation of the house of Israel for defiling the land

with their behaviors and actions that are contrary to the covenant God had made with them. God charges them with idol worship and offering sacrifices to idols, which, in the prophet's mind, would be considered an extreme act of dishonor toward God. Therefore, God is justified in responding to their actions by scattering the people across the lands. Israel's dispersion (scattering) further dishonors God because the nations, to which Israel was scattered, question the power of a God who cannot maintain the people in their own land. Therefore, God decides to show his holiness by withdrawing

the punishment on Israel and promising to regather Israel and bring them back to their own land. But God states clearly, "Not for your sakes do I act, house of Israel, but for the sake of my holy name, which you profaned among the nations to which you came."

Further, God says that he intends to perform a ritual cleansing for Israel in order to remove the impurities of their idolatry. From this point on, the vocabulary is highly covenantal, but this covenant is new and different. God says that he will give Israel a new heart and a new spirit. Ancient people

God is so worked up, he begins quoting himself!

Note the shift into the future tense. The tone doesn't change significantly, but from here to the conclusion of the reading, God is speaking about the future.

God wants to cleanse the future of its impurities.

And give people a new heart.

God's hope: this is his covenant.

For meditation and context:

Therefore say to the house of Israel: **Thus** says the Lord GOD:
  Not for **your sakes** do I act, house of Israel,
  but for the **sake** of my holy **name**,
  which you **profaned** among the **nations** to which you **came**.
I will **prove** the holiness of my great **name**, profaned among
    the **nations**,
  in whose **midst** you have **profaned** it.
Thus the **nations** shall know that **I** am the LORD, says the
    Lord GOD,
  when in their **sight** I prove my **holiness** through **you**.
For I will take you **away** from among the **nations**,
  gather you from **all** the foreign lands,
  and bring you **back** to your own land.
I will **sprinkle** clean water upon you
  to **cleanse** you from all your **impurities**,
  and from **all** your idols I will **cleanse** you.
I will give you a new **heart** and place a new spirit **within** you,
  taking from your bodies your **stony hearts**
  and **giving** you **natural** hearts.
I will put my **spirit** within you and make you **live** by my statutes,
  careful to observe my **decrees**.
You shall **live** in the land I **gave** your fathers;
  you shall be my **people**, and I will be your **GOD**.

RESPONSORIAL PSALM   Psalm 42:3, 5; 43:3, 4 (2)
WHEN BAPTISM IS CELEBRATED.

R. Like a deer that longs for running streams, my soul longs for you, my God.

Athirst is my soul for God, the living God.
  When shall I go and behold the face
    of God?

I went with the throng
  and led them in procession to the house
    of God,
amid loud cries of joy and thanksgiving,
  with the multitude keeping festival.

Or:

Send forth your light and your fidelity;
  they shall lead me on
and bring me to your holy mountain,
  to your dwelling-place.

Then will I go in to the altar of God,
  the God of my gladness and joy;
then will I give you thanks upon the harp,
  O God, my God!

understood the heart to be the seat of thinking and loving. The prophet says that God will remove their hearts of stone and give them a fleshly or human heart. The new spirit that God will give is described further in the next oracle, the vision of the dry bones, where God's spirit or breath gives new life to the community of Israel. Thus, God restores God's honor by returning the people to their land and reaffirming that he will be their God and they will be God's people. What can we say in response? God's faithfulness endures, even in spite of our sin.

EPISTLE The structure of the Easter Vigil liturgy is different from our normal Masses, as evidenced by the number of readings we have. Another unique element of it is that the Gloria is sung before the Epistle reading, rather than before the first reading. This joyful hymn leads us into this reading from Paul's Letter to the Romans, where we are reminded of the meaning of baptism, the foundation of our faith, and the reason for our joyful songs and celebrations. Hearing Paul's theology of baptism is extremely significant for this Easter feast because it grounds our

participation in the sacrament of baptism in the paschal mystery, the mystery of Jesus' death and resurrection for our salvation. Prior to this reading, Paul had been writing about the efficacy of God's justification of sinful humanity. The word "justification," also translated as "righteousness," has legal overtones and involves acquittal of the charges brought against humanity, where God is the judge and humanity is the accused. Be aware that acquittal in a court of law is not the same as being declared innocent. Humanity cannot earn justification. It is purely and in every way grace,

For meditation and context:

RESPONSORIAL PSALM Isaiah 12:2–3, 4bcd, 5–6 (3)
WHEN BAPTISM IS NOT CELEBRATED.

R. You will draw water joyfully from the springs of salvation.

God indeed is my savior;
    I am confident and unafraid.
My strength and my courage is the LORD,
    and he has been my savior.
With joy you will draw water
    at the fountain of salvation.

Give thanks to the LORD, acclaim his name;
    among the nations make known his deeds,
    proclaim how exalted is his name.

Sing praise to the LORD for his glorious
        achievement;
    let this be known throughout all
        the earth.
Shout with exultation, O city of Zion,
    for great in your midst
        is the Holy One of Israel!

Or:

For meditation and context:

RESPONSORIAL PSALM Psalm 51:12–13, 14–15, 18–19 (12a)
WHEN BAPTISM IS NOT CELEBRATED.

R. Create a clean heart in me, O God.

A clean heart create for me, O God,
    and a steadfast spirit renew within me.
Cast me not out from your presence,
    and your Holy Spirit take not from me.

Give me back the joy of your salvation,
    and a willing spirit sustain in me.
I will teach transgressors your ways,
    and sinners shall return to you.

For you are not pleased with sacrifices;
    should I offer a holocaust, you would not
        accept it.
My sacrifice, O God, is a contrite spirit;
    a heart contrite and humbled, O God, you
        will not spurn.

EPISTLE Romans 6:3–11

A reading from the Letter of Saint Paul to the Romans

Brothers and **sisters**:
Are you **unaware** that **we** who were **baptized** into Christ **Jesus**
    were **baptized** into his **death**?
We were **indeed** buried with him through **baptism** into **death**,
    so that, **just** as Christ was **raised** from the dead
    by the **glory** of the Father,
    we **too** might live in **newness** of life. »

A short reading focused on baptism. Because the Easter Vigil often includes the baptism of the elect, you should imagine you are speaking directly to those about to be baptized.

Paul begins by making a connection between Baptism, life and death, and resurrection. These are the terms that define this passage from his letter to the Romans.

that is, a gift from God. But, of course, someone will ask, "Shall we persist in sin that grace may abound?" to which Paul says, "Of course not!" (Romans 6:1).

Paul then likens a Christian's baptism to being baptized into Christ's death. The Greek verb *baptizó* means "to dip, immerse, or submerge" into Christ, which means that the Christian is also buried with Christ. And because baptized Christians are immersed into Christ, they can also hope to be raised from the dead "as Christ was raised from the dead by the glory of the Father." This word "glory" is important. In the Exodus sto-

ries, miracles are attributed to God's glory (see Exodus 15:7, 11; 16:7, 10). Likewise, Paul attributes the miracle of Jesus' resurrection to God's glory, which invests the risen Christ with life-giving power (Romans 1:4; see also 1 Corinthians 15:44).

But Paul has not forgotten that question about whether Christians can keep on sinning because God's grace abounds. Beginning with the notion that the Christian is united with Christ through baptism, he notes that it is our old self that dies when we die with Christ. Our old self, which was under the power of sin since the fall, is

freed from its slavery to sin. Moreover, when Christ was raised from the dead, he would not die again because "death no longer has power over him." Rather, now Christ lives for God. So, too, those of us who are united with Christ in his death are no longer under the power of sin. Our new selves are "living for God in Christ Jesus."

For if we have **grown** into union with him through a **death** like his,
   we shall also be **united** with him in the **resurrection**.
We know that our **old self** was **crucified** with him,
   so that our sinful **body** might be done **away** with,
   that we might no longer be in **slavery** to **sin**.
For a **dead** person has been **absolved** from sin.
If, then, we have **died** with Christ,
   we **believe** that we shall also **live** with him.
We know that **Christ**, **raised** from the **dead**, **dies** no more;
   death no longer has **power** over him.
As to his **death**, he **died** to **sin once** and for **all**;
   as to his **life**, he lives for **God**.
Consequently, **you too** must think of yourselves as being **dead** to sin
   and **living** for God in Christ **Jesus**.

> *To die with Christ is also to live with him, to be resurrected with him. Baptism is rebirth.*

> *Paul reemphasizes this point about resurrection in these concluding words.*

> *For meditation and context:*

RESPONSORIAL PSALM   Psalm 118:1–2, 16–17, 22–23

R. Alleluia, alleluia, alleluia.

Give thanks to the LORD, for he is good,
   for his mercy endures forever.
Let the house of Israel say,
   "His mercy endures forever."

The right hand of the LORD has struck with power;
   the right hand of the LORD is exalted.
I shall not die, but live,
   and declare the works of the LORD.

The stone which the builders rejected
   has become the cornerstone.
By the LORD has this been done;
   it is wonderful in our eyes.

GOSPEL The Gospel reading for the vigil of the celebration of Christ's resurrection is from Matthew's Gospel. The synoptic Gospels' versions of the empty tomb story share a basic plot, but they differ quite a bit in the details. In Matthew's version, two women come to the tomb after the sabbath but before the dawn on the first day of the week, which would be a Sunday. The women are identified as Mary Magdalene and the other Mary, who is likely the woman mentioned in Matthew 27:55–56 and 61. These two are listed as witnesses to Jesus' death, the place of his burial, and also the empty tomb, but, under Jewish law, women were not considered to be reliable witnesses. The fact that they are mentioned here in all three places is significant, but the Gospel writer does not explain. What do you think? What meaning might you attach to this detail?

A consistent feature of first-century burial sites in Israel was the large stone used to cover the entrance to the tomb so that animals could not enter the tomb and devour parts of the body or so that it would be harder for grave robbers to steal the body and any items of value that were placed in the tomb. Matthew's Gospel notes that the Jewish religious authorities requested and were granted permission to have Roman soldiers placed at the tomb to prevent Jesus' disciples from stealing his body and claiming that he had been raised from death (Matthew 27:62–66). The period of their assignment was three days, because after that time it was believed that resuscitation was not possible.

We are also told that the women "came to see the tomb," but there is no mention of them coming to wash and anoint the body, as women would have

GOSPEL   Matthew 28:1–10

A reading from the holy Gospel according to Matthew

After the **sabbath**, as the **first day** of the **week** was **dawning**,
  Mary **Magdalene** and the other **Mary came** to see the **tomb**.
And **behold**, there was a **great earthquake**;
    for an **angel** of the **Lord descended** from **heaven**,
    approached, **rolled** back the **stone**, and **sat upon** it.
His **appearance** was like **lightning**
    and his **clothing** was **white** as **snow**.
The **guards** were **shaken** with **fear** of him
    and **became** like **dead men**.
Then the **angel** said to the **women** in reply,
    "**Do not** be **afraid**!
I know that you are seeking **Jesus** the **crucified**.
He **is not here**, for he has been **raised just** as he **said**.
Come and see the **place** where he **lay**.
Then go **quickly** and tell his **disciples**,
    'He has been **raised** from the **dead**,
    and he is going **before** you to **Galilee**;
    there you will **see** him.'
    Behold, I have **told** you."
Then they went away **quickly** from the **tomb**,
    fearful yet **overjoyed**,
    and **ran** to **announce** this to his **disciples**.
And **behold**, Jesus **met** them on their **way** and **greeted** them.
They **approached**, embraced his **feet**, and did him **homage**.
Then Jesus **said** to them, "**Do not** be **afraid**.
Go tell my **brothers** to go to **Galilee**,
    and **there** they will **see** me."

The tone of this reading, which comes from the last chapter of Matthew, is conclusive. Its focus is on vision. The witnesses of this vision are women. State their names clearly.

Despite the exclamation point, the tone of this statement is soothing and calm.

Slight pause between "raised" and "just."

The tone of this reading overall is characterized by this line, "fearful yet overjoyed."

The reading concludes on a note of vision/seeing.

done in a normal burial. Was it because they expected that the soldiers would not have allowed it? Certainly, they would have known that they could not open the tomb by themselves. Were they simply coming to mourn in a ritual way, as in later Jewish traditions such as *shiva*?

Imagine the women's surprise and terror when they arrive at the tomb and see an angel come down from heaven in a mighty earthquake to remove the stone and sit on it. But we might also imagine their curiosity at witnessing such a sight! The earthquake, the angel's lightning-like appearance, and

radiant clothing are all signs of divine presence. The soldiers, likewise, are terrified, so much so that they become "like dead men." But now the angel's mission becomes clear. He comforts the women by telling them not to be afraid and showing them the empty tomb as proof of the resurrection. He also sends them on a mission: "go quickly and tell his disciples, 'He has been raised from the dead, and he is going before you to Galilee; there you will see him.'" They leave immediately, we are told, "fearful yet overjoyed."

But here is another interesting detail in Matthew's story of the empty tomb.

Jesus' disciples are not present at the tomb—this is not their finest day—and they will need to wait to see Jesus until they receive the message from the women to meet him in Galilee. But Mary Magdalene and the other Mary, who have no status as witnesses to the resurrection, will have a chance to greet the risen Jesus now! The women prostrate themselves and kiss Jesus' feet indicating that they recognize his divinity but also that they are not just seeing ghosts. Jesus has a real, resurrected body and he is truly raised from the dead. Alleluia! C.C.

EASTER SUNDAY OF THE RESURRECTION OF THE LORD

LECTIONARY #42

READING I   Acts of the Apostles 10:34a, 37–43

A reading from the Acts of the Apostles

In this reading, Peter is telling an assembled crowd the story of Jesus' life and the important lessons learned from his instructions

Judea = joo-DEE-uh

Peter **proceeded** to speak and said:
   "You **know** what has **happened** all over **Judea**,
   beginning in **Galilee** after the **baptism**
   that **John** preached,
   how **God** anointed **Jesus** of **Nazareth**
   with the Holy **Spirit** and **power**.

Here is the first point: Jesus went about doing good.

He went **about** doing **good**
   and healing all those **oppressed** by the **devil**,
   for **God** was **with** him.
We are **witnesses** of all that he **did**
   both in the country of the **Jews** and in **Jerusalem**.

Here is the second point: He was crucified.

They put him to **death** by hanging him on a **tree**.

Here is the third point: He was resurrected. Mostly even stresses on the words in this line.

This man God raised on the third day and **granted**
      that he be **visible**,
   not to all the people, but to **us**,
   the **witnesses** chosen by **God** in advance,
   who **ate** and drank with him after he **rose** from the dead.

Here is the fourth point: He commissioned Peter and the other disciples to preach.

He **commissioned** us to preach to the **people**
   and **testify** that he is the one **appointed** by God
   as **judge** of the **living** and the **dead**.

And finally, the fifth point: If you believe in Jesus, your sins will be forgiven. This point speaks directly to the assembly.

To him all the **prophets** bear **witness**,
   that everyone who **believes** in him
   will receive **forgiveness** of sins through his **name**."

There are options for today's readings. Contact your parish staff to learn which readings will be used.

READING I   Our first reading is a speech attributed to Peter on the occasion of his visit to the household of Cornelius, a Roman centurion who was posted in Caesarea and who was a generous supporter of the Jewish community there. One day, in a vision, Cornelius is told to call for Peter to come to his home. The next day, Peter receives a vision that he does not understand at first but that appears to cancel certain food prohibitions that kept Jews separate from Gentiles at meals and from entering each other's homes. Therefore, when Cornelius' men arrived at his home, Peter knew that he could go with them (see Acts 10:1–23).

When Peter enters Cornelius' home, he discovers that his entire household along with relatives and friends were gathered there. The first thing Peter does is acknowledge publicly that Jews were not supposed to associate with Gentiles, but that God showed him that no human person is to be considered "profane or unclean" (Acts 10:28). This is a radical break with tradition.

After Cornelius explains to Peter why he was summoned, Luke presents Peter in today's reading as delivering a testimony to his audience about the central mystery of Christian faith: that Jesus was sent by God to bring the Good News to the world, that he was crucified, that God raised him, and that he appeared to the apostolic witnesses. Finally, calling on the witness of the prophets, Peter says, "everyone who believes in him will receive forgiveness of sins through [Jesus'] name."

For meditation and context:

RESPONSORIAL PSALM   Psalm 118:1–2, 16–17, 22–23 (24)

R. This is the day the Lord has made; let us rejoice and be glad.
or
R. Alleluia.

Give thanks to the Lord, for he is good,
　for his mercy endures forever.
Let the house of Israel say,
　"His mercy endures forever."

"The right hand of the Lord has struck
　　with power;
　the right hand of the Lord is exalted.
I shall not die, but live,
　and declare the works of the Lord.

The stone which the builders rejected
　has become the cornerstone.
By the Lord has this been done;
　it is wonderful in our eyes.

READING II   Colossians 3:1–4

A reading from the Letter of Saint Paul to the Colossians

Brothers and **sisters**:
If then you were raised with **Christ**, seek what is **above**,
　where **Christ** is seated at the **right hand** of God.
Think of what is **above**, not of what is on **earth**.
For you have **died**, and your **life** is hidden with **Christ** in God.
When Christ your life **appears**,
　then **you too** will appear with him in **glory**.

Or:

Colossians = kuh-LOSH-uhnz

An exhortatory reading, compressed in its length but powerful in its message.

The focal word in this reading is "above."

The syntax here is strange. Be sure to practice.

As if to testify to the quality of faith found among his Gentile audience, we hear in the verses following today's reading that the Holy Spirit comes down upon everyone gathered at Cornelius' home and they begin speaking in tongues. What else could Peter conclude from this glorious event, but that everyone should be baptized in Jesus' name (Acts 10:47–48)!

READING II **Colossians.** Our second reading comes from the latter half of Colossians, in which the author gives practical advice for living as Christians.

Before going into the specifics of this, the letter writer exhorts the community to "seek what is above," that is, to seek the resurrected Christ, who is "seated at the right hand of God." Most likely, this is the snippet of a creedal statement based on Psalm 110:1. In this context, it affirms the summation of the paschal mystery: once crucified and buried, Jesus Christ was raised from the dead and now is exalted in glory.

But the key to fully understanding this text is a theology of baptism that appears to be similar to what Paul describes in Romans 6:1–11. Christian believers are bap-

tized into Christ's death, and their old self is now dead to sin. This is what the author of the Letter to the Colossians means when he says, "for you have died." And just as, in baptism, Christian believers are united with Christ in his death, they are united in his resurrection and emerge to newness of life. This is what the author of this letter means at the beginning of this reading when he writes, "If then you were raised with Christ." But for now, Christian believers live in the "between times," after Jesus' salvific death and resurrection but before he returns at the end time. This is what the

Corinthians = kohr-IN-thee-uhnz

A reading in which Paul makes use of an ingenious metaphor.

Yeast is Paul's metaphor for Christ's sacrifice. Just as there would be no feast without bread, so there is no spiritual life without leaven.

READING II   1 Corinthians 5:6b–8

A reading from the first Letter of Saint Paul to the Corinthians

Brothers and **sisters**:
Do you not **know** that a little **yeast** leavens all the **dough**?
Clear **out** the old **yeast**,
    so that you may become a fresh **batch** of **dough**,
    inasmuch as you are **unleavened**.
For our **paschal lamb**, Christ, has been **sacrificed**.
Therefore, let us **celebrate** the **feast**,
    not with the **old yeast**, the yeast of **malice** and **wickedness**,
    but with the **unleavened bread** of **sincerity** and **truth**.

SEQUENCE   Victimae paschali laudes

Christians, to the Paschal Victim
    Offer your thankful praises!
A Lamb the sheep redeems;
    Christ, who only is sinless,
    Reconciles sinners to the Father.
Death and life have contended in that
      combat stupendous:
    The Prince of life, who died,
      reigns immortal.

Speak, Mary, declaring
    What you saw, wayfaring.
"The tomb of Christ, who is living,
    The glory of Jesus' resurrection;
Bright angels attesting,
    The shroud and napkin resting.
Yes, Christ my hope is arisen;
    to Galilee he goes before you."
Christ indeed from death is risen, our new
      life obtaining.
    Have mercy, victor King, ever reigning!
    Amen. Alleluia.

TO KEEP IN MIND
Sequences originated as extensions of the sung Alleluia before the proclamation of the Gospel, although they precede the Alleluia now. The Easter Sequence is an ancient liturgical hymn that praises Christ, the paschal victim, for his victory over death. Mary Magdalene recounts her experience at Christ's tomb, proclaiming, "Christ my hope is arisen."

letter writer means when he says, "your life is hidden with Christ in God."

1 Corinthians. The situation described in today's reading concerns a report that Paul received about a member of the Christian community who has been sleeping with his mother or stepmother. Of course, Paul is not happy! He is equally displeased with the rest of the community, because they seem not to consider the harm that this does to everyone else.

To explain his position regarding what should happen to this man, Paul appeals to the metaphor of Passover preparation, for which every form of leavening must be removed from the house before Passover can begin, as a way of indicating one's commitment to a new beginning for a people no longer in slavery. Although the Christian community at Corinth consisted mostly of Gentiles, they would have known about this practice, because many would have already been attending synagogue or because they were introduced to the message of Jesus Christ by Paul, who was himself a Jew. Paul likens this man to the yeast that must be removed from the house

before Passover. Further, he likens the crucified Jesus to the Passover lamb that was sacrificed in the Temple on the day before Passover, and he wants the Corinthian community to be the new "unleavened bread of sincerity and truth."

GOSPEL | Today's Gospel reading, taken from John's account of the empty tomb, is constructed as an intercalation, a story within a story. The lectionary reading only consists of the opening section of the outer story (with Mary) and the inner story (with Peter and the Beloved

GOSPEL   John 20:1–9

A reading from the holy Gospel according to John

On the **first day** of the week,
   Mary of **Magdala** came to the tomb **early** in the morning,
   while it was still **dark**,
   and saw the **stone removed** from the **tomb**.
So she ran and went to Simon **Peter**
   and to the other **disciple** whom Jesus **loved**, and told them,
   "They have **taken** the Lord from the **tomb**,
   and we don't **know** where they **put** him."
So Peter and the other **disciple** went out and came to the **tomb**.
They both **ran**, but the other **disciple** ran faster than **Peter**
   and **arrived** at the tomb **first**;
   he bent **down** and saw the **burial cloths** there,
      but did **not** go in.
When Simon **Peter** arrived **after** him,
   he went into the **tomb** and saw the **burial cloths** there,
   and the **cloth** that had covered his **head**,
   not **with** the burial cloths but rolled **up** in a separate **place**.
Then the **other** disciple also went **in**,
   the one who had arrived at the tomb **first**,
   and he **saw** and **believed**.
For they did not yet **understand** the Scripture
   that he had to **rise** from the **dead**.

A reading relating a scene of enduring power and strangeness.
Magdala = MAG-duh-luh

The detail of the burial cloths is important. When Peter recognizes that the head cloth has been folded up, he understands that the body of Jesus was not stolen (since thieves wouldn't take the time to fold up the linens).

Seeing is believing: belief dawns on them here.
Believing and understanding are two separate things. Understanding can take more time than belief.

Disciple). It does not include the conclusion to the outer story about Mary still at the empty tomb (John 20:10–18).

In the first half of the outer story, Mary of Magdala arrives at the tomb very early in the morning when it is still dark outside, which would have been an extremely dangerous time for a woman to be out and about, especially alone. Only John's Gospel describes the tomb as being in a garden, perhaps an allusion to the paradisal garden of the first chapters of Genesis (John 19:41). When she sees that the tomb is open, she immediately assumes the worst! Her fright

is evidenced in the detail about her running to find Peter and the Beloved Disciple to tell them the horrifying news, that Jesus' body had been taken from the tomb and "we don't know where they put him." To whom does "we" refer? Is the Gospel writer using Mary to speak for the entire Johannine community? They must have struggled, at first, to understand the significance of Jesus' exaltation and return to the Father. Or perhaps there were other women with her, as in the other Gospel accounts.

The inner story begins with the narrator indicating that Peter and another disci-

ple, presumably the Beloved Disciple, went to the tomb. They run to the tomb and the Beloved Disciple arrives first, but he waits for Peter to enter into the tomb. This is an indication of the community's acknowledgement of Peter's authority in church leadership. But, while the Beloved Disciple is waiting, he looks in and sees the burial cloths. Likewise, when Peter arrives, he looks in and sees the burial cloths as well as the head covering, which is rolled up and set away from the other cloths. Why such detail? Some of the vocabulary in this story reminds us of the Lazarus story, in which

AFTERNOON GOSPEL   Luke 24:13–35

A reading from the holy Gospel according to Luke

That very day, the first **day** of the week,
  two of Jesus' **disciples** were going
  to a **village** seven miles from Jerusalem called **Emmaus**,
  and they were **conversing** about all the things that
    had occurred.
And it **happened** that while they were **conversing** and debating,
  Jesus **himself** drew **near** and walked **with** them,
  but their **eyes** were prevented from **recognizing** him.
He asked them,
  "What are you **discussing** as you walk **along**?"
They **stopped**, looking downcast.
One of them, named **Cleopas**, said to him in **reply**,
  "Are you the **only visitor** to Jerusalem
  who does not **know** of the things
  that have taken **place there** in these days?"
And he **replied** to them, "What **sort** of things?"
They said to him,
  "The **things** that happened to **Jesus** the Nazarene,
  who was a **prophet** mighty in **deed** and **word**
  before **God** and all the **people**,
  how our **chief priests** and rulers both **handed** him **over**
  to a **sentence** of **death** and **crucified** him.
But we were **hoping** that he would be the **one** to redeem Israel;
  and **besides** all this,
  it is now the **third day** since this took **place**.
Some women from our group, however, have **astounded** us:
  they were at the tomb **early** in the morning
  and did not find his **body**;
  they came **back** and reported
  that they had **indeed seen** a vision of **angels**
  who **announced** that he was **alive**.

A reading with great drama built into it. You can easily imagine it being filmed. The focus on the reading is recognition, specifically the time it takes Jesus' two disciples to recognize that he has been raised from the dead. The build-up of the narrative intensifies the excitement and joy of their recognition.

This phrase introduces the motif of recognition that guides the passage. Recognition is connected initially to seeing.

It's interesting that only one of these two disciples are named.

Note that "they" are speaking, both of them, even though it's one unified speech. The purpose of this description of Jesus' deeds and words is to build toward recognition.

Note "a vision of angels." Recognition and seeing are still urgently connected.

Jesus orders Lazarus to come forth from his tomb (John 11:44). When he emerges, he is still bound by the burial cloths and the head covering, but Jesus' situation is different. How was Jesus freed from the burial clothes? Was this God's doing? And what does it mean that the head covering was rolled or folded up by itself? Certainly, we can assume that Jesus' body was not stolen. After all, grave robbers who are in such a hurry as to steal a body are not going to take the time to undress the corpse and neatly fold up the face covering! Still, the

disciples did not fully understand what had happened.

This passage in John continues beyond the lectionary reading with the note that the disciples went home. What a strange ending! This inner story reminds us that Mary Magdalene, Peter, and the Beloved Disciple are all persons of limited faith at this point. This is important for us to acknowledge because they are us. We, too, find ourselves to be of limited faith more often than we would like to admit.

In the second half of the outer story (John 20:11–18), we learn that Mary remained at the tomb weeping. She encounters someone whom she assumes to be the gardener, but when he calls her by name, she recognizes him to be the risen Christ. Sent off by Jesus with a message to deliver to the disciples, she is able to proclaim, "I have seen the Lord," (John 20:18), making her the first apostle of the resurrection. But seeing is believing in John's Gospel. Mary's journey to full faith is now complete!

"Then some of those with us went to the **tomb**
  and found things **just as** the women had **described**,
  but him they did not **see**."
And he said to them, "**Oh**, how **foolish** you are!
How slow of heart to believe **all** that the prophets **spoke**!
Was it not **necessary** that the Christ should **suffer** these things
  and **enter** into his **glory**?"
Then beginning with **Moses** and all the **prophets**,
  he **interpreted** to them what referred to him
  in all the **Scriptures**.
As they **approached** the village to which they were **going**,
  he gave the **impression** that he was going on **farther**.
But they **urged** him, "**Stay** with us,
  for it is **nearly evening** and the day is almost **over**."
So he went in to **stay** with them.
And it happened that, while he was **with** them at table,
  he took bread, said the **blessing**,
  broke it, and **gave** it to them.
With **that** their eyes were **opened** and they **recognized** him,
  but he **vanished** from their **sight**.
Then they **said** to each other,
  "Were not our **hearts** burning **within** us
  while he **spoke** to us on the **way** and opened the **Scriptures**
    to us?"
So they set out at once and **returned** to Jerusalem
  where they found **gathered together**
  the eleven and those with them who were **saying**,
  "The **Lord** has truly been **raised** and has **appeared** to Simon!"
Then the two recounted
  what had taken **place** on the **way**
  and how he was made **known** to them in the **breaking**
    of **bread**.

After spending time with Jesus (whom they still don't recognize), these disciples have a desire for further fellowship with him. They are beginning to sense something different than seeing something.

In the breaking of the bread—the ritual that repeats the Passover when they last were in Jesus' company—there is recognition. Ritual reveals presence.

Confirmation of their recognition, repeated in the phrase "the breaking of bread," the message of this reading.

AFTERNOON GOSPEL As Luke tells the story in this Gospel reading, this encounter with the risen Christ takes place on the same day that Jesus was raised from the dead. We learn that two of Jesus' disciples are deep in conversation as they make their way to Emmaus, which is approximately seven miles from Jerusalem. The narrator notes that they appear sad or downcast and, when the risen Jesus joins them on the road, they do not recognize him.

As Jesus engages these two disciples in conversation, he prompts them to tell the story of what happened to him in Jerusalem. Their response reads like a credal formula, but noticeably absent is any mention of the resurrection. This is at odds with what they reveal next, that news of the resurrection had been proclaimed to them earlier that day. Thus, the risen Jesus confronts them, calling them foolish and slow of heart and scolding them about not understanding the Scriptures that describe the necessity of Jesus' suffering and glorification as part of God's plan from the start.

Then, at their evening meal, Jesus blessed, broke, and shared the bread in much the same way he did at his last meal before his death. It is only in the breaking of the bread do the disciples complete their journey from unbelief to full faith. Certainly, this is cause for great joy. C.C.

SECOND SUNDAY OF EASTER (SUNDAY OF DIVINE MERCY)

LECTIONARY #43

READING I   Acts of the Apostles 2:42–47

A reading from the Acts of the Apostles

The tone of this reading, from early in Acts, is one of awe at the vocation of the apostles, as well as purpose, as the work of that vocation reveals itself.

They **devoted** them**selves**
  to the **teaching** of the **apostles** and to the **communal life**,
  to the **breaking** of **bread** and to the **prayers**.
Awe came upon **everyone**,
  and **many wonders** and **signs** were **done** through the **apostles**.
All who **believed** were **together** and had **all things** in **common**;
  they would **sell** their **property** and **possessions**
  and **divide** them among **all according** to each one's **need**.

Slight pause between "all" and "according."

Every day they **devoted** themselves
  to **meeting together** in the **temple area**
  and to **breaking bread** in their **homes**.
They ate their **meals** with **exultation** and **sincerity** of **heart**,
  praising **God** and enjoying **favor** with all the **people**.
And **every day** the **Lord** added to their **number those** who were
  being **saved**.

Slight pause between "number" and "those."

READING I In today's first reading, from the Acts of the Apostles, Luke describes his vision for the life of the early Church community, which he places immediately after Peter's speech to the Jews who had come to Jerusalem from many parts of the world for the feast of Pentecost and the subsequent baptism of some three thousand people that day (Acts 2:14–41). It will be followed by a story in which Peter heals a crippled man who used to beg at the Beautiful Gate of the Temple (Acts 3:1–10), perhaps intended as an example of the "wonders and signs [that] were done through the apostles."

The defining elements of this ideal Christian community are that they hold fast to the teachings of the apostles and to the common life of Christian fellowship and that they share in the breaking of the bread (i.e., Eucharist) and the prayers. The Greek word translated here as "communal life" is *koinonia*, meaning "partnership or communion." Although this is the only place it appears in Acts, Paul uses *koinonia* multiple times in his letters to refer to the notion of church. Further, we are told that they were together in one place and that they shared everything in common (Greek, *koinos*) and distributed things to those who had needs. What might it look like today for our parishes and families to be inspired by this life of common care, fellowship, and faith?

READING II Biblical scholars have wrestled with several questions related to the First Letter of Peter, including authorship and date of composition. Because the document contains hints that it was written after Peter's martyrdom, perhaps between AD 70 and 90, most bibli-

For meditation and context:

RESPONSORIAL PSALM   Psalm 118:2–4, 13–15, 22–24 (1)

R. Give thanks to the Lord for he is good, his love is everlasting.
or
R. Alleluia.

Let the house of Israel say,
   "His mercy endures forever."
Let the house of Aaron say,
   "His mercy endures forever."
Let those who fear the LORD say,
   "His mercy endures forever."

I was hard pressed and was falling,
   but the LORD helped me.
My strength and my courage is the LORD,
   and he has been my savior.
The joyful shout of victory
   in the tents of the just.

The stone which the builders rejected
   has become the cornerstone.
By the LORD has this been done;
   it is wonderful in our eyes.
This is the day the LORD has made;
   let us be glad and rejoice in it.

READING II   1 Peter 1:3–9

A reading from the first Letter of Saint Peter

Blessed be the **God** and **Father** of our **Lord Jesus Christ**,
   who in his **great mercy** gave us a **new birth** to a **living hope**
   through the **resurrection** of **Jesus Christ** from the **dead**,
   to an **inheritance** that is **imperishable**, **undefiled**,
      and **unfading**,
   kept in **heaven** for you
   who by the **power** of **God** are **safeguarded** through **faith**,
   to a **salvation** that is **ready** to be **revealed** in the **final time**.
In **this** you **rejoice**, although **now** for a **little while**
   you may have to **suffer** through **various trials**,
   so that the **genuineness** of your **faith**,
   more **precious** than **gold** that is **perishable** even though
      tested by **fire**,
   may **prove** to be for **praise**, **glory**, and **honor**
   at the **revelation** of **Jesus Christ**. »

Blessed = BLES-uhd
This reading begins a series of readings during Easter Time from the First Letter of St. Peter, the tone of which is thoughtful, joyful, hopeful, and gentle.

"Faith" is Peter's watchword. Give it a little added emphasis here and at the end of the reading.

cal scholars believe that it is a pseudonymous work intended to preserve Peter's memory and extend his influence into the next generation of Christians. Additionally, biblical scholars have entertained questions about whether this document is a letter or some other literary genre. It has an opening and closing like a letter, but instead of a thanksgiving, it has a blessing. The rest of the document reads more like a homily or an exhortation on baptism and Christian living.

Today's reading begins with the words "Blessed be the God," which is similar to other blessings that we find in Jewish prayers (e.g., Genesis 9:26; Psalms 66:20; 68:20; 72:18), and it goes on to describe how the recipients of this document are God's chosen ones. By the great mercy of God, they are begotten again to a life of hope in and through Jesus' resurrection. To what else are they born anew? To an imperishable inheritance that is reserved in the heaven for those who have been kept secure by God's power and the gift faith. And for what end? For the salvation that will be revealed at the end time. But we are not yet in the end time. The author tells his readers that they will have to endure suffering in order to test the genuineness of their faith. The imagery is that of the refiner's fire. One of the ways that Scripture explains suffering is to say that God is like the refiner who heats metal to separate gold from the impurities in order to create a more beautiful piece of handiwork (e.g., Malachi 3:2–4). Thus, suffering is not punishment, but rather it is purifying and educative in order to prepare the sufferer for a more beautiful reality, in this case, the salvation of their souls.

Although you have not **seen** him you **love** him;
    even though you do not **see** him **now** yet **believe** in him,
    you **rejoice** with an **indescribable** and **glorious** joy,
    as you **attain** the **goal** of your **faith**, the **salvation** of your **souls**.

GOSPEL   John 20:19–31

A reading from the holy Gospel according to John

On the **evening** of that first day of the **week**,
    when the **doors** were locked, where the **disciples** were,
    for **fear** of the **Jews**,
    Jesus came and stood in their **midst**
    and said to them, "**Peace** be with you."
When he had **said** this, he **showed** them his hands and his **side**.
The disciples **rejoiced** when they saw the **Lord**.
Jesus said to them again, "**Peace** be with you.
As the **Father** has sent me, so I send **you**."
And when he had **said** this, he **breathed** on them and **said**
    to them,
    "**Receive** the Holy Spirit.
Whose sins you **forgive** are **forgiven** them,
    and whose **sins** you **retain** are **retained**."

Thomas, called **Didymus**, one of the **Twelve**,
    was not **with** them when Jesus **came**.
So the other disciples said to him, "We have **seen** the Lord."
But he said to them,
    "Unless I see the **mark** of the nails in his **hands**
    and put my **finger** into the nailmarks
    and put my **hand** into his side, I will **not** believe."

A passage containing a great deal of inherent and relatable mystery. Thomas not only stands for the person who needs to see in order to believe; he is also a stand-in for the reluctant believer or for anyone struggling with belief, giving his recognition of Jesus and his expression of faith even greater resonance.

Jesus announces his presence with the word "peace" in this passage. The word is focal.

Repetition of "peace."

Thomas' expressions of doubt in this passage should be treated with care.

GOSPEL   Today's Gospel is taken from the post-resurrection story in the Gospel of John. Mary Magdalene, who encountered the risen Jesus in the garden tomb in Jerusalem, is sent to tell the disciples that Jesus has been raised from the dead. She does so, beginning with the words "I have seen the Lord" (John 20:18). In John's Gospel, seeing is closely connected to belief or full faith in Jesus.

As this reading opens, we find that Jesus' disciples are in hiding "for fear of the Jews." Since these disciples are also Jews, we should not interpret statements like this one in John's Gospel as encouraging fear or hatred of Jewish people. Instead, most Johannine scholars suggest that the author is writing out of a context in which Jewish Jesus followers, including the author of this Gospel, are being persecuted by their fellow Jews over the idea that Jesus was the long-awaited messiah. In most cases, "the Jews" is used interchangeably with references to the religious authorities in Jerusalem, so we can safely assume that they are the target of the author's ire.

The first part of this scene bears some similarities to Luke 24:36–40, in which the risen Jesus appears suddenly and displays his hands and feet to the disciples to allay their fears and show that he is truly alive. However, John's version of the story includes a greeting, "Peace be with you," along with a conferral of the Holy Spirit for the forgiveness of sin. The greeting of peace is a reminder of Jesus' words to the disciples during the farewell discourse, when he says "Peace I leave with you; my peace I give to you. . . . Do not let your hearts be troubled" (John 14:27). The conferral of the Holy Spirit here, when Jesus breathes upon the disciples, should bring

Now a **week later** his disciples were **again** inside
and **Thomas** was with them.
Jesus came, although the doors were **locked**,
and stood in their **midst** and said, "**Peace** be with you."
Then he said to Thomas, "Put your finger **here** and see my **hands**,
and bring your **hand** and put it into my **side**,
and do not be **unbelieving**, but **believe**."
Thomas answered and said to him, "My **Lord** and my **God**!"
Jesus said to him, "Have you come to **believe** because you have
seen me?
Blessed are those who **have not seen** and have **believed**."

Now, Jesus did many other signs in the presence of his **disciples**
that are not **written** in this **book**.
But these are **written** that you may come to **believe**
that **Jesus** is the **Christ**, the Son of **God**,
and that **through this belief** you may have **life** in his name.

Another repetition of "peace."

Jesus' words to Thomas are spoken with gentleness.

Thomas' recognition is joyful—its expression conveys the joy. No need to overemphasize it.

The conclusion of this Gospel reading speaks directly to the assembly, using the second person pronoun. Even though the word isn't rhythmically emphasized, it is thematically focal.

---

to mind the second creation story of Genesis where God creates a man, Adam, and breathes into him the breath of life (Genesis 2:7). The disciples are made "new" insofar as they have a new mission, which is to continue the work that God had given Jesus to do—to be the light that casts out darkness (John 8:12).

The second part of this scene is about the apostle Thomas. It is a reminder that not all of us come to faith in the same way and at the same time. The narrator of the story provides no new setting, suggesting that the disciples are still in hiding on this first day of the week, when Thomas arrives. When the disciples tell him, "We have seen the Lord," he adamantly refuses to believe. But when the risen Jesus appears again after eight days to respond to Thomas' demand to see the risen Jesus' wounds, Thomas makes a profound expression of faith: "My Lord and my God." The blessing directed toward those who have not seen but believe is intended for the Johannine community and by extension to us. Such is the mercy of God! C.C.

THIRD SUNDAY OF EASTER

LECTIONARY #46

READING I   Acts of the Apostles 2:14, 22–33

A reading from the Acts of the Apostles

This reading consists of a rich and spirited proclamation by Peter to his fellow apostles. It's filled with his enthusiasm for the meaning of the work they are beginning to do.

Nazorean = naz-uh-REE-uhn

Slight pause between "man" and "commended."

Slight pause between "worked" and "through."

Then **Peter** stood **up** with the **Eleven**,
  raised his **voice**, and **proclaimed**:
  "**You** who are **Jews**, indeed **all** of you **staying** in **Jerusalem**.
Let **this** be **known** to you, and **listen** to my **words**.
You who are **Israelites**, **hear** these **words**.
Jesus the **Nazorean** was a **man commended** to you by **God**
  with **mighty deeds**, **wonders**, and **signs**,
  which **God worked through** him in your **midst**,
    as **you** yourselves **know**.
This man, **delivered up** by the **set plan** and **foreknowledge** of **God**,
  you **killed**, using **lawless men** to **crucify** him.
But **God** raised him **up**, **releasing** him from the **throes** of **death**,
  because it was **impossible** for **him** to be **held** by it.
For **David says** of him:
  *I saw the **Lord** ever **before** me,*
    *with **him** at my **right hand** I shall **not be disturbed**.*
  ***Therefore** my **heart** has been **glad** and my **tongue** has **exulted**;*
    *my **flesh**, **too**, will **dwell** in **hope**,*
  *because you **will not abandon** my soul to the **netherworld**,*
    ***nor** will you **suffer** your **holy** one to see **corruption**.*
  *You have **made known** to me the **paths** of **life**;*
    *you will **fill** me with **joy** in your **presence**.*

In quoting from King David, Peter lets David speak for himself and, therefore, for us.

READING I Our first reading for this Third Sunday of Easter is part of a much longer speech attributed to Peter in the Acts of the Apostles. The setting is Jerusalem on the Jewish feast of Pentecost, also known as *Shavuot*, which occurs fifty days after the second day of Passover. Originally, this was a harvest festival, but by the first century, it included a commemoration of the giving of the Law on Sinai. Pentecost was one of three pilgrimage feasts in early Judaism, the other two being Passover and Tabernacles.

Luke, the author of the Acts of the Apostles, notes that the city was filled with "devout Jews from every nation" (Acts 2:5) and, when they heard the noise of the descent of the Holy Spirit upon Jesus' disciples, they all gathered round, wanting to know what was going on. The wind and fire from heaven certainly would have attracted attention, but even more confusing was the fact that members of the crowd were able to understand the disciples in their own tongue. But others in the crowd mocked them, saying that they were drunk.

Therefore, in the first part of his speech, Peter is presented as defending his companions, arguing that they are not drunk at this early hour of the day. Rather, he explains that their condition should be understood in terms of an oracle of the prophet Joel, which he quotes somewhat differently: "I will pour out a portion of my spirit in those days, and they shall prophesy. And I will work wonders in the heavens above and signs on the earth below. . . . And it shall be that everyone shall be saved who calls on the name of the Lord" (Acts 2:18–19, 21; see Joel 3:1–5).

Slight pause between "descendants" and "upon."

"My **brothers**, one can **confidently say** to you
    about the **patriarch David** that he **died** and was **buried**,
    and his **tomb** is in our **midst** to this **day**.
But since he was a **prophet** and **knew** that **God** had **sworn** an
    oath to him
    that he would set **one** of his **descendants upon** his **throne**,
    he **foresaw** and **spoke** of the **resurrection** of the **Christ**,
    that **neither** was he **abandoned** to the **netherworld**
    nor did his **flesh** see **corruption**.
God **raised** this **Jesus**;
    of **this** we are all **witnesses**.
Exalted at the **right hand** of **God**,
    he **received** the **promise** of the **Holy Spirit** from the **Father**
    and poured him **forth**, as you **see** and **hear**."

The reading concludes with an emphatic statement of belief and purpose.

For meditation and context:

RESPONSORIAL PSALM   Psalm 16:1–2, 5, 7–8, 9–10, 11 (11a)

R. Lord, you will show us the path of life.
or
R. Alleluia.

Keep me, O God, for in you I take refuge;
    I say to the LORD, "My Lord are you."
O LORD, my allotted portion and my cup,
    you it is who hold fast my lot.

I bless the LORD who counsels me;
    even in the night my heart exhorts me.
I set the LORD ever before me;
    with him at my right hand I shall not
    be disturbed.

Therefore my heart is glad and my
    soul rejoices,
    my body, too, abides in confidence;
because you will not abandon my soul
    to the netherworld,
    nor will you suffer your faithful one to
    undergo corruption.

You will show me the path to life,
    abounding joy in your presence,
    the delights at your right hand forever.

But today's reading focuses on the second part of Peter's speech. It begins with one of several kerygmatic statements— that is, brief initial proclamations of the good news about Jesus Christ, that are found throughout Acts of the Apostles (e.g., Acts 3:12–26; 4:8–12; 5:29–32; 10:34–43; 13:16–41). They often begin with a statement about Jesus' words and deeds followed by a proclamation of his death and resurrection. The kerygmatic statements in Acts of the Apostles are typically directed toward Jewish audiences, and they often include an exhortation to forgiveness of

sin. They have a somewhat accusatory tone, but the primary thing to notice is that the events described in this kerygmatic statement amount to a declaration that everything is under the power of God and in keeping with God's plan of salvation.

In the closing sections of this speech, Luke focuses on David, because he believed him to be the author of the Psalms and of this psalm in particular. However, today we would attribute a much more complex history of composition to the Psalms. Luke identifies David as a prophet who spoke in Jesus' name, when he com-

posed Psalm 16:8–10, and he sees these verses as testimony to Jesus' resurrection, in fulfillment of a promise made to David that God would make one of his descendants the king of the Jewish people to reign forever (see 2 Samuel 7:12–17). Thus, Peter also quotes Psalm 110:1 to say that Jesus, who was crucified, is this messiah-king, who now sits exalted on God's throne.

READING II   Our second reading is taken from the First Letter of Peter, which was most likely not written by Peter but by a pseudonymous author in

READING II   1 Peter 1:17–21

A reading from the first Letter of Saint Peter

Beloved:
If you **invoke** as **Father him** who judges **impartially**
    according to e**ach one's works**,
    conduct yourselves with **reverence** during the **time**
        of your **sojourning**,
    realizing that you were **ransomed** from your **futile conduct**,
    handed **on** by your **ancestors**,
    not with **perishable things** like **silver** or **gold**
    but with the **precious blood** of **Christ**
    as of a **spotless unblemished lamb**.

He was **known** before the **foundation** of the **world**
    but **revealed** in the **final time** for **you**,
    who **through** him believe in **God**
    who **raised** him from the **dead** and **gave** him **glory**,
    so that your **faith** and **hope** are in **God**.

Slight pause between "Father" and "him."

sojourning = SOH-jern-ing

"Reverence": This is the focal word in this passage. Reverence is foremost a form of care; Peter wants to endow the recipients of his letter with care.

Note the rhythm that concludes this reading, where a stressed element near the beginning of the phrase leads to stressed elements toward the end of the phrase.

TO KEEP IN MIND
Pause to break up separate thoughts, set apart significant statements, or indicate major shifts. Never pause in the middle of a thought. Your primary guide for pauses is punctuation.

AD 79–90, who wanted to extend Peter's memory and his teachings to future generations. Although we call this document a letter, it reads more like a homily on baptism and Christian living or as an exhortation to holiness.

This reading is preceded by statements about how believing Christians enjoy a new life that is lived in the hope of Christ's resurrection and how God protects them, sustaining them in faith for the time of their salvation. The author of this letter goes on to speak directly to his audience, acknowledging that they will suffer as their faith is tested, but will find joy in knowing Christ as their savior.

Now, at the beginning of our reading, we are reminded of the intimate relationship that we have as children of our God, who is called Father in the best and purest sense of the word. This is a God who judges justly and with mercy, and therefore is deserving of our reverence. The Greek word *phobos*, translated here as "reverence," can also mean "fear or dread." But "fear of God" is not a concept that resonates well with modern readers. Instead, "awe" might be a better word to use.

Reread that part of this reading with "awe of God" replacing "reverence." We are to act out of awe for our God, who is so intimately tied to our lives as to treat us as his own dear children.

To expand on the notion of the awe or reverence that is due to God, the author of 1 Peter wants us to know that we are ransomed by the "precious blood of Christ" from our old way of life that goes back generations. A ransom is something that is paid or agreed upon for the release of someone living in captivity. The Greek word *timios*, translated here as "precious," also

GOSPEL   Luke 24:13–35

A reading from the holy Gospel according to Luke

That very day, the first **day** of the week,
   two of Jesus' **disciples** were going
   to a **village** seven miles from Jerusalem called **Emmaus**,
   and they were **conversing** about all the things that
      had occurred.
And it **happened** that while they were **conversing** and debating,
   Jesus **himself** drew **near** and walked **with** them,
   but their **eyes** were prevented from **recognizing** him.
He asked them,
   "What are you **discussing** as you walk **along**?"
They **stopped**, looking downcast.
One of them, named **Cleopas**, said to him in **reply**,
   "Are you the **only visitor** to Jerusalem
   who does not **know** of the things
   that have taken **place there** in these days?"
And he **replied** to them, "What **sort** of things?"
They said to him,
   "The **things** that happened to **Jesus** the Nazarene,
   who was a **prophet** mighty in **deed** and **word**
   before **God** and all the **people**,
   how our **chief priests** and rulers both **handed** him **over**
   to a **sentence** of **death** and **crucified** him.
But we were **hoping** that he would be the **one** to redeem Israel;
   and **besides** all this,
   it is now the **third day** since this took **place**.
Some women from our group, however, have **astounded** us:
   they were at the tomb **early** in the morning
   and did not find his **body**;
   they came **back** and reported
   that they had **indeed seen** a vision of angels
   who **announced** that he was **alive**. »

Side notes:

A reading with great drama built into it. You can easily imagine it being filmed. The focus on the reading is recognition, specifically the time it takes Jesus' two disciples to recognize that he has been raised from the dead. The build-up of the narrative intensifies the excitement and joy of their recognition.

This phrase introduces the motif of recognition that guides the passage. Recognition is connected initially to seeing.

It's interesting that only one of these two disciples are named.

Note that "they" are speaking, both of them, even though it's one unified speech. The purpose of this description of Jesus' deeds and words is to build toward recognition.

Note "a vision of angels." Recognition and seeing are still urgently connected.

means "held in honor, esteemed, or especially dear." Jesus' blood is especially dear, because it is the blood of the Passover lamb, poured out for our salvation. Coupled with the ancient belief that blood was the life-force of all living beings, it is no small matter that it is given up for us. Moreover, this was part of God's plan from the beginning of time so that our "faith and hope are in God." We stand in awe!

GOSPEL This Gospel reading is the story of the disciples on the road to Emmaus. As Luke tells the story, this encounter with the risen Christ takes place on the same day that Jesus was raised from the dead. We learn that two of Jesus' disciples are deep in conversation as they make their way to Emmaus, which is approximately seven miles from Jerusalem. The narrator notes that they appear sad or downcast and, when the risen Jesus joins them on the road, they do not recognize him.

As Jesus engages these two disciples in conversation, he prompts them to tell the story of what happened to him in Jerusalem. Their response reads like a credal formula, but noticeably absent is any mention of the resurrection. This is at odds with what they reveal next, that news of the resurrection had been proclaimed to them earlier that day. Thus, the risen Jesus confronts them, calling them foolish and slow of heart and scolding them about not understanding the Scriptures that describe the necessity of Jesus' suffering and glorification. We do not know what texts Luke had in mind, but more important is the message that Jesus' death and resurrection were all part of God's plan from the start.

The last scene in this story explains how and why the eyes and hearts of these

After spending time with Jesus (whom they still don't recognize), these disciples have a desire for further fellowship with him. They are beginning to sense something different than seeing something.

In the breaking of the bread—the ritual that repeats the Passover when they last were in Jesus' company—there is recognition. Ritual reveals presence.

Confirmation of their recognition, repeated in the phrase "the breaking of bread," the message of this reading.

"Then some of those with us went to the **tomb**
    and found things **just as** the women had **described**,
    but him they did not **see**."
And he said to them, "**Oh**, how **foolish** you are!
How slow of heart to believe **all** that the prophets **spoke**!
Was it not **necessary** that the Christ should **suffer** these things
    and **enter** into his **glory**?"
Then beginning with **Moses** and all the **prophets**,
    he **interpreted** to them what referred to him
    in all the **Scriptures**.
As they **approached** the village to which they were **going**,
    he gave the **impression** that he was going on **farther**.
But they **urged** him, "**Stay** with us,
    for it is **nearly evening** and the day is almost **over**."
So he went in to **stay** with them.
And it happened that, while he was **with** them at table,
    he took bread, said the **blessing**,
    broke it, and **gave** it to them.
With **that** their eyes were **opened** and they **recognized** him,
    but he **vanished** from their **sight**.
Then they **said** to each other,
    "Were not our **hearts** burning **within** us
    while he **spoke** to us on the **way** and opened the **Scriptures**
        to us?"
So they set out at once and **returned** to Jerusalem
    where they found **gathered together**
    the eleven and those with them who were **saying**,
    "The **Lord** has truly been **raised** and has **appeared** to Simon!"
Then the two recounted
    what had taken **place** on the **way**
    and how he was made **known** to them in the **breaking**
        of **bread**.

two disciples were finally opened. Having arrived at Emmaus, they invite Jesus to stay with them. At their evening meal, Jesus blessed, broke and shared the bread in much the same way he did at his last meal before his death. They remembered and were able to recognize Jesus for who he was. They also remembered how they felt when he was teaching them on their journey and how their hearts were set afire. Finally then, in the breaking of the bread, they complete their journey from unbelief to full faith. Certainly, this is cause for great joy. C.C.

FOURTH SUNDAY OF EASTER

LECTIONARY #49

READING I   Acts of the Apostles 2:14a, 36–41

A reading from the Acts of the Apostles

Then **Peter** stood **up** with the **Eleven**,
    raised his **voice**, and **proclaimed**:
"Let the **whole house** of **Israel** know for **certain**
    that **God** has made both **Lord** and **Christ**,
    this **Jesus** whom you **crucified**."

Now when they **heard** this, they were **cut** to the **heart**,
    and they asked **Peter** and the other **apostles**,
    "**What** are we to **do**, my **brothers**?"
Peter **said** to them,
    "**Repent** and be **baptized**, **every one** of you,
    in the **name** of Jesus **Christ** for the **forgiveness** of your **sins**;
    and you will **receive** the **gift** of the **Holy Spirit**.
For the **promise** is **made** to **you** and to your **children**
    and to **all those far off**,
    whomever the **Lord** our **God** will **call**."
He **testified** with **many other arguments**, and was **exhorting** them,
    "**Save** yourselves from this **corrupt generation**."
Those who **accepted** his **message** were **baptized**,
    and about **three thousand persons** were **added** that **day**.

There is an urgent tone to this reading, with the sense especially of getting busy to fulfill the work of the Lord.

This statement expresses Peter's focus: repentance and baptism.

Slight pause between "those" and "far."

There's an emphasis here on the numbers, suggesting a sense of the apostles' initial success.

READING I Peter's speech takes place in the context of the Jewish feast of Pentecost. Acts reports that "devout Jews from every nation under heaven staying in Jerusalem" (2:5) had assembled to celebrate this agricultural feast of the firstfruits. In order to underscore the fact that Peter's speech is in complete continuity with historic roots in Judaism, Acts notes that the eleven apostles were with Peter, thereby fully representing the twelve tribes of Israel. Peter addresses "the whole house of Israel," upon whom he places the guilt of Jesus'

crucifixion. In the context of this speech, Peter uses this accusation to point to the sovereignty of God and a call to conversion. To underscore the seriousness of the matter, Peter emphasizes that God has transformed this perceived criminal into "both Lord and Christ."

The reading suggests that the crowd is deeply wounded by Peter's accusation and questions how they could possibly repent for such a sin. Peter's solution is baptism. Some in the crowd would surely recall the baptism of John as they heard Peter's summons to "repent and be baptized." However,

unlike the baptism of John, this is not a baptism undertaken in preparation for the eschatological future, this is a baptism that imparts the gift of the Holy Spirit.

Peter concludes his exhortation with the assurance that the call to conversion goes out not only to the Jewish community but to the Gentiles (those who are "far off"). Unlike the Jewish understanding of the covenant, in which God carves out a special people destined for salvation, this message is given to whomever God wishes. Thus, God is not limited in whom he can elect for salvation. Acts suggests the far-

For meditation and context:

RESPONSORIAL PSALM   Psalm 23:1–3a, 3b–4, 5, 6 (1)

R. The Lord is my shepherd; there is nothing I shall want.
or
R. Alleluia.

The LORD is my shepherd; I shall not want.
  In verdant pastures he gives me repose;
beside restful waters he leads me;
  he refreshes my soul.

He guides me in right paths
  for his name's sake.
Even though I walk in the dark valley
  I fear no evil; for you are at my side,
with your rod and your staff
  that give me courage.

You spread the table before me
  in the sight of my foes;
you anoint my head with oil;
  my cup overflows.

Only goodness and kindness follow me
  all the days of my life;
and I shall dwell in the house of the LORD
  for years to come.

READING II   1 Peter 2:20b–25

A reading from the first Letter of Saint Peter

Peter is urging patience to this letter's recipients; imagine you are offering the same advice to the assembly.

Beloved:
If you are **patient** when you **suffer** for **doing** what is **good**,
  this is a **grace** before **God**.
For to **this** you have been **called**,
  because **Christ also suffered** for you,
  leaving you an **example** that you should **follow** in his **footsteps**.
*He **committed** no **sin**, and no **deceit** was **found** in his **mouth**.*

At "When," Peter shifts directly into the lesson he wants to give, about patience in the face of insult.

Even emphasis on "He himself bore."

When he was **insulted**, he **returned** no **insult**;
  when he **suffered**, he did not **threaten**;
  instead, he **handed** himself **over** to the **one** who judges **justly**.
He himself bore our **sins** in his **body** upon the **cross**,
  so that, **free** from **sin**, we might **live** for **righteousness**.
By his **wounds** you have been **healed**.
For you had **gone astray** like **sheep**,
  but you have **now returned** to the **shepherd** and **guardian**
    of your **souls**.

The reading concludes with the image of Jesus as shepherd, which will reappear immediately in the reading from the Gospel of John. Allow the words "sheep," "shepherd," and "guardian" to resonate.

---

reaching power of God's call when it reports that around three thousand people believed Peter's message and were baptized.

READING II — This reading from this epistle attributed to St. Peter is thought to be part of an early Christian hymn based on the fifty-third chapter of Isaiah (Isaiah 53:4–12) that describes the lot of a "suffering servant" sent by God to heal the world. The author names Christ as this servant, who undergoes suffering without returning any sort of retribution. Christ is depicted here as the perfect model of suf-

fering. The author's point is to remind Christians that while Christ's suffering was undertaken in their name, they must be willing to patiently endure similar suffering in their present-day reality. The ability to suffer along with Christ is both a grace and something Christians are called to by God.

What are the practical ways in which a Christian must patiently endure suffering? The author provides several answers: commit no sin, speak no words of deception, offer no insult when insulted, and make no threat when threatened. The proper response to all things that will test the

patience of a Christian is to surrender the self just as Christ freely gave himself over to "the one who judges justly." This just judge is his own Father, and thus, suffering is to be seen as an offering of love.

Finally, the reading ends with a call to "live for righteousness," which is made possible because Christians have been healed by Christ's suffering. The suffering servant is now likened to a shepherd who is faithful in watching over his flock. The author accuses his readers of having once wandered from the flock but have now returned to the fold. The Greek word here

GOSPEL   John 10:1–10

A reading from the holy Gospel according to John

Jesus said:
"**Amen**, **amen**, **I say** to **you**,
  whoever does not **enter** a **sheepfold** through the **gate**
  but **climbs over elsewhere** is a **thief** and a **robber**.
But whoever **enters** through the **gate** is the **shepherd** of the **sheep**.
The **gatekeeper opens** it for him, and the **sheep hear** his **voice**,
  as the **shepherd** calls his **own sheep** by **name** and **leads**
    them **out**.
When he has **driven out all** his **own**,
  he walks **ahead** of them, and the **sheep follow** him,
  because they **recognize** his **voice**.
But they w**ill not follow** a **stranger**;
  they will run **away** from him,
  because they **do not recognize** the **voice** of **strangers**."
Although **Jesus** used this **figure** of **speech**,
  the **Pharisees** did not **realize** what he was **trying** to **tell** them.

So **Jesus** said **again**, "**Amen**, **amen**, I **say** to you,
  I am the **gate** for the **sheep**.
All who came **before** me are **thieves** and **robbers**,
  but the **sheep** did not **listen** to them.
I am the **gate**.
Whoever enters through **me** will be **saved**,
  and will come **in** and go **out** and find **pasture**.
A **thief** comes only to **steal** and **slaughter** and **destroy**;
  I came so that they might have **life** and have it
    more **abundantly**."

An allegorical reading from John's Gospel with the potent, forceful quality repeated in its two parts. In the first part, John presents his allegory. In the second part, John explains the allegory. Don't let the repetition trip you up. John is extending his example with his explanation.
Slight pause between "sheep" and "hear."

Slight pause between "out" and "all."

Here begins the explanation of the allegory.

Emphasis on "I."

---

for "guardian" is *episkopos*, the word used for "bishop." Thus, this early Christian hymn can be understood to be both a profession of belonging both to Christ and to the authority of the Church.

GOSPEL The beginning of the tenth chapter of John introduces us to the theme of the "Good Shepherd." Here Jesus employs two different shepherding images to illustrate his care for all those who follow him. The first reference to a shepherd emphasizes the legitimacy of his authority. The legitimate shepherd is the one whose voice is known by the sheep and who in turn knows each of the sheep by name. This shepherd does not lead them astray or take advantage of them by stealing. Instead, this shepherd has a genuine relationship of trust with his sheep. The Pharisees fail to recognize that Jesus is likening them to these false shepherds.

The second image Jesus uses at the outset of the "Good Shepherd" discourse is that of a "gate." He refers to himself as a gate that protects the sheep; it will keep the "thieves and robbers" (the false shepherds) away from the sheep. This reference also applies to salvation, as those who pass through the gate, namely those who come to believe in Jesus and hear his voice, will have access to the Father. False shepherds seek to destroy the sheep (here we can read "Church"), whereas Jesus is the "Good Shepherd" who wishes to give life in abundance. Jesus is the one reliable "gate" that leads to God, and thus he is the way to true salvation. S.W.

FIFTH SUNDAY OF EASTER

LECTIONARY #52

READING I   Acts of the Apostles 6:1–7

A reading from the Acts of the Apostles

As the **number** of **disciples continued** to **grow**,
    the **Hellenists complained** against the **Hebrews**
    because their **widows**
    were being **neglected** in the **daily distribution**.
So the **Twelve** called **together** the **community** of the **disciples**
        and **said**,
    "It **is not right** for us to **neglect** the **word** of **God** to **serve**
        at **table**.
Brothers, **select** from **among** you s**even reputable men**,
    filled with the **Spirit** and **wisdom**,
    whom we shall **appoint** to this **task**,
    whereas **we** shall **devote ourselves** to **prayer**
    and to the **ministry** of the **word**."
The **proposal** was **acceptable** to the **whole community**,
    so they chose **Stephen**, a man **filled** with **faith** and the
        Holy Spirit,
    also **Philip**, **Prochorus**, **Nicanor**, **Timon**, **Parmenas**,
    and **Nicholas** of **Antioch**, a **convert** to **Judaism**.
They **presented** these **men** to the **apostles**
    who **prayed** and laid **hands** on them.

Hellenists = HEL-uh-nists

This reading hinges on a dispute between the Hellenists and the Hebrews. The Hellenists were presumably Greek-speaking Jewish Christians, where the Hebrews were Aramaic-speaking Jewish Christians. The Hellenists are feeling short-changed at the communal meals.

Emphasis on "we." The apostles want to give over management of meals to community members so that that can devote themselves to the ministry of the word.

Prochorus = PRAH-kuh-ruhs
Nicanor = nī-KAY-nuhr
Timon = Tī-muhn
Parmenas = PAHR-muh-nuhs
Antioch = AN-tee-ahk

Names. No need to overdo it but add some reverence to your voice as you speak the names of these early members of the Church.

READING I   Acts of the Apostles provides the account of the calling and the "ordaining" of the first deacons in the Church. Revealed in this short passage is an infant Church that is struggling with growing pains. Acts wishes to portray the early Church as striving to persevere in unity in community life, in worship, and in charitable outreach (see Acts 2:42–47). However, here we see unrest in the community as some members are complaining that their needs are being ignored while others are receiving special treatment. In particular, it is the Greek-speaking members of the community who are arguing that their widows are being neglected "in the daily distribution." The growing pains experienced here are those of growing diversity within the Church; the Hellenists represent both a different culture and a different language. This accusation of bias serves as a bridge between the early Church centered in Jerusalem and the expansion of the Church into missionary territory.

It is significant to note that the seven men chosen for the task of diaconal service all have Greek names. Because they are Hellenists, they remain subordinate to the apostles, who maintain the tradition of handing a portion of their authority through prayer and the laying on of hands. Acts is very clear to list the responsibilities of the apostles: theirs is the ministry of prayer and preaching the Word. The specific role of the seven men chosen for service is not specified, but we may assume that it is attending to the needs of those who are often overlooked, namely the widows whom God promised to sustain (see Jeremiah 49:11). Luke tells us that this decision to expand apostolic leadership had great success, as the apostles were able to

The reading concludes on a note of the success of the apostles' intervention.

The **word** of **God continued** to **spread**,
and the **number** of the **disciples** in **Jerusalem increased greatly;**
even a **large group** of **priests** were becoming **obedient**
to the **faith**.

For meditation and context:

RESPONSORIAL PSALM   Psalm 33:1–2, 4–5, 18–19 (22)

R. **Lord, let your mercy be on us, as we place our trust in you.**
or
R. **Alleluia.**

Exult, you just, in the LORD;
    praise from the upright is fitting.
Give thanks to the LORD on the harp;
    with the ten-stringed lyre chant
        his praises.

Upright is the word of the LORD,
    and all his works are trustworthy.
He loves justice and right;
    of the kindness of the LORD the earth
        is full.

See, the eyes of the LORD are upon those who
        fear him,
    upon those who hope for his kindness,
to deliver them from death
    and preserve them in spite of famine.

READING II   1 Peter 2:4–9

A reading from the first Letter of Saint Peter

This section of Peter's letter is built on the unusually powerful metaphor of "living stone." Something both foundational and animated.

Peter uses Scripture to draw out his metaphor.

Zion = Zī-uhn or Zī-ahn

Beloved:
Come to him, a **living stone**, **rejected** by human **beings**
    but **chosen** and **precious** in the **sight** of **God**,
    and, like **living stones**,
    let **yourselves** be **built** into a **spiritual house**
    to be a **holy priesthood** to offer **spiritual sacrifices**
    acceptable to **God** through **Jesus Christ**.
For it **says** in **Scripture**:
    Behold, I am **laying** a **stone** in **Zion**,
    a **cornerstone**, **chosen** and **precious**,
    and **whoever believes** in it shall **not** be put to **shame**. ❯❯

---

spread the Word of God, and the Church continued to grow in numbers. This internal conflict allows Luke to show the need to broaden various ministries as the Church continues to grow and mature.

READING II   The First Letter of St. Peter addresses a group of persecuted Christians in Asia Minor around the time of Nero and the burning of the city of Rome in AD 64. As one of the seven "catholic epistles," or universal letters, it employs the authorship of Peter as a means of encouraging Christians to persevere in the

hope of salvation through Christ, despite harsh rejection from the world.

Vivid language is used in this passage to express both the strength of individual and communal faith of those who come to Christ. Christians are portrayed here as stones that are being "built up into a spiritual house" with Christ as the foundation stone. Even though he has been rejected by humans, God has chosen him. With this "living stone," the temple of the Church surely cannot be destroyed. Referring to Isaiah 28:16, the author describes the cor-

nerstone of the church, which is Christ, as "chosen and precious."

Therefore, faith in Christ is seen as a valuable gift for those who believe. For people without faith, it makes sense that they choose to reject the gift, since they do not have the means of perceiving its value. Again, employing the writing of the prophet Isaiah, this rejected stone becomes a problem for his own people; Christ is called "a stone that will make people stumble" for those who do not believe (see Isaiah 8:14). The failure to believe is blamed on the people's disobedience.

Peter is quoting here from Psalm 118:22—even though it is very familiar, proclaim it afresh.

Therefore, its **value** is for **you** who have **faith**, but for **those**
> **without** faith:
> *The **stone** that the **builders rejected***
> *has **become** the **cornerstone**,*
and
> *a **stone** that will make **people stumble**,*
> *and a **rock** that will **make** them **fall**.*
They **stumble** by **disobeying** the **word**, as is their **destiny**.

The tone of the reading's conclusion is rousing.

You are "a **chosen race**, a **royal priesthood**,
> a **holy nation**, a **people** of his **own**,
> so that you may **announce** the **praises**" of him
> who **called** you out of **darkness** into his **wonderful light**.

GOSPEL   John 14:1–12

A reading from the holy Gospel according to John

A declarative tone pervades this reading. When Jesus speaks, he is doing so forcefully.

Jesus said to his **disciples**:
> "**Do not** let your **hearts** be **troubled**.
You have **faith** in **God**; have **faith also** in **me**.
In my **Father's house** there are **many dwelling** places.
If there were **not**,
> would I have **told** you that I am **going** to **prepare** a **place**
> for you?
And if **I go** and **prepare** a **place** for you,
> I will **come back again** and **take** you to **myself**,
> so that **where I am you also** may **be**.
Where I am **going** you know the **way**."

Slight pause between "am" and "you."

Thomas said to him,
> "**Master**, we **do not know** where you are **going**;
> **how** can we know the **way**?"
Jesus **said** to him, "I am the **way** and the **truth** and the **life**.
No one comes to the **Father except** through **me**.
If you **know** me, then you will **also know** my **Father**.

Familiar though this declaration is, proclaim it as though it is being said for the first time.

Slight pause between "Father" and "except."

Finally, the passage concludes with a description of the value of being built up together as living stones. Christians enjoy chosen status because of their faith in Christ. However, just as in the Book of Exodus which the author of 1 Peter references, when God chose the Israelites as "a people of his own," calling them "a royal priesthood, a holy nation" (see Exodus 19:6), this designation comes with responsibility. Even in persecution, Christians are not meant to hide away in secret, but rather, they must proclaim God's praises. Coming to Christ involves rejecting the darkness of ignorance and sin and basking in "his wonderful light."

GOSPEL   Chapter 14 of the Gospel of John is part of Jesus' farewell discourse to his disciples at the Last Supper. John depicts Jesus as fully aware of his disciples' fragile faith, as they will struggle to know what direction to take when he is no longer with them to guide them. As Jesus commands his disciples to have no fear, he alludes to his death and resurrection and even of his return. By the time John writes his Gospel, the understanding of the parousia had changed significantly from an ushering in of a royal and mighty power to the belief that Christ would return to gather together all who had believed in him in this life. For this reason, Jesus speaks of preparing "many dwelling places" ahead of time for all who wait expectantly for his return.

In response to this talk about Jesus' leave-taking, Thomas utters the basic concern of all the disciples: "we do not know where you are going." The answer that Jesus gives is that he is "the way and the truth and the life." In the Acts of the Apostles,

The pervasive tone of the conclusion of this Gospel reading is mysterious. But don't discount Jesus' slight irritation at Philip. You can color your proclamation in very slight irritation.

From **now on** you **do know** him and have **seen** him."
Philip **said** to him,
   "**Master**, show us the **Father**, and that will be **enough** for us."
Jesus **said** to him, "Have I been **with** you for so **long** a **time**
   and you **still** do not **know** me, Philip?
Whoever has **seen** me has **seen** the **Father**.
How can you **say**, '**Show** us the **Father**'?
Do you not **believe** that **I** am in the **Father** and the **Father**
   is in **me**?
The **words** that I **speak** to you I do not **speak** on my **own**.
The **Father** who **dwells** in me is **doing** his **works**.
Believe me that I am in the **Father** and the **Father** is in **me**,
   or **else**, **believe** because of the **works themselves**.
Amen, **amen**, I **say** to you,
   whoever **believes** in me will do the **works** that I **do**,
   and will do **greater ones** than **these**,
   because I am **going** to the **Father**."

Christian life is called "the way" (Acts 9:2). The words "truth" and "life" are means of explaining the way. Very simply, in the Gospel of John having faith is the source of truth and life. Writing at a time when many Christians were beginning to leave the faith because Jesus had not yet returned, Jesus' self-description here is meant to bolster the confidence of Christians to remain in the faith.

Jesus contends that adherence to him is the only way that one finds access to God. And yet this continues to be a concern for his disciples; they will not be satisfied until they have "seen" God. In addressing this issue put on the lips of Phillip, Jesus chastises his followers for not being able to see and understand the intimate connection between himself and his Father. This intimacy is prevalent throughout John's Gospel, beginning with the prologue in which the author's high Christology describes Jesus as the Word who was with God before the world began (see John 1:1). For readers of John's Gospel, who are unable to see Jesus in the flesh, trusting in their faith and accomplishing great works in his name ought to be signs enough that the Son and the Father are one. Those who see with the eyes of faith see the way, the truth, and the life; this sight is far greater than anything perceived by human sight alone. S.W.

SIXTH SUNDAY OF EASTER

LECTIONARY #55

READING I   Acts of the Apostles 8:5–8, 14–17

A reading from the Acts of the Apostles

Philip went **down** to the **city** of **Samaria**
    and **proclaimed** the **Christ** to them.
With **one accord**, the **crowds** paid **attention** to what was **said**
        by **Philip**
    when they **heard** it and saw the **signs** he was **doing**.
For **unclean spirits**, crying **out** in a **loud voice**,
    came out of **many possessed people**,
    and **many paralyzed** or **crippled people** were **cured**.
There was **great joy** in that **city**.

Now when the **apostles** in **Jerusalem**
    heard that **Samaria** had **accepted** the **word** of **God**,
    they sent them **Peter** and **John**,
    who went **down** and **prayed** for them,
    that they might **receive** the **Holy Spirit**,
    for it had **not yet fallen** upon **any** of them;
    they had **only** been **baptized** in the **name** of the **Lord Jesus**.
Then they **laid hands** on them
    and they **received** the **Holy Spirit**.

Samaria = suh-MAYR-ee-uh
This reading describes what it was like for the Holy Spirit to work through the early apostles of the Church, in this case, Philip, who is the focal figure of this reading.

Emphasis on "unclean spirits." Their negative energy is exorcised by Philip's work.

The conclusion of this reading emphasizes the work of the Holy Spirit. Emphasis here and at the end of the reading on "Holy Spirit."

READING I In hearing of the success of Philip's preaching of the Gospel in the land of Samaria, we note a shift in the long-standing rift between the Samaritans and the Jews. We hear in Luke's Gospel of Jesus' healing of the ten lepers with one being a Samaritan (Luke 17:11–19) and the telling of the parable of the Good Samaritan (Luke 10:25–37). These accounts, and the historical witness of the time, inform us about the discord between the Jews and the Samaritans. Yet here in the Acts of the Apostles we see Philip going to Samaria to preach to them about Christ.

Philip was one of the seven chosen to assist the twelve apostles in their ministry after the dispute broke out between the Hebrews and the Hellenists (Acts 6:1–7). Additionally, after the martyrdom of Stephen (who was one of the seven) and the persecution of the Church in Jerusalem, Philip and the other men were scattered but continued to preach the Good News (Acts 7:54—8:1; 8:1–4).

Arriving at the passage we hear in today's first reading, Philip goes to Samaria and God makes good use of these circumstances in which he finds himself. The crowds were mesmerized by what Philip was both saying and doing. They heard the Gospel and they were moved by the signs Philip performed, such as freeing people who were possessed and curing those who were paralyzed. The author of Acts notes that "there was great joy in that city."

The discovery of Philip's success by the apostles in Jerusalem affirms the growth of the Church even more. They send Peter and John to impart the gift of the Holy Spirit to those newly baptized. While these people had been baptized in the Lord's name, Acts suggests that apos-

For meditation and context:

RESPONSORIAL PSALM   Psalm 66:1–3, 4–5, 6–7, 16, 20 (1)

R. Let all the earth cry out to God with joy.
or
R. Alleluia.

Shout joyfully to God, all the earth,
  sing praise to the glory of his name;
  proclaim his glorious praise.
Say to God, "How tremendous are
    your deeds!"

"Let all on earth worship and sing praise
    to you,
  sing praise to your name!"
Come and see the works of God,
  his tremendous deeds among the children
    of Adam.

He has changed the sea into dry land;
  through the river they passed on foot;
  therefore let us rejoice in him.
He rules by his might forever.

Hear now, all you who fear God,
  while I declare
  what he has done for me.
Blessed be God who refused me not
  my prayer or his kindness!

READING II   1 Peter 3:15–18

A reading from the first Letter of Saint Peter

Beloved:
Sanctify Christ as **Lord** in your **hearts**.
Always be **ready** to give an **explanation**
    to **anyone** who **asks** you for a **reason** for your **hope**,
    but **do** it with **gentleness** and **reverence**,
    keeping your **conscience clear**,
    so that, when you are **maligned**,
    those who **defame** your **good conduct** in **Christ**
    may **themselves** be put to **shame**.
For it is **better** to **suffer** for doing **good**,
    if **that** be the **will** of **God**, than for **doing evil**.

For **Christ also suffered** for **sins** once,
    the **righteous** for the **sake** of the **unrighteous**,
    that he might **lead** you to **God**.
Put to **death** in the **flesh**,
    he was brought to **life** in the **Spirit**.

This selection from Peter's letter is in the imperative voice. He is deliberately offering advice to the recipients of this letter.

Note the power here of using Christ as an example for suffering. Your assembly is meant to identify emphatically and empathetically with Jesus.

---

tolic authority is necessary for the completion of baptism through the conferral of the Holy Spirit. Receiving the giving of the Holy Spirit from the apostles underscores the importance of the Spirit's role in unifying the universal church. For Luke, the authority of the apostles and the unity of the Church are inseparable.

READING II | The first of two epistles attributed to St. Peter is addressed to the Christians of several Roman provinces in Asia Minor. A primary purpose of the letter is to encourage Christians to

maintain their belief and continue acting in a way that reflects their faith. The short excerpt that we read today is part of the author's encouragement to endure persecution for the sake of Christ. It opens with the command "Sanctify Christ as Lord in your hearts." This provides a solid foundation upon which Christians can make a defense of their faith in light of persecution. A Christian's response to the challenge of a nonbeliever must be the profession of Christ's name in a gentle and reverent manner.

The author continues by suggesting that a Christian's "good conduct" will not only serve to reveal loyalty to Christ, but it will eventually "shame" the one who scoffs at it. Just as the innocence of Christ led him to suffer for the guilty, so too are those who live virtuously in Christ to consider themselves as suffering for the sake of the unrighteous. In the same way that suffering led to Christ's glorification, so will persecuted Christians be raised up in the power of the Spirit. By putting to death the things "in the flesh" (things that are the opposite of gentleness, reverence, and a clear con-

Emphasis, from the beginning, on "love" and "keep."

In somewhat oblique terms, Jesus is speaking of the Holy Spirit.

Jesus in John's Gospel makes mysterious and complex statements that your slow and steady proclamation rewards.

TO KEEP IN MIND

When you proclaim of the Word you participate in catechizing the faithful and those coming to faith. Understand what you proclaim so those hearing you may also understand.

GOSPEL John 14:15–21

A reading from the holy Gospel according to John

Jesus said to his **disciples**:
  "If you **love** me, you will **keep** my **commandments**.
And I will **ask** the **Father**,
  and he will **give** you another **Advocate** to **be** with you **always**,
  the **Spirit** of **truth**, whom the **world** cannot **accept**,
  because it neither **sees** nor **knows** him.
But **you** know him, because he **remains** with **you**,
  and will **be** in you.
I will not leave you **orphans**; I will **come** to you.
In a **little while** the **world** will no longer **see** me,
  but **you** will see me, because **I** live and **you** will live.
On **that day** you will **realize** that **I** am in my **Father**
  and **you** are in **me** and **I** in **you**.
Whoever has my **commandments** and **observes** them
  is the **one** who **loves** me.
And **whoever loves** me will be **loved** by my **Father**,
  and I will **love** him and **reveal** myself to him."

---

scious), the Christian will experience newness of life "in the Spirit." Suffering for the sake of Christ is not based on pacifism but on an ethical mandate to embody the virtues of the Lord.

GOSPEL Today's reading continues Jesus' farewell discourse given to his friends. Jesus has just finished telling them that he is the way that leads to the Father and to life eternal. The inheritance of a room in God's eternal dwelling place depends upon believing that Jesus and the Father are one. Now Jesus instructs them that the keeping of his commandments is an expression of their love for him and their ongoing relationship with him. Observing the commandments that Jesus leaves is real proof that God dwells with them.

The major point that we are called to focus on today is the sending of a second Advocate, with Jesus understood as the first. This Advocate's role will be to animate a "seeing" of the Lord's presence; believers will see what the world fails to see. Recognition of the Son's ongoing presence through the work of the Spirit will also reassure disciples of the intimate relationship that exists between the Father and the Son. Ongoing divine revelation is made known by keeping the commands and persevering in love of the Lord. Doing these things also expresses the theological theme of remaining in the Lord as a description of Christian life, which John will articulate in the following chapter when Jesus employs the image of a vine and branches to express the need to cling to him (John 15:1–17). Although Jesus must die and return to the Father, his followers should not feel abandoned. S.W.

THE ASCENSION OF THE LORD

LECTIONARY #58

READING I   Acts of the Apostles 1:1–11

A reading from the Acts of the Apostles

In the **first** book, Theophilus,
   I dealt with **all** that Jesus **did** and **taught**
   until the **day** he was taken **up**,
   after giving **instructions** through the Holy **Spirit**
   to the **apostles** whom he had **chosen**.
He presented himself **alive** to them
   by many **proofs** after he had **suffered**,
   appearing to them during forty **days**
   and **speaking** about the **kingdom** of God.
While **meeting** with them,
   he **enjoined** them not to **depart** from **Jerusalem**,
   but to wait for "the **promise** of the **Father**
   about which you have **heard** me **speak**;
   for John baptized with **water**,
   but in a few days you will be **baptized** with the Holy **Spirit**."

When they had gathered **together** they asked him,
   "**Lord**, are you at this time going to **restore** the **kingdom**
     to Israel?" »

Theophilus = thee-AWF-uh-luhs

A reading that recounts the Ascension of Jesus, along with some of Jesus' last words to the disciples before he departs for heaven. The reading is dramatic and visionary. You will only need to proclaim it with care for its power to come through.

"The day he was taken up": the Ascension. The vertical direction is important.

This question allows Jesus to provide the disciples specific details of their task as well as advice before he departs.

READING I   Acts opens with the announcement that this book is intended to be a sequel to the first correspondence addressed to Theophilus, which was the Gospel of Luke (see Luke 1:1–4). While the Gospel of Luke was designed to tell the story Jesus' life and ministry during his time on earth, Acts turns to the mission bestowed upon the apostles to witness to Jesus' resurrection and to make believers of all the nations. Luke's Gospel ends with an extremely brief depiction of Jesus' ascension. Now in Acts, Luke provides a much more detailed account of what took place between the time of Jesus' death and resurrection and his ascension into heaven.

Acts tells us that the apostles were instructed to remain together in Jerusalem for several days before they would be "baptized with the Holy Spirit." The risen Lord diligently prepares his followers for the work of continuing his mission. He offers them "many proofs" during the forty days following his resurrection, enlightening them about the kingdom of God. Yet Acts portrays the apostles as failing to truly understand the Lord's teaching, as they question him on the possibility of restoring the kingdom of Israel rather than God's kingdom. Jesus gently corrects them and refocuses their vision on the kingdom, which the arrival of the Spirit will enable them to help build up. Through the instructions of the resurrected Jesus, Luke tells us that the mission will be rooted in Jerusalem and Judea, will go out to the partially Jewish region of Samaria, and will extend even beyond "to the ends of the earth." This order guides the growth and mission of the Church in the overall scheme of Acts.

He answered them, "It is not for you to know the **times**
> or **seasons**
> that the **Father** has established by his own **authority**.
But you will **receive** power when the Holy **Spirit** comes
> upon you,
> and you will be my **witnesses** in Jerusalem,
> throughout **Judea** and **Samaria**,
> and to the **ends** of the **earth**."
When he had **said** this, as they were looking **on**,
> he was lifted **up**, and a **cloud** took him from their **sight**.
While they were looking **intently** at the sky as he was **going**,
> suddenly two men **dressed** in white **garments** stood
> **beside** them.
They said, "Men of **Galilee**,
> why are you **standing** there looking at the **sky**?
This Jesus who has been taken **up** from you into **heaven**
> will **return** in the same way as you have **seen** him going
> into **heaven**."

Emphasize "witnesses." Witnessing is essential to discipleship.
Judea = joo-DEE-uh
Samaria = suh-MAYR-ee-uh

The reading concludes with a vision of two angelic beings. Give their speech that follows emphasis by slowing your pace ever so slightly.

For meditation and context:

RESPONSORIAL PSALM   Psalm 47:2–3, 6–7, 8–9 (6)

R. God mounts his throne to shouts of joy: a blare of trumpets for the Lord.
or
R. Alleluia.

All you peoples, clap your hands,
> shout to God with cries of gladness,
for the LORD, the Most High, the awesome,
> is the great king over all the earth.

God mounts his throne amid shouts of joy;
> the LORD, amid trumpet blasts.
Sing praise to God, sing praise;
> sing praise to our king, sing praise.

For king of all the earth is God;
> sing hymns of praise.
God reigns over the nations,
> God sits upon his holy throne.

The account of Jesus' ascension in Acts concludes with his being "lifted up" in the midst of a cloud with the apostles looking on. The dramatic portrayal is meant to bring to an end the earthly work of Jesus so that the ministry may begin anew under the guidance of the Holy Spirit and through the work of the disciples. Luke includes "two men dressed in white garments" who observe the apostles' reaction and provide a commentary on Jesus' ascent into heaven. Keeping the movement of Jesus into heaven at the ascension in context of his larger mission, they inform the apostles that Jesus

will someday return just as he departed (the parousia). It is a call to action for the apostles and there is an urgency with which they are to testify to the glorified Lord.

READING II   The Letter to the Ephesians is an encouragement to Christian communities to understand themselves as united with Christ and in Christ so that they might continue his work. In the passage we hear today, the author offers a prayer for the community for their further enlightenment in Christ. First, he asks that the Ephesians may be given the

wisdom to come to know the mystery of God. Next, the prayer asks that this knowledge include an understanding of the "hope" of what it means to belong to Christ, namely, to be counted among the "holy ones," and those destined to inherit the "riches of glory."

The prayer for the Church in Ephesus continues by describing the mighty power of God. Not only did God raise Jesus from the dead, but he also seated him "at his right hand" to glorify him, allowing him to reign over every imaginable power. Far mightier than "every principality, authority,

---

READING II Ephesians 1:17–23

A reading from the Letter of Saint Paul to the Ephesians

Brothers and **sisters**:

May the **God** of our Lord Jesus **Christ**, the Father of **glory**,
    give you a Spirit of **wisdom** and **revelation**
    resulting in **knowledge** of him.
May the **eyes** of your hearts be **enlightened**,
    that you may **know** what is the **hope** that belongs to his **call**,
    what are the **riches** of glory
    in his **inheritance** among the holy **ones**,
    and what is the surpassing **greatness** of his **power**
    for **us** who **believe**,
    in **accord** with the exercise of his **great might**,
    which he **worked** in **Christ**,
    raising him from the **dead**
    and **seating** him at his right **hand** in the **heavens**,
    far above every **principality**, **authority**, **power**, and **dominion**,
    and every **name** that is **named**
    not only in this **age** but also in the one to **come**.
And he put **all things** beneath his **feet**
    and gave him as **head** over all things to the church,
    which is his **body**,
    the **fullness** of the one who fills **all things** in every **way**.

Ephesians = ee-FEE-zhuhnz

An exhortatory reading, filled with high-hearted blessings.
The first blessing comes from God to the people of Ephesus.

The second blessing comes from Paul to the people of Ephesus, including knowledge, hope, and the riches of glory. Give each aspect of this blessing its due by emphasizing it slightly.

These are the traditional names of some of the angelic powers.

Paul concludes by invoking the power of Jesus himself.

---

power, and dominion," all things will be subjected to the power of Christ for all eternity. Christ's authority is complete and universal.

The prayer concludes with a further mention that God subjects "all things" to the reign of Christ, including, and perhaps most especially, the Church. In keeping with other Pauline epistles, the Church is described as a body, with Christ as its head (see Colossians 1:18 and Romans 12:4–8). The head is understood as giving direction to the body. Because the body enacts the command of the head, the reign of Christ is

handed on to the Church to be exercised in the world. With the Church filled with "a spirit of wisdom and revelation" and with Christ as its head, the Christian community is meant to reveal the authority of the glorified Lord, cooperating with his work.

GOSPEL The setting for Jesus' ascension in Matthew is very similar to the one found in the evangelist's rendering of the transfiguration in chapter 17. There Jesus leads Peter, James, and John up a mountain where he is transfigured, glorified by the voice of God, and

then proceeds to tell the disciples about his resurrection from the dead. Now, in the final verses of Matthew's Gospel, Jesus orders the eleven to a mountain in Galilee where he reminds them of his divine authority and commissions them to go "make disciples of all nations."

An important detail of this short passage is the reaction of the disciples when they discover Jesus on this mountain. Matthew states that "they worshiped, but they doubted." Unlike Mark's account of the Gospel, in which there are several appearances of the risen Lord prior to his

GOSPEL   Matthew 28:16–20

A reading from the holy Gospel according to Matthew

This reading comes from the concluding words of Matthew's Gospel. Therefore, they have a valedictory quality to them.

Matthew's Gospel concludes with these words of Jesus, which function as a concise and moving summation of his teachings. He is encouraging his disciples while also saying farewell to them.

This last statement in light of Jesus' imminent departure is especially poignant.

The **eleven disciples** went to **Galilee**,
   to the **mountain** to which **Jesus** had **ordered** them.
When they **saw** him, they **worshiped**, but they **doubted**.
Then **Jesus approached** and **said** to them,
   "**All power** in **heaven** and on **earth** has been **given** to me.
Go, therefore, and make **disciples** of all **nations**,
   baptizing them in the name of the **Father**,
   and of the **Son**, and of the **Holy Spirit**,
   teaching them to observe **all** that I have **commanded** you.
And **behold**, I am with you **always**, until the **end** of the **age**."

ascension (see Mark 16:9–14), the resurrected Lord in Matthew appears only to the women at the tomb before he meets the eleven in Galilee. Thus, the doubt they experience should not surprise us, as this is their first encounter with the risen Jesus. Their act of worship is meant to override their doubt.

After the Lord reveals the authority given to him from above, his commissioning of the apostles contains two components that go into the making of disciples. First, they are commanded to baptize in the name of the triune God—Father, Son, and Holy Spirit. No longer is baptism simply about immersion into the kingdom and repentance (as John the Baptist's baptism was; see Matthew 3:11), but now it is to unite the recipient with God. The second important aspect of the apostles' mission to "all nations" is that they are to teach all that Jesus has handed on to them. Thus, baptism is inseparable from the preaching of the Gospel. In word and sacrament, Jesus remains with the church "until the end of the age." S.W.

SEVENTH SUNDAY OF EASTER

LECTIONARY #59

READING I   Acts of the Apostles 1:12–14

A reading from the Acts of the Apostles

After **Jesus** had been taken **up** to **heaven** the **apostles**
   returned to **Jerusalem**
   from the **mount** called **Olivet**, which is near **Jerusalem**,
   a **sabbath day's journey away**.

When they **entered** the **city**
   they went to the **upper room** where they were **staying**,
   Peter and **John** and **James** and **Andrew**,
   Philip and **Thomas**, **Bartholomew** and **Matthew**,
   James son of **Alphaeus**, **Simon** the **Zealot**,
   and **Judas** son of **James**.
All these devoted themselves with **one accord** to **prayer**,
   together with some **women**,
   and **Mary** the mother of **Jesus**, and his **brothers**.

Drawn from the opening chapter of Acts, this reading has something of the quality of "setting the story up," by describing the location and listing the characters.
Olivet = OL-ih-vet
Each word here has even emphasis.

Note the names, all of them men. These are the apostles; speak their names with some emphasis and reverence.
Bartholomew = bahr-THAHL-uh-myoo
Alphaeus = AL-fee-uhs

Note how "some women" are added at the end, including Mary the mother of Jesus.

READING I Today's brief passage from Acts takes place between the Lord's ascension and the choosing of Matthias to replace Judas. If there is a theological message that Luke wishes to impart in these three verses it is that the apostles are resolved to preserve their unity and do so through shared prayer. Furthermore, Luke maintains the location of Jerusalem as their meeting place, placing it as the center of the emerging Church. Even though Jesus tells the apostles at the time of his ascension that they will be his witnesses to the world, Jerusalem continues to be the epicenter for the apostles' mission.

Luke mentions the names of the apostles just as he did in the Gospel (Luke 6:12–16). The one name missing from the list this time is that of Judas. We will discover in a few verses that Peter deems it necessary that Judas be replaced so that their ministry may continue on. Mary is present with the apostles in the upper room as they devote themselves to prayer and discernment. It is important that Mary is present here at the beginning of the early Christian community, since she was present from the beginning of Jesus' life and is a model of Christian discipleship. Also, Luke mentions that the "brothers" of Jesus were in the room together with women other than Mary. As we see in Luke's Gospel account, these women and men were likely to have been present throughout much of Christ's ministry (for example, see Luke 8:1–3, 19–21 and 23:49, 55). All in all, the overall theme of this passage is that the apostles are acting as one and are engaging in the work of discernment vis-à-vis their prayer.

For meditation and context:

RESPONSORIAL PSALM   Psalm 27:1, 4, 7–8 (13)

R. **I believe that I shall see the good things of the Lord in the land of the living.**
or
R. **Alleluia.**

The LORD is my light and my salvation;
   whom should I fear?
The LORD is my life's refuge;
   of whom should I be afraid?

One thing I ask of the LORD;
    this I seek:
to dwell in the house of the LORD
   all the days of my life,
that I may gaze on the loveliness
    of the LORD
    and contemplate his temple.

Hear, O LORD, the sound of my call;
   have pity on me, and answer me.
Of you my heart speaks; you my glance
   seeks.

READING II   1 Peter 4:13–16

A reading from the first Letter of Saint Peter

Beloved:
Rejoice to the **extent** that you **share** in the sufferings of **Christ**,
   so that when his **glory** is **revealed**
   you may also **rejoice exultantly**.
If you are **insulted** for the **name** of **Christ**, **blessed** are **you**,
   for the **Spirit** of **glory** and of **God** rests **upon** you.
But let **no one among** you be **made** to **suffer**
   as a **murderer**, a **thief**, an **evildoer**, or as an **intriguer**.
But **whoever** is **made** to **suffer** as a **Christian** should **not**
    be **ashamed**
   but **glorify God because** of the **name**.

This reading is in the imperative voice. Peter is offering encouraging advice to the recipients of this letter.

This claim sets up an unusual contrast. He seems to be saying, if you suffer because you've committed a vile crime, your suffering is your own, whereas if you suffer because of Christ, you glorify God.

Slight pause between "God" and "because."

READING II The First Letter of Peter is addressed to Christians living in the "diaspora," namely cities in Asia Minor where Christians are very much in the minority. It is designed to help these churches embrace a lifestyle suitable to following the Christian way as opposed to following the values and the way of life of the pagan world that surrounds them. The author's theology of Christian suffering is very much in keeping with that of Paul's: as baptized Christians, they have been immersed into the Lord's suffering, death, and resurrection (see Romans 6) which gives them strength to face their own persecution.

The letter calls blessed those who are willing to bear insult for Christ and those who endure suffering on his behalf. However, it also suggests that a Christian has no business seeking to suffer needlessly. The author describes several forms of suffering, such as killing and stealing, which may produce suffering that is duly justified; Christianity is only about the way of innocent suffering. The one who is made to suffer and the one who sacrifices the desires of the flesh is worthy of God's glory and has life in the Spirit.

GOSPEL Today's passage takes place near the end of Jesus' "farewell discourse," in which he seeks to strengthen his disciples for the task of remaining in him after he is gone from this world (John 14–17). Chapter 17 is a long prayer in which Jesus prays for himself to glorify the Father's name and for his disciples to persevere in the world. The eschatological tone of this prayer is revealed in the very first line of this prayer, as Jesus

---

GOSPEL John 17:1–11a

A reading from the holy Gospel according to John

Jesus raised his **eyes** to **heaven** and **said**,
   "**Father**, the **hour** has **come**.
Give **glory** to your **son**, so that your **son** may **glorify** you,
   just as you gave him **authority** over **all people**,
   so that your **son** may give eternal **life** to **all** you **gave** him.
Now **this** is eternal **life**,
   that they should **know** you, the **only true God**,
   and the **one** whom you **sent**, **Jesus Christ**.
I **glorified** you on **earth**
   by **accomplishing** the **work** that you **gave** me to **do**.
Now **glorify** me, **Father**, **with** you,
   with the **glory** that I **had** with you before the **world began**.

"I **revealed** your **name** to **those** whom you **gave** me **out**
      of the **world**.
They **belonged** to you, and you **gave** them to me,
   and they have **kept** your **word**.
Now they **know** that **everything** you gave me is **from** you,
   because the **words** you **gave** to me I have **given** to **them**,
   and they **accepted** them and truly **understood** that I **came**
      from you,
   and they have **believed** that you **sent** me.
I **pray** for them.
I **do not pray** for the **world** but for the **ones** you have **given** me,
   because they are **yours**, and **everything** of **mine** is **yours**
   and **everything** of **yours** is **mine**,
   and I have been **glorified** in them.
And **now** I will **no longer be** in the **world**,
   but **they** are in the world, while **I** am coming to **you**."

This reading consists almost entirely of words Jesus is speaking directly to the Father. They are as confident as they are complex. Proclaim them with deference to their complexity.

Emphasis on "glorified," "glorify," and "glory."

Even emphasis on "do not pray."

Note the inclusive inversion, from "everything of mine is yours" to "everything of yours is mine."

---

acknowledges that "the hour has come." In referring to his death, Jesus prays to be given the Father's glory in order to return glory to the Father. With this chapter's placement immediately before Jesus' arrest and crucifixion, the reader immediately connects this prayer with the courage and perseverance Jesus will exercise in accepting God's will that he suffer and die.

While the first part of the prayer concentrates on the glory that the cross bestows, Jesus soon turns to the future of the disciples. He makes clear that he did everything he could to reveal the Father to those who believed. They are privileged recipients of divine revelation, and Jesus confidently states that they now know the connection between the Father and the Son. Knowing this relationship between Jesus and the Father places the disciples in a new relationship with the Father, as belonging to him and living for him through their continued commitment to Christ.

Near the end of this passage, Jesus states clearly that the prayer he utters is to benefit those who have believed in him. He does not pray for the world as a whole, because the world has not accepted him or the Father's message that he reveals. While John's Gospel envisions a universal mission for the Word of God, the evangelist clearly recognizes that the world is also home to much that is evil and opposed to the reception of divine love. The strengthening of the disciples for the mission ahead is signaled by Jesus calling them the Father's possession (just as he is). Thus, those who believe in the Son and know that the Father has sent him into the world are also a sign of God's glory. S.W.

PENTECOST SUNDAY: VIGIL

LECTIONARY #62

READING I Genesis 11:1–9

A reading from the Book of Genesis

The whole **world** spoke the same **language**, using the
> same **words**.
While the **people** were migrating in the east,
> they came upon a **valley** in the land of **Shinar** and
> settled there.
They said to one another,
> "**Come**, let us mold **bricks** and harden them with **fire**."
They used **bricks** for stone, and **bitumen** for mortar.
Then they said, "**Come**, let us **build** ourselves a **city**
> and a **tower** with its **top** in the **sky**,
> and so make a **name** for ourselves;
> otherwise we shall be **scattered** all over the **earth**."

The Lord came down to see the **city** and the **tower**
> that the **people** had built.
Then the Lord said: "If **now**, while they are one **people**,
> all **speaking** the same **language**,
> they have **started** to do this,
> **nothing** will later stop them from doing **whatever**
> they **presume** to do.
Let us then go **down** there and **confuse** their language,
> so that **one** will not **understand** what another **says**."
Thus the Lord **scattered** them from **there** all over the **earth**,
> and they **stopped** building the city.

Genesis = JEN-uh-sihs

A reading of a story absorbed in mysterious power. As much a parable as it is a demonstration of the incomprehensible mind of God, it can seem almost like science fiction. It's probably best to treat it that way in terms of proclaiming it: Read what's in the text, straightforwardly and clearly.

Shinar = SHĪ-nahr

The two repetitions of "Come" stand for the aspirations—or arrogance—of the people. Give a little edge to the word when you speak it.

bitumen = bih-TYOO-m*n

God's use of "let us" repeats the use of the builders of the tower. Here, God's intention is unhelpful, destructive even. "Confuse" is the loaded word.

There are options for today's readings. Contact your parish staff to learn which readings will be used.

READING I The first eleven chapters of Genesis contain the primeval history of the world's creation and its need for salvation. While the world is deemed "good" by God, with all things manifesting perfect order and complementarity, and with humanity made in God's image, sin quickly enters the world through the human desire to possess the knowledge that belongs to God alone (Genesis 1–3).

God's frustration with humanity comes to a highpoint in Genesis in the story of Noah, when God decides to destroy creation with a flood but then relents and establishes a new order of creation with Noah in the giving of a covenant that renews the face of the earth (Genesis 6:5—9:17). However, as the descendants of Noah begin to repopulate the earth, with everyone speaking the same language, the story unfolds in yet another rupture in the relationship with God. Once again, humanity forgets the providence of God and chooses to strive to become as great as God.

The story of the tower of Babel opens with the image that the whole world is united by the ability to communicate without difficulty. Nevertheless, the unity experienced by the human family is cause for the development of a fear. They come to believe that they must make a great name for themselves, or they will become separated from one another. Thus, they decide to build a tower that rises high into the sky in order to demonstrate their greatness on the face of the earth and to preserve their unity.

However, the Lord comes down to earth to observe what the people are doing

That is why it was called **Babel**,
  because **there** the Lord **confused** the speech of **all** the world.
It was from **that** place that he **scattered** them all over the **earth**.

RESPONSORIAL PSALM Psalm 33:10–11, 12–13, 14–15

R. Blessed the people the Lord has chosen to be his own.

The Lord brings to nought the plans
  of nations;
he foils the designs of peoples.
But the plan of the Lord stands forever;
  the design of his heart, through
  all generations.

Blessed the nation whose God is the Lord,
  the people he has chosen for his own
  inheritance.
From heaven the Lord looks down;
  he sees all mankind.

From his fixed throne he beholds
  all who dwell on the earth,
He who fashioned the heart of each,
  he who knows all their works.

READING II Exodus 19:3–8a, 16–20b

A reading from the Book of Exodus

Moses went up the **mountain** to God.
Then the Lord **called** to him and said,
  "**Thus** shall you say to the house of **Jacob**;
  tell the **Israelites**:
  You have **seen** for yourselves how I **treated** the Egyptians
  and how I **bore** you up on **eagle wings**
  and **brought** you here to **myself**.
Therefore, if you **hearken** to my voice and **keep** my covenant,
  you shall be my **special** possession,
  dearer to me than **all** other people,
  though **all** the earth is **mine**.
You shall be to me a **kingdom** of priests, a **holy** nation.
That is what you must **tell** the Israelites."
So **Moses** went and summoned the **elders** of the people.
When he set **before** them
  all that the Lord had **ordered** him to tell them, »

in the construction of a tower. The people have abused their gift of unity and are moving along a path where they become so grandiose in their self-assessment that they will feel they no longer need God. Thus, God's punishment is to inflict upon the people precisely what they feared from the outset: they will forever be "scattered," separated from one another "all over the earth." The primeval account of creation thus ends with an explanation as to why there is a diversity of languages in the world that causes communication to be difficult. Confusion of speech thereby prevents the human family from pursuing the destructive path of trying to be God's equal.

READING II This passage from the Book of Exodus is in two parts. The first half of the passage details the Lord's choice of Israel as his own possession and the promise of the covenant. The second portion focuses on the great theophany at Mount Sinai, when God makes the mountain come alive with his awesome presence. First God speaks, and then God manifests his power using the tangible means of natural wonders.

At the beginning of this passage we witness Moses climbing the mountain in order to meet privately with God. This takes place three months after the Israelites began their journey of freedom out of Egypt. The Lord calls Moses and commands him to speak to the Israelites, reminding them of God's action in their exodus from Egypt. It was God alone who carried them out of Egypt as if borne on "eagle wings." Furthermore, God tells Moses that this newfound freedom comes with an important responsibility. The people are to respond to God's voice, keep his covenant,

"Everything the Lord has said, we will do":
With these words, the covenant is sealed.
Emphasis on "do."

Natural forces express themselves vividly
in response.

Even stresses on the words in this line.

the people all answered together,
    "**Everything** the Lord has **said**, we will **do**."

On the **morning** of the third **day**
    there were **peals** of thunder and lightning,
    and a heavy **cloud** over the mountain,
    and a very loud trumpet blast,
    so that all the **people** in the camp **trembled**.
But **Moses** led the people **out** of the camp to meet **God**,
    and they **stationed** themselves at the foot of the **mountain**.
Mount **Sinai** was all wrapped in **smoke**,
    for the LORD came down **upon** it in **fire**.
The smoke **rose** from it as though from a **furnace**,
    and the whole **mountain** trembled **violently**.
The trumpet blast grew **louder** and **louder**, while Moses
        was speaking,
    and God **answering** him with **thunder**.

When the LORD came **down** to the top of Mount **Sinai**,
    he summoned **Moses** to the top of the **mountain**.

The vision of smoke and fire signals the
power of God. These words paint a potent
picture. No need, however, to raise your
voice. Keep it steady.

RESPONSORIAL PSALM   Daniel 3:52, 53, 54, 55, 56

R. Glory and praise for ever!

"Blessed are you, O Lord, the God of
    our fathers,
    praiseworthy and exalted above
    all forever;
and blessed is your holy and glorious name,
    praiseworthy and exalted above all for
    all ages."

"Blessed are you in the temple of your
    holy glory,
    praiseworthy and glorious above
    all forever."

Or:

"Blessed are you on the throne of
    your Kingdom,
    praiseworthy and exalted above
    all forever."

"Blessed are you who look into the depths
    from your throne upon the cherubim,
    praiseworthy and exalted above
    all forever."

"Blessed are you in the firmament of heaven,
    praiseworthy and glorious forever."

TO KEEP IN MIND
The responsorial psalm "has great
liturgical and pastoral importance,
since it fosters meditation on the
Word of God," the *General Instruction on the Roman Missal* says. Pray
it as you prepare.

and display before all the world what it means to be his "special possession." Israel is to take on a priestly identity, suggesting that they are set apart from every other nation. Their holiness is to be a sign of God's power and fidelity, and as the Book of Exodus will show, of God's great mercy. When Moses speaks to the people, represented by a group of leaders, the people answer in unison that they will do all that the Lord has commanded.

Verses 9 through 15 of this chapter, which are omitted in our hearing of Exodus today, contains the preparations the

Israelites make to ready themselves for God's formal giving of the law. The people are to ritually purify themselves and are told not to go anywhere near God's holy mountain. With these preparations, the Israelites are made ready to behold the fearsome wonder of God. Thus we hear the second portion of this reading, the theophany at Sinai. With thunder and lightning, dense clouds and the sounding of the trumpet, the people tremble as God makes himself known. As they look on, Moses and God carry on an intense conversation, which is made visibly present in fire and

smoke, trumpet and thunder. Made ready for the deepening of his personal encounter with God, Moses leaves the people and ascends the mountain, where he will receive instruction on the covenant from the mouth of God. This magnificent theophany reveals in a very physical way that God's power and might is beyond compare. Yet God will later come to demonstrate that his greatest strength of all is the ability to show mercy and compassion to his sinful people (for example, Exodus 34:6–7).

RESPONSORIAL PSALM   Psalm 19:8, 9, 10, 11

R. Lord, you have the words of everlasting life.

The law of the LORD is perfect,
  refreshing the soul;
The decree of the LORD is trustworthy,
  giving wisdom to the simple.

The precepts of the LORD are right,
  rejoicing the heart;
The command of the LORD is clear,
  enlightening the eye.

The fear of the LORD is pure,
  enduring forever;
The ordinances of the LORD are true,
  all of them just.

They are more precious than gold,
  than a heap of purest gold;
Sweeter also than syrup
  or honey from the comb.

READING III   Ezekiel 37:1–14

A reading from the Book of the Prophet Ezekiel

The **hand** of the LORD came **upon** me,
  and he led me **out** in the **spirit** of the LORD
  and set me in the **center** of the **plain**,
  which was now **filled** with **bones**.
He made me **walk** among the **bones** in every **direction**
  so that I saw how **many** they were on the **surface** of the plain.
How **dry** they were!
He asked me:
  Son of **man**, can these **bones** come to **life**?
I answered, "Lord GOD, you **alone know** that."
Then he said to me:
  Prophesy over these **bones**, and **say** to them:
  Dry bones, **hear** the **word** of the LORD!
Thus **says** the Lord GOD to these **bones**:
  See! I will bring spirit into you, that you may come to **life**.
I will put **sinews** upon you, make flesh grow **over** you,
  cover you with **skin**, and put spirit **in** you
  so that you may come to **life** and **know** that I am the LORD. ❯❯

Ezekiel = ee-ZEE-kee-uhl

A reading with visionary passages of exquisite strangeness and power. God speaks to and through Ezekiel throughout this reading. Because the punctuation isn't entirely clear, it's useful to have markers for yourself for when God is speaking and when Ezekiel is speaking for himself. Also, this reading makes use of the verb "prophesy" as well as its past tense, "prophesied." Pronunciation is important. Prophesy = PROF-uh-sī (not PROF-uh-see); Prophesied = PROF-uh-sīd (not PROF-uh-seed). Be sure to practice

God begins to speak here.

The vision, which is frightening, begins here with the valley of dry bones. The life of this vision relies on these dry bones coming to life.
sinews = sin-yooz

Emphasis on "know."

READING III The context for Ezekiel's prophecy is the utter desolation of Israel. The Temple in Jerusalem has been leveled, the people have been banished to the land of Babylon, and the entire nation begins to doubt that God no longer wishes to be in relationship with them anymore. The Israelites had to ask themselves this basic question: how can we consider ourselves to be God's chosen people when our life situation only speaks of doom and gloom, despair and death?

Ezekiel uses this bleak outlook to provide the people with a new sense of hope.

His vision of dry bones being put back together again with life and vitality not only forecasts the future of Israel as a new and vibrant nation, but it can also be seen as an image of resurrection in general. In the recreation of the human body, it is the Spirit who is hard at work providing the gift of new life.

The reading begins with Ezekiel testifying to the Lord's inspiration and to the Spirit's guidance in the vision that has been given to him. He sees a vast plain filled with decaying human bones. These are not just bones, but they are "dry bones," indicating

even greater lifelessness than can be seen from the outside. God commands Ezekiel to prophesy over the dry bones; they are to "hear the word of the LORD!" The word God speaks is also to communicate the giving of spirit that will make new life spring up in the seemingly worthless bones.

When Ezekiel follows the Lord's command and prophesies over the field of bones, they begin to take human form again, but they lack the invigorating life of the spirit. Thus, God commands Ezekiel to call upon the Spirit directly. When he does so, Ezekiel witnesses a "vast army" before him

Ezekiel himself is speaking here.

God begins to speak again here.

Ezekiel himself is speaking again here.

From here to the end of the reading, God is speaking, even as he quotes the house of Israel.

I, **Ezekiel**, **prophesied** as I had been **told**,
  and even as I was **prophesying** I heard a **noise**;
  it was a **rattling** as the bones came together,
    bone joining **bone**.
I saw the **sinews** and the **flesh** come **upon** them,
  and the skin **cover** them, but there was no spirit in them.
Then the LORD said to me:
  Prophesy to the **spirit**, **prophesy**, son of man,
  and **say** to the spirit: **Thus** says the Lord GOD:
  From the **four winds come**, O spirit,
  and **breathe** into these **slain** that they may **come** to life.
I **prophesied** as he told me, and the spirit came **into** them;
  they came **alive** and stood **upright**, a vast **army**.
Then he said to me:
  Son of **man**, these **bones** are the **whole house** of Israel.
They have been **saying**,
  "Our **bones** are dried up,
  our **hope** is lost, and we are cut **off**."
Therefore, **prophesy** and say to them: **Thus** says the Lord GOD:
  O my **people**, I will open your **graves**
  and have you **rise** from them,
  and bring you **back** to the land of **Israel**.
Then you shall **know** that I am the **LORD**,
  when I open your **graves** and have you **rise** from them,
  O my **people**!
I will put my **spirit** in you that you may **live**,
  and I will **settle** you upon your **land**;
  thus you shall **know** that I am the LORD.
I have **promised**, and I will **do** it, says the LORD.

full of energy and life. God then interprets the scene to Ezekiel stating that the dry bones represent the nation of Israel that cries out for new life fearing that they have nothing to hope for in their return to the land God provided. Yet the Lord promises the gift of new life. He will open their graves and restore them to life. Even more, God promises to provide them with the enduring power of his spirit who will ensure their prosperity in the land. In the context of Pentecost, this reading from Ezekiel may renew in us the frequent utterance of the simple prayer "Come, Holy Spirit," seeking to find new life in what might appear as hopeless, death-dealing situations in our own lives.

READING IV The Book of Joel is a two-part prophecy. The first part of the book, chapters 1 and 2, tell the story of a plague of locusts that serves to provoke the lamentation of the people of Israel. Joel calls the nation to repentance and prayer and is given the vision of a restored land that produces fruit in abundance. The second part of the book, chapters 3 and 4, issues forth God's judgment upon all the nations, with the assurance that God will spare everyone "who calls on the name of the LORD"

Our reading today is the opening of the book's second half. It begins with the outpouring of the spirit of God on all people. In other words, there is a universality in God's giving of the Spirit—all people on earth are recipients of this gift and therefore have the opportunity to respond to God's initiative. The reading continues by

For meditation and context:

RESPONSORIAL PSALM   Psalm 107:2–3, 4–5, 6–7, 8–9

R. Give thanks to the Lord; his love is everlasting.
or
R. Alleluia.

Let the redeemed of the LORD say,
   those whom he has redeemed from the
     hand of the foe
And gathered from the lands,
   from the east and the west, from the north
     and the south.

They went astray in the desert wilderness;
   the way to an inhabited city they did
     not find.
Hungry and thirsty,
   their life was wasting away within them.

They cried to the LORD in their distress;
   from their straits he rescued them.
And he led them by a direct way
   to reach an inhabited city.

Let them give thanks to the LORD for
   his mercy
   and his wondrous deeds to the children
     of men,
Because he satisfied the longing soul
   and filled the hungry soul with
     good things.

A reading of a prophetic vision of a cataclysmic event. Scripture often shifts into this visionary mode—which can be exciting to proclaim because the language is so vivid.

prophesy = PROF-uh-sī

READING IV   Joel 3:1–5

A reading from the Book of the Prophet Joel

Thus says the LORD:
I will **pour out** my spirit upon all **flesh**.
Your **sons** and **daughters** shall **prophesy**,
   your old men shall dream **dreams**,
   your young men shall see **visions**;
even upon the **servants** and the **handmaids**,
   in those days, I will pour out my **spirit**.
And I will work **wonders** in the **heavens** and on the **earth**,
   blood, **fire**, and columns of **smoke**;
the sun will be turned to **darkness**,
   and the **moon** to **blood**,
at the **coming** of the day of the LORD,
   the **great** and terrible **day**.
Then **everyone** shall be **rescued**
   who **calls** on the name of the LORD;
for on Mount **Zion** there shall be a **remnant**,
   as the LORD has said,
and in **Jerusalem** survivors
   whom the LORD shall **call**.

"The great and terrible day": with these words, Joel concludes his vision.

The vision is immediately followed by the promise of rescue from God, which continues to the end of the reading. Don't overdo your reading, but you can shift to a slightly more optimistic tone.

outlining those who will attempt to awaken all people to God's power; the young and the old, men and women, servants and handmaids will all be charged with the responsibility to prophesy in God's name.

Joel's vision proceeds to describe the wonders that God will perform in announcing his judgement upon earth. Blood, fire, and smoke will cover the land, the sun will not shine, the moon will be darkened. Joel refers to the dawning of this day as "great and terrible." Implanting this fear in the

hearts of those who have just been released from the destruction of the plague of locusts, Joel assures the people that those who remain faithful to the Lord and call upon his name will be preserved in the new world that is to come. Those who recognize God's great power and authority and respond to the promptings of the spirit by making God's greatness known will survive any peril that may come as a part of God's vindication.

EPISTLE   Living in a time when there were eyewitnesses to Christ himself, many early Christians were eager for Christ to return as he had promised. However, as time went on, some of these early Christians began to lose hope in the Lord's promise. The words we hear today in Paul's Letter to the Romans offer encouragement for Christians awaiting the coming kingdom of God. Their efforts are not made in vain but are done in cooperation with the Spirit.

For meditation and context:

RESPONSORIAL PSALM   Psalm 104:1–2a, 24, 35c, 27–28, 29bc–30 (30)

R. Lord, send out your Spirit, and renew the face of the earth.
or
R. Alleluia.

Bless the LORD, O my soul!
    O LORD, my God, you are great indeed!
You are clothed with majesty and glory,
    robed in light as with a cloak.

How manifold are your works, O LORD!
    In wisdom you have wrought them all—
the earth is full of your creatures;
    bless the LORD, O my soul! Alleluia.

Creatures all look to you
    to give them food in due time.
When you give it to them, they gather it;
    when you open your hand, they are filled
        with good things.

If you take away their breath, they perish
    and return to their dust.
When you send forth your spirit,
    they are created,
    and you renew the face of the earth.

EPISTLE   Romans 8:22–27

A reading from the Letter of Saint Paul to the Romans

Brothers and **sisters**:
We **know** that all creation is **groaning** in labor pains even
        until **now**;
    and not only **that**, but we **ourselves**,
    who have the **firstfruits** of the **Spirit**,
    we also groan within **ourselves**
    as we wait for **adoption**, the **redemption** of our **bodies**.
For in **hope** we were **saved**.
Now hope that **sees** is not **hope**.
For who **hopes** for what one **sees**?
But if we **hope** for what we do not see, we wait with **endurance**.

In the **same way**, the Spirit too comes to the aid of our weakness;
    for we do not **know** how to pray as we **ought**,
    but the Spirit himself **intercedes** with inexpressible **groanings**.
And the one who searches **hearts**
    knows what is the **intention** of the Spirit,
    because he **intercedes** for the **holy** ones
    according to God's **will**.

A reading that contains a potent and not easily digested message: That life is challenging—Paul compares it to childbirth—and its pain does not abate, even as we hope for its end. Nevertheless, we hope.

The first line after the greeting contains the core of Paul's message. Emphasize "know," "groaning," and "now."

Slight extra emphasis on "endurance."

"In the same way": Paul intends to compare our life to the work of the Holy Spirit, who comes to our aid. In the Spirit lies our hope.

The opening words of this reading are vivid in their imagery of creation groaning out with labor pains, waiting for the fullness of the day of redemption. Paul uses this image to connect with Christians awaiting Christ; they yearn from the depths of their beings for the coming of this day. Followers of Jesus are accompanied by the Spirit, who assists in guiding and directing the hope that looks forward to the day of final salvation. Paul provides an important reminder as to the true nature of hope. Hope looks to what has not been attained, and it is the Spirit who provides the hope necessary to endure the unknown. This applies also to the action of our prayer. By one's own power, prayer lacks confidence, but with the aid of the Spirit, one discovers how to pray and be heard by God.

Echoing his first imagery of creation groaning and laboring, Paul notes that in our prayer "the Spirit himself intercedes with inexpressible groanings." The Christian's effort must be attuned to cooperating with the movement of the Holy Spirit. Through this intercession of the Spirit, the Christian is guided along the path of holiness. When left to themselves, humans will always fall short of comprehending the will of God. However, with the power of the Spirit at work within them and in the world, disciples can hope that all of creation is moving toward God.

GOSPEL   Today's passage from the Gospel of John takes place at the conclusion of the eight-day feast of Tabernacles. The feast of Tabernacles was one of the three great pilgrimage festivals—

GOSPEL   John 7:37–39

A reading from the holy Gospel according to John

On the **last** and greatest **day** of the **feast**,
    Jesus stood up and **exclaimed**,
    "Let anyone who **thirsts** come to me and **drink**.
    As Scripture says:
    *Rivers of living water will **flow** from within him who
        believes in me.*"

He said this in reference to the **Spirit**
    that **those** who came to **believe** in him were to **receive**.
There was, of course, no **Spirit** yet,
    because **Jesus** had not yet been **glorified**.

A brief reading with an extraordinary exhortation embedded in it.

"Rivers of living water" is an especially evocative phrase, especially as a sign of belief.

The reading concludes with an anticipatory claim about Jesus' eventual glorification.

Pesach (Passover), *Shavuot* (Pentecost), and *Sukkot* (Tabernacles)—all of which required an annual journey to the Temple in Jerusalem in order to offer a sacrifice. The late-summer/early-autumn feast of Tabernacles celebrates the harvest and asks God for the blessing of plentiful rain for the fruition of next year's crops. It also commemorates the Israelite's freedom from slavery in Egypt and God's protection of his people. Building on the theme of abundant rain, Jesus speaks within this context and invites people to come to him

for "living water." In a not-so-subtle way, Jesus is using this traditional Jewish feast to reveal himself as the one who has the ability to bestow life in abundance. These words of Jesus cause the crowds to discuss anew how it is that he could be the Christ, the anointed one of God (in the verses following today's reading; see John 7:40–52).

This short passage moves from Jesus' proclamation about the true source of life to John's interpretation that Jesus' words serve as a foreshadowing of the giving of the Holy Spirit. John notes that it is the

Spirit himself who is the "living water" that flows from the source of the glorified Lord. These explanatory comments from John are consistent with Johannine theology that reserves the giving of the Spirit to the Church after the Lord's resurrection (for example, John 20:22). While Jesus provides the invitation to the people around him to come to him to quench their thirst, he is also looking toward the time of the Church, when the Spirit will guide and support his followers after he has returned to the Father. S.W.

PENTECOST SUNDAY: DAY

LECTIONARY #63

READING I   Acts of the Apostles 2:1–11

A reading from the Acts of the Apostles

When the **time** for Pentecost was **fulfilled**,
    they were all in one place **together**.
And suddenly there came from the **sky**
    a **noise** like a strong driving **wind**,
    and it filled the entire **house** in which they **were**.
Then there appeared to them **tongues** as of fire,
    which **parted** and came to **rest** on each **one** of them.
And they were all **filled** with the Holy **Spirit**
    and began to **speak** in different **tongues**,
    as the Spirit **enabled** them to **proclaim**.

Now there were devout **Jews** from every **nation** under **heaven**
    staying in **Jerusalem**.
At this sound, they gathered in a large **crowd**,
    but they were **confused**
    because each one heard them **speaking** in his own **language**.
They were **astounded**, and in amazement they **asked**,
    "Are not all these **people** who are speaking **Galileans**?
Then how does each of us **hear** them in his native **language**?
We are **Parthians**, **Medes**, and **Elamites**,
    inhabitants of **Mesopotamia**, Judea and **Cappadocia**,
    Pontus and **Asia**, **Phrygia** and **Pamphylia**,
    Egypt and the districts of **Libya** near **Cyrene**,
    as well as **travelers** from **Rome**,

A reading that directly inverts the Tower of Babel passage from Genesis. (See the first reading for the Pentecost Vigil.) This kind of inverted symmetry is one of the enduring pleasures of reading Scripture. Babel doesn't need to be mentioned in order for your assembly to sense its presence.

Air and fire are the two elements associated with the Holy Spirit. Here, it's air in the form of wind.

And here in the form of tongues of fire.

Read all of these names with care. Be sure to practice their pronunciation:
Parthians = PAHR-thee-uhnz
Medes = meedz
Elamites = EE-luh-mīts
Mesopotamia = mes-uh-poh-TAY-mee-uh
Judea = joo-DEE-uh
Cappadocia = cap-uh-DOH-shee-uh
Pontus = PON-tuhs
Phrygia = FRIJ-ee-uh
Pamphylia = Pam-FIL-ee-uh
Libya = LIB-ee-uh
Cyrene = sī-REE-nee

READING I   On this feast of Pentecost, our first reading is taken from the Acts of the Apostles. The setting is the Jewish feast of Pentecost, also known as *Shavuot*. As Luke tells the story, Jesus' disciples and followers remained in the Jerusalem area after Jesus' ascension into heaven. Because it was a pilgrimage feast, Jews from other parts of the world had also come to Jerusalem. On this particular day, Jesus' followers were gathered together in a house. Suddenly, they receive the Holy Spirit in the forms of a strong wind from the sky and tongues of fire that come down

upon each of them. Wind and fire are signs of a theophany, a manifestation of the divine.

The New Testament associates a wide variety of gifts and abilities with the Holy Spirit, including speaking in tongues. When Jesus' followers in this story begin to speak to the crowd, the crowd is aware that each hear them in their own language. Notice the crowd's reaction first to the sound coming from the house and later to the followers of Jesus speaking in tongues but try not to get caught up in the drama. It is most important to observe that the Spirit moves Jesus' followers and uses them as his

agents to preach "the mighty acts of God," and they do so with great gusto!

READING II   Today's second reading also focuses on the gifts of the Holy Spirit. Paul begins by making the point that a person cannot proclaim faith in Jesus Christ without the Holy Spirit. Apparently, some members of the Christian community at Corinth were "puffed up" over their ability to go into ecstatic trance in prayer and prophecy and to speak in tongues. Paul asserts that there are not different spirits to whom people can lay claim

both **Jews** and converts to **Judaism**, **Cretans** and **Arabs**,
yet we **hear them** speaking in our own **tongues**
of the **mighty acts** of **God**."

Cretans = KREE-tuhnz

For meditation and context:

RESPONSORIAL PSALM   Psalm 104:1, 24, 29–30, 31, 34 (30)

R. Lord, send out your Spirit, and renew the face of the earth.
or
R. Alleluia.

Bless the LORD, O my soul!
   O LORD, my God, you are great indeed!
How manifold are your works, O LORD!
   the earth is full of your creatures.

If you take away their breath, they perish
   and return to their dust.
When you send forth your spirit,
   they are created,
and you renew the face of the earth.

May the glory of the LORD endure forever;
   may the LORD be glad in his works!
Pleasing to him be my theme;
   I will be glad in the LORD.

READING II   1 Corinthians 12:3b–7, 12–13

Corinthians = kohr-IN-thee-uhnz

A reading with claims of enduring force.

The invocation of the Holy Spirit is meant to echo the same in the first reading at Pentecost. Here the Holy Spirit is understood in terms of spiritual gifts.

A reading from the first Letter of Saint Paul to the Corinthians

Brothers and **sisters**:
No one can say, "**Jesus** is Lord," **except** by the Holy Spirit.

There are different **kinds** of spiritual gifts but the same **Spirit**;
   there are different **forms** of service but the same **Lord**;
   there are different **workings** but the same **God**
   who produces **all** of them in **everyone**.
To each individual the **manifestation** of the Spirit
   is **given** for some **benefit**.

Even stress on these three words: "so also Christ."

The vision of radical equality that Paul stresses in these lines is something the Church continues to aspire to.

As a **body** is one though it has many **parts**,
   and all the **parts** of the body, though **many**, are one **body**,
   so also Christ.
For in one **Spirit** we were all **baptized** into one **body**,
   whether **Jews** or **Greeks**, **slaves** or free **persons**,
   and we were all **given** to drink of one **Spirit**.

---

for their own benefit. Rather, it is the *one* Spirit, who motivates and enlivens the life of the Christian community.

   Further, Paul categorizes the manifestations of the Spirit, noting that there are different types of spiritual gifts, ways of service or ministering to others, and activities or workings or things wrought. All of these manifestations of the Spirit are necessary for healthy and fruitful communities of faith. Thus, Paul says elsewhere, "Do not quench the Spirit" (1 Thessalonians 5:19). The Greek word translated here as "quench"

also has the meaning of "extinguish, suppress, or stifle."

   Finally, to reinforce the idea that the Spirit's role or mission is to foster unity, Paul uses the metaphor of a body. Just as the body has fingers and toes, a heart and a nose, each with different functions for the benefit of the body, so too does the Christian community, which is the body of Christ, have different manifestations of the Spirit. It does not matter who we are or what is our status in life, we all have been "given to drink of one Spirit."

GOSPEL   The setting for today's Gospel reading is described as "on the evening of that first day of the week." A lot has happened already on that day. Before dawn, Mary Magdalene had been to the garden tomb where Jesus was buried and found it empty. Peter and the Beloved Disciple ran to the tomb to find it empty. Mary met the risen Jesus and then told the disciples about Jesus' resurrection. Despite all of this, we still find them hiding behind locked doors "for fear of the Jews." Most frequently in John's Gospel, "the Jews" is used interchangeably with refer-

TO KEEP IN MIND
Sequences originated as extensions of the sung Alleluia before the proclamation of the Gospel, although they precede the Alleluia now. The Pentecost Sequence, also called the Golden Sequence, is an ancient liturgical hymn praising the Holy Spirit. It is the source of the hymn "Come, Holy Ghost."

SEQUENCE Veni, Sancte Spiritus

Come, Holy Spirit, come!
And from your celestial home
　Shed a ray of light divine!
Come, Father of the poor!
Come, source of all our store!
　Come, within our bosoms shine.
You, of comforters the best;
You, the soul's most welcome guest;
　Sweet refreshment here below;
In our labor, rest most sweet;
Grateful coolness in the heat;
　Solace in the midst of woe.
O most blessed Light divine,
Shine within these hearts of yours,
　And our inmost being fill!
Where you are not, we have naught,

Nothing good in deed or thought,
　Nothing free from taint of ill.
Heal our wounds, our strength renew;
On our dryness pour your dew;
　Wash the stains of guilt away:
Bend the stubborn heart and will;
Melt the frozen, warm the chill;
　Guide the steps that go astray.
On the faithful, who adore
And confess you, evermore
　In your sevenfold gift descend;
Give them virtue's sure reward;
Give them your salvation, Lord;
　Give them joys that never end. Amen.
　Alleluia.

GOSPEL John 20:19–23

A reading from the holy Gospel according to John

On the **evening** of that first day of the **week**,
　when the **doors** were locked, where the **disciples** were,
　for **fear** of the Jews,
　Jesus came and **stood** in their midst
　and **said** to them, "**Peace** be with you."
When he had **said** this, he **showed** them his hands and his side.
The disciples **rejoiced** when they saw the Lord.
Jesus said to them again, "**Peace** be with you.
As the **Father** has sent me, so I send **you**."
And when he had **said** this, he **breathed** on them and
　said to them,
　"**Receive** the Holy Spirit.
Whose sins you **forgive** are **forgiven** them,
　and whose **sins** you **retain** are **retained**."

A narrative reading that depicts the transmission of the Holy Spirit through Jesus himself to his disciples.

Jesus enters the scene with the word "Peace."

Breath is the most ancient sign of life in scripture. Here, Jesus' powers are transmitted directly through his breath.
Note the parallel construction: forgive/forgiven; retain/retained.

ences to the religious authorities in Jerusalem, so we must be careful not to assume that this mention of Jews applies to our Jewish brothers and sisters today or even to Jews in Jesus' time.

This story of the appearance of the risen Jesus to his disciples bears some similarities with Luke 24:36–40, in which the risen Jesus appears suddenly and shows his hands and feet to the disciples to allay their fears and show that he is truly alive. However, there are some important differences, as well. The greeting Jesus gives them, "Peace be with you," reminds us of

Jesus' words to the disciples earlier in John's Gospel, when during the farewell discourse and before his arrest and crucifixion he says "Peace I leave with you; my peace I give to you. . . . Do not let your hearts be troubled" (John 14:27).

John's version of the story also has the detail about Jesus breathing upon the disciples and saying, "Receive the Holy Spirit." This statement should recall for us the second creation story of Genesis, when God creates a man, Adam, and breathes into him the breath of life and he "became a living being" (Genesis 2:7). When Jesus

breathes on the disciples, they become "new" living beings insofar as they have a new mission, which is to continue the work that God had given to Jesus to do—to be the light that casts out darkness (John 8:12; see also John 1:5; 3:19–21). When we hear the command, "Whose sins you forgive are forgiven them, and whose sins you retain are retained," we can see how it fits in as part of this larger mission of Jesus' disciples to be light in darkness. C.C.

THE MOST HOLY TRINITY

LECTIONARY #164

READING I Exodus 34:4b–6, 8–9

A reading from the Book of Exodus

Early in the **morning Moses** went up **Mount Sinai**
as the LORD had **commanded** him,
taking along the two stone tablets.

Having come **down** in a **cloud**, the LORD stood with **Moses** there
and **proclaimed** his **name**, "**LORD**."
Thus the **Lord** passed **before** him and cried **out**,
"The LORD, the LORD, a **merciful** and **gracious God**,
slow to **anger** and **rich** in **kindness** and **fidelity**."
Moses at once **bowed down** to the **ground** in **worship**.
Then he **said**, "If I find **favor** with you, O LORD,
do come **along** in our **company**.
This is **indeed** a **stiff-necked people**;
yet **pardon** our **wickedness** and **sins**,
and **receive** us as your **own**."

Exodus = EK-suh-duhs
Moses = MOH-zihz or MOH-zihs
Sinai = SĪ-nī
Slight pause between "morning" and "Moses."

God is speaking this exhortation to Moses.

"Stiff-necked people": Moses is speaking for all of us in our stubbornness when he uses these words.

READING I Our first reading is part of the story about God restoring the tablets of the Law that Moses broke when he came down the mountain and saw the Israelites engaged in worshiping a golden calf (Exodus 32:19). The Book of Exodus describes Moses as having an intimate relationship with God, and the narrator of Exodus 33:11 tells us "the LORD used to speak to Moses face to face, as a person speaks to a friend." At one point, Moses asks to see God's glory, and God consents, saying, "I will proclaim my name, 'LORD,' before you. . . . But you cannot see my face, for no one can see me and live" (Exodus 33:19–20).

This is where today's reading begins. God tells Moses to prepare to return to the top of the mountain with two new stone tablets so that God can remake the tablets of the covenant with the Israelites. God comes down to the mountain to meet Moses and "proclaimed his name, 'LORD.'" What is the significance of this action? If we look at the description of God's covenant with Moses and the Israelites in Exodus 20, we will find an important clue. There too God proclaims his name, that is, identifies himself, as the one making the covenant. God does so by saying, "For I, the LORD, your God, am a jealous God, inflicting punishment for their ancestors' wickedness on the children of those who hate me, down to the third and fourth generation; but showing love down to the thousandth generation of those who love me and keep my commandments" (Exodus 20:5–6).

However, in this story of the restoration of the tablets of the Law, God proclaims his name differently. Here, God says, "The LORD, the LORD, a merciful and gracious God, slow to anger and rich in kind-

For meditation and context:

RESPONSORIAL PSALM   Daniel 3:52, 53, 54, 55 (52b)

R. Glory and praise for ever!

Blessed are you, O Lord, the God
    of our fathers,
  praiseworthy and exalted above all
    forever;
and blessed is your holy and glorious name,
  praiseworthy and exalted above all for
    all ages.

Blessed are you in the temple of your
    holy glory,
  praiseworthy and glorious above
    all forever.

Blessed are you on the throne
    of your kingdom,
  praiseworthy and exalted above all forever.

Blessed are you who look into the depths
    from your throne upon the cherubim,
  praiseworthy and exalted above all forever.

READING II   2 Corinthians 13:11–13

A reading from second Letter of Saint Paul to the Corinthians

Brothers and **sisters**, **rejoice**.
Mend your **ways**, **encourage** one **another**,
  agree with one **another**, live in **peace**,
  and the **God** of **love** and **peace** will be **with** you.
Greet one another with a **holy kiss**.
All the **holy** ones **greet** you.

The **grace** of the **Lord Jesus Christ**
  and the **love** of **God**
  and the **fellowship** of the **Holy Spirit** be with **all** of you.

Corinthians = kohr-IN-thee-uhnz

This reading comes from the conclusion of Paul's second letter to the Corinthians, the so-called valediction. Its tone is encouraging and uplifting, meant to convey Paul's conclusive feelings of hope.

ness and fidelity." Immediately Moses bowed his head—the Hebrew word suggests worship or submission—and asks God to be with them. All that remains is for God to deliver the Law, the Israelites' obligation to the covenant.

READING II Today's second reading is the conclusion of Paul's Second Letter to the Corinthians. Paul's exhortations to good behavior are general in nature—like what a parent might say to an adolescent child before leaving them

alone—but Paul's big concern is peace within the community. If we could reconstruct the life of this Christian community at Corinth based on Paul's two letters, we would be amazed at this colorful and unruly group of Christians. Their story would make a great soap opera! But the reason that this reading is noteworthy, especially today on the solemnity of the Most Holy Trinity, is the final sentence. It is the clearest and most illuminating acclamation of the trinitarian God in the entire New Testament.

GOSPEL John's Gospel provides us with an equally beautiful and profound statement about Jesus, his relationship with the Father, and his role in the salvation of the world. The verbs in the phrases "he gave his only Son" and "God did not send his Son" have related meanings. Likewise, the verbs "to perish" and "to condemn" have related meanings, as do "to have eternal life" and "to be saved." But there is even more going on here. There are several Greek words for love, including sexual attraction, friendship love, and uncondi-

GOSPEL John 3:16–18

A reading from the holy Gospel according to John

God **so** loved the **world** that he gave his **only Son**,
    so that **everyone** who **believes** in him might not **perish**
    but might **have eternal life**.
For **God** did not send his **Son** into the **world** to **condemn**
    the world,
    but that the **world** might be **saved through** him.
Whoever **believes** in him will **not** be **condemned**,
    but whoever **does not believe** has **already** been **condemned**,
    because he has **not believed** in the **name** of the **only Son**
    of **God**.

A brief reading with a very familiar message. Try not to proclaim the opening as a slogan. Instead, proclaim as if it is being said for the first time.

Slight pause between "saved" and "through."

Note the repetition and the inversion: "believes" and "not condemned"; "does not believe" and "already condemned."

---

tional love without expectation for return. The Greek word for this third kind of love is *agapaó*. Although the author of John's Gospel is not entirely consistent regarding the use of these synonyms for love, clearly, in this instance, John has in mind unconditional love. Also, the author of this Gospel has what we call a "realized eschatology," meaning that he understands himself and his community to be already in the throes of the end time.

Why would early Christians think this way? Among first-century Jewish views

about what happens after death, there was a segment of the population who believed that resurrection of the dead was a sign of the end time. Therefore, when people began to proclaim Jesus Christ raised from the dead, these same people thought that the end time was already underway. This is why there is no "in between" in the talk about salvation and condemnation. Either you are already committed to God and his Son Jesus, or you are already condemned. Today, most Christians who anticipate an end time return of Christ have a future

eschatology, which significantly defers people's anxiety about the end time. Regardless, the point of this reading for today's believers is that God is so generous and unconditional with divine love that he is willing to give his only Son to effect salvation for the whole world. How else can we respond but in gratitude? C.C.

THE MOST HOLY BODY AND BLOOD OF CHRIST (CORPUS CHRISTI)

LECTIONARY #167

READING I   Deuteronomy 8:2–3, 14b–16a

A reading from the Book of Deuteronomy

Moses said to the **people**:
  "**Remember** how for **forty years now** the LORD, your **God**,
  has **directed** all your **journeying** in the **desert**,
  so as to **test** you by **affliction**
  and find **out** whether or **not** it was your **intention**
  to **keep** his **commandments**.
He **therefore** let you be **afflicted** with **hunger**,
  and then **fed** you with **manna**,
  a **food unknown** to **you** and your **fathers**,
  in order to **show** you that **not** by **bread alone** does one **live**,
  but by **every word** that comes **forth** from the **mouth**
    of the LORD.

"**Do not forget** the LORD, your **God**,
  who **brought** you out of the **land** of **Egypt**,
  that **place** of **slavery**;
  who **guided** you through the **vast** and **terrible desert**
  with its **saraph serpents** and **scorpions**,
  its **parched** and **waterless ground**;
  who **brought forth water** for you from the **flinty rock**
  and **fed** you in the **desert** with **manna**,
  a **food unknown** to your **fathers**."

Deuteronomy = doo-ter-AH-nuh-mee

Moses = MOH-zihz or MOH-zihs

This reading consists of two parts, the first introduced by "Remember," recalling the past of the Israelites, the second introduced by "Do not forget," offering advice about how to proceed.

manna = MAN-uh
Manna is a focus of this reading.

Note the rhythm of the second part of the reading, in which the verb in the phrase is emphasized to lead to a noun related to the Israelites' desert exile.

Once again, manna is mentioned.

READING I The first reading for today's feast is taken from the Book of Deuteronomy. The title of the book means "second law," and it presents Moses as the great law giver. Traditionally, Moses was thought to be the author of this book, but today biblical scholars understand it to have been written over several centuries, starting in the eighth century BC and possibly extending to the exile in the sixth century BC.

Today's reading is part of a unit that begins with the words "Be careful to observe this whole commandment that I enjoin on you today" (Deuteronomy 8:1). It provides a recollection of the past to urge obedience to the covenant. The recollection is of the manna that God provided to the Israelites in their sojourn in the wilderness (Exodus 16:4–15) and the water from the rock that God provided when the Israelites were thirsty (Exodus 17:1–7). The reward associated with observing the commandments is to live and prosper in the land that was promised to their ancestors.

But Moses observes that the commandments are God's way of teaching discipline to God's people, like a father would teach his son (see Deuteronomy 8:5). And what does God want to teach the people? He wants them to learn reliance on God so that they never assume that their prosperity comes from their own hands. Thus, the stories of the manna and the water from the rock are perfect illustrations of God's benevolence even to an unruly and grumpy people.

READING II Our second reading is an excerpt from a section of the First Letter to the Corinthians in which Paul warns the community about the dan-

For meditation and context:

RESPONSORIAL PSALM   Psalm 147:12–13, 14–15, 19–20 (12)

R. Praise the Lord, Jerusalem.
or
R. Alleluia.

Glorify the LORD, O Jerusalem;
    praise your God, O Zion.
For he has strengthened the bars
        of your gates;
    he has blessed your children within you.

He has granted peace in your borders;
    with the best of wheat he fills you.
He sends forth his command to the earth;
    swiftly runs his word!

He has proclaimed his word to Jacob,
    his statutes and his ordinances to Israel.
He has not done thus for any other nation;
    his ordinances he has not made known
        to them. Alleluia.

READING II   1 Corinthians 10:16–17

Corinthians = kohr-IN-thee-uhnz

An elegantly simple reading that condenses into its few lines a whole theology of the Eucharist. Emphasis throughout especially on "body," "blood," "loaf," and "cup."

A reading from the first Letter of Saint Paul to the Corinthians

Brothers and **sisters**:
The **cup** of **blessing** that we **bless**,
    is it **not** a **participation** in the **blood** of **Christ**?
The **bread** that we **break**,
    is it **not** a **participation** in the **body** of **Christ**?
Because the **loaf** of **bread** is **one**,
    we, though **many**, are **one body**,
    for we **all partake** of the **one loaf**.

gers of overconfidence, telling them that even God's chosen ones can fall into idolatry. He uses the Exodus story to illustrate his point by noting that, while they were in the wilderness, all were given safe passage through the sea and all received the same spiritual nourishment. Thus, the Israelites experienced the same manifestations of God's benevolence. Despite these miraculous interventions, they grumbled against God and practiced idolatry. They were punished, Paul says, to give an example to others so that they might avoid the temptation of evil things (1 Corinthians 10:1–13).

Transitioning from this general warning about overconfidence, Paul addresses the problem of idolatry more directly. Major social gatherings, such as banquets, games, and other forms of entertainment in Corinth would have involved sacrifices to idols, and these early Christians would have felt compelled to participate, if they wanted to be part of the social scene. But Paul wants the Corinthian community to judge based on their own experience. Which is better or more fulfilling: idol worship or the Eucharist? To make his case, he uses two rhetorical questions that antici-

pate a response of "Yes, of course!" The Greek word translated here as "participation" is *koinonia*, which also means "fellowship or partnership." Paul uses it frequently to refer to the communion of believers. In today's more secular society, you might think, "Why can't the Corinthian Christian community just go ahead and participate in these events?" Paul says, "You cannot drink the cup of the Lord and also the cup of demons. You cannot partake of the table of the Lord and of the table of demons" (1 Corinthians 10:21). In other words, you must choose!

SEQUENCE   Lauda, Sion, Salvatorem

Laud, O Zion, your salvation,
Laud with hymns of exultation,
　　Christ, your king and shepherd true:

Bring him all the praise you know,
He is more than you bestow.
　　Never can you reach his due.

Special theme for glad thanksgiving
Is the quick'ning and the living
　　Bread today before you set:

From his hands of old partaken,
As we know, by faith unshaken,
　　Where the Twelve at supper met.

Full and clear ring out your chanting,
Joy nor sweetest grace be wanting,
　　From your heart let praises burst:

For today the feast is holden,
When the institution olden
　　Of that supper was rehearsed.

Here the new law's new oblation,
By the new king's revelation,
　　Ends the form of ancient rite:

Now the new the old effaces,
Truth away the shadow chases,
　　Light dispels the gloom of night.

What he did at supper seated,
Christ ordained to be repeated,
　　His memorial ne'er to cease:

And his rule for guidance taking,
Bread and wine we hallow, making
　　Thus our sacrifice of peace.

This the truth each Christian learns,
Bread into his flesh he turns,
　　To his precious blood the wine:

Sight has fail'd, nor thought conceives,
But a dauntless faith believes,
　　Resting on a pow'r divine.

Here beneath these signs are hidden
Priceless things to sense forbidden;
　　Signs, not things are all we see:

Blood is poured and flesh is broken,
Yet in either wondrous token
　　Christ entire we know to be.

Whoso of this food partakes,
Does not rend the Lord nor breaks;
　　Christ is whole to all that taste:

Thousands are, as one, receivers,
One, as thousands of believers,
　　Eats of him who cannot waste.

Bad and good the feast are sharing,
Of what divers dooms preparing,
　　Endless death, or endless life.

Life to these, to those damnation,
See how like participation
　　Is with unlike issues rife.

When the sacrament is broken,
Doubt not, but believe 'tis spoken,
　　That each sever'd outward token
　　　doth the very whole contain.

Nought the precious gift divides,
Breaking but the sign betides
　　Jesus still the same abides,
　　　still unbroken does remain.

[Shorter form begins here.]
Lo! the angel's food is given
To the pilgrim who has striven;
　　See the children's bread from heaven,
　　　which on dogs may not be spent.

Truth the ancient types fulfilling,
Isaac bound, a victim willing,
　　Paschal lamb, its lifeblood spilling,
　　　manna to the fathers sent.

Very bread, good shepherd, tend us,
Jesu, of your love befriend us,
　　You refresh us, you defend us,
　　Your eternal goodness send us
In the land of life to see.

You who all things can and know,
Who on earth such food bestow,
　　Grant us with your saints, though lowest,
　　Where the heav'nly feast you show,
Fellow heirs and guests to be. Amen.
　　Alleluia.

TO KEEP IN MIND

Sequences originated as extensions of the sung Alleluia before the proclamation of the Gospel, although they precede the Alleluia now. St. Thomas Aquinas composed the hymn that is now the sequence for the Most Holy Body and Blood of Christ in the thirteenth century.

GOSPEL   The Gospel reading for today is part of the "Bread of Life" discourse from the Gospel of John, which is often described as a midrash on the sentence "He gave them bread from heaven to eat" (John 6:31), a paraphrase and conflation of Exodus 16:4 and Psalm 78:24. A midrash is a type of Jewish literature in which the author provides commentary on a Scripture text, sometimes taking it apart phrase by phrase or word by word, and giving it a new contemporary meaning.

As a preface to this midrash, the narrator tells us that the crowds try to follow Jesus after he performs a miracle of multiplying loaves and fishes (John 6:1–15). The next day, they catch up with Jesus again. After a brief conversation about doing the works of God, they ask Jesus for a sign so that they might believe in him, saying, "Our ancestors ate manna in the desert, as it is written: 'He gave them bread from heaven to eat.'" In the midrash that follows, Jesus clarifies that "he," in this sentence, refers to God not Moses, and "gave" becomes "gives." Also, "bread from heaven" is no longer manna but rather Jesus, who comes from the Father to do God's work.

Today's Gospel is the last part of this midrash, where Jesus explains what "to eat" means. John's Gospel does not have a Last Supper/institution of the Eucharist narrative, but here we have lots of eucharistic imagery: bread, food, flesh, blood, and so on. When Jesus declares that he is the living bread and that "whoever eats this bread will live forever," "the Jews" (i.e., Jewish religious authorities) argue about what this means. In the simplest of terms, they think Jesus is inviting the crowd to be cannibals! The author of John's Gospel regularly uses this literary technique, in which

---

GOSPEL   John 6:51–58

A reading from the holy Gospel according to John

Jesus said to the **Jewish crowds**:
"I am the **living bread** that came **down** from **heaven**;
whoever **eats** this **bread** will **live forever**;
and the **bread** that I will **give**
is my **flesh** for the **life** of the **world**."

The **Jews quarreled among** themselves, saying,
"**How** can this **man** give us his **flesh** to **eat**?"
Jesus **said** to them,
"**Amen**, **amen**, I **say** to you,
unless you **eat** the **flesh** of the **Son** of **Man** and **drink**
his **blood**,
you **do not have life** with**in** you.
Whoever **eats** my **flesh** and **drinks** my **blood**
has **eternal life**,
and I will **raise** him on the **last** day.
For my **flesh** is **true food**,
and my **blood** is **true drink**.
Whoever **eats** my **flesh** and **drinks** my **blood**
remains in **me** and I in **him**.
Just as the **living Father sent** me
and I have **life because** of the **Father**,
so also the **one** who **feeds** on me
will have **life because** of me.
This is the **bread** that came **down** from **heaven**.
Unlike your **ancestors** who **ate** and still **died**,
whoever **eats** this **bread** will **live forever**."

A reading that draws out the potent metaphor of Jesus as the "living bread."

Even emphasis on "do not have life." Note the emphasis on "-in" in "within."

Do not sell the strangeness of this promise short. Eating flesh and drinking blood together were strictly forbidden in Jewish dietary laws (and still are for those who keep kosher). In those terms, what Jesus is saying here is appalling.

Slight pause between "Father" and "sent."

Slight pause between "life" and "because."

Jesus says something deliberately ambiguous, and characters in the story understand only the plain meaning of his words, which allows Jesus to explain further. But, in this case, the Johannine Jesus piles on even more offensive language. No wonder people were upset!

The phrase "Amen, amen I say to you" is like saying "Sit up and pay attention! This is important!" The Greek verb *trógó* translated here as "to eat" more often means "to gnaw on or to crunch on." Elsewhere, in this reading, the less repulsive *phago*, meaning "to eat," is used. Consider how these pas-sages read with this understanding of the difference in "to eat": "Whoever eats (*phago*) my flesh and drinks my blood has eternal life." "Whoever gnaws on (*trógó*) my flesh and drinks my blood remains in me and I in him." "The one who feeds on (*trógó*) me will have life because of me." "Whoever crunches on (*trógó*) this bread will live forever."

Although we cannot fully know what the author of this Gospel intended to say with the use of such graphic language, at the very least we can say that Jesus was not a phantom; he was truly incarnated in flesh and blood, which he gave up for our salvation. We can also say that Jesus continuously invites us to share in this eucharistic experience so that we can remain in him and he in us. This is the fullness of life! C.C.

ELEVENTH SUNDAY IN ORDINARY TIME

LECTIONARY #91

READING I   Exodus 19:2–6a

Exodus = EK-suh-duhs

Sinai = SĪ-nī

Visually, the focus in this reading is Moses' ascent of the holy mountain to speak to God.

The content of the reading is focused on the promise of God conveyed in his speech to Moses. God's promise is uplifting and encouraging.

A reading from the Book of Exodus

In **those days**, the **Israelites** came to the **desert** of **Sinai** and
    pitched camp.
While **Israel** was **encamped** here in **front** of the **mountain**,
    Moses went up the **mountain** to **God**.
Then the LORD **called** to him and **said**,
    "**Thus** shall you **say** to the **house** of **Jacob**;
    tell the **Israelites**:
    You have **seen** for **yourselves** how I **treated** the **Egyptians**
    and how I **bore** you **up** on **eagle wings**
    and **brought** you **here** to **myself**.
Therefore, if you **hearken** to my **voice** and **keep** my **covenant**,
    you shall be my **special possession**,
    dearer to **me** than **all other people**,
    though **all** the **earth** is **mine**.
You shall be to me a **kingdom** of **priests**, a **holy nation**."

For meditation and context:

RESPONSORIAL PSALM   Psalm 100:1–2, 3, 5 (3c)

R. We are his people: the sheep of his flock.

Sing joyfully to the LORD, all you lands;
    serve the LORD with gladness;
    come before him with joyful song.

Know that the LORD is God;
    he made us, his we are;
    his people, the flock he tends.

The LORD is good:
    his kindness endures forever,
    and his faithfulness to all generations.

READING I   Chapter 19 of the Book of Exodus, which we hear the beginning of today, begins the third part of Exodus and tells the story of God establishing a covenant with the children of Israel and bestowing upon them a code of law. It has taken the newly released exiles three months to journey out of Egypt beyond the Red Sea through the desert wilderness to finally arrive and set up camp at Mount Sinai, the holy mountain of God.

Upon their arrival, the first order of business is for God to speak individually to Moses. In revealing his covenant to the people, God will proceed to call Moses apart from them to instruct him and to foster the development of a relationship that symbolizes the one God will come to establish with the Israelite nation as a whole. The words God speaks to Moses here are meant to serve as a personal introduction that will remind the former slaves of how God has acted in the past on their behalf in order that they might expect his divine assistance in the future. God highlights his actions against the Egyptians as the care he showed the Israelites by stating that he "bore you up on eagle wings and brought you here to myself." Instead of belonging to Pharaoh and all of Egypt, they are now God's "special possession." God demonstrates here a preferential option for Israel, as he desires to make them a people set apart. The notion of being separated from other nations is made clear in choosing them to be a holy people. It is not simply that Israel is made sacred to God but that they are to perform the role of mediating on behalf of other peoples as priests are set apart to minister to others and be in God's presence.

READING II   Romans 5:6–11

A reading from the Letter of Saint Paul to the Romans

Brothers and **sisters**:
Christ, while we were still **helpless**,
   yet **died** at the **appointed time** for the **ungodly**.
Indeed, only with **difficulty** does one **die** for a **just person**,
   though **perhaps** for a **good person**
   one might **even** find **courage** to **die**.
But **God** proves his **love** for us
   in that while we were **still sinners** Christ **died** for us.
How much more then, since we are now **justified** by his **blood**,
   will we be **saved** through **him** from the **wrath**.
Indeed, if, **while** we were **enemies**,
   we were **reconciled** to **God** through the **death** of his **Son**,
   how much more, once **reconciled**,
   will we be **saved** by his **life**.
Not only **that**,
   but we also **boast** of **God** through our **Lord Jesus Christ**,
   through whom we have **now received reconciliation**.

GOSPEL   Matthew 9:36—10:8

A reading from the holy Gospel according to Matthew

At the **sight** of the **crowds**, Jesus' **heart** was **moved**
    with **pity** for them
  because they were **troubled** and **abandoned**,
  like **sheep** without a **shepherd**.
Then he **said** to his **disciples**,
   "The **harvest** is **abundant** but the **laborers** are **few**;
   so ask the **master** of the **harvest**
   to send out **laborers** for his **harvest**." »

Paul's letter makes a complex argument about reconciliation. Proclaim at an even pace to allow its subtleties to register with the assembly.

Even emphasis on "How much more."

Even emphasis on "now received reconciliation."

Jesus uses the image of sheep without a shepherd to instruct his disciples. Not only is Jesus their shepherd but the disciples themselves are shepherds as they go out.

READING II This passage from Romans comes immediately after Paul's declaration of the justification by faith that Christians have through the grace of God. This is cause for the faithful to be filled with hope, even in times of persecution. Thus, Paul sets out to answer why Christians have reason to be hopeful. He begins by acknowledging that Christ chose to die for sinners not the righteous. The decision not to die for only the holy ones demonstrates God's immense love, since it would be far easier to die for those who do not dwell in sin.

Thus, for Paul, justification is the reconciliation of sinners to Christ through his death on the cross. But salvation is a different thing. Sin must first be remitted before salvation can be given. Paul will go on to say that this is precisely what baptism will ensure (Romans 6:1–11). Having been reconciled to God by the blood of the cross, Christians are baptized into Christ in order to look forward in hope to the fullness of the gift that is salvation.

GOSPEL Jesus' words that "the harvest is abundant but the laborers are few" serve as a transition between several public cures and demonstrations of Jesus' authority and his commissioning of the twelve apostles. Jesus has discovered in a very short time of proclaiming the kingdom of God that the people in the countryside are in desperate need of spiritual leadership. Matthew states quite clearly that Jesus "was moved with pity" for the people because they were "like sheep without a shepherd." He turns to his disciples and acknowledges the great amount of work that needs to be done. They are to

Don't rush through these names of the disciples. And don't give unnecessary emphasis to the name of Judas Iscariot.

Zebedee = ZEB-uh-dee

Bartholomew = Bahr-THAHL-uh-myoo

Alphaeus = AL-fee-uhs

Thaddeus = THAD-ee-uhs

Cana = KAY-nuh

Iscariot = ih-SKAYR-ee-uht

Samaritan = suh-MAYR-uh-tuhn

Here the image of the lost sheep returns.

Jesus provides instruction as clear and direct as possible as to what his disciples are to do. Proclaim these tasks forcefully.

Then he **summoned** his twelve **disciples**
and gave them **authority** over **unclean spirits**
to drive them **out** and to cure **every disease** and **every illness**.
The **names** of the twelve **apostles** are **these**:
first, **Simon** called **Peter**, and his brother **Andrew**;
James, the son of **Zebedee**, and his brother **John**;
Philip and **Bartholomew**, **Thomas** and **Matthew** the
tax collector;
James, the son of **Alphaeus**, and **Thaddeus**;
Simon from **Cana**, and **Judas Iscariot** who **betrayed** him.

Jesus sent **out** these **twelve** after **instructing** them **thus**,
"**Do not go** into **pagan territory** or enter a **Samaritan town**.
Go rather to the **lost sheep** of the **house** of **Israel**.
As you **go**, make **this proclamation**: 'The **kingdom** of **heaven**
is at **hand**.'
Cure the **sick**, **raise** the **dead**, **cleanse lepers**, **drive out demons**.
Without **cost** you have **received**; without **cost** you are to **give**."

pray for more people to assist with bringing people into the fold, or into God's kingdom.

After his honest assessment that the work to come will be arduous, Jesus gives authority to the twelve disciples—who are referred to by Matthew here as apostles, meaning those who are sent out—to heal people and combat the works of evil. Essentially, Jesus invites these disciples to share in his ministry in a particular way. He then names them and from this we have a list of the twelve apostles. Earlier in Matthew we have heard the names of five of them: Peter, Andrew, James, and John were

mentioned when Jesus called these fishermen away from their father, their boats, and their nets (Matthew 4:18–22) and Matthew was called away from his post as a tax collector (Matthew 9:9); the remaining seven names are listed here for the first time here.

Before releasing the disciples on to the world, Jesus provides them with instructions that begin with a caution to avoid the territory of the Gentiles and Samaritans and to focus exclusively on "the lost sheep of the house of Israel." Remember that Jesus has been ministering amongst this people and has come to pity them. For Matthew's audi-

ence, who is primarily a community of Jewish Christians struggling to understand their faith in a rapidly changing society where they are no longer accepted by the Jewish community, and in the wake of the Temple's destruction, this command by Jesus to minister within given boundaries would have been reassuring. But this is only the beginning of the work of the kingdom, as Jesus instructs them to announce that "the kingdom of heaven is at hand." This work of the harvest is still ongoing today as we take up the Christian mission and give in abundance without expecting to be repaid. S.W.

TWELFTH SUNDAY IN ORDINARY TIME

LECTIONARY #94

READING I   Jeremiah 20:10–13

A reading from the Book of the Prophet Jeremiah

Jeremiah said:
"I **hear** the **whisperings** of **many**:
  '**Terror** on **every side**!
  Denounce! let us **denounce** him!'
All those who were my **friends**
  are on the **watch** for any **misstep** of mine.
'**Perhaps** he will be **trapped**; then **we** can **prevail**,
  and take our **vengeance** on him.'
But the LORD is **with** me, like a **mighty champion**:
  my **persecutors** will **stumble**, they **will not triumph**.
In their **failure** they will be **put** to **utter shame**,
  to **lasting, unforgettable confusion**.
O LORD of **hosts**, **you** who **test** the **just**,
  who probe **mind** and **heart**,
let me **witness** the **vengeance** you **take** on them,
  for to **you** I have **entrusted** my **cause**.
Sing to the LORD,
  praise the LORD,
for he has **rescued** the **life** of the **poor**
  from the **power** of the **wicked**!"

Jeremiah = jer-uh-MĪ-uh

The tone that opens this reading is fearful. Jeremiah is terrified.

Here, with "But," the tone shifts, becoming more hopeful. Jeremiah is talking himself into persevering.

"O Lord" begins a petition, one in which Jeremiah asks to witness the vengeance God will take on his persecutors, a common enough request but nevertheless worth noting.

With this conclusion, Jeremiah shifts into the imperative voice: Jeremiah is speaking to the assembly through these words.

READING I   This passage is a portion of one of Jeremiah's "confessions," a term scholars use to describe passages of Jeremiah in which the prophet reveals personal anguish and lament to God. This confession follows Jeremiah's encounter with the priest Pashhur, who was one of the Temple priests who persecuted Jeremiah for his prediction of the destruction of Jerusalem by the Babylonians. In hearing Jeremiah's distress, it is important to keep in mind that he never sought the life of a prophet and even, in this moment of lamentation, considers himself deceived by God to accept this life as a prophet (Jeremiah 20:7).

Our reading begins with the announcement "Terror on every side!" Jeremiah uses these words to foretell the destruction of Jerusalem, but they also come from the lips of those who oppose the prophet. Like Job, Jeremiah believes that his friends have turned against him (Job 19:19). What acts of "vengeance" they plot for the demise of the prophet we can only imagine. However, Jeremiah confronts fear and turns to the Lord who will act as a hero on his behalf and cause his enemies to "stumble." Jeremiah counts himself among the just whose mind and heart is known well by God, and he prays that he will be able to witness the power of the Lord bringing Jeremiah's enemies to shame.

The final words of Jeremiah's "confession" turns from lament to praise. He commands that songs of praise ring out before the Lord because he has defended the poor—who may be understood as the lowly ones of Israel—from the "power of the wicked." It is clear that God defends the poor not because of their economic status but rather because of their dependence

For meditation and context:

RESPONSORIAL PSALM   Psalm 69:8–10, 14, 17, 33–35 (14c)

R. Lord, in your great love, answer me.

For your sake I bear insult,
    and shame covers my face.
I have become an outcast to my brothers,
    a stranger to my children,
because zeal for your house consumes me,
    and the insults of those who blaspheme
        you fall upon me.

I pray to you, O LORD,
    for the time of your favor, O God!
In your great kindness answer me
    with your constant help.
Answer me, O LORD, for bounteous is
    your kindness;
    in your great mercy turn toward me.

"See, you lowly ones, and be glad;
    you who seek God, may your hearts revive!
For the LORD hears the poor,
    and his own who are in bonds he
        spurns not.
Let the heavens and the earth praise him,
    the seas and whatever moves in them!"

READING II   Romans 5:12–15

A reading from the Letter of Saint Paul to the Romans

Brothers and **sisters:**
Through **one man sin entered** the **world,**
    and through **sin, death,**
    and thus **death** came to **all men, inasmuch** as **all sinned—**
for **up** to the **time** of the **law, sin** was in the **world,**
    though **sin** is not **accounted** when there **is no law.**
But **death reigned** from **Adam** to **Moses,**
    even over **those** who **did not sin**
    after the **pattern** of the **trespass** of **Adam,**
    who is the **type** of the **one** who was to **come.**

But the **gift** is not like the **transgression.**
For if by the **transgression** of the **one** the **many died,**
    how much more did the **grace** of **God**
    and the **gracious gift** of the **one man Jesus Christ**
    overflow for the **many.**

Slight pause between "man" and "sin." Paul uses the example of Adam to make a complex argument about sin and sinfulness, especially its durability in Scripture. Like reading a nuanced legal argument aloud, proclaim at a slow and even pace to allow its contents to register with your assembly.

Note the inversion that concludes the reading: "transgression of the one" and "many died"; the "gracious gift" of "one man" benefitting the "many."

---

upon him. Although the prophet did not ask for this task of proclaiming the word of God, he never falters in his obedience and his dependence on the goodness of God.

READING II These verses from the fifth chapter of the Letter to the Romans serve as part of the prelude to Paul's foundational theology of baptism. Baptism is participation in Christ's death and burial so that sin can reign in the body no more and we will have life in Christ (Romans 6). The passage we read today provides the background as to why bap-

tism is necessary. Sin entered the world through the disobedience of Adam, and this resulted in the dawning of death. Adam brings about a universal predicament for all humans, namely that all participate in sin and will experience death.

The appearance of Moses in this passage is important for Paul's theology. Moses represents the giving of the law by God. Thus, from the time between Adam and Moses, humanity was without the direction of the law. This means that humanity could not be (legally) responsible for sin during this time since it did not have an understanding

of the law. Nevertheless, sin did exist at this point because death had already entered the world. Sin cannot be separated from death; death is the result of sin.

Paul's major point here is that God provides a gift in the death of his Son that far outweighs the consequences of Adam's disobedience. By his own death, Jesus destroys death once and for all. With the destruction of death comes the banishment of all sin. The grace of God that is provided in this gift is to be accessed by baptism into Christ Jesus.

Jesus is speaking to his disciples and offering them advice. There is a somewhat stern and mysterious tone that prevails.

The example of the sparrows at first seems to be out of context with what comes before, yet Jesus persists in the example, connecting it with his message about overcoming fear.

Note the inversion Matthew uses to conclude Jesus' speech in this passage, contrasting acknowledgment and denial.

GOSPEL   Matthew 10:26–33

A reading from the holy Gospel according to Matthew

Jesus said to the **Twelve**:
  "Fear **no** one.
Nothing is **concealed** that will **not** be **revealed**,
  nor **secret** that will **not** be **known**.
What I **say** to **you** in the **darkness**, **speak** in the **light**;
  what you hear **whispered**, **proclaim** on the **housetops**.
And **do not** be **afraid** of **those** who **kill** the **body**
    but **cannot** kill the **soul**;
  rather, be **afraid** of the **one** who can **destroy**
  both **soul** and **body** in **Gehenna**.
Are not **two sparrows sold** for a **small coin**?
Yet not **one** of them **falls** to the **ground**
    without your Father's **knowledge**.
Even **all** the **hairs** of your **head** are **counted**.
So **do not** be **afraid**; you are worth **more** than many **sparrows**.
Everyone who **acknowledges** me before **others**
  I will **acknowledge** before my heavenly **Father**.
But whoever **denies** me before **others**,
  I will **deny** before my heavenly **Father**."

GOSPEL   Jesus' instructions to the twelve apostles as he sends them out to gather the harvest of the kingdom speak of: the necessary boldness of discipleship that will turn whispers into a message shouted from the housetops. Jesus has just finished informing his disciples that when he sends them into the world, they can expect to be persecuted by those who refuse to listen to them. Their response to such persecution must be quite simply "Fear no one." In fact, in this one reading, Jesus tells them three times that fear is not an acceptable attitude for disciples.

The quiet nature of the message of the kingdom by which Jesus instructs his disciples, spoken in "darkness" and heard "whispered," also calls our attention to the commission of the disciples after the resurrection. The fullness of Jesus' message can't be proclaimed yet, even by the those closest to Jesus because the disciples lack a full understanding of the kingdom and what Jesus' death and resurrection will mean; at the end of Matthew's Gospel, the disciples are called to share the Good News with all peoples. Returning our attention to

this moment, the disciples do go out and proclaim it as they can at that time.

The dire warning that death is a possible outcome of this mission is cause for fear, yet Jesus helps the disciples to shift their focus from the fear of bodily harm and death to the importance of preserving one's soul in the face of the wicked. Because of their identity as followers of God, they are cared for by God. They must act in a manner that illustrates this, trusting in God and remaining in him. S.W.

THIRTEENTH SUNDAY IN ORDINARY TIME

LECTIONARY #97

READING I   2 Kings 4:8–11, 14–16a

A reading from the second Book of Kings

Elisha = ee-LĪ-shuh
Shunem = SHOO-nuhm
Slight pause between "day" and "Elisha." This reading recounts a powerful narrative of generosity and reward. It's almost like a fable and can be proclaimed with that sense of wonder.

One day Elisha came to **Shunem**,
     where there was a **woman** of **influence**, who **urged** him
          to **dine** with her.
Afterward, **whenever** he passed **by**, he used to **stop** there to **dine**.
So she **said** to her **husband**, "I know that **Elisha** is a **holy** man
          of **God**.
Since he **visits** us **often**, let us **arrange** a little **room** on the **roof**
     and **furnish** it for him with a **bed**, **table**, **chair**, and **lamp**,
          so that when he **comes** to us he can **stay** there."
Sometime **later Elisha** arrived and **stayed** in the **room overnight**.

Slight pause between "later" and "Elisha."

Slight pause between "Later" and "Elisha."
Gehazi = geh-HAY-zī

Later Elisha asked, "Can **something** be **done** for her?"
His servant **Gehazi** answered, "**Yes**!
     She has **no son**, and her **husband** is getting **on** in **years**."
Elisha said, "**Call** her."
When the **woman** had been **called** and **stood** at the **door**,
     Elisha **promised**, "**This time next year**
     you will be **fondling** a **baby son**."

Even emphasis on "this time next year."

READING I   On this Thirteenth Sunday of Ordinary Time, we are invited to reflect on the gifts that come to us when we practice hospitality with no strings attached. Today's first reading tells the story of the prophet Elisha, who regularly stopped at the home of a wealthy couple when he was passing through Shunem, located approximately thirty miles northeast of Samaria, in the land given to the tribe of Issachar, one of the twelve tribes of Israel. The woman remains unnamed, but she is the one who first invited Elisha to dinner, and she is the one who told her husband that they should prepare a room for him to stay when he comes to Shunem, for no other reason than she believed him to be a holy man. Perhaps her wealth gave her privilege, but we should not ignore the fact that most women in the ancient world did not enjoy such power or influence. In response to her generous hospitality, Elisha asks his servant what he might offer as a gift of gratitude, and he learns that she has no son.

This is a very serious problem. Without a son, there was no one to take care of the couple in their old age and no way to pass on the husband's legacy to the next generation. Ancients thought that the woman determined the gender of their child, so it was her responsibility and shame that they had no son. Therefore, Elisha's prophecy is a huge gift to the couple.

We learn from the verses that follow this reading that the woman is skeptical and pleads with him not to give her false hope (2 Kings 4:16), and Elisha does not disappoint. Just as he prophesied, in the following year she had a healthy son, but tragedy struck when the son complained of a headache and died later that day (2 Kings

For meditation and context:

RESPONSORIAL PSALM   Psalm 89:2–3, 16–17, 18–19 (2a)

R. For ever I will sing the goodness of the Lord.

The promises of the LORD I will
    sing forever,
  through all generations my mouth shall
    proclaim your faithfulness.
For you have said, "My kindness is
    established forever";
  in heaven you have confirmed your
    faithfulness.

Blessed the people who know the
    joyful shout;
  in the light of your countenance,
    O LORD, they walk.
At your name they rejoice all the day,
    and through your justice they are exalted.

You are the splendor of their strength,
    and by your favor our horn is exalted.
For to the LORD belongs our shield,
    and to the Holy One of Israel, our king.

READING II   Romans 6:3–4, 8–11

A reading from the Letter of Saint Paul to the Romans

Brothers and **sisters**:
Are you **unaware** that **we** who were **baptized** into **Christ Jesus**
    were **baptized** into his **death**?
We were **indeed buried** with him through **baptism** into **death**,
    so that, **just** as **Christ** was **raised** from the **dead**
    by the **glory** of the **Father**,
    we too might **live** in **newness** of **life**.

If, **then**, we have **died** with **Christ**,
    we **believe** that we shall also **live** with him.
We **know** that **Christ**, **raised** from the **dead**, **dies** no more;
    death no longer has **power** over him.
As to his **death**, he **died** to **sin once** and for **all**;
    as to his **life**, he **lives** for **God**.
Consequently, **you too** must **think** of **yourselves** as **dead** to **sin**
    and **living** for **God** in **Christ Jesus**.

Paul's argument is staged in two parts. In the first part, he introduces his argument about baptism, death, and life with a question. The question allows the argument to proceed.

4:18–20). This brave and determined woman seeks out Elisha to bring her dead son back to life, which he does, thus rewarding her doubly for her hospitality (2 Kings 4:22–37).

 As in the most recent Sundays in Ordinary Time, our second reading comes from Paul's Letter to the Romans. Today's reading is an excerpt from his teaching on baptism. Water is a fitting element to be associated with the ritual of baptism, since the Greek word *baptizó* means "to dip, submerge, or immerse." Paul describes baptism as a participation in

the death of Jesus Christ "so that, just as Christ was raised from the dead," we can enter into newness of life and live with Christ. Further, because he understood that death entered the world because of sin, Jesus' resurrection was a triumph over sin *and* death. Therefore, being submerged in the water is an apt symbol for going into death and emerging from the water is a symbol for coming into new life. Paul goes on to assure his audience that Jesus, now resurrected, will never die again. So too, we are "dead to sin," that is, to our old way of

life, and should consider ourselves "living for God in Christ Jesus."

GOSPEL   Today's Gospel reading is taken from a section of Matthew's Gospel sometimes called the "mission discourse." The mission discourse begins with the narrator listing the twelve disciples (Matthew 10:1–4) and describing how Jesus commissioned them to go out among the people of the house of Israel and to teach and heal (Matthew 10:5–15). But before they depart on their mission, Jesus prepares them for what they might

The words of Jesus in this reading, divided into two parts, are challenging. In this first part, Jesus argues for worthiness in his followers based on how they feel about their family members. Then as now, these are hard words to reconcile to the ways we actually feel about our family members. Though unstressed, let the repetitions of "whoever" anchor your proclamation.

The second part of the reading focuses on the spiritual and moral sense of reward that Jesus wants to impart on his disciples and those who would heed his teachings.

TO KEEP IN MIND
Pause to break up separate thoughts, set apart significant statements, or indicate major shifts. Never pause in the middle of a thought. Your primary guide for pauses is punctuation.

GOSPEL   Matthew 10:37–42

A reading from the holy Gospel according to Matthew

Jesus said to his **apostles**:
  "Whoever loves **father** or **mother more** than **me** is not
      worthy of me,
  and whoever loves **son** or **daughter more** than **me** is not
      worthy of me;
  and whoever does not **take up** his **cross**
  and follow **after** me is not **worthy** of me.
Whoever **finds** his **life** will **lose** it,
  and **whoever loses** his life for **my sake** will **find** it.

"Whoever receives **you** receives **me**,
  and whoever receives **me** receives the **one** who **sent** me.
Whoever receives a **prophet** because he is a **prophet**
  will receive a **prophet's reward**,
  and whoever receives a **righteous man**
  because he is a **righteous man**
  will receive a **righteous man's reward**.
And whoever gives only a **cup** of **cold water**
  to one of these **little ones** to **drink**
  because the **little** one is a **disciple**—
  amen, I **say** to you, he will **surely not lose** his **reward**."

face along the way; they will face persecution and must muster their courage, but they should also be encouraged because God protects even the sparrows, so why would he not protect them? He also warns them that they will experience Jesus as a source of division in the communities they visit and among families (Matthew 10:16–36).

This is the background for today's Gospel teaching on discipleship. It is a call to radical discipleship! We are told that we must love Jesus more than father or mother and son or daughter. We must be willing to take up our crosses and follow Jesus even

to death. But as radical as this call to discipleship is, its success depends on a corresponding ministry of hospitality. Ancient cultures of the Near East operated on the patronage system. Patrons were responsible for providing certain protections or resources for their clients, and clients performed certain services for their patron. In some cases, this meant that the client would serve as an agent of the patron such that whatever he said or did in the name of his patron had the power and authority of the patron himself. Thus, the disciples are about to be sent out to be Jesus' presence

among the people they meet, and, as Jesus' representatives, they are likewise agents of God. Similarly, if we insist on holding onto what we value in our daily lives, Jesus says that we will lose it. But if we perform acts of hospitality, even if only a cup of water for the least of God's children, we will receive God's reward. C.C.

FOURTEENTH SUNDAY IN ORDINARY TIME

LECTIONARY #100

READING I   Zechariah 9:9–10

A reading from the Book of the Prophet Zechariah

> **Thus** says the LORD:
> Rejoice **heartily**, O **daughter Zion**,
>   **shout** for **joy**, O **daughter Jerusalem**!
> **See**, your **king** shall **come** to you;
>   a **just savior** is **he**,
> **meek**, and **riding** on an **ass**,
>   on a colt, the foal of an ass.
> He shall **banish** the **chariot** from **Ephraim**,
>   and the **horse** from **Jerusalem**;
> the **warrior's bow** shall be **banished**,
>   and he shall proclaim **peace** to the **nations**.
> His **dominion** shall be from **sea** to **sea**,
>   and from the **River** to the **ends** of the **earth**.

Zechariah = zek-uh-RĪ-uh

Zion = ZĪ-uhn or ZĪ-ahn

A rich and exhortatory reading, in which the words of the Lord ring out joyfully and forcefully. Let your tone be guided by the joy and force that come through this reading, as much like a poem as it is Scripture.

Ephraim = EE-fray-im; EF-r*m

READING I Today's readings invite us to consider God's benevolence as we face the challenges of our daily lives. We can reimagine what our life is like when God's promise of salvation is fulfilled and we accept its grace into our lives.

The Book of Zechariah is a collection of two or perhaps three smaller prophetic units written by different authors but having somewhat similar themes. Although parts of this book are more universal in tone, it was probably compiled after the return from the Babylonian Exile in the sixth century BC. This period of rebuilding the

Jerusalem Temple and reestablishing a working society in Judea was a perilous time, so messages of consolation would have been most welcome.

This first reading is the second oracle in the second section (chapters 9 through 11) of the Book of Zechariah. Its interpretation depends on the meaning of the first oracle. Briefly, the first oracle describes how God, the great warrior, will protect Judea by setting up his home in the Jerusalem Temple and establishing his garrison there, not because Judea has earned

God's protection, but because God has seen their affliction.

Subsequently, in this second oracle, which is today's first reading, God urges Jerusalem to rejoice, because God is sending a king who is just—in right relationship to God—and humble. This one who is to come will be a king of peace, riding on a donkey, an animal used for farming and commerce, and vanquishing the implements of war (bows and arrows, chariots and horses). The Hebrew word translated "meek" to describe the king also has the connotation of "poor," "weak," or "lowly." Thus, we can

For meditation and context:

RESPONSORIAL PSALM   Psalm 145:1–2, 8–9, 10–11, 13–14 (1)

R. I will praise your name for ever, my king and my God.
or
R. Alleluia.

I will extol you, O my God and King,
   and I will bless your name for ever
      and ever.
Every day will I bless you,
   and I will praise your name for ever
      and ever.

The LORD is gracious and merciful,
   slow to anger and of great kindness.
The LORD is good to all
   and compassionate toward all his works.

Let all your works give you thanks, O LORD,
   and let your faithful ones bless you.
Let them discourse of the glory of
      your kingdom
   and speak of your might.

The LORD is faithful in all his words
   and holy in all his works.
The LORD lifts up all who are falling
   and raises up all who are bowed down.

READING II   Romans 8:9, 11–13

A reading from the Letter of Saint Paul to the Romans

Brothers and **sisters**:
You are **not** in the **flesh**;
   on the **contrary**, you are in the **spirit**,
   if **only** the **Spirit** of **God dwells** in you.
Whoever does not have the **Spirit** of **Christ** does not **belong**
      to him.
If the **Spirit** of the one who raised **Jesus** from the **dead**
      dwells in you,
   the one who raised **Christ** from the **dead**
   will give **life** to your **mortal bodies also**,
   through his **Spirit** that **dwells** in you.
Consequently, **brothers** and **sisters**,
   we are not **debtors** to the **flesh**,
   to live **according** to the **flesh**.
For if you live **according** to the **flesh**, you will **die**,
   but if by the **Spirit** you put to **death** the **deeds** of the **body**,
   you will **live**.

In this portion of his letter to the Romans, Paul instructs his audience about the nature of life in the Spirit. His watchwords are "death" and "life," the "body" and "flesh," and "spirit." Less does he contrast these terms than he works them into his argument like ingredients into dough, in which the Spirit is the leavening agent. Read slowly and carefully, to allow the terms of Paul's argument to sink into your assembly.

surmise that this king will come from among his own people. But when God establishes him in power, he will have dominion over all the peoples of the world. As you can imagine, the early Church associated this prophecy with Jesus and his entrance into Jerusalem on a donkey (see Matthew 21:1–11).

READING II Today's second reading is a continuation of our recent Sunday readings from Paul's Letter to the Romans. It is part of a longer section that began in chapter 5, in which Paul expounds

on the nature of Christian life for those who have been justified by faith. Justification can be a difficult concept to understand, but, briefly, Paul asserts that fallen humanity has been set right with God through the death and resurrection of Jesus. This justification is available to all who open themselves in faith to receive this free gift. Further, he argues that the lives of the justified are transformed insofar as they are now free from sin and death (Romans 5), free from their old selves (Romans 6) and free from the belief that Jewish law will put them right with God (Romans 7). Finally, as

we see in this reading, Paul asserts that the Christian life is lived in the Spirit. We leave behind our old way of life—what Paul calls living "according to the flesh"—and now live in the Spirit of God who dwells in us. And because the Spirit of God dwells in us, we can be assured that we will be raised from the dead, just as Jesus was raised from the dead. This is not our doing, but it is God's free gift.

GOSPEL This reading from Matthew's Gospel is an example of the wisdom teachings of Jesus. Something sim-

Though all the words in this opening line are evenly emphasized, there is a slight pause between "time" and "Jesus."
The first half of this reading has Jesus directly addressing God the Father. It has a quality of public intimacy.

The second half of this reading begins with these familiar and comforting words of Jesus. Imagine they are being said for the first time as you proclaim them.

Beautiful and reassuring.

GOSPEL Matthew 11:25–30

A reading from the holy Gospel according to Matthew

At that time Jesus exclaimed:
    "I give **praise** to you, **Father**, Lord of **heaven** and **earth**,
    for although you have **hidden** these **things**
    from the **wise** and the **learned**
    you have **revealed** them to **little ones**.
Yes, **Father**, **such** has been your **gracious will**.
All things have been handed **over** to me by my **Father**.
No one knows the **Son** except the **Father**,
    and **no one knows** the **Father** except the **Son**
    and **anyone** to whom the Son **wishes** to **reveal** him.

"**Come** to me, all you who **labor** and are **burdened**,
    and **I** will **give** you **rest**.
Take my **yoke upon** you and **learn** from me,
    for I am **meek** and **humble** of **heart**;
    and you will find **rest** for **yourselves**.
For my **yoke** is **easy**, and my **burden light**."

---

ilar can be found in Sirach 51:23–30. In keeping with Matthew's Jewish-Christian audience, Jesus begins with a traditional Jewish blessing formula—"I give praise to you, Father, Lord of heaven and earth"—but with the addition of the divine attribute, "Father," which appears five times in this short text. He is offering praise and thanks for God's revelation, which will be channeled through Jesus according to God's "gracious will." The Greek *eudokia* here expands our understanding of God's attitude; it includes the notion that these actions are taken with "good will, kindly

intent, or benevolence." Moreover, it is not something that can be attained through superior intellect. Rather, it is revealed to "little ones," metaphorically speaking, the simple and uneducated. And what is this revelation? It is knowledge or experience of God's very self, to which Jesus has unique access as Son of the Father. In other words, we come to know God through the person of Jesus.

Thus, Jesus, like personified Wisdom in Sirach, invites all of us who are exhausted and weighed down to come to him and to take rest in him and be refreshed. The ref-

erence to taking on Jesus' yoke is probably in juxtaposition to the obligations of Torah law, since first- and second-century rabbis used the term in the phrases "yoke of the Torah" and "yoke of the kingdom of heaven" with a similar meaning. The words translated here as "meek" and "humble of heart" have similar meanings and can be translated, respectively, as "gentle or humble" and "lowly or deferring oneself as a servant to others." Let us ask ourselves, then, what does it mean to say that Jesus' yoke is easy and his burden light? C.C.

JULY 16, 2023

FIFTEENTH SUNDAY IN ORDINARY TIME

LECTIONARY #103

READING I   Isaiah 55:10–11

A reading from the Book of the Prophet Isaiah

Thus says the LORD:
Just as from the heavens
 the rain and snow come down
and do not return there
 till they have watered the earth,
 making it fertile and fruitful,
giving seed to the one who sows
 and bread to the one who eats,
so shall my word be
 that goes forth from my mouth;
my word shall not return to me void,
 but shall do my will,
 achieving the end for which I sent it.

Isaiah = ī-ZAY-uh

A simple and elegant reading in poetic language that makes a direct and powerful comparison between nourishing water and the word of God.
Even emphasis on "do not return."

READING I   Today's readings invite us to reflect on the full flourishing of God's Word in the world and the way it bears fruit in our lives.

The first reading comes from the section of the Book of Isaiah referred to as Second Isaiah (Isaiah 40–55), which is generally understood to have been written by a disciple of the eighth-century BC prophet during the time of the Babylonian Exile.

This short reading is part of the last oracle of consolation in Second Isaiah, which begins with an invitation from God to come to the one who nourishes all of life. In the first part of the oracle, God acknowledges that Israel has sinned but invites them to turn to him for mercy (Isaiah 55:7). God also tells them that he will make a covenant with them and be steadfast and loyal to them (Isaiah 55:3). This is where we pick up today's reading. The prophet, speaking for God, says that God's Word is not out in the ether somewhere. Rather, it comes gently to earth like rain or snow that nourishes the earth and makes it sprout with new growth that returns to God as plants and trees. Think of this as a metaphor for the human experience of the divine. Like gentle rain or sparkling snow, God's Word comes down upon us and infuses our being with God's life-giving Spirit, and we can trust that God will make his Word fruitful in us to the praise and glory of God.

READING II   Today's second reading continues our recent Sunday readings from Paul's Letter to the Romans. Here Paul is writing about the destiny that awaits Christians in the end time. He uses

212

For meditation and context:

RESPONSORIAL PSALM   Psalm 65:10, 11, 12–13, 14 (Luke 8:8)

R. The seed that falls on good ground will yield a fruitful harvest.

You have visited the land and watered it;
  greatly have you enriched it.
God's watercourses are filled;
  you have prepared the grain.

Thus have you prepared the land: drenching
    its furrows,
  breaking up its clods,
softening it with showers,
  blessing its yield.

You have crowned the year with your bounty,
  and your paths overflow with a
    rich harvest;
the untilled meadows overflow with it,
  and rejoicing clothes the hills.

The fields are garmented with flocks
  and the valleys blanketed with grain.
  They shout and sing for joy.

READING II   Romans 8:18–23

A reading from the Letter of Saint Paul to the Romans

Brothers and **sisters**:
I **consider** that the **sufferings** of this **present time** are as **nothing**
    compared with the **glory** to be **revealed** for us.
For **creation awaits** with **eager expectation**
    the **revelation** of the **children** of **God**;
    for **creation** was made **subject** to **futility**,
    not of its **own accord** but **because** of the **one** who **subjected** it,
    in **hope** that **creation itself**
    would be **set free** from **slavery** to **corruption**
    and **share** in the **glorious freedom** of the **children** of **God**.
We **know** that all **creation** is **groaning** in **labor** pains **even**
        until **now**;
    and **not** only **that**, but **we ourselves**,
    who have the **firstfruits** of the Spirit,
    we also groan within **ourselves**
    as we wait for **adoption**, the **redemption** of our **bodies**.

In this letter, Paul discusses the role of suffering as a metaphysical condition that defines life. It's a challenging argument he is making. Proclaim slowly and carefully so that his words can sink in.

"Expectation" is a focal word in this reading.

One of the more powerful images in Paul's letters. Emphasis on "all creation."

---

the metaphor of a woman in labor pains to describe the "sufferings of this present time." The pain is great in the moment, but so is the hope of a glorious new life. Paul recognizes that all of creation was negatively affected by humanity's first sin, but that creation has within it a deep longing to share in humanity's redemption in Christ. Paul says that human sin subjects all of creation to the slavery of corruption or decay. But we have hope because humanity possesses "the firstfruits of the Spirit." In the Jewish sacrificial system, the firstfruits

were the first and best of the harvest offered to God as a pledge of what is to come for the entire harvest. And so we groan as we await the full flourishing of the harvest or what Paul calls "the redemption of our bodies." To redeem is to "buy back," in this case, from the forces of sin and evil. As our bodies are redeemed through the death and resurrection of Jesus, we become fully children of God.

GOSPEL   The short form of today's Gospel is the very familiar parable of the sower and the seed. The long form includes Jesus' explanation for why he teaches in parables, as well as an interpretation of this parable. Parables are riddles that take the form of fictional stories designed to engage the listener in active thought. This parable is about a farmer who goes out to sow seed, which falls on four different types of soil and bears fruit in proportion to the type of soil on which it falls. The riddle or surprising

GOSPEL   Matthew 13:1–23

A reading from the holy Gospel according to Matthew

[On that day, **Jesus** went **out** of the **house** and sat **down**
  by the **sea.**
Such **large crowds gathered** around **him**
  that he **got** into a **boat** and sat **down,**
  and the **whole crowd stood** along the **shore.**
And he **spoke** to them at **length** in **parables,** saying:
  "A **sower** went **out** to **sow.**
And **as** he **sowed, some seed fell** on the **path,**
  and **birds** came and **ate** it up.
Some fell on **rocky ground,** where it had **little soil.**
It **sprang up** at **once** because the **soil** was not **deep,**
  and when the **sun rose** it was **scorched,** and it **withered** for
    lack of **roots.**
Some seed fell among **thorns,** and the **thorns** grew **up** and
    choked it.
But **some seed fell** on **rich soil,** and produced **fruit,**
  a **hundred** or **sixty** or **thirtyfold.**
Whoever has **ears** ought to **hear.**"]

The **disciples approached** him and **said,**
  "**Why** do you **speak** to them in **parables?**"
He **said** to them in **reply,**
  "Because **knowledge** of the **mysteries** of the **kingdom**
    of **heaven**
  has been **granted** to **you,** but to **them** it has **not** been **granted.**
To **anyone** who **has, more** will be **given** and he will **grow rich;**
  from **anyone** who has **not, even** what he **has** will be
    taken away.
This is **why I speak** to them in **parables,** because
  *they **look** but do not **see** and **hear** but do not **listen***
    *or **understand**.*
Isaiah's prophecy is **fulfilled** in them, which says:

Margin notes (left column):

Slight pause between "crowds" and "gathered." The first part of this reading relates a well-known parable, as straightforward as it is compelling.

Slight pause between "seed" and "fell."

Here, speaking to his disciples about the parable he has spoken, Jesus initiates them into the mysteries of the kingdom of heaven. A revelatory tone pervades.

Jesus uses Scripture to underscore the mysteries he is revealing. They are ancient mysteries.

---

element of this parable is the bountiful harvest that the good soil produces. Even today with our advanced techniques of farming, a hundred-fold yield is impossible! Hence, we need to look more deeply into the message of the parable.

Gospel parables often do not include an interpretation, but this one does. The seed is the "word of the kingdom" or message about the reign of God. The four types of soil represent the categories of people who are invited to respond to the Word. The path is so hard that the seed cannot

penetrate the soil or begin to germinate, so the evil one is able to steal it away. The rocky soil receives the Word and quickly responds, but, as the plants begin to grow, the heat and lack of moisture—i.e., persecutions—causes the produce to wither and die. Likewise, the thorny soil does not produce results because "worldly anxiety" keep us from responding to God's word. The questions for us, then, are "What kind of soil am I?" and "How do I open myself to be like the good soil that receives it and produces more?"

The longer form of today's Gospel also has a section that explains why Jesus taught in parables, and it is not what you might expect. First, he offers a proverb that still holds true today; some have been given more than others, and the ones who have more will receive more. Second, he quotes from Isaiah 6:9–10, essentially saying that God ordained it that some would accept God's Word and others would not. As Christianity began to separate itself from Judaism in the second century AD, Christians used this text to argue that the

*You shall **indeed hear** but **not understand**,*
  *you shall **indeed look** but **never see**.*
***Gross** is the **heart** of this **people**,*
  *they will **hardly hear** with their **ears**,*
  *they have **closed** their **eyes**,*
  *lest they **see** with their **eyes***
  *and **hear** with their **ears***
*and **understand** with their **hearts** and be **converted**,*
  *and I **heal** them.*

Here, he boosts the confidence of his disciples. By extension, this boosts our own confidence that we too are being initiated into these mysteries.

"But **blessed** are your **eyes**, because they **see**,
  and your **ears**, because they **hear**.
Amen, I **say** to you, **many prophets** and **righteous people**
  longed to **see** what **you** see but **did not see** it,
  and to **hear** what **you** hear but **did not hear** it.

The explanation of the parable begins with "Hear."

"**Hear** then the **parable** of the **sower**.
The **seed sown** on the **path** is the **one**
  who **hears** the **word** of the **kingdom without understanding** it,
  and the **evil** one **comes** and **steals** away
  what was **sown** in his **heart**.
The **seed sown** on **rocky ground**
  is the **one** who **hears** the **word** and **receives** it at **once** with **joy**.
But he has **no root** and lasts **only** for a **time**.
When **some tribulation** or **persecution** comes **because** of
    the **word**,
  he **immediately** falls **away**.
The **seed sown** among **thorns** is the **one** who **hears** the **word**,
  but then **worldly anxiety** and the **lure** of **riches choke**
    the **word**
  and it **bears** no **fruit**.

Slight pause between "riches" and "choke."

But the **seed sown** on **rich soil**
  is the one who **hears** the **word** and **understands** it,
  who **indeed** bears **fruit** and yields a **hundred** or **sixty**
    or **thirtyfold**."

[Shorter: Matthew 13:1–9 (see brackets)]

Jews' refusal to accept Jesus as the messiah resulted in God's covenant being extended to Gentile believers (see Acts 28:23–28). C.C.

SIXTEENTH SUNDAY IN ORDINARY TIME

LECTIONARY #106

READING I   Wisdom 12:13, 16–19

A reading from the Book of Wisdom

There is **no god besides** you who **have** the **care** of **all**,
    that you **need show** you have not **unjustly condemned**.
For your **might** is the **source** of **justice**;
    your **mastery** over **all things** makes you **lenient** to all.
For you **show** your **might** when the **perfection** of your **power**
    is **disbelieved**;
    and in **those** who **know** you, you **rebuke temerity**.
But **though** you are **master** of **might**, you **judge**
    with **clemency**,
    and with **much lenience** you **govern** us;
    for **power**, whenever you **will**, **attends** you.
And you **taught** your **people**, by **these deeds**,
    that **those** who are **just** must be **kind**;
and you gave your **children good ground** for **hope**
    that you would **permit repentance** for their **sins**.

A poetic and forceful reading with an uplifting message and a somewhat complex delivery. Proclaim with care to let its language settle on your assembly.

temerity = tuh-MER-uh-tee (audacity)

clemency = KLEM-*n-see

Slight pause between "children" and "good."

READING I   Our first reading is taken from the Book of Wisdom, also called the Wisdom of Solomon. Although the author is anonymous, we can surmise that he was a well-educated, Greek-speaking Jew, possibly from Alexandria, Egypt. Biblical scholars are divided about its date of composition, but sometime between the end of the first century BC and the beginning of the first century AD is reasonable. Catholics classify this book as deuterocanonical, meaning "second list of authoritative books," and part of the Bible, but most of our Protestant brothers and sisters consider it to be apocryphal, meaning "of doubtful authenticity," and include it in a separate section of the Bible.

To best appreciate this reading, we should try to get a sense of the big picture. It is part of a lengthy reflection on God's faithfulness and providential care of the Israelites during the Exodus, which begins at Wisdom 11:2 and extends to Wisdom 19:22. The first element of this reflection is a brief retelling of the Exodus narrative based on Psalm 107. Second, the author introduces the theme of his reflection: the Israelites benefited from the very things that God did to punish the Egyptians. Third, the author presents five examples, each in the form of diptych, that is, a text in two related parts. The five diptychs appear in this order: the miracle of water from the rock as compared to the plague of blood in the Nile, the miracle of quail in the wilderness as compared to the plagues of locusts and flies, the miracle of manna in the wilderness as compared to the plague of storms, the miracle of the column of fire as compared to the plague of darkness, and the tenth plague that brought freedom to

For meditation and context:

RESPONSORIAL PSALM   Psalm 86:5–6, 9–10, 15–16 (5a)

R. Lord, you are good and forgiving.

You, O LORD, are good and forgiving,
   abounding in kindness to all who call
      upon you.
Hearken, O LORD, to my prayer
   and attend to the sound of my pleading.

All the nations you have made shall come
   and worship you, O LORD,
   and glorify your name.
For you are great, and you do
      wondrous deeds;
   you alone are God.

You, O LORD, are a God merciful
   and gracious,
   slow to anger, abounding in kindness
      and fidelity.
Turn toward me, and have pity on me;
   give your strength to your servant.

A brief and incisive reading from Paul in which he offers up a challenging teaching, that our ignorance might be interceded upon by the Spirit. The emphasis is on our weakness.

Slight pause between "himself" and "intercedes."

READING II   Romans 8:26–27

A reading from the Letter of Saint Paul to the Romans

Brothers and **sisters**:
The **Spirit comes** to the **aid** of our **weakness**;
   for we **do not know** how to **pray** as we **ought**,
   but the **Spirit himself intercedes** with i**nexpressible groanings**.
And the **one** who **searches hearts**
   knows what is the **intention** of the **Spirit**,
   because he **intercedes** for the **holy** ones
   according to **God's will**.

---

the Israelites and death to the Egyptians' first born.

The second of these diptychs is interrupted by several digressions, including the one from which today's reading is taken. The topic of this digression is God's power and mercy. Our author begins by praising God, who is all-powerful and who cares for the needs of everyone; there is no other god who can accuse God of dealing unjustly with his people. The author argues further that God's power is the "source of justice," which also allows God to be lenient, balancing justice with mercy. Although the

author's comparison is not obvious in this short excerpt, we should be reminded of the words of the wicked expressed earlier in the book, "Let our strength be our norm of righteousness; for weakness proves itself useless" (Wisdom 2:11). The wicked are the ones who by their words and deeds bring about their own destruction (Wisdom 1:12). The author of this excerpt concludes by saying that, just as God tempers justice with mercy, so too we must be kind in our dealings with others. Knowing that God allows for repentance of sin gives us hope for ourselves and all of humanity.

READING II Once again, our second reading is a continuation of recent Sunday readings from Paul's Letter to the Romans. In the verses that immediately precede this reading, Paul writes about how Jesus' followers await with great hope the birth of a new creation. In today's reading, he explains that having been made children of God, "the Spirit comes to the aid of our weakness." Implied here is the recognition that human aspirations will never reach their mark without assistance, because of the limitations brought on by sin. But the Spirit will inter-

A lengthy reading that consists of three different parables and the explanation of the first. The tone is instructive, of course, but also mysterious. The first parable is the most detailed.

Slight pause between "weeds" and "all."

GOSPEL   Matthew 13:24–43

A reading from the holy Gospel according to Matthew

[**Jesus proposed another parable** to the **crowds**, saying:
"The **kingdom** of **heaven** may be **likened** to a **man**
   who **sowed good seed** in his **field**.
While **everyone** was **asleep** his **enemy** came
   and sowed **weeds all through** the **wheat**, and **then** went **off**.
When the **crop grew** and **bore fruit**, the **weeds** appeared as **well**.
The **slaves** of the **householder came** to him and said,
   '**Master**, did you not **sow good seed** in your **field**?
Where have the **weeds** come from?'
He **answered**, 'An **enemy** has done this.'
His **slaves said** to him,
   'Do you **want** us to **go** and pull them **up**?'
He replied, '**No**, if you **pull up** the **weeds**
   you might **uproot** the **wheat** along **with** them.
Let them grow together until **harvest**;
   then at **harvest** time I will **say** to the **harvesters**,
   "**First** collect the **weeds** and tie them in **bundles** for **burning**;
   but **gather** the **wheat** into my **barn**."'"]

This second parable involves a very familiar teaching. Proclaim it as if for the first time.

He proposed **another** parable to them.
"The **kingdom** of **heaven** is like a **mustard** seed
   that a **person took** and **sowed** in a **field**.
It is the **smallest** of **all** the **seeds**,
   yet when **full-grown** it is the **largest** of **plants**.
It becomes a **large bush**,
   and the '**birds** of the **sky** come and **dwell** in its **branches**.'"

The third parable consists of a powerful image.

He **spoke** to them another **parable**.
"The **kingdom** of **heaven** is like **yeast**
   that a **woman took** and **mixed** with **three measures**
      of **wheat** flour
   until the **whole batch** was **leavened**."

cede for us over and above our human limitations, with "inexpressible groanings." The phrase "who searches hearts" is a reference to God, who can understand what the Spirit says, as it intercedes on our behalf. What a wondrous mystery! And what consolation to know that God hears us through the agency of the Spirit, even when we are unable to pray as we want.

GOSPEL   Today's Gospel reading consists of a collection of three parables from Matthew's Gospel. The longer form of this Gospel reading also includes an interpretation of the first of these parables. Parables are puzzles that take the form of fictional stories designed to engage the listener in active thought. Most, though not all, begin with a phrase like "the kingdom of heaven is like . . . ." In other words, parables are comparisons. Also, "the kingdom of heaven" is not heaven. Rather, it describes the anticipated reality in which God's authority will manifest itself fully in creation and rid the world of discord, pain, and suffering.

The first of these parables is often referred to as the Parable of the Weeds and Wheat. However, on a deeper level, it should be called the Parable of Feuding Farmers, because the weeds are merely instruments designed to dishonor one's enemy. In the ancient Near East and in many parts of the world even today, societies operated on the notion that the enemies of one's grandparents and parents are your enemies as well. To maintain your family's honor, you were obligated to challenge the social status of those enemies in some way—even if meant introducing weeds into your enemy's field! The typical farmer would have felt obligated to respond

All these things Jesus **spoke** to the **crowds** in **parables**.
He **spoke** to them **only** in **parables**,
to **fulfill** what had been **said** through the **prophet**:
  *I will **open** my **mouth** in **parables**,*
    *I will **announce** what has lain **hidden***
      *from the **foundation** of the **world**.*

Then, **dismissing** the **crowds**, he **went** into the **house**.
His **disciples approached** him and said,
  "**Explain** to us the **parable** of the **weeds** in the **field**."
He **said** in **reply**, "**He** who sows **good seed** is the **Son** of **Man**,
  the **field** is the **world**, the **good seed** the **children**
    of the **kingdom**.
The **weeds** are the **children** of the **evil** one,
  and the **enemy** who **sows** them is the **devil**.
The **harvest** is the **end** of the **age**, and the **harvesters** are **angels**.
Just as **weeds** are **collected** and burned **up** with **fire**,
  so will it **be** at the **end** of the **age**.
The **Son** of **Man** will send his **angels**,
  and they will **collect** out of his **kingdom**
    all who cause others to **sin** and **all evildoers**.
They will **throw** them into the **fiery furnace**,
  where there will be **wailing** and **grinding** of **teeth**.
Then the **righteous** will **shine** like the **sun**
  in the **kingdom** of their **Father**.
Whoever has **ears** ought to **hear**."

[Shorter: Matthew 13:24–30 (see brackets)]

When the disciples ask for an explanation, they are asking Jesus to deepen their initiation into the mysteries he is revealing to them. That Jesus complies eagerly is part of the excitement of this Gospel reading.

The tone that concludes this reading is decidedly apocalyptic.

in kind, but this farmer does not retaliate and instead allows his honor to be compromised for an entire season until harvest, which is a symbol of God's end time judgment, when the instruments of hatred can be destroyed in fire.

The second and third parables in this reading compare the kingdom of heaven to something that begins its existence very small but becomes very large when it comes to completeness. The mustard seed is very small, though in fact not the smallest seed found in Israel and elsewhere, and it can grow to as much as six feet. However, it is not a tree. Rather, it is a gangly bush that sways easily in the wind, so it is unlikely to hold a bird's nest. Anyone walking the villages and fields of the time would know that this is hyperbole, but it clearly makes the point: the reign of God will surely grow, and it will grow beyond imagining. Likewise, the parable about the yeast is surprising, but this time it is because of the enormous amount of flour involved. Biblical scholars do not have consensus about how big a measure was in first-century Palestine, but three measures likely would have amounted to forty to sixty pounds of flour, which, when leavened, would create an enormous amount of bread! But such is the coming reign of God, encompassing all and being the source of nourishment for all. C.C.

SEVENTEENTH SUNDAY IN ORDINARY TIME

LECTIONARY #109

READING I   1 Kings 3:5, 7–12

A reading from the first Book of Kings

The **LORD** appeared to **Solomon** in a **dream** at **night**.
God said, "**Ask** something of me and I will **give** it to you."
Solomon answered:
"O **LORD**, my **God**, you have **made** me, your **servant**, **king**
  to **succeed** my **father David**;
  but **I** am a **mere youth**, not **knowing** at **all** how to **act**.
I **serve** you in the **midst** of the **people** whom you have **chosen**,
  a **people** so **vast** that it **cannot** be **numbered** or **counted**.
Give your **servant**, therefore, an **understanding heart**
  to judge your **people** and to distinguish **right** from **wrong**.
For **who** is **able** to **govern** this **vast people** of yours?"

The **LORD** was **pleased** that **Solomon** made this **request**.
So God **said** to him:
"**Because** you have **asked** for this—
  not for a **long life** for **yourself**,
  nor for **riches**,
  nor for the **life** of your **enemies**,
  but for **understanding** so that you may **know** what is **right**—
  I **do** as you **requested**.
I give you a **heart** so **wise** and **understanding**
  that there has **never** been **anyone like** you up to **now**,
  and **after** you there will come **no one** to **equal** you."

Solomon = SOL-uh-muhn

A reading like a fairy tale, in which a request is granted, as instructive as it is full of wonder.

Part of the power of the reading comes from the way that Solomon draws out his request. Allow it to unfold in your proclamation.

Note the rhythm, especially in the repetitions of "not" and "nor."

READING I Our first reading comes from the First Book of Kings. It tells the story about how King Solomon had a powerful nighttime vision of a conversation with God. In the chapter and verses that precede this reading, we learn that Solomon ascended the throne of Israel in Jerusalem after his father David died. Before David died, he instructed Solomon to follow God's ordinances in the law of Moses. David tells his son to settle scores with some of his enemies, which he does. Solomon also had his brother Adonijah killed, because he perceived him to be a threat to his kingship. Finally, when he had established his kingdom, he began to build his home and the Temple in Jerusalem.

The narrator of the story tells us that Solomon "loved the Lord, walking in the statutes of David his father" (1 Kings 3:3). This is why God said to Solomon, "Ask something of me and I will give it to you." Solomon's response is comprised of three statements. The first, which is not included in today's reading, is about God's past relationship with his father David, who was loved by God for his faithfulness (literally, walking in truth), his righteousness as a ruler, and the upright nature of his heart. Ancients believed that the heart was associated with emotions but also thought, insight, discernment, and will. The second statement is about Solomon's present relationship with God. He describes himself as God's servant, chosen to be king in his father's place, even though he feels greatly inadequate to the job. The third statement is a request for the future that he be given "an understanding heart" literally, "a listening heart," so that he can govern well and act with proper discernment toward God's people. God responds by praising him for

For meditation and context:

RESPONSORIAL PSALM Psalm 119:57, 72, 76–77, 127–128, 129–130 (97a)

R. Lord, I love your commands.

I have said, O LORD, that my part
   is to keep your words.
The law of your mouth is to me more
    precious
   than thousands of gold and silver pieces.

Let your kindness comfort me
   according to your promise to
    your servants.
Let your compassion come to me that
   I may live,
   for your law is my delight.

For I love your commands
   more than gold, however fine.
For in all your precepts I go forward;
   every false way I hate.

Wonderful are your decrees;
   therefore I observe them.
The revelation of your words sheds light,
   giving understanding to the simple.

Paul's teaching in this letter is complex and challenging. Read it with care because its content might easily be misconstrued.

READING II Romans 8:28–30

A reading from the Letter of Saint Paul to the Romans

Brothers and **sisters**:
We **know** that **all things work** for **good** for **those** who **love God**,
   who are **called** according to his **purpose**.
For **those** he **foreknew** he also **predestined**
   to be **conformed** to the **image** of his **Son**,
   so that he might be the **firstborn**
   among **many brothers** and **sisters**.
And those he **predestined** he also **called**;
   and those he **called** he also **justified**;
   and those he **justified** he also **glorified**.

> **TO KEEP IN MIND**
> Read the Scripture passage and its commentary in Workbook. Then read it from your Bible, including what comes before and after it, so that you understand the context.

not asking for things that kings typically wanted and by granting Solomon's request for wisdom and discernment, adding that Solomon is unique among the kings of Israel. Sadly, Solomon's reign would end much differently than it began, because he stopped observing God's commandments (see 1 Kings 11:1–13).

READING II Today's second reading follows immediately after last Sunday's reading from Paul's Letter to the Romans, in which Paul explained how the Spirit would come to our aid in our weak-

ness and intercede for us before God when we do not know how to pray. In this reading, Paul goes on to assure his readers that God is in control and everything that we experience is part of God's plan. And what is God's plan for those who love God? Paul is thinking of the community as a whole here, not individuals on their own merit. But notice that Paul does not use the term "predestined" as modern theologians do, suggesting that God has determined beforehand who would be saved and who would not. Rather, it means something like "God decided beforehand" that he wanted

humanity to be formed in a way similar to the image or likeness of Christ. Thus, God called us and justified us—put us in right relationship with God—so that we can also be glorified with Christ. Essentially, Paul is talking about the invitation God has given us to participate in the paschal mystery, dying with Christ so that we can come to fullness of life in Christ.

GOSPEL Today's Gospel provides us with three more parables about the reign of God or what Matthew calls "the kingdom of heaven." The first

---

GOSPEL   Matthew 13:44–52

A reading from the holy Gospel according to Matthew

[**Jesus** said to his **disciples**:
   "The **kingdom** of **heaven** is like a **treasure buried** in a **field**,
   which a **person finds** and **hides again**,
   and out of **joy** goes and sells **all** that he **has** and **buys** that **field**.
Again, the **kingdom** of **heaven** is like a **merchant**
     searching for **fine pearls**.
When he finds a **pearl** of great **price**,
   he goes and **sells all** that he **has** and **buys** it.]
Again, the **kingdom** of **heaven** is like a **net thrown** into the **sea**,
   which **collects fish** of **every kind**.
When it is **full** they **haul** it **ashore**
   and sit **down** to put what is **good** into **buckets**.
What is **bad** they throw **away**.
Thus it will **be** at the **end** of the **age**.
The **angels** will go out and **separate** the **wicked**
     from the **righteous**
   and **throw** them into the **fiery furnace**,
   where there will be **wailing** and **grinding** of **teeth**.

"Do you **understand all** these **things**?"
They answered, "**Yes**."
And he **replied**,
   "Then **every scribe** who has been **instructed** in the **kingdom**
    of **heaven**
   is like the **head** of a **household**
   who **brings** from his **storeroom** both the **new** and the **old**."

[Shorter: Matthew 13:44–46 (see brackets)]

This reading consists of a series of vivid comparisons and likenesses to the kingdom of heaven that Jesus provides for his disciples.

After providing the likenesses, Jesus' tone becomes more pointedly apocalyptic.

With this question, Jesus concludes the initiation into the mysteries of heaven he has undertaken with the disciples.

Let the strangeness of this imagery abide with the members of your assembly.

---

two—the parable of the treasure and the parable of the pearl of great price—have some important similarities, and therefore most likely are intended to have a similar message. In both cases, the values of the treasure and the pearl are noted. Such is the reign of God; it is a treasure of immeasurable value. Nothing can compare to it anywhere on earth. And what about the person who seeks out the treasure or pearl? Having found this object of great price, the person goes off and sells everything he has in order to secure it. Again, such is the reign of God; the wise person recognizes it in joy and commits to it so fully that he gives up everything he has to participate in it.

The third parable sounds a lot like the parable of the weeds and wheat from the previous Sunday's Gospel reading. The sea is filled with good fish and bad fish. Likewise, the field has wheat and weeds growing together until harvest. Thus, the netting and sorting of fish in this parable serves the same purpose as the gathering of the harvest and burning of the weeds in the previous parable. Both are symbols of God's end time judgment, when the righteous will be separated from the wicked. But to be clear, God is the judge. It is not our place to judge others but to act with patience and charity. God will judge when the time is right. Moreover, there is hope for all of us because God's judgment is best described as justice tempered with mercy.
C.C.

THE TRANSFIGURATION OF THE LORD

LECTIONARY #614

READING I   Daniel 7:9–10, 13–14

A reading from the book of the Prophet Daniel.

As I **watched**:
　Thrones were set **up**
　　and the **Ancient One** took his **throne**.
　His **clothing** was **bright** as **snow**,
　　and the **hair** on his **head** as **white** as **wool**;
　His **throne** was **flames** of **fire**,
　　with **wheels** of **burning fire**.
　A **surging stream** of fire
　　flowed **out** from where he **sat**;
　Thousands upon **thousands** were **ministering** to him,
　　and **myriads** upon **myriads attended** him.
The **court** was **convened** and the **books** were **opened**.

As the **visions** during the **night continued**, I saw:
　One like a **Son** of **man coming**,
　　on the **clouds** of **heaven**;
　when he **reached** the **Ancient One**
　　and was **presented before** him,
　the **one** like a **Son** of **man** received **dominion, glory**,
　　　and **kingship**;
　all **peoples**, **nations**, and **languages serve** him.
　His **dominion** is an everlasting **dominion**
　　that shall **not** be **taken away**,
　　his **kingship** shall **not** be **destroyed**.

A powerful, visionary reading that is a thrill to proclaim. The images are so vivid and the language so exciting and strange, be careful not to get carried away. Proclaim in a firm and steady voice and let the contents of the reading come through in your clarity.

myriads = MEER-ee-uhdz (a large amount/countless)

The focus of the reading shifts with this new vision of Daniel's, one that foretells the coming of Jesus, lending this vision a special power.

READING I In the verses preceding today's reading, the prophet receives a vision of four great beasts that emerge from the sea, which are thought to represent four great empires in succession: the Babylonians, the Medes, the Persians, and the Greeks. Each beast has a number of horns that represent kings associated with that dynasty. As Daniel's vision continues, a tiny horn sprouts on the fourth beast, replacing three of its ten horns. This is the Seleucid King Antiochus IV Epiphanes, who was notorious for his violence and who launched a persecution of the Jews in mid-second century BC. He took the name "Epiphanes" which means "god manifest," but his eccentric behavior earned him the name Epimanes, meaning "the mad one," among his contemporaries.

This background about Antiochus IV is important for understanding today's reading because it explains the expansiveness and elegance of Daniel's vision of God's throne room. The "Ancient One" is God, and the details of his appearance speak to his divine status of wisdom and purity. The throne and river of fire suggest God's supremacy over cosmic phenomena. Daniel sees that God has so many court ministers and such a large number of subjects that it was impossible to count them. So much for Antiochus claiming to be Epiphanes, "god manifest!" In contrast to Antiochus' tiny horn with eyes and a mouth (Daniel 7:8), the Ancient One is what a real God looks like! Also, in contrast to whatever power Antiochus IV might have, there is "one like a Son of man," or someone in human form, who is presented before the Ancient One to receive "dominion, glory, and kingship" from God. Moreover, his kingship will last forever. Most likely Daniel understood this

223

RESPONSORIAL   Psalm 97:1–2, 5–6, 9 (1a, 9a)

R. The Lord is king, the Most High over all the earth.

The LORD is king; let the earth rejoice;
    let the many islands be glad.
Clouds and darkness are round about him,
    justice and judgment are the foundation
        of his throne.

The mountains melt like wax before
        the LORD,
    before the LORD of all the earth.
The heavens proclaim his justice,
    all peoples see his glory.

Because you, O LORD, are the Most High
        over all the earth,
    exalted far above all gods.

READING II   2 Peter 1:16–19

A reading from the second Letter of Saint Peter

Beloved:
We **did not follow cleverly devised myths**
    when we made **known** to you
        the **power** and **coming** of our **Lord Jesus Christ**,
    but we had been **eyewitnesses** of his **majesty**.
For he received **honor** and **glory** from **God** the **Father**
    when that **unique declaration came** to him from the
        majestic glory,
    "**This** is my **Son**, my **beloved**, with **whom** I **am** well **pleased**."
We ourselves heard this **voice come** from **heaven**
    while we were **with** him on the holy **mountain**.
Moreover, we possess the **prophetic message** that is
        altogether reliable.
You will **do well** to be **attentive** to it,
    as to a **lamp shining** in a **dark place**,
        until **day dawns** and the **morning star rises** in your **hearts**.

Even emphasis on "did not follow cleverly devised myths," with a slight pause between "follow" and "cleverly."

Slight pauses between "ourselves" and "heard," and between "voice" and "come."

Slight pause between "star" and "rises."

---

one like a son of man to be a representative of God's chosen people (see Daniel 7:18) or Israel's messiah. Early Christians associated this text with Jesus, and the Gospels use Son of Man as a title for Jesus though the origin of that title is unclear.

READING II Our second reading is from the Second Letter of Peter. Although attributed to Peter, this work is most likely pseudonymous, written in approximately AD 100–125, by a disciple or admirer of Peter to keep his memory alive some forty to fifty years after his martyrdom.

One of the topics that this document addresses is the delay of the parousia, the return of Christ at the end time. Because resurrection from the dead was one of the signs of the end time, the earliest Christians believed that the Christ's return would happen very soon. In fact, Paul thought it would be within his lifetime (1 Thessalonians 4:13–18). Now, some seventy to ninety years after Jesus' resurrection, early Christians were still waiting for the parousia. The reference to "cleverly devised myths" appears to be a response to an accusation that was leveled against people who made up stories about

rewards and punishment in the end time in order to control people's behavior. This writer asserts that he does not spout such myths. Rather, writing as if he were Peter, he declares that he actually witnessed Jesus' prophecy about the end time in the power and glory of his transfigured appearance and in the voice from heaven. This prophecy we can rely on, he says.

GOSPEL The story of Jesus' transfiguration on a high mountain is included in all three of the synoptic Gospels. The mountain that provides the

GOSPEL Matthew 17:1–9

Jesus took **Peter**, **James**, and his brother, John,
and led them up a **high mountain** by **themselves**.
And he was **transfigured before** them;
his **face** shone like the **sun**
and his **clothes** became **white** as **light**.
And **behold**, **Moses** and **Elijah appeared** to them,
conversing with him.
Then **Peter** said to **Jesus** in **reply**,
"**Lord**, it is **good** that we are **here**.
If you **wish**, I will make **three tents** here,
one for **you**, one for **Moses**, and one for **Elijah**."
While he was **still speaking**, **behold**,
a **bright cloud** cast a **shadow** over them,
then from the **cloud** came a **voice** that said,
"**This** is my beloved **Son**, with **whom** I am well **pleased**;
listen to him."
When the **disciples heard** this, they fell **prostrate**
and were **very much afraid**.
But **Jesus** came and **touched** them, saying,
"**Rise**, and do **not** be **afraid**."
And when the disciples **raised** their **eyes**,
they saw **no one else** but **Jesus** alone.

As they were **coming down** from the **mountain**,
Jesus **charged** them,
"Do not **tell** the **vision** to **anyone**
until the **Son** of **Man** has been **raised** from the **dead**."

"Transfigured" focuses this reading, sets its tone. This is a celestial event.

Moses = MOH-zihz or MOH-zihs
Elijah = ee-LI-juh
Initially, the appearance of Moses and Elijah intensifies the focus.

But then Peter humanizes things in his desire to set up a shrine.
At "behold," the focus shifts back to a heavenly perspective that overwhelms the earthly perspective.

Even emphasis on "very much afraid."

The mystery of this final command of Jesus is worth lingering over as you conclude your proclamation.

---

setting for this story is unnamed, but tradition has identified it with Mount Tabor, though Mount Carmel or Mount Hermon is also a possibility. However, the precise location does not matter. More important to know is that ancient peoples believed mountains to be the site of divine revelations. Jesus is radiant with light, which is how ancients would have understood a divine presence. Moses and Elijah, who appear with Jesus, represent the Law and the Prophets, respectively.

Though this is a familiar story, there are several things that we can learn anew in this reading of it. Peter's desire to put up tents for the three heavenly beings suggests the Feast of Tabernacles, which is a commemoration of the giving of the Law on Sinai and an anticipation of the coming reign of God at the end time. The tents are a reminder of the forty years living in temporary dwellings in the wilderness. Today, this Jewish feast is usually celebrated at the end of September.

God's voice from heaven announcing that Jesus is God's beloved Son is similar to the words that came from heaven at Jesus' baptism (see Matthew 3:13–17), except that now the words are addressed to the disciples. Only Matthew includes the detail about the disciples bowing down in fear and adoration. But their fear is reasonable, because many ancient peoples believed that humans could not see God face to face and remain alive. Matthew has Jesus describe this event as a vision, suggesting that it symbolizes an event that will happen later, though it can be helpful to remember that the Gospel was written after the resurrection of Jesus and with the after-the-fact insight that goes with the experience. C.C.

NINETEENTH SUNDAY IN ORDINARY TIME

LECTIONARY #115

READING I   1 Kings 19:9a, 11–13a

A reading from the first Book of Kings

At the **mountain** of **God**, **Horeb**,
  Elijah came to a **cave** where he took **shelter**.
Then the Lord **said** to him,
  "**Go outside** and **stand** on the **mountain** before the Lord;
  the Lord will be passing **by**."
A **strong** and **heavy wind** was **rending** the **mountains**
  and **crushing rocks** before the Lord—
  but the Lord was **not** in the **wind**.
After the **wind** there was an **earthquake**—
  but the Lord was **not** in the **earthquake**.
After the **earthquake** there was **fire**—
  but the Lord was **not** in the **fire**.
After the **fire** there was a **tiny whispering sound**.
When he **heard this**,
  Elijah hid his **face** in his **cloak**
  and went and **stood** at the **entrance** of the **cave**.

Horeb = HOHR-eb
A bracing and poetic reading, with the quality of both a myth and a parable. There is a magical clarity that defines it.

Elijah = ee-LĪ-juh

The rhythm here is important, especially the *"Lord* was *not . . . "*

 READING I Today's first reading is the story of Elijah's encounter with God. To better understand this reading, we should know that Elijah was a prophet of God in the time of King Ahab, whose wife was Jezebel, a foreigner and worshiper of Baal. After Elijah slayed the prophets of Baal in the Wadi Kishon in Galilee, Jezebel vowed to kill him, so he ran all the way to Beer-sheba, a distance of more than one hundred miles, and escaped into the wilderness, where he laid down under a broom tree and prayed for death. Miraculously, an angel came to wake him and tell him to eat and drink what was left for him. When the angel came again to waken him, Elijah was told again to eat and drink in preparation for a journey, which takes him to Mount Horeb, also known as Sinai (1 Kings 19:1–8).

Having arrived at Horeb, God asks Elijah what he's doing there. Elijah responds with a complaint about how God's people had abandoned the covenant, destroyed God's altars, and killed his prophets. Elijah adds, "I alone remain, and they seek to take my life" (1 Kings 19:10). Arriving at the beginning of our first reading, we hear God telling Elijah to go out and stand on the mountain before God. The phrase "stand before the Lord" is another way of saying that Elijah is being called to service. The fierce wind, earthquake, and fire are all accompaniments to a theophany—a manifestation of the divine—but it is only in the "tiny whispering sound" that Elijah knows God's presence. Thus, he emerged from the cave but hid his face because ancients believed that no one could see God face to face and live. Today, too, we might not see God face to face, but we can see God's activity in the world if we look attentively. Where is God at work in your life?

For meditation and context:

RESPONSORIAL PSALM Psalm 85:9, 10, 11–12, 13–14 (8)

R. Lord, let us see your kindness, and grant us your salvation.

I will hear what God proclaims;
 the LORD—for he proclaims peace.
Near indeed is his salvation to those who
  fear him,
 glory dwelling in our land.

Kindness and truth shall meet;
 justice and peace shall kiss.
Truth shall spring out of the earth,
 and justice shall look down from heaven.

The LORD himself will give his benefits;
 our land shall yield its increase.
Justice shall walk before him,
 and prepare the way of his steps.

READING II Romans 9:1–5

A reading from the Letter of Saint Paul to the Romans

Even emphasis on "do not lie."

Brothers and **sisters**:
I speak the **truth** in **Christ**, I **do not lie**;
 my **conscience joins** with the **Holy Spirit** in **bearing**
  me **witness**
 that I have **great sorrow** and **constant anguish** in my **heart**.
For I could **wish** that **I myself** were **accursed** and cut off
  from **Christ**
 for the **sake** of my own **people**,
 my **kindred according** to the **flesh**.
They are **Israelites**;
 theirs the **adoption**, the **glory**, the **covenants**,
 the **giving** of the **law**, the **worship**, and the **promises**;
 theirs the **patriarchs**, and **from** them,
 according to the **flesh**, is the **Christ**,
 who is **over all**, **God blessed forever**. Amen.

Note the unusual rhythm/rhetoric of the phrases beginning with "theirs."

Slight pause between "all" and "God."

Strong emphasis on the whole phrase, "over all, God blessed forever."

READING II Our second reading is a continuation of Paul's Letter to the Romans, which we have been hearing during recent Sundays in Ordinary Time. This reading is the opening section of a long diatribe that extends from Romans 9:1 through 11:36. Although our modern understanding of diatribe usually has negative connotations and anger associated with it, in literature and during the time period of Paul, a diatribe is a type of argument in which the speaker, or writer in this case, imagines a hypothetical respondent who challenges the speaker or asks questions of him at different points in the argument. The speaker or writer's responses then become the starting point for another section of the argument. Paul's concern is immediately evident. He is worried about his fellow Jews who have not accepted Jesus Christ as the messiah and have not joined the Jesus movement. Hopefully you can get a sense of the profound grief and anguish that he carries in his heart. He says that he would rather be cut off from Christ—the worst possible thing that Paul could imagine—for the sake of his people. He also lists seven privileges that God has given to the chosen people and adds an eighth—the sending of Christ, the preeminent descendant of the patriarchs—whom some of his Jewish brethren refuse to accept. At the end of Paul's diatribe, he will conclude that the reason for his Jewish brethren's rejection of Jesus is to make it possible for the expansion of God's covenant to include the Gentiles.

GOSPEL Today's Gospel reading tells the story of another theophany or manifestation of the divine. In Matthew's Gospel, this story appears immediately after the first of two miracles of the

GOSPEL   Matthew 14:22–33

A reading from the holy Gospel according to Matthew

After he had **fed** the **people**, **Jesus** made the **disciples** get
    into a **boat**
   and **precede** him to the other **side**,
   while he **dismissed** the **crowds**.
After **doing** so, he went **up** on the **mountain** by **himself** to **pray**.
When it was **evening** he was there **alone**.
Meanwhile the **boat**, **already** a **few miles offshore**,
   was being **tossed about** by the **waves**, for the **wind** was
    against it.
During the **fourth watch** of the **night**,
   he came **toward** them **walking** on the **sea**.
When the **disciples saw** him **walking** on the **sea** they
    were **terrified**.
"It is a **ghost**, " they said, and they cried **out** in **fear**.
At once Jesus spoke to them, "Take **courage**, it is **I**; do **not**
   be **afraid**."
Peter said to him in **reply**,
  "**Lord**, if it is **you**, **command** me to **come** to you on the **water**."
He said, "**Come**."
Peter got **out** of the **boat** and began to **walk** on the **water**
    toward **Jesus**.
But when he **saw** how strong the **wind** was he became
    frightened;
   and, **beginning** to **sink**, he cried out, "**Lord**, **save** me!"
Immediately Jesus stretched out his **hand** and caught **Peter**,
   and **said** to him, "O **you** of little **faith**, **why** did you **doubt**?"
After they **got** into the **boat**, the **wind** died **down**.
Those who were in the **boat** did him **homage**, saying,
   "**Truly**, **you** are the **Son** of **God**."

This reading depicts such a vivid scene, it's like a short film.

That Jesus is alone suggests something of the power he is feeling/gathering.

Seeing Jesus, the disciples are truly frightened. Fear is the mood of this reading.

The disciples' fear is contrasted by Jesus telling them not to be afraid.

Once again, fright.

When Jesus rebukes Peter for his doubt, he seems especially to be calling him out for letting his fear master him.

---

multiplication of loaves and fishes (Matthew 14:13–21 and 15:32–39). In this reading, Jesus first directs his disciples to go to the other side of the Sea of Galilee, away from the crowds that had gathered in the wilderness and were fed from the five loaves and two fish. Then he goes off by himself to pray. The Sea of Galilee is a large freshwater lake measuring approximately thirty-three miles in circumference. Because of its geography, nighttime storms on the lake are common even today.

The narrator of this story tells us that the boat that holds the disciples is already a few miles offshore when Jesus observes their predicament, presumably because of the high winds that they are encountering. He went out to them very early in the morning, likely before or close to dawn. The disciples must have been exhausted after fighting the storm all night. But then they see a figure walking toward them on the water and are beside themselves in fear. Stormy water suggested that its monsters were exerting their powers. They thought this figure was a ghost or a haunting spirit, but finally when Jesus spoke, they realized it was Jesus.

The scene in which Peter asks Jesus to have him come to Jesus across the water is only in Matthew's Gospel (compare it with Mark 6:45–52). Peter is extremely enthusiastic at first, but he quickly doubts and begins to sink into the water. Finally, when Jesus calms the storm, they know his true identity, because only God can control the forces of nature. Thus, the disciples bow down in worship and acknowledge him as the Son of God. C.C.

THE ASSUMPTION OF THE BLESSED VIRGIN MARY: VIGIL

LECTIONARY #621

READING I   1 Chronicles 15:3–4, 15–16; 16:1–2

A reading from the first Book of Chronicles

David assembled **all Israel** in **Jerusalem** to bring the **ark**
    of the **LORD**
to the **place** that he had **prepared** for it.
David also called together the sons of **Aaron** and the **Levites**.

The **Levites** bore the **ark** of God on their **shoulders** with **poles**,
    as **Moses** had **ordained** according to the **word** of the LORD.

David commanded the **chiefs** of the **Levites**
    to **appoint** their **kinsmen** as **chanters**,
    to play on **musical** instruments, **harps**, **lyres**, and **cymbals**,
    to make a **loud sound** of **rejoicing**.

They brought in the **ark** of **God** and set it **within** the **tent**
    which **David** had **pitched** for it.
Then they offered up **burnt offerings** and **peace offerings** to **God**.
When **David** had finished offering up the **burnt offerings** and
    peace offerings,
    he **blessed** the people in the **name** of the LORD.

Chronicles = KRAH-nih-k*ls

A reading that describes the preparation and then the activities of a celebration ordained by King David.
Aaron = AYR-uhn
Levites = LEE-vīts

Don't rush through the details. These— including the musical instruments signify the nature and quality of the celebration.

Note the parallel emphases on "burnt offerings" and "peace offerings."

The feast of the Assumption of Mary is both ancient and new. It has been celebrated as part of the Christian tradition since the fifth century, but the Catholic dogma (doctrine) of the assumption of Mary did not become official until 1950 under Pope Pius XII. The readings for the vigil Mass point to the holiness of those objects or people that bear the presence of God; Mary is honored by God for her discipleship and holiness in bearing Christ into the world and so we believe she was taken up, body and soul, into heaven.

READING I Our first reading is a narrative account of King David bringing the ark of God into Jerusalem. This is the ark that had traveled with the Israelites from the time of the Exodus. It was said to have contained the tablets of the Ten Commandments and to have special powers of protection for the Israelites. Except for the times that their warriors carried it into battle, it was kept in a special tent attended by Israelite priests and Levites, the tribe of Jacob that was set aside for religious service.

When David first rose to power, the ark was housed at Kirjath-jearim, but after he built his palace in Jerusalem, he ordered that the ark be brought to Jerusalem, where it continued to reside in a tent, as it had throughout the Exodus. This reading gives us a glimpse into the honor and splendor associated with the ark of God. The descendants of Aaron, whom David gathered for the transport of the ark, are the priests. The Levites, who carried the ark over its nine-mile journey to Jerusalem, did so with poles on their shoulders in order not to touch the ark itself. The event

For meditation and context:

RESPONSORIAL PSALM   Psalm 132:6–7, 9–10, 13–14 (8)

R. Lord, go up to the place of your rest, you and the ark of your holiness.

Behold, we heard of it in Ephrathah;
   we found it in the fields of Jaar.
Let us enter into his dwelling,
   let us worship at his footstool.

May your priests be clothed with justice;
   let your faithful ones shout merrily for joy.
For the sake of David your servant,
   reject not the plea of your anointed.

For the LORD has chosen Zion;
   he prefers her for his dwelling.
"Zion is my resting place forever;
   in her will I dwell, for I prefer her."

READING II   1 Corinthians 15:54b–57

Corinthians = kohr-IN-thee-uhnz

A reading in which Paul insists on the victory over death that results from the defiance of sin gained through Christ's sacrifice.

In this quotation, emphasize the first and last word in each italicized line.

Note the rhythm of these two lines, each of which has three beats: sting, death, sin, and power, sin, law.

A reading from the first Letter of Saint Paul to the Corinthians

Brothers and **sisters**:
When **that** which is **mortal** clothes **itself** with **immortality**,
   then the **word** that is **written** shall come **about**:

   Death *is swallowed up in* ***victory***.
   Where, *O death, is your* ***victory***?
   Where, *O death, is your* ***sting***?

The **sting** of **death** is **sin**,
   and the **power** of **sin** is the **law**.
But **thanks** be to **God** who gives us the **victory**
   through our **Lord** Jesus **Christ**.

TO KEEP IN MIND
Make eye contact with the assembly. This helps keep the assembly engaged with the reading.

---

was so sacred that the musical instruments could only be played by members of the tribe of Levi, and David himself offered the offerings of well-being before the ark. The offering of well-being was a burnt offering, part of which was given to God and part to the people, thus establishing communion with God. What a splendid affair!

READING II In today's second reading, Paul completes his lengthy teaching on resurrection of the body with a powerful exclamatory statement about what it will be like to inherit the kingdom of God at the end time. He has already made the point that the corruptible body—that is, the physical body which decays—cannot inherit the kingdom of God. Rather, at the end time, a trumpet will sound, and the dead will be raised incorruptible—that is, with an immortal spiritual body. When this happens, Paul says, the words of Scripture will be fulfilled. Paul's quotation is a loose conflation of Isaiah 25:8 and Hosea 13:14, which results in a beautifully poetic statement about death being swallowed up in victory.

In his Letter to the Romans, Paul states even more clearly than in today's reading that death came into the world through sin (see Romans 5:12) and that humanity did not know sin except through Jewish law, but that sin took advantage of the law to make us want what we should not have (Romans 7:7–13). This is what Paul means here, when he says, "the sting of death is sin" and "the power of sin is the law." But just as God raised Jesus from the dead in triumph over sin and death, we too, with our transformed bodies, will be raised in victory over death.

A short but intense Gospel reading in which an exhortation is embedded in a brief narrative. This reading can seem like a rebuke or at least a correction on Jesus' part. Instead, consider it an intensification of the excited statement made by the woman in the crowd.

Don't change your tone at "Rather." Instead, treat what Jesus says as an affirmation and furthering of what the woman has said.

GOSPEL   Luke 11:27–28

A reading from the holy Gospel according to Luke

While **Jesus** was **speaking**,
    a **woman** from the crowd called **out** and **said** to him,
    "**Blessed** is the **womb** that **carried** you
    and the **breasts** at which you **nursed**."
He replied,
    "**Rather**, blessed are **those**
    who **hear** the **word** of **God** and **observe** it."

GOSPEL   Our Gospel reading is very short but certainly relevant for this feast. It is part of a longer segment of Luke's Gospel in which Jesus responds to the accusation from some in the crowd that he drives out demons by the power of Satan (Luke 11:14–26) and to their demand for a sign from heaven before they will accept his testimony (Luke 11:29–36). In the first response, Jesus argues that he is actually the enemy of Satan and that he drives out demons by the power of God. In the second response, he turns the tables on his accusers, calling them an evil generation and telling them that the only sign he will give them is the sign of Jonah—a reference to how the people of Nineveh repented when they heard Jonah's preaching—and the great distance from which the queen of the south came to hear Solomon's words. Finally, Jesus delivers the decisive blow against his opponents by saying that they have someone greater than Solomon or Jonah in their midst and they do not see him because their they are living in darkness and cannot see the light of truth.

This is the backdrop for today's Gospel reading. Against Jesus' opponents who refuse to acknowledge the power of his word, a woman in the crowd shouts out "Blessed is the womb that carried you." In so doing, she is defending Jesus' honor and countering the charge that his power comes from Satan. Jesus' response to her encapsules all that needs to be said about discipleship—"Blessed are those who hear the word of God and observe it." Thankfully, we can call on Mary to be our guide in our journey of discipleship, because she is blessed on both counts! C.C.

THE ASSUMPTION OF THE BLESSED VIRGIN MARY: DAY

LECTIONARY #622

A reading full of vivid depictions and visionary intensity. Avoid the temptation to exaggerate your tone; instead, proclaim this text directly and straightforwardly, allowing its inherent drama to ring out to your assembly. Proclaim at an even pace so that the extraordinary details can be clearly imagined.

Slight pause between woman and clothed.

READING I   Revelation 11:19a; 12:1–6a, 10ab

A reading from the Book of Revelation

God's **temple** in **heaven** was **opened**,
  and the **ark** of his **covenant** could be **seen** in the **temple**.

A great **sign appeared** in the **sky**, a **woman clothed** with the **sun**,
  with the **moon** under her **feet**,
  and on her **head** a crown of **twelve stars**.

She was with **child** and **wailed aloud** in **pain** as she **labored**
    to give **birth**.

Note the repeated use of the word birth in this reading. Themes and visualizations of birth dominate the details.

Then another **sign** appeared in the **sky**;
  it was a **huge red dragon**, with seven **heads** and ten **horns**,
  and on its **heads** were seven **diadems**.

Its tail swept away a **third** of the **stars** in the **sky**
  and hurled them **down** to the **earth**.

Slight pause between "woman" and "about."

Then the **dragon** stood before the **woman about** to give **birth**,
  to **devour** her **child** when she gave **birth**.

Once again, the theme of birth.

She gave **birth** to a **son**, a **male child**,
  destined to **rule** all the **nations** with an iron **rod**.

Her **child** was caught up to **God** and his **throne**.

Slight pause between herself and fled.

The woman **herself fled** into the **desert**
  where she had a **place prepared** by **God**.

READING I A brief history of the origin of the feast of the Assumption of Mary and the doctrine associated with the feast is provided in the preface to the commentary on the readings for the vigil of this feast. In 1950, when Pope Pius XII defined the doctrine of the Assumption of Mary in the apostolic constitution *Munificentissimus Deus*, he noted many Scripture passages that theologians have used to contribute to our understanding of this teaching of Mary's assumption. Two Scripture texts that are part of the liturgy for the vigil of this feast, namely,

1 Corinthians 15:54–57 and Psalm 132, are referenced in his writing. He also mentions the vision of the woman clothed with the sun from the Book of Revelation (chapter 12), which is our first reading for today's feast. The identity of this woman is not evident from the text, but some Christian theologians in the early Church understand her to be Mary. Over time, this became the traditional Catholic interpretation of our text, but other suggestions include the Church, the heavenly Jerusalem, the people of Israel, and personified wisdom.

In this vision, John, the author of the Book of Revelation, saw a pregnant woman, who was adorned as a goddess, hovering in the sky. Her labor pains are a reminder of the consequences of Adam and Eve's fall (see Genesis 3:16), suggesting to some that she is the new Eve. He also saw a great red dragon waiting to devour her child when it was born. The dragon is a reminder of the serpent in the Adam and Eve story (Genesis 3:1–7), who is later identified with Satan. The dragon's ten horns introduce a detail from Daniel's vision of the four great oppressive empires of the world (Daniel

Then I heard a **loud voice** in heaven **say**:
  "**Now** have **salvation** and **power** come,
    and the **Kingdom** of our **God**
    and the **authority** of his **Anointed One**."

The loud voice indicates the Anointed One. You don't need to raise your voice any more than you already have. Instead, you can slow your pace just slightly.

For meditation and context:

RESPONSORIAL PSALM Psalm 45:10, 11, 12, 16 (10bc)

R. The queen stands at your right hand, arrayed in gold.

The queen takes her place at your right
  hand in gold of Ophir.

Hear, O daughter, and see; turn your ear,
  forget your people and your father's house.

So shall the king desire your beauty;
  for he is your lord.

They are borne in with gladness and joy;
  they enter the palace of the king.

READING II 1 Corinthians 15:20–27

Corinthians = kohr-IN-thee-uhnz

A reading in which Paul makes a set of forceful claims he wants the members of the early Church in Corinth to understand.

Paul uses analogy here to contrast the original sin of Adam to the redemption from sin of Christ.

Note the repetition of the biblical word "firstfruits."

The conclusion of this reading is quite forceful; note the emphatic connection between "enemies" and "death."

A reading from the first Letter of Saint Paul to the Corinthians

Brothers and **sisters**:
Christ has been **raised** from the **dead**,
  the **firstfruits** of **those** who have fallen **asleep**.
For since **death** came through **man**,
  the **resurrection** of the **dead** came **also** through **man**.
For just as in **Adam** all **die**,
  so too in **Christ** shall all be **brought** to **life**,
  but each **one** in proper **order**:
  Christ the **firstfruits**;
  then, at his **coming**, **those** who **belong** to **Christ**;
  then comes the **end**,
  when he hands **over** the **Kingdom** to his **God** and **Father**,
  when he has **destroyed** every **sovereignty**
  and every **authority** and **power**.
For he must **reign** until he has put all his **enemies** under
    his **feet**.
The last **enemy** to be **destroyed** is **death**,
  for "he subjected **everything** under his **feet**."

7:7). In general, horns represented power, and ten was the number representing fullness in the Greco-Roman world. Also, the detail about the dragon throwing down stars from the sky recalls a myth about a rebellious chaos monster that went so far as to attack the stars (see Daniel 8:10).

Likewise, the detail about the dragon waiting to devour the woman's baby would have reminded the initial readers of this text of the Greco-Roman myth of the birth of Apollo, whose mother Leto was attacked by the mythical dragon Python in order to kill the child and preserve his power over

the oracle at Delphi. But Apollo's father, Zeus, intervened to secure protection for Leto, and after Apollo was born, the child killed Python. It appears that John used these cultural images to depict the birth of the messiah, who was destined to rule with "an iron rod." Finally, the detail about the woman escaping to the desert, there to be taken care of by God, is a reminder of the Exodus. The length of her stay—one thousand two hundred sixty days—is about three and a half years. Half of seven, a number of fullness, this number represents a limited time.

Our first reading ends with a heavenly voice declaring that God's salvation and his kingdom have arrived, and Christ's authority is made known. This saying makes a beautiful *inclusio* with the opening sentence of the reading (a literary device used to frame a portion of text). Also, because this reading is intended to honor Mary's heavenly reality, the lectionary leaves out the intercalated vision of how the archangel Michael defeated the dragon and its minions (Revelation 12:7–9). This, too, is cause for rejoicing.

GOSPEL   Luke 1:39–56

A reading from the holy Gospel according to Luke

Mary set out
    and **traveled** to the hill country in **haste**
    to a town of **Judah**,
    where she **entered** the house of **Zechariah**
    and greeted **Elizabeth**.
When Elizabeth heard Mary's **greeting**,
    the infant **leaped** in her **womb**,
    and **Elizabeth**, filled with the **Holy Spirit**,
    cried **out** in a **loud** voice and **said**,
    "**Blessed** are **you** among **women**,
    and **blessed** is the **fruit** of your **womb**.
And how does this **happen** to me,
    that the **mother** of my **Lord** should **come** to me?
For at the **moment** the **sound** of your **greeting** reached my **ears**,
    the **infant** in my **womb** leaped for **joy**.
Blessed are **you** who **believed**
    that what was **spoken** to you by the **Lord**
    would be **fulfilled**."

And Mary said:
    "My **soul** proclaims the **greatness** of the **Lord**;
    my **spirit** rejoices in **God** my **Savior**
    for he has looked with **favor** on his lowly **servant**.
From **this day** all **generations** will call me **blessed**:
    the **Almighty** has done great **things** for me
    and **holy** is his **Name**.
He has **mercy** on those who **fear** him
    in every **generation**.
He has shown the **strength** of his **arm**,
    and has scattered the **proud** in their **conceit**.

A reading from Luke's gospel included in the nativity story. Its familiarity to your assembly will not diminish its power. No need to over-dramatize it; let the words of the reading convey its power.

Judah = JOO-duh
Zechariah = zek-uh-RĪ-uh

The focus of this reading is on sound, especially of Mary's voice. Let that voice ring out.

Words at the core of one of our most familiar prayers.

Once again, the emphasis is on the sound of Mary's voice and the joy it brings.

Here, Mary proclaims the words of the Magnificat, one of the most solemn hymns in the Church. We aren't necessarily accustomed to hearing these words nowadays. These are the words of a joyful affirmation the Gospels uniquely possess.

"He has shown," "He has cast down," "He has filled," "He has come": These phrases drive the rhythm of the Magnificat as it is proclaimed in this Gospel reading.

READING II   Our second reading comes from the same section of the First Letter to the Corinthians as did the second reading for the vigil of this feast. Paul has been making the argument that Christians who believe that Jesus was raised from the dead must also believe that they will be raised bodily from the dead—not with our present, physical bodies but with our new, transformed bodies. If we believe otherwise, then Jesus did not triumph over sin and death.

    In this reading, Paul writes about Christ as the firstfruits the first and best of the harvest offered to God as a symbol and consecration of all God's chosen ones who have fallen asleep. Paul also uses a method of interpretation called typology, an investigation of patterns of persons or events from the Old Testament that are fully realized in the New Testament. Here, Adam, who brought death into the world, is a type of Christ, who brings fullness of life. The "coming" of Christ is a reference to the parousia at the end time when Christ returns and God's reign is fully manifest to the world.

GOSPEL   Today's Gospel reading is the beautiful story of Mary's visitation to her cousin Elizabeth's home, after she learns that Elizabeth, who was old and barren, is six months pregnant and Mary herself is newly pregnant. This story is told only in Luke's Gospel.

    On the surface of this story, it could appear that there is little to say beyond the fact that Mary is presented as a charitable, young Jewish girl who is concerned for the welfare of her aged relative. However, let's dig a little deeper. Why does the narrator say that Mary traveled in haste? Also, was

He has cast down the **mighty** from their **thrones**,
  and has **lifted up** the lowly.
He has filled the **hungry** with **good things**,
  and the **rich** he has sent away **empty**.
He has come to the **help** of his servant **Israel**
  for he has **remembered** his promise of **mercy**,
  the **promise** he made to our **fathers**,
  to **Abraham** and his children for **ever**."

Mary **remained** with her about three **months**
  and then **returned** to her **home**.

she travelling alone or with a caravan? Why would she have been allowed to make this approximately ninety-mile, four-day journey alone? The chances of being raped or killed along the way would have been extremely high. Though we don't have the details of her journey, the manner in which she undertook it is significant.

Perhaps Luke's intention in having Mary travel "in haste" was to maintain a close connection between the announcement of the conception of these women's children and the acclamation of their sons' relationship to one another. Both the narra-tor and Elizabeth comment on her unborn baby leaping in her womb when she hears Mary's greeting, further suggesting that her child, John, recognized Jesus even before either was born. In all four Gospels, John is the one who precedes Jesus and paves the way for his ministry in the world. Elizabeth also acclaims Mary's blessedness and the blessedness of her unborn baby. She is the mother of their Lord! She is also the model of faith for all believers.

Mary responds with words that have come to be known as the Magnificat or the Canticle of Mary. It is patterned after the Song of Hannah (1 Samuel 2:1–10), which Hannah prayed to God when she brought her son Samuel to the house of the Lord in Shiloh to dedicate him to God, after she had endured years of bullying and shame because of her barrenness. Here, in the Magnificat, Mary attributes her blessed-ness to God, who in his mercy has raised up the lowly and brought down the proud of heart. Luke highlights this reversal theol-ogy throughout his Gospel. C.C.

TWENTIETH SUNDAY
IN ORDINARY TIME

READING I   Isaiah 56:1, 6–7

Isaiah = ī-ZAY-uh

A reading charged with poetry. Be attentive to its rhythms, which convey a lot of its power.

A reading from the Book of the Prophet Isaiah

> **Thus** says the LORD:
> **Observe** what is **right**, **do** what is **just**;
>   for my **salvation** is about to **come**,
>   my **justice**, about to be **revealed**.
>
> The **foreigners** who **join** themselves to the LORD,
>   **ministering** to him,
> **loving** the **name** of the LORD,
>   and **becoming** his **servants**—
> **all** who keep the **sabbath free** from **profanation**
>   and **hold** to my **covenant**,
> **them** I will **bring** to my **holy mountain**
>   and make **joyful** in my **house** of **prayer**;
> their **burnt offerings** and **sacrifices**
>   will be **acceptable** on my **altar**,
> for my **house** shall be **called**
>   a **house of prayer** for all **peoples**.

profanation = prah-fuh-NAY-shuhn
Slight pause between "sabbath" and "free."

The conclusion shifts into an uplifting register.

READING I Chapters 55–66 of Isaiah constitute the section known as Trito-Isaiah, a collection of prophetic material spoken to the Israelites after their return to Jerusalem following the Babylonian Exile. By the time this portion of Isaiah had been written, the Temple had been rebuilt and there needed to be a rethinking of what constituted the true nature of the religion. Sacrifice in the Temple was an established means of expressing fidelity to the covenant, but in the time that passed during the absence of the Temple, the people deepened their understanding of what God truly looks for in choosing them as his beloved possession.

The primary theme of this passage is that the covenant is about justice, especially demonstrated in the acceptance of outsiders. The Lord's voice speaks to the people, reminding them that his justice will dawn very soon. Furthermore, the Israelites must not see themselves as having exclusive access to the fruits of God's justice. Instead, all those who love the Lord and find a way to serve him will be welcomed on God's mountain. The Lord suggests that those who have been gifted with the law ought to teach those who do not know the law how to serve God, as well as how to keep the covenant and honor the Sabbath. Undoubtedly, those who have returned from exile rejoice in the restoration of God's house in the city of Jerusalem, but now they must extend God's household far beyond the Temple precincts. The truly acceptable sacrifice is to participate in the construction of a unity among all peoples so that God's house may become "a house of prayer for all peoples."

For meditation and context:

RESPONSORIAL PSALM   Psalm 67:2–3, 5, 6, 8 (4)

R. O God, let all the nations praise you!

May God have pity on us and bless us;
    may he let his face shine upon us.
So may your way be known upon earth;
    among all nations, your salvation.

May the nations be glad and exult
    because you rule the peoples in equity;
    the nations on the earth you guide.

May the peoples praise you, O God;
    may all the peoples praise you!
May God bless us,
    and may all the ends of the earth fear him!

READING II   Romans 11:13–15, 29–32

A reading from the Letter of Saint Paul to the Romans

Brothers and **sisters**:
I am **speaking** to you **Gentiles**.
Inasmuch as I am the **apostle** to the **Gentiles**,
    I glory in my **ministry** in order to make my **race jealous**
    and **thus save some** of them.
For if their **rejection** is the **reconciliation** of the **world**,
    what will their **acceptance** be but **life** from the **dead**?

For the **gifts** and the **call** of **God** are **irrevocable**.
Just as you once **disobeyed God**
    but have now **received mercy because** of their **disobedience**,
    so **they** have now **disobeyed** in **order** that,
    by **virtue** of the **mercy shown** to you,
    they too may now receive **mercy**.
For **God delivered all** to **disobedience**,
    that he might have **mercy** upon **all**.

An uplifting message Paul addresses directly to the Gentiles.

Slight pause between "race" and "jealous."
Slight pause between "save" and "some."

irrevocable = ir-REV-uh-kuh-b*l

Slight pause between "mercy" and "because."

READING II In addressing his fellow Christians in Rome, whom he identifies as Gentiles or outsiders, Paul refers to himself as their apostle. Beginning in chapter 9, Paul begins a long exhortation regarding the privilege granted to the people of Israel as well as their responsibility to see that the law is fulfilled in Christ (Romans 10:4). It is Paul's hope that Israel will accept the mercy of God and choose to recognize Jesus as their savior. In today's reading we see that Paul hopes that his ministry to the Gentiles will make his own people "jealous" and lead at least some of them (a "remnant") to seek the way of conversion. Paul acknowledges that just as Israel's rejection of the Christian way has led to the blossoming of the Church in foreign lands, the opportunity for them to embrace Christ will be a great sign of resurrected life in the world.

In the second half of this reading, Paul illuminates the triumphant power of God's mercy. Both the gifts of God and his call are "irrevocable." This is certainly true for the mercy of God. The Gentiles did not ask for mercy, but because the Jews rejected the Gospel, Paul has preached God's merciful word to them. The "disobedience" of some has allowed others to benefit from God's forgiveness. The bottom line is that sin and disobedience become the means by which God is able to display his very nature to the world, for he is a God that desires to "have mercy upon all."

GOSPEL Take note that all three readings today deal with Gentiles, or outsiders. Given the fact that Matthew is writing to a community primarily composed of Jewish Christians, it is not surprising that the tenor of this encounter

GOSPEL   Matthew 15:21–28

A reading from the holy Gospel according to Matthew

At that time, **Jesus withdrew** to the **region** of **Tyre** and **Sidon**.
And **behold**, a **Canaanite woman** of that district **came**
    and called **out**,
  "Have **pity** on me, **Lord**, **Son** of **David**!
My **daughter** is **tormented** by a **demon**."
But **Jesus** did not say a **word** in **answer** to her.
Jesus' disciples came and **asked** him,
  "**Send** her **away**, for she keeps **calling out after** us."
He **said** in **reply**,
  "I was sent **only** to the **lost sheep** of the **house** of **Israel**."
But the **woman came** and did **Jesus homage**, saying,
    "**Lord**, **help** me."
He **said** in **reply**,
  "It **is not right** to take the **food** of the **children**
  and **throw** it to the **dogs**."
She said, "**Please**, **Lord**, for even the **dogs** eat the **scraps**
  that **fall** from the **table** of their **masters**."
Then **Jesus said** to her in **reply**,
  "O **woman**, **great** is your **faith**!
Let it be **done** for you as you **wish**."
And the woman's **daughter** was **healed** from that **hour**.

Tyre = tīr
Sidon = Sī-duhn
Even emphasis on the opening words of this reading: "At that time, Jesus withdrew . . . "

Jesus' refusal to answer the Canaanite woman, and his subsequent responses, may seem startling to us.

At last, Jesus' mood changes when he recognizes the depth of the Canaanite woman's faith.

between Jesus and the Canaanite woman seems to display exclusion. We may even wonder why Jesus would want to find seclusion in this northern region near the border of Phoenicia. He will announce that his mission is "only to the lost sheep of the house of Israel," and yet he has placed himself squarely in foreign territory.

Nevertheless, the location has a great surprise in store for Jesus. He is able to discover an outsider to the Jewish world who has incredible faith. Three times the Canaanite woman begs Jesus to release her daughter from the torment of a demon.

After the first request, Jesus simply ignores her, while the disciples beg him to send her away. This gives Jesus the opportunity to announce the parameter of his mission as extending only for the people of Israel. In turn, the woman seems to ignore Jesus, as she performs some act of homage and states boldly, "Lord, help me." Now, Jesus replies with a rather startling comment, comparing her to a dog. Even in the face of this insult, the woman does not relent, but instead suggests that even dogs are worthy of table scraps. Her persistent pleading now causes Jesus to appreciate the depths

of her faith, and he cures the daughter from a distance at that very moment. Matthew uses the story to demonstrate an expansion of the mission in the vision of Jesus himself. S.W.

TWENTY-FIRST SUNDAY IN ORDINARY TIME

LECTIONARY #121

READING I   Isaiah 22:19–23

Isaiah = ī-ZAY-uh

Shebna = SHEB-nah
A poetic reading in whose rhythms express the powers and convictions of the Lord.

Eliakim = ee-LĪ-uh-kim
Hilkiah = hil-KĪ-uh

A reading from the Book of the Prophet Isaiah

> **Thus** says the LORD to **Shebna**, **master** of the **palace**:
> "I will **thrust** you from your **office**
>   and **pull** you **down** from your **station**.
> On **that day** I will **summon** my **servant**
>   **Eliakim**, son of **Hilkiah**;
> I will **clothe** him with your **robe**,
>   and **gird** him with your **sash**,
>   and give **over** to him your **authority**.
> He shall be a **father** to the **inhabitants** of **Jerusalem**,
>   and to the **house** of **Judah**.
> I will **place** the **key** of the **House** of **David** on
>   **Eliakim's shoulder**;
>   when he **opens**, no one shall **shut**,
>   when he **shuts**, no one shall **open**.
> I will **fix** him like a **peg** in a **sure spot**,
>   to be a **place** of **honor** for his **family**."

Take note of the inversion: "opens"/"shut"; "shuts"/"open." Give them emphasis.

TO KEEP IN MIND
If you are assigned to proclaim the first reading, read the Gospel for that week as well. They are connected in thematic ways.

READING I This reading exhibits a popular literary theme based on the "keeper of the keys," wherein someone has power and insider knowledge because of the responsibility given to them to control entry into the place. Here we have Shebna, who holds the keys that will allow the king entrance, being replaced by a new steward named Eliakim. This exchange takes place during the reign of Hezekiah, the thirteenth king of Judah who ruled in the late eighth to early seventh century BC. The Lord has determined that the king's chief steward must be replaced because he has become prideful by building a tomb for himself and taking pride in his chariots, among other things that might bring shame to the king (Isaiah 22:16–18).

The Lord describes the confidence he has in selecting Eliakim to replace Shebna by the vesture of his office. He will be clothed with Shebna's own robe and sash, which serves to mark the transition of authority from Shebna to Eliakim. Unlike Shebna's display of infidelity, Eliakim will be like a "father" to the people. This means that he will not take advantage of the role entrusted to him. Finally, Eliakim will be given the "key of the House of David." Keys are often used as a symbol of authority. It will be Eliakim's decision whom to admit to the king's palace and whom to reject. He is not to be understood as any mere doorkeeper, but he is to be a steward who has great care and concern for all in his responsibility. Because the Lord's confidence in this servant is so great, he will become an honor for his family.

READING II Paul's hymn of wonder over the wisdom revealed in God's plan must be read within the frame-

For meditation and context:

RESPONSORIAL PSALM   Psalm 138:1–2, 2–3, 6, 8 (8bc)

R. Lord, your love is eternal; do not forsake the work of your hands.

I will give thanks to you, O LORD, with all
    my heart,
  for you have heard the words of my mouth;
in the presence of the angels I will sing
    your praise;
  I will worship at your holy temple.

I will give thanks to your name,
  because of your kindness and your truth:
when I called, you answered me;
  you built up strength within me.

The LORD is exalted, yet the lowly he sees,
  and the proud he knows from afar.
Your kindness, O LORD, endures forever;
  forsake not the work of your hands.

READING II   Romans 11:33–36

A reading from the Letter of Saint Paul to the Romans

Oh, the **depth** of the **riches** and **wisdom** and **knowledge** of **God**!
How **inscrutable** are his **judgments** and how **unsearchable**
    his **ways**!
  For *who* has **known** the **mind** of the **Lord**
    or **who** has been his **counselor**?
  Or *who* has given the **Lord anything**
    that he may be **repaid**?
For **from** him and **through** him and **for** him are **all things**.
To **him** be **glory forever. Amen.**

A short and powerful reading from Paul,
expressed with great passion.

inscrutable = in-SKROO-tuh-b*l (unknowable)

Note how the prepositions supply the
power: "from," "through," and "for."

work of the apostle's overall mission to the Gentiles. Paul himself surely must have been utterly amazed at the work of God in his own conversion from being a strident persecutor of the Christian way to leading the charge to spread the Gospel to peoples far removed from Jerusalem. Paul has just reminded the Romans that while the Jewish people continue to receive God's favor, the conversion of the Gentiles to Christ has allowed God to display the gift of his mercy, which the chosen people of Israel are invited to accept (Romans 11:1–29).

This brief hymn proclaims there is no wisdom and knowledge comparable to God's. This theme of praise can be seen in Old Testament texts that champion God's wisdom (for example, Wisdom 17:1). For Paul, it is simply impossible to plumb the depths of God's knowledge. Furthermore, the hymn proclaims that God acts alone and has no need of advice in carrying out his plan for creation. Though human beings may not understand God's ways, God is the beginning, the sustainer, and the end of all that is. As the conclusion of Paul's exhortation on the place of the people of Israel in

God's plan of salvation, this hymn conveys the message that it would be utter foolishness to do anything but cooperate fully with God's wisdom and thus work toward a bond of unity between Jews and Gentiles.

GOSPEL Today's reading from Matthew is generally considered to be the chief evangelical text for our understanding of the Church's foundation. While the story of Peter's profession of faith is recorded in Mark 8:27–30 and in Luke 9:18–21, it is only in Matthew that Jesus calls Simon "Peter," or "the Rock"

GOSPEL   Matthew 16:13–20

A reading from the holy Gospel according to Matthew

Jesus went into the **region** of **Caesarea Philippi** and
he **asked** his **disciples**,
"**Who** do **people say** that the **Son** of **Man is**?"
They **replied**, "**Some** say **John** the **Baptist**, **others Elijah**,
still **others Jeremiah** or **one** of the **prophets**."
He said to them, "But who do you say that I am?"
Simon Peter said in **reply**,
"**You** are the **Christ**, the **Son** of the **living God**."
Jesus said to him in **reply**,
"**Blessed** are **you**, **Simon** son of **Jonah**.
For **flesh** and **blood** has not **revealed** this to you, but my
heavenly Father.
And so I **say** to you, you are **Peter**,
and **upon this rock** I will **build** my **church**,
and the **gates** of the **netherworld** shall not **prevail against** it.
I will give you the **keys** to the **kingdom** of **heaven**.
Whatever you **bind** on **earth** shall be **bound** in **heaven**;
and whatever you **loose** on **earth** shall be **loosed** in **heaven**."
Then he **strictly ordered** his **disciples**
to tell **no one** that he was the **Christ**.

Caesarea Philippi = sez-uh-REE-uh fih-LIP-ī

This reading is a set piece in which Jesus, in asking the disciples to tell him what people are saying about him, designates Peter as the one to receive the keys to his kingdom. As such, it has a vivid, narrative quality.

Slight pause between "Peter" and "said."

Even emphasis on "upon this rock."

Note the parallel: bind-earth-bound-heaven || loose-earth-loosed-heaven.
The conclusion is mysterious. You can allow some of that mystery and slight confusion to slip into your tone.

(from the Greek, *petra/Petros*; and the Aramaic, *kēpā'/Kēphas*), and gives him the power to forgive sins. What is evident here is the influence of the early Church, which presents itself as solid, authoritative, and clearly organized.

The location for this story, in the land north of Galilee, very near to Gentile territory, is important. Matthew designs his Gospel so that the first profession of faith is uttered not in Jerusalem but in a place some distance from the center. When asked by Jesus "Who do people say that the Son of Man is?" the disciples reply with a variety of well-known figures in the Hebrew faith— John the Baptist, Elijah, and Jeremiah—but the follow-up question "But who do you say that I am?" suggests that the disciples are more insiders than these classic figures. Furthermore, Peter's profession of Jesus' identity being both "the Christ" and "the Son of the living God" suggests divine wisdom. True knowledge of Jesus can only be granted by God himself. "Flesh and blood" alone, meaning human knowledge, is incapable of grasping the mystery of God revealed in Jesus; this gift comes from above.

At such a profound statement of faith and openness to the Spirit, Jesus does not simply offer words of praise but instead grants him complete authority over his future mission. "The Rock" is to provide a firm foundation for the earthly Church and to make heavenly entrance possible by the forgiveness of sins. The Church is completely life-giving, with no power of death able to conquer it. Like Eliakim being in charge of the keys to the palace in the first reading, Peter is a righteous steward called to manage well the affairs of God's household. S.W.

TWENTY-SECOND SUNDAY IN ORDINARY TIME

Jeremiah = jayr-uh-MĪ-uh

"Duped": It's a strong word! This helps set the tone for this reading, which is one of weariness and frustration.

Take care not to over-dramatize Jeremiah's frustration. It will come through clearly in the words themselves as you proclaim them.

Extra emphasis on "cannot endure."

LECTIONARY #124

READING I   Jeremiah 20:7–9

A reading from the Book of the Prophet Jeremiah

You **duped** me, O LORD, and I **let myself** be **duped**;
   you were **too strong** for me, and you **triumphed**.
All the **day** I am an **object** of **laughter**;
   everyone **mocks** me.

Whenever I **speak**, I must **cry out**,
   violence and **outrage** is my **message**;
the **word** of the LORD has **brought** me
   derision and **reproach** all the **day**.

I **say** to **myself**, I will not **mention** him,
   I will **speak** in his **name** no **more**.
But then it **becomes** like **fire burning** in my **heart**,
   imprisoned in my **bones**;
I grow **weary** holding it **in**, I **cannot endure** it.

READING I The words that we read from Jeremiah today are some of the strongest words of lamentation found in the Old Testament. The prophet has just completed three forecasts of Jerusalem's downfall (Jeremiah 19:1–3, 14–15, and 20:1–5). The most recent prediction of the city's demise was made to the Temple priest Pashhur, who had placed him in the stocks outside of the Temple's gate (Jeremiah 20:2). After announcing that Pashhur and all his family will die in captivity in Babylon, Jeremiah turns his attention to God and calls out in his agony.

Jeremiah claims that God had "duped" him by calling him into service as a prophet. The Hebrew word *pātâ* may also be translated as "seduced," thereby making the accusation more comparable to sexual allurement. The prophet's point is to address God as boldly as possible, revealing the frustration he has internalized for a long period of time. Jeremiah complains that his work as a prophet has been met with utter rejection, as the people treat him with "derision and reproach."

However, in the final verse Jeremiah seems to surrender to God once more.

While he would like to forget God, refusing to bring him to mind or utter his name, God's call surges up in him again "like fire burning in my heart." Although he knows he will make every attempt to contain this fire within, it must be released. The language of this passage of lament suggests that to attempt to restrain the Word of God that must be spoken is simply impossible.

READING II Chapter 12 of Romans contains an exhortation on humility and charity. He has just finished proclaiming a hymn honoring the wisdom

For meditation and context:

RESPONSORIAL PSALM   Psalm 63:2, 3–4, 5–6, 8–9 (2b)

R. My soul is thirsting for you, O Lord my God.

O God, you are my God whom I seek;
   for you my flesh pines and my soul thirsts
   like the earth, parched, lifeless and
      without water.

Thus have I gazed toward you in
      the sanctuary
   to see your power and your glory,
for your kindness is a greater good than life;
   my lips shall glorify you.

Thus will I bless you while I live;
   lifting up my hands, I will call upon
      your name.
As with the riches of a banquet shall my soul
      be satisfied,
   and with exultant lips my mouth shall
      praise you.

You are my help,
   and in the shadow of your wings I shout
      for joy.
My soul clings fast to you;
   your right hand upholds me.

READING II   Romans 12:1–2

A reading from the Letter of Saint Paul to the Romans

I **urge** you, **brothers** and **sisters**, by the **mercies** of **God**,
   to **offer** your **bodies** as a **living sacrifice**,
   holy and **pleasing** to **God**, your **spiritual worship**.
Do not **conform** yourselves to this **age**
   but be **transformed** by the **renewal** of your **mind**,
   that you may **discern** what is the **will** of **God**,
   what is **good** and **pleasing** and **perfect**.

A short and potent reading whose urgency presents a challenge to your assembly.

As challenging a teaching when Paul made it as it remains today.

of God's mercy (Romans 11:33–36), and now he wishes to impress upon the Romans the need to live and to behave in a manner appropriate to the Christian way. In keeping with the mercy freely given by God, Paul opens this part of the letter by suggesting that God's grace makes it possible for one to offer the entirety of oneself (one's "body") "as a living sacrifice." The use of sacrificial language underscores that Paul is demanding complete and total surrender of the self. This is conversion not only of the mind and heart but of the way in which the body is used as well.

To accomplish this conversion—always to be done in cooperation with God's will—disciples are urged to resist conforming to the world. Since the transformation of a Christian into the life of Christ is an ongoing process, the mind must be constantly discerning what is "good and pleasing and perfect." Before Paul outlines concretely the ways in which disciples must live in this world with humility and charity, he prevails upon the Christians in Rome to envision life as constant transformation. Even though the world in which human beings live is temporary (see

1 Corinthians 7:31), Paul wants believers to understand the hard work of Christian life as a sacrifice pleasing to God.

GOSPEL   This passage marks a shift in the structure of Matthew's Gospel. Immediately prior to today's reading Jesus asks his disciples about his identity and Peter offers his great profession of faith (Matthew 16:13–20, see last week's Gospel reading). Matthew's Gospel now turns to focus on the cross. While Peter is able to identify Jesus as the Christ, he is unwilling to accept Jesus' hum-

GOSPEL　Matthew 16:21–27

A reading from the holy Gospel according to Matthew

The tone of this Gospel reading begins gloomily, even apocalyptically.

Jesus began to **show** his **disciples**
　　that he must **go** to **Jerusalem** and **suffer greatly**
　　from the **elders**, the **chief priests**, and the **scribes**,
　　and be **killed** and on the **third day** be **raised**.
Then **Peter** took **Jesus aside** and **began** to **rebuke** him,
　　"**God forbid, Lord! No such thing** shall **ever happen** to you."
He **turned** and said to **Peter**,
　　"Get **behind** me, **Satan! You** are an **obstacle** to me.
You are thinking **not** as **God does**, but as **human beings** do."

"Rebuke": This is a strong word. Peter is upset.

But Jesus is bothered, even more so than Peter is upset.

Then **Jesus said** to his **disciples**,
　　"Whoever **wishes** to come **after** me must **deny** himself,
　　take up his **cross**, and **follow** me.
For whoever **wishes** to save **his** life will **lose** it,
　　but whoever **loses** his **life** for **my sake** will **find** it.
What **profit** would there **be** for one to **gain** the **whole world**
　　and **forfeit** his **life**?
Or what can **one give** in **exchange** for his **life**?
For the **Son** of **Man** will come with his **angels** in his
　　Father's glory,
　　and then he will **repay all according** to his **conduct**."

Familiar though Jesus' command may be, it is challenging, something even the most devout Christian might not be able to live up to.

Note the inversion: wishes-life-lose compared to loses-life-find.

Slight pause between "all" and "according."

ble acceptance of God's will, which would lead to his suffering and eventual death. Thus, the juxtaposition of these two passages demonstrates the difficulty of holding together the horror of the cross with the messianic nature of the person Jesus.

　　In his private rebuke of Peter (Peter had taken Jesus aside) for attempting to shield him from suffering, Jesus reminds Peter that he is failing to discern the will of God. Peter is viewing power and authority as humans naturally would. However, Jesus turns to his disciples as a whole and tells them the true nature of power and author-

ity, namely, what will come to be celebrated in the Church as the paschal mystery. Discipleship involves the willingness to die to self in order to find life again in service of others. Jesus outlines this as a threefold movement: denial of self, taking up the cross, and following after him. Far from seeking the reward of glory, the very purpose of following Jesus is the carrying of the cross. Profit and gain are overturned in Christian discipleship; Christians are to give themselves away in order to receive all that Christ will have in store for them when he returns in glory. The final verse of the

reading foreshadows Matthew's story of the Son of Man separating the sheep from the goats on the day of his return (25:31–46). S.W.

TWENTY-THIRD SUNDAY IN ORDINARY TIME

LECTIONARY #127

READING I Ezekiel 33:7–9

A reading from the Book of the Prophet Ezekiel

Thus says the LORD:
> **You**, son of **man**, I have appointed **watchman** for the **house** of **Israel**;
> when you **hear** me say **anything**, you shall **warn** them for me.
> If I tell the **wicked**, "O **wicked one**, you shall **surely die**,"
> and you **do not speak out** to **dissuade** the **wicked** from his **way**,
> the **wicked** shall **die** for his **guilt**,
> but I will hold **you responsible** for his **death**.
> But if you **warn** the **wicked**,
> trying to **turn** him from his **way**,
> and he **refuses** to **turn** from his **way**,
> he shall **die** for his **guilt**,
> but **you** shall **save yourself**.

Ezekiel = ee-ZEE-kee-uhl

An ominous reading in which God makes a challenging command. God speaks directly to the assembly through Ezekiel.

Slight pause between "you" and "responsible."

Emphasis on "you."

TO KEEP IN MIND
As you prepare your proclamation, make choices about what emotions need to be expressed. Some choices are evident from the text, but some are harder to discern. Understanding the context of the Scripture passage will help you decide.

READING I The prophet Ezekiel experienced the forced exile of the Israelites by the Babylonians. During that time, he received his call by God to watch over Israel and to challenge the ways of the wicked. Ezekiel was one of the few Old Testament prophets who received his calling outside the land of Israel, which can shed light on his understanding of God's universal judgment—in Ezekiel, God judges not only the deeds of his chosen people but those of all the nations.

Foretelling of the impending destruction of Jerusalem, the voice of the Lord summons Ezekiel to be a "watchman" during the time of conflict. He is to provide a warning to the wicked to renounce their ways. Ezekiel is told quite clearly that failing to enact this task will result in his own demise. This is the second instance of Ezekiel being called to be a watchman and communicate God's message to those who sin, the first being in Ezekiel 3:17–21. The reading we hear today takes place after the prophet has called many nations to conversion and has prophesied the eventual restoration of Israel. Once again, like a trustworthy sentinel who is to protect the people, Ezekiel receives the call to address the ways of the wicked with challenging words. As watchman, Ezekiel is to make very clear the seriousness of failing to turn from evil in order to pursue the way of righteousness. While Israel has certainly suffered from their deportation to Babylon, they ought to be bolstered in God's care and concern for them by his placing such great responsibility in Ezekiel, a trustworthy and vigilant prophet.

For meditation and context:

RESPONSORIAL PSALM   Psalm 95:1–2, 6–7, 8–9 (8)

R. If today you hear his voice, harden not your hearts.

Come, let us sing joyfully to the LORD;
  let us acclaim the rock of our salvation.
Let us come into his presence
    with thanksgiving;
  let us joyfully sing psalms to him.

Come, let us bow down in worship;
  let us kneel before the LORD who made us.
For he is our God,
  and we are the people he shepherds,
    the flock he guides.

Oh, that today you would hear his voice:
  "Harden not your hearts as at Meribah,
    as in the day of Massah in the desert,
where your fathers tempted me;
    they tested me though they had seen
      my works."

READING II   Romans 13:8–10

A reading from the Letter of Saint Paul to the Romans

The reading begins with a potent exhortation that shifts into a more subtle teaching.

The recitation of these commandments has a rote quality . . .

. . . which leads to this distillation of the wisdom of the Scriptures.
Even emphasis on "Love does no evil."

Brothers and **sisters**:
Owe **nothing** to **anyone**, except to **love** one **another**;
  for the one who **loves another** has **fulfilled** the **law**.
The **commandments**, "You shall **not** commit **adultery**;
  you **shall not kill**; you **shall not steal**; you **shall not covet**,"
  and **whatever other commandment** there may **be**,
  are **summed up** in this **saying**, **namely**,
  "You shall **love** your **neighbor** as **yourself**."
Love does no evil to the **neighbor**;
  hence, **love** is the **fulfillment** of the law.

READING II This reading on the commandment to love follows Paul's instruction to the Romans to obey the rule of civil authorities. Paul understands all civil authority as subject to the law of God. Thus, since God is the ultimate authority, obedience ought to be given to the law of the land since rupture in society is ultimately in conflict with the unity God desires.

Paul tells the Romans that the only debt they are to incur is "to love one another." While the foundation of Hebrew law is based on the command to avoid certain wrongdoings such as murder, theft,

and lust (see Exodus 20:13–17), Paul speaks of the law's foundation in a proactive manner. Love is not simply avoiding actions that are evil, but love involves moving outside of oneself in order to support the lives of others. The command to love in no means replaces the ancient law, but instead, it buffers it and demands more than mere passivity. In the next chapter, Paul will provide concrete examples as to how love unfolds in charitable outreach to others. We see him begin to explore this idea at the end of this reading by bringing together the law and the life of the Christian: "Love does

no evil to the neighbor; hence, love is the fulfilment of the law."

GOSPEL In the verses preceding today's Gospel passage, Jesus tells his disciples the parable of the lost sheep among the flock of one hundred. Great effort is expended by the caring shepherd who leaves the ninety-nine in order to seek out the one who has gone astray. Jesus then likens the Father to the shepherd who is vigilant in guarding his flock and making sure that none are lost.

A reading that demonstrates, in part, the way that Jesus sequences his thoughts, one following from another, building his argument.

GOSPEL   Matthew 18:15–20

A reading from the holy Gospel according to Matthew

Jesus said to his **disciples**:
  "If your **brother** sins **against** you,
  go and **tell** him his **fault** between **you** and him **alone**.
If he **listens** to you, you have won **over** your **brother**.
If he **does not listen**,
  take **one** or **two others along** with you,
  so that '**every fact** may be **established**
  on the **testimony** of **two** or **three witnesses**.'
If he **refuses** to **listen** to them, tell the **church**.
If he **refuses** to listen even to the **church**,
  then **treat** him as you would a **Gentile** or a **tax** collector.
Amen, I **say** to you,
  whatever you **bind** on **earth** shall be **bound** in **heaven**,
  and **whatever** you **loose** on **earth** shall be **loosed** in **heaven**.
Again, **amen**, I **say** to **you**,
  if **two** of you **agree** on **earth**
  about **anything** for which they are to **pray**,
  it shall be **granted** to them by my **heavenly Father**.
For where **two** or **three** are **gathered together** in my **name**,
  there am **I** in the **midst** of them."

Slight pause between "others" and "along."

Note the parallel: bind-earth-bound-heaven || loose-earth-loosed-heaven.

Try to proclaim this familiar insistence as if saying these words for the first time.

It is in this context that we are to read today's teaching on how disputes within the community are not to lead to permanent division but must be resolved through a process of forgiveness. Jesus tells his disciples that the first step in this process is to confront the one responsible for a "fault." If this private encounter proves unsuccessful, several witnesses may assist in exposing the culpability of the one who denies his sin. The authority of the Church is to be consulted as a third option to correct the wrongdoing, and if this fails, the sinner is to be treated as "a Gentile or a tax collector."

In other words, the person is to be treated as someone who is outside the faith of the Church.

All of this culminates in Jesus alluding to the ministry of reconciliation as carried out by the Church. The Church as a whole is given the authority to determine what sins are to be "bound" and "loosed." This is an authority that was earlier handed over by Jesus to Peter alone (Matthew 16:19). Furthermore, Jesus concludes the instruction by ensuring his disciples of the efficacy of prayer and the importance of community. When two or more come together to pray, they must believe that the Father will hear their prayer. The source of this confidence is found in the presence of the Lord in the midst of his assembled Church. Thus, in their ministry of forgiveness and in their petition of the Lord's aid, the community of believers experiences the presence of Jesus in their midst. S.W.

TWENTY-FOURTH SUNDAY IN ORDINARY TIME

LECTIONARY #130

READING I   Sirach 27:30—28:7

A reading from the Book of Sirach

> **Wrath** and **anger** are **hateful things**,
>   yet the **sinner hugs** them **tight**.
> The **vengeful** will **suffer** the LORD'S **vengeance**,
>   for he **remembers** their **sins** in **detail**.
> **Forgive** your **neighbor's injustice**;
>   **then** when you **pray**, your **own sins** will be **forgiven**.
> Could **anyone nourish anger** against **another**
>   and **expect healing** from the LORD?
> Could **anyone** refuse **mercy** to **another** like **himself**,
>   can he seek **pardon** for his **own sins**?
> If **one** who is but **flesh cherishes wrath**,
>   **who** will **forgive** his **sins**?
> **Remember** your **last days**, set e**nmity aside**;
>   **remember death** and **decay**, and **cease** from **sin**!
> **Think** of the **commandments**, **hate not** your **neighbor**;
>   **remember** the Most **High's covenant**, and **overlook faults**.

Sirach = SEER-ak or SĪ-ruhk

A poetic reading drawn along by its powerful rhythm. Slight pause between "sinner" and "hugs."

These emphatic questions set the tone of the reading.

Slight pause between "flesh" and "cherishes."

The reading concludes with an exhortation whose timeliness remains relevant.

READING I The wisdom of the Hebrew scribe Ben Sira is believed to have been compiled between the years 200 and 175 BC. As a collection of ethical instructions, this book attempts to provide practical advice on primary relationships, such as those with mother and father, siblings, the rich and the poor. Today's reading offers wisdom on the issue of holding a grudge against others. Ben Sira opens this section with the image of the sinner hugging tightly to "wrath and anger."

He proceeds to instruct his hearers that those who inflict vengeance upon others will in turn receive the Lord's vengeance. In order to be forgiven by God, one must extend forgiveness to others. The same is true with anger; if one harbors anger in one's heart, then one should not be surprised when God will not heal the situation. In the final portion of his instruction on why a person should avoid hatred and vengeance, the author employs the image of death. The threat of death is indeed the gravest of all of his warnings. By remembering the last moments of life, a person ought to recognize that it would be ultimate destruction to die in a state of holding hatred against another. Ben Sira's message is abundantly clear: live constantly the virtue of dismissing the faults of others, and God will respond in kind.

For meditation and context:

RESPONSORIAL PSALM   Psalm 103:1–2, 3–4, 9–10, 11–12 (8)

R. The Lord is kind and merciful, slow to anger, and rich in compassion.

Bless the Lord, O my soul;
  and all my being, bless his holy name.
Bless the Lord, O my soul,
  and forget not all his benefits.

He pardons all your iniquities,
  heals all your ills.
He redeems your life from destruction,
  he crowns you with kindness and
    compassion.

He will not always chide,
  nor does he keep his wrath forever.
Not according to our sins does he deal
  with us,
  nor does he requite us according
    to our crimes.

For as the heavens are high above the earth,
  so surpassing is his kindness toward
    those who fear him.
As far as the east is from the west,
  so far has he put our transgressions
    from us.

READING II   Romans 14:7–9

A reading from the Letter of Saint Paul to the Romans

Brothers and **sisters**:
None of us **lives** for **oneself**, and **no one dies** for **oneself**.
For if we **live**, we **live** for the **Lord**,
  and if we **die**, we **die** for the **Lord**;
  so **then**, whether we **live** or **die**, we are the **Lord's**.
For **this** is why **Christ died** and **came** to **life**,
  that he might be **Lord** of both the **dead** and the **living**.

A short and potent reading that makes use of the opposition of "live" to "die," using these words to drive home its insistence that Jesus embodies both "the dead" and "the living."

READING II | The wisdom of Ben Sira flows nicely into today's reading from Romans. Paul has just cautioned the Romans against judging one another, and now he tells them quite clearly that the nature of the Christian life is to live totally and completely for the Lord. In other words, as love and mercy flow from the heart of God, so too must all Christians embody these key virtues.

For Paul, conforming oneself to Christ is a matter of life and death. In life, a Christian lives "for the Lord," and in death, a Christian dies "for the Lord." Paul presents such absolute commitment in the framework of belonging. Christians live and die for Christ because they belong completely to him. We know that Paul's understanding of belonging is rooted in baptism. Through baptism, Christians are immersed into his death in order to have new life in him (Romans 6:1–11). Freedom is based no longer on a law written upon a scroll but rather on a relationship of complete allegiance. This covenantal relationship applies not only to the living but to the dead as well. Those who have already died belong to Christ as much as those who live. Jesus, who experienced both human life and human death, will give life to all who belong to him.

GOSPEL | Jesus has just finished instructing his disciples on the important role of forgiveness and prayer in uniting the community of disciples when Peter asks him how far a person should go in being willing to forgive. Peter attempts to provide a potential answer to

GOSPEL   Matthew 18:21–35

A reading from the holy Gospel according to Matthew

A very challenging Gospel reading in which a quite descriptive parable is used to illuminate Jesus' extravagant teaching about forgiveness.

Peter approached **Jesus** and **asked** him,
"**Lord**, if my **brother** sins **against** me,
how **often** must I **forgive**?
As many as **seven times**?"
Jesus **answered**, "I **say** to you, not **seven times**
but **seventy-seven times**.

Here begins the parable, which proceeds in an understandable way.

That is why the **kingdom** of **heaven** may be **likened** to a **king**
who **decided** to settle **accounts** with his **servants**.
When he **began** the **accounting**,
a **debtor** was brought **before** him who owed him
a **huge amount**.
Since he had **no way** of **paying** it **back**,
his master **ordered** him to be **sold**,
along with his **wife**, his **children**, and **all** his **property**,
in **payment** of the **debt**.

It is useful to keep in mind that the servants are subject to the king, their master.

At **that**, the **servant** fell **down**, did him **homage**, and **said**,
'Be **patient** with me, and I will **pay** you **back** in **full**.'
Moved with **compassion** the **master** of that **servant**
let him **go** and **forgave** him the **loan**.
When that **servant** had **left**, he found one of his **fellow servants**
who **owed** him a **much smaller amount**.
He **seized** him and started to **choke** him, demanding,
'**Pay back** what you **owe**.'

Note the differences between interactions in the scenes: the king toward the servant, the servant toward the other servant, and once again the king toward the first servant.

Falling to his **knees**, his **fellow servant begged** him,
'Be **patient** with me, and I will **pay** you back.'
But he **refused**.
Instead, he had the **fellow servant put** in **prison**
until he **paid back** the **debt**.
Now when his **fellow servants saw** what had **happened**,
they were **deeply disturbed**, and **went** to their **master**
and **reported** the **whole affair**.

his own question, suggesting seven times, or the biblical number of perfection. However, the saying uttered by Jesus transcends even perfection, as he contends that there must be no end to a disciple's willingness to forgive another. Thus, the number seventy-seven.

This discussion on forgiveness allows Jesus to tell the parable of the unforgiving debtor. While not exactly revealing the limitless need to forgive, the story certainly

underscores the importance of developing an attitude of empathy and being ready to forgive the one who sins. Jesus likens the kingdom of heaven to a king who wants his servants to pay back what they owe him. The first servant has accumulated a great debt of "a huge amount" that he owes the king. When the king threatens to balance the debt by selling the servant along with his entire household, the servant begs the king to treat him with patience. Jesus says

that this request caused the king to act with compassion, as he released the servant and forgave the debt.

But we quickly discover the lack of gratitude on the part of this servant, as he leaves the king's presence and demands that a fellow servant pay off the debt that owed him. This second servant utters to his debtor the same plea as the first: "Be patient with me, and I will pay you back." However, unlike the compassionate king,

His **master summoned** him and **said** to him, 'You
    wicked servant!
I **forgave** you your **entire debt** because you **begged** me to.
Should **you not** have had **pity** on your **fellow servant**,
    as I had **pity** on **you**?'
Then in **anger** his master **handed** him **over** to the **torturers**
    until he should **pay back** the **whole debt**.
So will my **heavenly Father do** to **you**,
    unless **each** of you forgives your **brother** from your **heart**."

The master's wrath is tangible.

The reading concludes on a challenging note: If you don't forgive, the heavenly Father will be wrathful and punish you like the master punishes his ungrateful servant!

the servant is not moved with pity nor does he forgive the debt. Instead, he has the servant thrown in prison. Clearly, this man represents the contrasting attitude to that of the king; he learns nothing from the king's kindness.

In a way that corresponds to the method for brotherly correction in last week's Gospel reading of Matthew 18:15–18, the parable continues by introducing other "fellow servants" who witness the injustice and approach the king with the story of the servant's sin. The king summons the servant before him and pronounces him "wicked." Thus, forgiveness is to be returned to the one who extends forgiveness, but to the one who fails to forgive no mercy will be shown in return. S.W.

SEPTEMBER 24, 2023

TWENTY-FIFTH SUNDAY IN ORDINARY TIME

LECTIONARY #133

READING I   Isaiah 55:6–9

Isaiah = ī-ZAY-uh

An intense and poetic reading. Let its language carry your proclamation.

A reading from the Book of the Prophet Isaiah

Seek the LORD while he **may** be **found**,
    call him while he is **near**.
Let the **scoundrel forsake** his **way**,
    and the **wicked** his **thoughts**;
let him **turn** to the LORD for **mercy**;
    to our **God**, who is **generous** in **forgiving**.
For **my thoughts** are not **your thoughts**,
    nor are **your ways my ways**, says the LORD.
As **high** as the **heavens** are **above** the **earth**,
    so **high** are my **ways above** your **ways**
    and my **thoughts above** your **thoughts**.

Slight pause between "ways" and "my."
In these last three lines, the Lord is presumably speaking, through Isaiah.

For meditation and context:

RESPONSORIAL PSALM   Psalm 145:2–3, 8–9, 17–18 (18a)

R. The Lord is near to all who call upon him.

Every day will I bless you,
    and I will praise your name forever
        and ever.
Great is the LORD and highly to be praised;
    his greatness is unsearchable.

The LORD is gracious and merciful,
    slow to anger and of great kindness.
The LORD is good to all
    and compassionate toward all his works.

The LORD is just in all his ways
    and holy in all his works.
The LORD is near to all who call upon him,
    to all who call upon him in truth.

READING I This reading comes from the final chapter of the second portion of Isaiah known as "Deutero-Isaiah." Chapters 40 to 55 were most likely written after Israel had been exiled to Babylon. The basic warning found in today's reading focuses on the temptation to make God operate in a way that corresponds to human understanding. God's ways do not always correspond with ours.

The reading opens with the command to "seek the Lord." Searching for the Lord is possible because he allows himself to be found, and the author says that God is indeed "near." Recall that the pattern of seeking God for the Israelites was generally found in the sacrifices offered in the Temple, now destroyed by the Babylonians. Because of their exile, the Israelites had to find a new way to seek the Lord, one that was more personal in nature. Isaiah suggests that the Lord can be found when one turns from evil and seeks the Lord's mercy. Because God "is generous in forgiving," one can trust that the past will be overturned as new way of living begins.

It is in the context of assuring Israel that the repentant sinner will be restored to relationship with God that Deutero-Isaiah cautions against trying to overly scrutinize God's ways. Searching for the Lord does not mean imposing human standards upon him. While the mercy of God is abundant, one should not attempt to measure it according to the world's sense of justice. The Lord transcends all human thought. Even though God's ways and wisdom are mysterious and beyond us, true worship of God demands conversion of life and constant journeying to find and follow the way of the Lord.

252

READING II Philippians 1:20c–24, 27a

A reading from the Letter of Saint Paul to the Philippians

Brothers and **sisters**:
Christ will be **magnified** in my **body**, whether by **life** or by **death**.
For to **me life** is **Christ**, and **death** is **gain**.
If I **go on living** in the **flesh**,
    that means **fruitful labor** for me.
And I **do not know** which I shall **choose**.
I am **caught** between the **two**.
I **long** to **depart** this **life** and **be** with **Christ**,
    for **that** is **far better**.
Yet that I **remain** in the **flesh**
    is more necessary for your **benefit**.

Only, **conduct yourselves** in a way **worthy** of the gospel of **Christ**.

GOSPEL Matthew 20:1–16a

A reading from the holy Gospel according to Matthew

Jesus told his **disciples** this **parable**:
    "The **kingdom** of **heaven** is like a **landowner**
    who went **out** at **dawn** to hire **laborers** for his **vineyard**.
After agreeing with them for the **usual daily wage**,
    he **sent** them into his **vineyard**.
Going **out** about **nine o'clock**,
    the **landowner** saw others standing **idle** in the **marketplace**,
    and he **said** to them, '**You too go** into my **vineyard**,
    and I will **give** you what is **just**.' »

Sidebar notes (left column):

Philippians – fih-LIP-ee-uhnz

A passionate exhortation, expressed in a tone of vulnerability.

Slight pause between "me" and "life."

Paul expresses a moving thought here: Though he longs to be united with Christ in heaven, he recognizes the value of remaining in the flesh to do God's work.

A long parable but one told with a clear-eyed economy whose message is crystal clear.

Slight pause between "too" and "go."

READING II At the beginning of the Letter to the Philippians, Paul greets them with thanksgiving and a prayer for the fruition of the community before he turns to a lengthy description of his state of imprisonment. Given the backdrop of prison, it is no wonder that Paul ruminates on the possibility of death in today's reading. Paul begins by acknowledging his body as a means of glorifying Christ. The analogy of the body suggests that Paul is totally dedicated to the Lord. Every part of his being, in life and in death, functions to serve Christ.

Paul continues by exploring the possible outcomes for himself, the value of his life versus the value of his death. On the one hand, continuing to live, even from the confines of jail, allows Paul the opportunity to spread the message of the Gospel. On the other hand, if Paul were put to death, he would enter into an even deeper relationship with Christ. While Paul assesses that the latter option of death and eternal union with Christ is far more valuable, he knows that it is better for the infant Church that he continue to live.

Omitted from our reading are verses 25 and 26, in which Paul announces that he will renew his commitment to encourage the community and will one day return to them. In the meantime, he expects that they will behave "in a way worthy of the gospel of Christ." He has provided them with all the tools they need to live in Christ; now it is up to them to put it into practice.

GOSPEL It is important to notice that the parable begins with the kingdom of heaven being likened to the "landowner" and not to the vineyard.

So they went **off**.
And he went out **again** around **noon**,
   and around **three o'clock**, and did **likewise**.
Going out about **five o'clock**,
   the **landowner** found **others standing around**, and **said**
      to them,
     'Why do you **stand** here **idle** all **day**?'
They **answered**, 'Because **no one** has **hired** us.'
He **said** to them, '**You too go** into my **vineyard**.'
When it was **evening** the **owner** of the **vineyard** said
     to his **foreman**,
     '**Summon** the **laborers** and **give** them their **pay**,
     beginning with the **last** and ending with the **first**.'
When **those** who had **started** about **five o'clock** came,
   each received the **usual daily wage**.
So when the **first came**, they **thought** that they would
     receive **more**,
   but each of them also got the **usual wage**.
And on **receiving** it they **grumbled** against the **landowner**, saying,
   'These **last** ones worked **only one hour**,
   and you have **made** them **equal** to us,
   who **bore** the **day's burden** and the **heat**.'
He **said** to one of them in **reply**,
   'My **friend, I am not cheating** you.
Did you not **agree** with me for the **usual daily wage**?
Take what is **yours** and go.
What if I **wish** to give this **last** one the **same** as you?
Or am I not **free** to **do** as I **wish** with my **own money**?
Are you **envious** because I am **generous**?'
Thus, the **last** will be **first**, and the **first** will be **last**."

Slight pause between "too" and "go."

Don't overdo the workers' grumbling tone.

Likewise, don't overdo the landowner's pedantic tone. Allow his equanimity to all the workers he hired to characterize your tone.

In fact, for those who heard this parable from the mouth of Jesus, the image of the vineyard most likely conjured up the idea of Israel. Isaiah 5 foretells the future of Israel as a vineyard that produced bad fruit and which God judged. The point of this parable is that the landowner's method of care is quite unlike anything we may expect.

The parable suggests that those who are waiting to be hired are loafing around rather than being proactive in their pursuit of work. When the landowner returns for a final time at five o'clock, he appears to be perplexed at their ongoing inactivity, as he asks them "Why do you stand here idle all day?" Their simple excuse that no one has hired them does not dissuade the landowner from sending these men into the vineyard. But what could they possibly accomplish with such short time left in the day?

This question does not seem to cross the landowner's mind as he instructs his foreman to begin paying those who began their work at the end of the day with the same "usual daily wage" that is due those who started work at nine in the morning. When the first workers get nothing more than those who arrived last in the vineyard their excitement turns to resentment, as they grumble and complain that they deserve more.

The generosity of the landowner does not pair with typical human understanding of justice, but that is the very point of this parable on the kingdom of heaven. God's invitation to share in the kingdom is far more universal than we might think. What matters the most is responding to the call of discipleship no matter the time in one's life. S.W.

TWENTY-SIXTH SUNDAY IN ORDINARY TIME

LECTIONARY #136

READING I   Ezekiel 18:25–28

A reading from the Book of the Prophet Ezekiel

Thus says the **LORD**:
You say, "The **LORD'S way** is not **fair**!"
Hear now, **house** of Israel:
   Is it **my way** that is **unfair**, or rather, are not **your ways unfair**?
When someone **virtuous** turns **away** from **virtue** to commit
      iniquity, and **dies**,
   it is because of the **iniquity** he **committed** that he must **die**.
But if he **turns** from the **wickedness** he has **committed**,
   and **does** what is **right** and **just**,
   he shall **preserve** his **life**;
   since he has turned **away** from all the **sins** that he
      has **committed**,
   he shall **surely live**, he **shall not die**.

Ezekiel = ee-ZEE-kee-uhl

The expression that begins this reading is familiar to anyone who has parented young children. There is a little of the petulance of a child in the house of Israel's complaint. God's argument is to turn the tables; he's not unfair but instead the house of Israel behaves unfairly toward him.

For meditation and context:

RESPONSORIAL PSALM   Psalm 25:4–5, 6–7, 8–9 (6a)

R. Remember your mercies, O Lord.

Your ways, O LORD, make known to me;
   teach me your paths,
guide me in your truth and teach me,
   for you are God my savior.

Remember that your compassion, O LORD,
   and your love are from of old.
The sins of my youth and my frailties
      remember not;
   in your kindness remember me,
   because of your goodness, O LORD.

Good and upright is the LORD;
   thus he shows sinners the way.
He guides the humble to justice,
   and teaches the humble his way.

READING I   The chapter of Ezekiel from which our reading comes deals with individual responsibility. Written during the time of Babylonian captivity, the mandates represented here reveal a new chapter in Israelite law. Up to this point, the emphasis was placed on corporate responsibility. Sins committed by parents were understood to be passed on to their children. However, the strong sense of guilt brought about by the destruction of Jerusalem and the exile to Babylon gave rise to a new sense of individual responsibility, whereby each person could develop

a relationship with God and was responsible for maintaining that relationship.

This reading deals with the consequences of departing from a virtuous way of life in order to pursue some form of wickedness. Speaking the Lord's own words to the people of Israel, Ezekiel begins by challenging them to adjust their understanding of fairness. While they may perceive a certain punishment given by the Lord to be unfair, it is really the actions of people themselves that are unfair. Ezekiel raises the topic of the punishment of death that is given to the one who turns from vir-

tue to wickedness. Death is deemed quite fair for this failure to act responsibly. Similarly, God's fairness will be executed in the life of the one who turns from wickedness to doing what is "right and just." That person's reward shall be the preservation of life. Thus, we see that God's justice—both punishment and reward—is not passed down through the generations; instead, it is a matter of personal culpability.

READING II   After reminding the Philippians of his imprisonment and of the need to persevere in faith,

READING II   Philippians 2:1–11

A reading from the Letter of Saint Paul to the Philippians

[**Brothers** and **sisters:**
If there is any **encouragement** in **Christ**,
    any **solace** in **love**,
       any **participation** in the **Spirit**,
       any **compassion** and **mercy**,
       complete my **joy** by being of the **same mind**, with the
          same love,
       united in **heart**, **thinking one thing**.
Do **nothing** out of **selfishness** or out of **vainglory**;
    rather, **humbly regard others** as more **important**
       than **yourselves**,
    each looking **out not** for his own **interests**,
    but **also** for **those** of **others**.

Have in **you** the same **attitude**
    that is **also** in **Christ Jesus**,]
      Who, though he was in the **form** of **God**,
         did not **regard equality** with **God**
         something to be **grasped**.
      Rather, he **emptied** himself,
         taking the **form** of a **slave**,
         coming in **human likeness**;
         and found **human** in **appearance**,
         he **humbled** himself,
         becoming **obedient** to the **point** of **death**,
         even **death** on a **cross**.
      Because of this, God **greatly exalted** him
         and **bestowed** on him the name
         which is **above every name**,
         that at the **name** of **Jesus**
         every **knee** should **bend**,

Margin notes

Philippians = fil-LIP-ee-uhnz

A reading of great and solemn mystery, offering a glimpse into the beliefs and expressions of the members of the early Church.

solace = SOL-uhs (comfort)

Slight pause between "out" and "not."

In this expression lies one of the mystical cores of Christian beliefs, Christ's self-emptying (kenosis). Proclaim it solemnly.

These words probably belong to an ancient hymn Paul records in this letter. Allow for their musical quality to echo in your speech.

Commentary

Paul turns to the topic of the Church's pursuit of unity in a spirit of humility. Employing the evidence of an early Christological hymn in which Christ's exaltation is revealed as a reward for his humility, Paul encourages Christians to have the "same attitude" as Christ.

This reading opens with the reason Christians must pursue the way of unity. Because they belong to Christ and participate in the Spirit, they ought to consider themselves as sharers in the "same mind" and the "same love" that flow from Christ. The way this oneness is most concretely displayed is in the way in which Christians reject any form of selfishness and consider the needs of others as more important than their own.

Halfway into this reading, Paul introduces what was an early Christian hymn the community might have been aware of to portray the humility of Christ. The first half of the hymn reveals Christ's humble attitude displayed in his rejection of divine power in order to share in the lot of humanity. Instead of grasping at or exploiting his divine nature, Christ became as lowly as a "slave." His humility continues to the cross where he becomes perfectly "obedient" by accepting his death as part of God's will.

The second half of the hymn praises Christ and describes the reward bestowed upon him by God. God exalts him, places his name over all things in the cosmos, and moves every being to proclaim that "Jesus Christ is Lord!" While this reading does not provide a suggestion as to how to put this hymn into practice, Paul's intention is very clear: Christ's humility and obedience ought to guide all Christian living.

of **those** in **heaven** and on **earth** and **under** the **earth**,
and **every tongue confess** that
Jesus Christ is **Lord**,
to the **glory** of **God** the **Father**.

[Shorter: Philippians 2:1–5 (see brackets)]

GOSPEL   Matthew 21:28–32

A reading from the holy Gospel according to Matthew

Jesus said to the **chief priests** and **elders** of the **people**:
    "**What** is your **opinion**?
A **man** had **two sons**.
He came to the **first** and **said**,
    '**Son**, go **out** and **work** in the **vineyard today**.'
He said in **reply**, 'I will **not**,'
    but **afterwards** changed his **mind** and **went**.
The **man came** to the **other son** and **gave** the **same order**.
He **said** in **reply**, '**Yes**, sir,' but **did not go**.
Which of the **two** did his **father's will**?"
They **answered**, "The **first**."
Jesus **said** to them, "**Amen**, **I say** to you,
    tax collectors and **prostitutes**
    are entering the **kingdom** of **God before** you.
When **John came** to you in the way of **righteousness**,
    you **did not believe** him;
    but **tax collectors** and **prostitutes did**.
Yet **even** when you **saw** that,
    you **did not later change** your **minds** and **believe** him."

In this reading, Jesus uses the techniques of a rabbi to demonstrate to the rabbis the weakness of their own understanding. It's as subtle as it is striking.

First, Jesus sets up a position of defiance followed by compliance.

Next, Jesus sets up compliance followed by defiance.

When Jesus says "Amen," he brings home his parable to the present situation, speaking with the chief priests and elders.

Slight pause between "later" and "change."

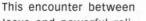 **GOSPEL** This encounter between Jesus and powerful religious leaders takes place in the Jerusalem Temple. These authorities have been questioning Jesus on the source of his authority to teach. Rather than providing a solid answer, Jesus tells them the parable of the two sons in order to point out their stubbornness in failing to recognize and respond to God's will when it ought to be fully apparent before their very eyes (that is, in the teaching and ministry of Jesus himself).

Jesus employs the image of a vineyard, which is a popular metaphor for the nation of Israel (Isaiah 5:1–7) as well as for the kingdom of God (Matthew 20:1; 21:33). However, the focus of this parable is not on the vineyard but on the attitude of the two sons. The first son, who blatantly tells his father that he will not work in the vineyard, changes his mind and responds obediently to his father's summons. This first son represents the "tax collectors" and "prostitutes," who are deemed sinners, and yet prove themselves open to conversion. The second son, who tells his father that he will work in the vineyard but does not go, represents those who have been questioning the authority of Jesus. They appear to be righteous, but they fail to be open to the coming of God's kingdom (alluded to here in the ministry of John the Baptist). This parable, which is unique to Matthew, clearly speaks to the infant Church of the constant need for conversion in carrying out the will of God; discipleship must involve no sense of hesitancy or complacency. S.W.

TWENTY-SEVENTH SUNDAY IN ORDINARY TIME

LECTIONARY #139

READING I   Isaiah 5:1–7

A reading from the Book of the Prophet Isaiah

Isaiah = ī-ZAY-uh

A lengthy, rich, and poetic reading whose point is the condemnation of the house of Israel for its wildness.

spaded = SPY-d*d

Let me now **sing** of my **friend,**
  my **friend's song concerning** his **vineyard.**
My **friend** had a **vineyard**
  on a **fertile hillside;**
he **spaded** it, **cleared** it of **stones,**
  and **planted** the **choicest vines;**
within it he built a **watchtower,**
  and **hewed** out a **wine press.**
Then he **looked** for the **crop** of **grapes,**
  but what it **yielded** was **wild grapes.**

Even emphasis on "What more was."

Even emphasis on "bring forth wild grapes."

Now, **inhabitants** of **Jerusalem** and **people** of **Judah,**
  judge between **me** and my **vineyard:**
What more was there to do for my vineyard
  that I **had not done?**
Why, when I **looked** for the **crop** of **grapes,**
  did it **bring forth wild grapes?**
Now, I will let you **know**
  what I **mean** to **do** with my **vineyard:**
take away its **hedge, give** it to **grazing,**
  break through its **wall, let** it be **trampled!**

READING I — Isaiah's prophecy takes the form of a poetic song in today's first reading, and reads as a parable for those in Israel who hear Isaiah's words. Using the image of a beautiful vineyard that will be made "a ruin," Isaiah addresses Israel's failure to remain faithful to the covenant. In the preceding chapters, Isaiah has revealed to the people that Jerusalem will soon be torn apart by great destruction. Although some inhabitants will survive as a remnant, the nation as a whole has gone astray from the way of God and will be dispersed from the land. Thus, the lamentation that follows in the song of the vineyard.

Isaiah states that the song is sung about his "friend" who, in reality, is God. Isaiah labors at length to describe the way in which this friend has invested his energy and his livelihood into his vineyard. First, the vineyard owner chooses the most fertile land on which to plant his grape vines. He spades the land, removes stones, and plants "the choicest vines." He constructs a tower from which he can watch over his vineyard, and he readies for a fruitful harvest by preparing a wine press.

Undoubtedly, this is a project of great pride for Isaiah's "friend."

With all the construction complete, he now waits for the growth of the vines and hopes for an abundant crop of beautiful, sweet grapes. But, alas, all this grand vineyard yields are "wild grapes" that are rotten. Still speaking from the viewpoint of the vineyard owner, Isaiah calls the people of Israel to pass judgement on the predicament presented in the song. What is the owner to do? Has he not done all that he can to assure a good harvest? At this point in the story, what might the hearers of this

258

Yes, I will **make** it a **ruin**:
  it **shall not** be **pruned** or **hoed**,
  but **overgrown** with **thorns** and **briers**;
I will **command** the **clouds**
  not to send **rain upon** it.
The **vineyard** of the LORD of **hosts** is the **house** of **Israel**,
  and the **people** of **Judah** are his **cherished plant**;
he looked for **judgment**, but **see**, **bloodshed**!
  for **justice**, but **hark**, the **outcry**!

Slight pause between "rain" and "upon."

For meditation and context:

RESPONSORIAL PSALM Psalm 80:9, 12, 13–14, 15–16, 19–20 (Isaiah 5:7a)

R. The vineyard of the Lord is the house of Israel.

A vine from Egypt you transplanted;
  you drove away the nations and planted it.
It put forth its foliage to the Sea,
  its shoots as far as the River.

Why have you broken down its walls,
  so that every passer-by plucks its fruit,
the boar from the forest lays it waste,
  and the beasts of the field feed upon it?

Once again, O LORD of hosts,
  look down from heaven, and see;
take care of this vine,
  and protect what your right hand
    has planted,
  the son of man whom you yourself
    made strong.

Then we will no more withdraw from you;
  give us new life, and we will call upon
    your name.
O LORD, God of hosts, restore us;
  if your face shine upon us, then we shall
    be saved.

---

be thinking? What is the lesson to be learned?

While the "friend" asked the people to decide the fate of the vineyard for themselves, the speaker then tells the listeners exactly what he intends to do with his failed project. The tone of the story builds with intensity as he begins to describe in detail how he will destroy his vineyard. He will begin by dismantling hedges and walls so that other may trample upon it. He will not care for it in any way, neither pruning the vines nor hoeing the soil, but instead will allow it to be "overgrown with thorns

and briers." He will go so far as to pray that no rain will fall upon it to keep it alive. It will become thoroughly lifeless. It is only here at the end of the song that Isaiah clearly identifies the vineyard as the "house of Israel," and the "cherished plant" is "the people of Judah." The Lord did all that he could to provide for Israel; his sense of justice leaves no other choice than to dismantle what he once favored.

READING II Before Paul closes his letter to the Philippians, he imparts further advice on living the Christian

life. First, he upholds the importance of prayer as a means of conquering all forms of anxiety. He contends that when one turns to God with "prayer and petition, with thanksgiving," making one's needs known to him, that the "peace of God" will fill believers. Prayer is the way believers communicate all things to God and express their complete dependence upon him. The divine peace that flows from prayer is the foundation of their Christian life and keep them in Christ.

This leads Paul to his second piece of advice for the Christians at Philippi. He

<table>
<tr><td>

Philippians = fih-LIP-ee-uhnz

This reading begins with an exhortation that seems easy to make but hard to believe—is it really possible to have no anxiety at all? Paul wants to encourage you that it might be so.

A really compelling rhythm picks up here.

The conclusion is especially uplifting.

</td><td>

READING II   Philippians 4:6–9

A reading from the Letter of Saint Paul to the Philippians

Brothers and **sisters**:
Have no anxiety at **all**, but in **everything**,
   by **prayer** and **petition**, with **thanksgiving**,
   make your **requests** known to **God**.
Then the **peace** of **God** that **surpasses** all **understanding**
   will **guard** your **hearts** and **minds** in **Christ Jesus**.

Finally, **brothers** and **sisters**,
   whatever is **true**, **whatever** is **honorable**,
   whatever is **just**, **whatever** is **pure**,
   whatever is lovely, **whatever** is **gracious**,
   if there is **any excellence**
   and if there is **anything worthy of praise**,
   think about these things.
Keep on doing what you have **learned** and **received**
   and **heard** and **seen** in me.
Then the **God** of **peace** will be **with** you.

</td></tr>
</table>

<table>
<tr><td>

Clear-eyed as many of Jesus' parables are, it must be admitted that some of them are completely opaque. This is one of the more challenging ones to fathom.

Don't be afraid to stress the viciousness of the tenants. It's part of the parable's power.

</td><td>

GOSPEL   Matthew 21:33–43

A reading from the holy Gospel according to Matthew

Jesus said to the **chief priests** and the **elders** of the **people**:
   "**Hear** another **parable**.
There was a **landowner** who planted a **vineyard**,
   put a **hedge** around it, dug a **wine press** in it, and built a **tower**.
Then he **leased** it to **tenants** and **went** on a **journey**.
When **vintage time** drew **near**,
   he sent his **servants** to the **tenants** to **obtain** his **produce**.
But the **tenants** seized the **servants** and **one** they **beat**,
   another they **killed**, and a **third** they **stoned**.

</td></tr>
</table>

proceeds to list several virtues that he connects with the gift of God's peace. These virtues are truth, honor, justice, purity, beauty, and graciousness. Some similar values are found in the philosophical movement of stoicism, which was prevalent during that time period and in that community. Their culture was very skilled at celebrating core human values that would ensure happiness in this life. Thus, Paul challenges the Philippians to strive for "excellence" in living out these virtues in their Christian life. Paul tells them that what they have "learned and received and

heard and seen" from his teaching and his actions is all that they need to follow the path of discipleship. In the end, Paul assures them that lives lived virtuously in Christ are sure to be filled with the grace of the "God of peace." Once again, there is no room for anxiety in the life of a Christian who has the mind and the heart of Christ.

GOSPEL | Just as in the story of the vineyard in the first reading, from Isaiah, today's Gospel text from Matthew also considers the owner of a vineyard. The landowner plants a vineyard, sur-

rounds it with a hedge, digs a wine press, and constructs a watch tower. However, rather than caring for this vineyard on his own as in Isaiah, the landowner entrusts its care to several tenants. Because he is confident that they will watch over it with the same level of care and concern that he put in to create it, he departs on a journey.

We can assume that an entire growing season has passed when the landowner sends his servants to the vineyard to collect his share of the harvest. However, the tenants, who have been watching over the vineyard, have no intention of sharing with

Again he sent **other servants**, more **numerous** than the **first** ones,
  but they **treated** them in the **same way**.
Finally, he sent his **son** to them, thinking,
  'They will **respect** my **son**.'
But when the **tenants** saw the **son**, they **said** to one **another**,
  '**This** is the **heir**.

Likewise, the brutality of the tenants.

Come, let us **kill** him and **acquire** his **inheritance**.'
They **seized** him, threw him **out** of the **vineyard**, and **killed** him.
What will the **owner** of the **vineyard do** to those **tenants** when
    he **comes**?"
They **answered** him,
  "He will **put** those **wretched men** to a **wretched death**
  and **lease** his **vineyard** to **other tenants**
  who will **give** him the **produce** at the **proper times**."

The parable pivots when Jesus quotes Scripture, as much to change its tone as to offer understanding.

Jesus **said** to them, "Did you **never read** in the **Scriptures**:
  *The **stone** that the **builders rejected**
    has **become** the **cornerstone**;
  by the **Lord** has this been **done**,
    and it is **wonderful** in our **eyes**?*
Therefore, I **say** to you,
  the **kingdom** of **God** will be **taken away** from you
  and **given** to a **people** that will **produce** its **fruit**."

This is a hard conclusion to a disturbing parable.

the landowner. Instead, they beat and kill the servants that the landowner sends them. As a final means of attempting to secure his portion of the harvest, the landowner sends his son to the tenants, thinking, "They will respect my son." Seeing the son as the heir to all that belongs to the landowner, they put him to death as well.

When Jesus asks the chief priests and elders, who have been listening to the parable, what will happen to the wicked tenants, they reply that the landowner will put them to death and hand the vineyard over to the care of responsible tenants. Jesus responds by reminding them of Psalm 118, which the early Church understood as a prophetic allusion to Jesus being rejected by his own people. Although rejected, the "cornerstone" of the Church, namely Christ himself, was deemed "wonderful" in the eyes of those who received him and cared for his Father's vineyard. Matthew's Jesus ends the passage by suggesting that God will not look so favorably upon those who reject the gift that has been sent specifically to them, and that gift is his very Son. S.W.

TWENTY-EIGHTH SUNDAY IN ORDINARY TIME

LECTIONARY #142

READING I   Isaiah 25:6–10a

Isaiah = ī-ZAY-uh

A luminously poetic and uplifting reading offering a powerful vision of eternal life.

A reading from the Book of the Prophet Isaiah

On **this mountain** the LORD of **hosts**
    will **provide** for all **peoples**
a **feast** of **rich food** and **choice wines**,
    juicy, **rich food** and **pure**, **choice wines**.
On **this mountain** he will **destroy**
    the **veil** that **veils** all **peoples**,
the **web** that is **woven** over all **nations**;
    he will **destroy death forever**.
The **Lord GOD** will **wipe away**
    the **tears** from **every face**;
the **reproach** of his **people** he will **remove**
    from the **whole earth**; for the LORD has **spoken**.
    On **that day** it will be **said**:
"**Behold** our **God**, to whom we **looked** to **save** us!
    This is the LORD for **whom** we **looked**;
    let us **rejoice** and be **glad** that he has **saved** us!"
For the **hand** of the LORD will **rest** on this **mountain**.

An intoxicating promise.

Let the image with which the reading concludes linger with your assembly by pausing for a long moment before saying "The Word of the Lord."

READING I Isaiah 24 to 27 constitutes what scholars call the "Apocalypse of Isaiah," which concludes ten chapters of prophesies on the future of various nations. Although Isaiah has prophesied that Israel has lost favor with God and will witness the destruction of Jerusalem, he is also clear that nations at odds with Israel will also be subject to God's judgment. Chapter 24 compares Jerusalem to a vine that is withering away (Isaiah 24:7), and yet there is the hope that Israel's repentance will result in God's forgiveness.

In chapter 25, which our reading is from today, we read about a sense of universal eschatology. The Lord will welcome people from every nation to his mountain with a feast of abundant joy. After the Lord has destroyed all that is evil in the world, including the ultimate enemy found in death, he will gather to his holy place all those who heard his voice and turned from their wicked ways.

Isaiah says that God will destroy "the veil that veils all people." This "veil," that he also calls "the web," is an allusion to death. In the past, all peoples were tangled in the powers of death, but now God "will destroy death forever." God will not only destroy death, but he will take away all pain and suffering; all the toils and struggles, the "tears" and the "reproach" experienced by his people will be no more. We may assume that the words "his people" has expanded to include representatives from every nation and not simply from Israel alone.

The passage concludes with a chorus of voices heralding the presence and power of God "to whom we looked to save us!" At the end of time, when this power of God is revealed, it will indeed be a cause for joy

For meditation and context:

RESPONSORIAL PSALM   Psalm 23:1–3a, 3b–4, 5, 6 (6cd)

R. I shall live in the house of the Lord all the days of my life.

The LORD is my shepherd; I shall not want.
 In verdant pastures he gives me repose;
beside restful waters he leads me;
 he refreshes my soul.

He guides me in right paths
 for his name's sake.
Even though I walk in the dark valley
 I fear no evil; for you are at my side
with your rod and your staff
 that give me courage.

You spread the table before me
 in the sight of my foes;
you anoint my head with oil;
 my cup overflows.

Only goodness and kindness follow me
 all the days of my life;
and I shall dwell in the house of the LORD
 for years to come.

READING II   Philippians 4:12–14, 19–20

Philippians = flh-LIP-ee-uhnz

A conclusive reading that records the sentiments near the end of Paul's letter to the members of the early church at Philippi. Its tone is personal and thankful.

Slight pause between "being" and "well."

A reading from the Letter of Saint Paul to the Philippians

Brothers and **sisters**:
I **know** how to **live** in **humble circumstances**;
 I know **also** how to **live** with **abundance**.
In **every circumstance** and **in all things**
 I have **learned** the **secret** of **being well fed** and of **going hungry**,
 of **living** in **abundance** and of **being** in **need**.
I can **do all things** in **him** who **strengthens** me.
Still, it was **kind** of you to **share** in my **distress**.

My **God** will **fully supply whatever** you **need**,
 in **accord** with his **glorious riches** in **Christ Jesus**.
To our **God** and **Father**, **glory forever** and **ever**. **Amen**.

---

among all peoples who have recognized the truth of God and followed him.

READING II — In the verses immediately prior to this passage, Paul praises God for the support given to him by the Philippians, both for their monetary support and their spiritual growth that is a testament to the continued spread of the Good News. The latter, more than donation sent to him, is sure to bolster his spirit during his time of imprisonment and be a greater witness to the truth of his preaching.

Paul uses this as an opportunity to remind the Philippians of a Christian's true source of support: God. While striving to be self-sufficient in his own ministry, and having experienced both times of having "humble circumstances" and "abundance," Paul has come to learn true dependence on God. Today's reading omits verses 15–18, which comment on the previous generosity of the Philippians to Paul when he was just beginning to preach the Gospel. These verses lead into a final statement by Paul regarding his confidence that God will provide the Christian community with what-

ever it needs. In all things, they are to look to Christ, as Paul has done throughout his own ministry.

GOSPEL — Today's parable is addressed to the chief priests and elders gathered within the Temple precincts. Jesus opens the parable with the king's method of summoning guests to the wedding banquet for his son: servants are sent to extend the invitation. However, all the invited guests decline the invitation. The king tries a second time by sending other servants, who are not just to invite guests

GOSPEL   Matthew 22:1–14

A reading from the holy Gospel according to Matthew

[**Jesus again** in **reply spoke** to the **chief priests** and **elders**
    of the **people**
  in **parables**, saying,
  "The **kingdom** of **heaven** may be **likened** to a **king**
  who gave a **wedding** feast for his **son**.
He **dispatched** his **servants**
    to **summon** the **invited guests** to the **feast**,
    but they **refused** to **come**.
A **second time** he sent **other servants**, saying,
    '**Tell those invited**: "**Behold**, I have **prepared** my **banquet**,
    my **calves** and **fattened cattle** are **killed**,
    and **everything** is **ready; come** to the **feast**."'
Some ignored the **invitation** and went **away**,
    one to his **farm**, **another** to his **business**.
The **rest** laid **hold** of his **servants**,
    mistreated them, and **killed** them.
The **king** was **enraged** and **sent** his **troops**,
    destroyed those **murderers**, and **burned** their **city**.
Then he **said** to his **servants**, 'The **feast** is **ready**,
    but **those** who were **invited** were not **worthy** to **come**.
Go out, therefore, into the **main roads**
    and **invite** to the **feast whomever** you **find**.'
The **servants** went **out** into the **streets**
    and **gathered all** they **found**, **bad** and **good** alike,
    and the **hall** was **filled** with **guests**.]
But when the **king came in** to **meet** the **guests**,
    he saw a **man** there not **dressed** in a **wedding** garment.

Slight pause between "reply" and "spoke."

This parable seems straightforward but takes an unexpected turn, ending on a somewhat disturbing message. It could also be interpreted as having an ironic tone when one compares those who were invited originally with those who ended up actually celebrating with the king.

Even emphasis on "Tell those invited: 'Behold.'"

Don't overdo the king's rage.

The king's fixation on how this presumably vagrant wedding guest is dressed is yet another disturbing reaction, out of context and unrealistic to what the listeners expected to hear.

but are to lure them with words of bounty, describing what they would otherwise be missing. This time the rejection of the invitation is more forceful; while some are simply indifferent to it, others capture the servants and kill them.

The king's reaction is swift and severe. He sends an army to destroy the city of the guests who had been invited. Scholars believe this to be an allusion to the recent destruction of the Temple and the city of Jerusalem in AD 70, which the Matthean community would have experienced since this Gospel was compiled after that time.

Nevertheless, the king is unwilling to allow the abundant feast that he has prepared go to waste. Thus, he instructs his servants to go out "into the main roads" in order to invite whomever they might find. Jesus tells his listeners that these servants succeed in filling the hall with guests, both wicked and good. Here we are meant to understand that God, like this king, is willing to welcome anyone into his kingdom.

For this reason, the king's entrance into the hall and his reaction to the guest who is not dressed in the appropriate attire for a wedding feast is quite shocking. When

the king asks the man to explain himself for his attendance at the wedding feast, the man can give no reply. In response to his lack of "a wedding garment," the king has the man bound and thrown out into the darkness "where there will be wailing and grinding of teeth." This final portion of the parable is filled with symbols pertaining to eschatological judgment. The king's entrance into the wedding hall represents God's entrance into the world for its final judgment. The wedding garment is the sign of a person's repentance and participation in the Church; the man improperly dressed

The king **said** to him, 'My **friend**, how **is** it
that you **came** in **here** without a **wedding garment**?'
But he was **reduced** to **silence**.
Then the **king** said to his **attendants**, 'Bind his **hands** and **feet**,
and **cast** him into the **darkness outside**,
where there will be **wailing** and **grinding** of **teeth**.'
Many are **invited**, but **few** are **chosen**."

[Shorter: Matthew 22:1–10 (see brackets)]

This conclusion reinforces that sense of irony.

stands for those outside the Church's membership who have not turned their hearts to God. While the kingdom may be open to both the good and the bad, only those dressed in the garment of salvation will avoid being banished from the feast. Finally, the last line from the parable suggests that being called or invited does not necessarily mean being chosen among the elect. Matthew's theology suggests that salvation depends upon some level of transformation in Christ; responding to the invitation requires a sign of belonging. S.W.

OCTOBER 22, 2023

TWENTY-NINTH SUNDAY IN ORDINARY TIME

LECTIONARY #145

READING I Isaiah 45:1, 4–6

A reading from the Book of the Prophet Isaiah

> **Thus** says the **LORD** to his **anointed**, **Cyrus**,
>   whose **right hand I grasp**,
> **subduing nations before** him,
>   and making **kings run** in his **service**,
> opening **doors before** him
>   and **leaving** the **gates unbarred**:
> For the **sake** of **Jacob**, my **servant**,
>   of **Israel**, my **chosen** one,
> I have **called** you by your **name**,
>   giving you a **title**, though you **knew** me **not**.
> I am the **LORD** and there **is** no **other**,
>   there is no **God besides** me.
> It is **I** who **arm** you, though you **know** me **not**,
>   so that toward the **rising** and the **setting** of the **sun**
>   **people** may **know** that there is **none besides me**.
> I am the **LORD**, there is **no other**.

Isaiah = ī-ZAY-uh

Cyrus = SĪ-ruhs
A forceful reading whose tone is stern.

Slight pause between "kings" and "run."

These lines, echoing the first of the Ten Commandments, is the heart of this reading.

The concluding repetition requires emphasis on "is no other."

TO KEEP IN MIND
Read the Scripture passage and its commentary in Workbook. Then read it from your Bible, including what comes before and after it, so that you understand the context.

READING I Today's readings illustrate an interesting theme—namely, "How can God work for good in a world that does not believe in God?" This first reading is an example. King Cyrus was a Persian king who reigned in 559–530 BC and who created the largest empire known to date. Part of his success in managing his vast empire was allowing conquered peoples to have some governing powers at the regional level and respecting the religions and customs of his subjects. An edict by King Cyrus in 538 BC allowed the Judean exiles to return from Babylon to Jerusalem, and the author of Second Isaiah says this is God's doing.

In this first reading, God is speaking through the prophet, and he identifies Cyrus as God's anointed. The Hebrew word is *mashiach*, meaning "anointed" or "messiah" in English. Kings were anointed, so in some sense this title is not surprising, but the prophet goes on to describe Cyrus as chosen to advance his conquest of other nations on God's behalf and to demonstrate to the world that there is no god other than the God of Jacob and Israel. Moreover, he says that God called Cyrus by name and gave him a title—probably referring to his messiahship—even though Cyrus did not know the God of the Israelites. What a stunning declaration! God can work even through people who do not know God or acknowledge God as their savior.

READING II Our second reading is the opening section of Paul's First Letter to the Thessalonians. Here we see the standard letter opening of first-century Hellenistic writers: sender, recipients, greeting, and thanksgiving. Only Paul's letter to the Galatians deviates from this pat-

266

For meditation and context:

RESPONSORIAL PSALM Psalm 96:1, 3, 4–5, 7–8, 9–10 (7b)

R. Give the Lord glory and honor.

Sing to the LORD a new song;
   sing to the LORD, all you lands.
Tell his glory among the nations;
   among all peoples, his wondrous deeds.

For great is the LORD and highly
      to be praised;
   awesome is he, beyond all gods.
For all the gods of the nations are things
      of nought,
   but the LORD made the heavens.

Give to the LORD, you families of nations,
   give to the LORD glory and praise;
   give to the LORD the glory due his name!
Bring gifts, and enter his courts.

Worship the LORD, in holy attire;
   tremble before him, all the earth;
say among the nations: The LORD is king,
   he governs the peoples with equity.

Thessalonians = thes-uh-LOH-nee-uhnz

Silvanus = sil-VAY-nuhs

This reading comes from the opening of Paul's first letter to the members of the early church in Thessalonica. In effect, it is the salutation, which is meant to have a rousing, even cheerful quality.

This thanks being given is sincere; let your tone reflect that sincerity.

A rousing and spirited conclusion.

READING II 1 Thessalonians 1:1–5b

A reading from the first Letter of Saint Paul to the Thessalonians

Paul, **Silvanus**, and **Timothy** to the **church** of the **Thessalonians**
   in **God** the **Father** and the **Lord Jesus Christ**:
   grace to **you** and **peace**.
We give **thanks** to **God always** for **all** of you,
   remembering you in our **prayers**,
   unceasingly calling to **mind** your **work** of **faith** and **labor**
      of **love**
   and **endurance** in **hope** of our **Lord Jesus Christ**,
   before our **God** and **Father**,
   knowing, **brothers** and **sisters loved** by **God**,
   how you were **chosen**.
For our **gospel** did not **come** to you in **word alone**,
   but also in **power** and in the **Holy Spirit** and with
      much conviction.

---

tern, and that is because he was too mad at the Galatian churches and the people who were leading them astray to pray in thanksgiving to God for them. Instead, he gives them a good scolding (see Galatians 1:6–7)! Turning our attention back to today's reading, we see that Timothy, who was Paul's constant companion for much of his ministry, is mentioned here and in several other letters as a co-sender. Likewise, Silvanus is mentioned; he is most likely the one identified as Silas in Acts of the Apostles (e.g., Acts 15:22, 40). Paul's thanksgiving is in

the form of a prayer to God as he remembers the community's exercise of the theological virtues of faith, hope, and love. Notice that Paul does not view these virtues as abstractions, since he ties them to nouns that suggest activity: work, labor, and endurance, respectively. Finally, he identifies the source and sustainer of this activity—namely, the Holy Spirit. Notice, also, the affection that Paul has for this community. He calls them God's beloved and God's chosen ones.

GOSPEL Today's Gospel reading is found in all three of the synoptic Gospels with slight variations. It is a story about some Pharisees, teachers of the Law, teaming up with some Herodians to entrap Jesus so that they could make a formal complaint against him. The Herodians are often paired with the Pharisees in the synoptic Gospels as groups who were opposed to Roman rule, but the Herodians are so named because they wanted someone from the lineage of Herod the Great to be their ruler. Herod the Great was origi-

GOSPEL   Matthew 22:15–21

A reading from the holy Gospel according to Matthew

The **Pharisees** went **off**
  and **plotted** how they might **entrap Jesus** in **speech**.
They **sent** their **disciples** to him, with the **Herodians**, saying,
  "**Teacher**, we **know** that you are a **truthful man**
  and that you **teach** the **way** of **God** in **accordance**
    with the **truth**.
And you are **not concerned** with **anyone's opinion**,
  for you **do not regard** a **person's status**.
Tell us, then, **what** is your **opinion**:
  Is it **lawful** to **pay** the **census tax** to **Caesar** or **not**?"
Knowing their **malice**, Jesus said,
  "**Why** are you **testing** me, you **hypocrites**?
Show me the **coin** that **pays** the **census tax**."
Then they **handed** him the **Roman** coin.
He **said** to them, "**Whose image** is **this** and **whose inscription**?"
They replied, "**Caesar's**."
At **that** he **said** to them,
  "Then **repay** to **Caesar** what **belongs** to **Caesar**
  and to **God** what **belongs** to **God**."

Pharisees = FAYR-uh-seez
This reading consists of a set-up that backfires on the Pharisees. Its drama is inherent. No need to overplay it.

Especially, the wickedness of the Pharisees: Don't overplay it. It will come through in your steady proclamation.

Consider that Jesus' tone here is exasperation.

Pause before "Caesar's" to suggest the Pharisees' recognition that their plan to entrap Jesus has backfired.

---

nally from Edom, south of Judea, and was raised as a Jew by his parents.

As the scene unfolds, the Pharisees and Herodians heap (false) praise on Jesus for being impartial and sincere in his efforts to teach the way of God. This is their set-up to ensnare Jesus by flattery, but he recognizes their evil intent. They ask him whether it is lawful for Jews to pay taxes to the emperor. But Jesus calls them out as the hypocrites they are by demanding that they show him the coin used for paying the tax, a Roman denarius, and asking whose image is on the coin and what is written on it. The

image is that of the emperor, and its inscription would read something like "Tiberius Caesar, Augustus, son of divine Augustus." Jews who were strict observers of Jewish law would not admit to being in possession of a denarius, because of their strong belief there is no god except the God of Israel. But someone in the group pulls out the coin, probably with great embarrassment when they realize that Jesus has defeated them in this confrontation. Some interpreters of Jesus' response—"Repay to Caesar what belongs to Caesar and to God what belongs to God"—suggest that it is an argument for

the separation of church and state. However, in first-century Palestine, no such division existed. Rather, his words more likely reflect the notion that kinship is more important—in this case kinship with God—than polity, what we might call civil entities, though it has a place in society and should be respected as such. Thus, the second half of Jesus' statement is an accusation directed at the Pharisees and Herodians: they do not pay to God the honor that is due to God. C.C.

THIRTIETH SUNDAY IN ORDINARY TIME

LECTIONARY #148

READING I   Exodus 22:20–26

A reading from the Book of Exodus

Thus says the LORD:
"You **shall not molest** or **oppress** an **alien**,
   for you were **once aliens yourselves** in the **land** of Egypt.
You **shall not wrong** any **widow** or **orphan**.
If **ever** you **wrong** them and they cry **out** to me,
   I will **surely hear** their **cry**.
My **wrath** will **flare up**, and I will **kill** you with the **sword**;
   then your **own wives** will be **widows**, and your
      children orphans.

"If you lend **money** to **one** of your **poor neighbors** among
      my **people**,
   you **shall not act** like an **extortioner toward** him
   by **demanding interest from** him.
If you **take** your **neighbor's cloak** as a **pledge**,
   you shall **return** it to him before **sunset**;
   for this **cloak** of his is the **only covering** he **has** for his **body**.
What **else** has he to **sleep** in?
If he cries **out** to me, I will **hear** him; for **I** am **compassionate**."

Exodus = EK-suh-duhs

The tone of this powerful reading is unusually stern.

Note the violence of the Lord's wrath, flaring up. Give slight emphasis to "kill."

extortioner = ek-STOHR-shuhn-*r
Even emphasis on "shall not act."

The reading concludes with a note of contrast on the word "compassionate."

READING I Our first reading comes from a larger section of Exodus that biblical scholars call the Covenant Code (Exodus 20:22—23:33), which consists of a collection of case law, pronouncements, commands, and prohibitions. The Covenant Code follows immediately after God's appearance on Mount Sinai and delivery of the Ten Commandments. With the thunder, lightning, and smoke on the mountain, the Israelites became afraid and told Moses to speak God's commands to them instead of them directly encoun-

tering God. Thus, Moses became the mediator of God's covenant law to the people.

Today's reading provides us with two of these commands from the Covenant Code. Both fall into a category that today we might call social justice teaching. The first command is to protect and not abuse the resident alien. The Hebrew word is *ger*, meaning "stranger, temporary dweller, or sojourner." The reason given for this mandate is that God did the same for them when they were sojourners in the land. In the Old Testament especially, resident

aliens are regularly grouped with widows and orphans as the poorest and most vulnerable in society. The punishment due to those who do not observe this command speaks to its importance.

The second command has to do with money lending, which, in the ancient world, was more like the pawn broker today than our modern banking system. Only poor people who had no other access to financial resources used money lenders, who charged high interest and demanded significant collateral. This command forbids

For meditation and context:

RESPONSORIAL PSALM   Psalm 18:2–3, 3–4, 47, 51 (2)

R. I love you, Lord, my strength.

I love you, O LORD, my strength,
  O LORD, my rock, my fortress,
    my deliverer.

My God, my rock of refuge,
  my shield, the horn of my salvation,
    my stronghold!
Praised be the LORD, I exclaim,
  and I am safe from my enemies.

The LORD lives and blessed be my rock!
  Extolled be God my savior.
You who gave great victories to your king
  and showed kindness to your anointed.

READING II   1 Thessalonians 1:5c–10

A reading from the first Letter of Saint Paul to the Thessalonians

Brothers and sisters:
You know what sort of people we were among you for your sake.
And you became imitators of us and of the Lord,
  receiving the word in great affliction, with joy from the
    Holy Spirit,
  so that you became a model for all the believers
  in Macedonia and in Achaia.
For from you the word of the Lord has sounded forth
  not only in Macedonia and in Achaia,
  but in every place your faith in God has gone forth,
  so that we have no need to say anything.
For they themselves openly declare about us
  what sort of reception we had among you,
  and how you turned to God from idols
  to serve the living and true God
  and to await his Son from heaven,
  whom he raised from the dead,
  Jesus, who delivers us from the coming wrath.

Thessalonians = thes-uh-LOH-nee-uhnz

Paul is heaping praise in this reading onto the Thessalonians for how impressively they have become models for believers. His praise is as sincere as it is motivating, which you can convey to your assembly as you proclaim.

Macedonia = mas-eh-DOH-nee-uh
Achaia = uh-KAY-uh

Slight pause between "declare" and "about."

---

charging interest, and it places substantial limitations on what constitutes as collateral. For example, you cannot keep a person's cloak as collateral, because it likely serves as his bedding at night. Notice that God calls the poor "my people." How can we deny God's people the protections they need?

READING II Today's second reading is the second half of the thanksgiving section of the First Letter to the Thessalonians, which we began reading last week. The thanksgiving sections of

Paul's letters are interesting because they often contain the major themes of the letter. This one is no exception. One of his favorite themes is captured in the phrase, "And you became imitators of us and of the Lord." It might sound arrogant to modern listeners, but Paul repeatedly tells the communities that he founded to imitate him. He can say this because he sees his own life as imitating Christ, that is, dying with him so that he can come to new life in Christ (see Philippians 3:7–11). All of this is by God's grace.

A related theme that Paul previews in this thanksgiving is the affliction that they share. The Greek word for this is *thlipsis*, and it means "oppression, affliction, tribulation, or distress." Paul intends it to refer to the tribulations that were expected to accompany the parousia, the return of the risen Christ in the end time. Although he was mistaken about the timing of the parousia —he thought it would be in his lifetime (1 Thessalonians 4:14–18)—his message is sound. Despite afflictions, Christians should receive God's word with joy and live out their faith in service, so that they can be an

Pharisees = FAYH-uh-seez
Sadducees = SAD-yoo-seez

The greatest commandment; this reading is as consequential to Christian belief as it is powerful and concise. Its clarity is that of water from the clearest spring.

Slight pause between "prophets" and "depend."

The emphases on the words in this line are worth practicing to get right.

GOSPEL   Matthew 22:34–40

A reading from the holy Gospel according to Matthew

When the **Pharisees** heard that **Jesus** had **silenced** the **Sadducees**,
    they **gathered together**, and **one** of them,
    a **scholar** of the **law**, **tested** him by **asking**,
    "**Teacher**, **which commandment** in the **law** is the **greatest**?"
He **said** to him,
    "You shall **love** the **Lord**, your **God**,
    with all your **heart**,
    with all your **soul**,
    and with all your **mind**.
This is the **greatest** and the **first commandment**.
The **second** is **like** it:
    You shall **love** your **neighbor** as **yourself**.
The **whole law** and the **prophets depend** on **these**
        two commandments."

---

example to others until the coming of the risen Lord. Moreover, we can live in hope because, just as God raised Jesus, Jesus will rescue us at the end time.

GOSPEL Our Gospel reading picks up the subject of the Covenant Code in today's first reading. In the preceding verses, the Sadducees challenged Jesus with an issue related to teachings about resurrection of the dead, but Jesus bested them with his response (Matthew 22:23–33). The Sadducees were theologically conservative and did not

accept the possibility of resurrection. They were also part of the leadership in Jerusalem and Judea, though they were not well liked by the Jewish population because they colluded with the Romans to maintain their positions of power.

Knowing that the Sadducees failed in trying to bring Jesus down, now the Pharisees, who were scholars and interpreters of Jewish Law, try to challenge Jesus. Their designated speaker, a lawyer (Greek, *nomikos*, meaning someone who was an expert in the law) asks this question: "Teacher, which commandment in the

law is the greatest?" In essence, they are testing Jesus on what he thinks makes all of Jewish law meaningful and relevant. This is a monumental question fraught with potential landmines, but Jesus answers beautifully, quoting Deuteronomy 6:5 and Leviticus 19:18. To love God with all your heart, soul, and mind describes fidelity to God and to the covenant that God made with his people. To love your neighbor as you might love yourself is to abandon any tendency toward narcissism and to be focused on others in all we say and do. C.C.

ALL SAINTS

LECTIONARY #667

READING I Revelation 7:2–4, 9–14

A reading from the Book of Revelation

I, **John**, saw another **angel** come up from the **East**,
  holding the **seal** of the living **God**.
He cried **out** in a **loud voice** to the four **angels**
  who were given **power** to **damage** the **land** and the **sea**,
    "Do not **damage** the **land** or the sea or the **trees**
  until we put the **seal** on the **foreheads** of the **servants**
    of our **God**."
I heard the **number** of those who had been **marked** with the seal,
  one **hundred** and forty-four **thousand** marked
  from every **tribe** of the children of **Israel**.

After **this** I had a **vision** of a great **multitude**,
  which **no one** could count,
  from every **nation**, **race**, **people**, and **tongue**.
They stood before the **throne** and before the **Lamb**,
  wearing **white robes** and holding **palm branches** in
    their **hands**.
They cried out in a **loud voice**:

  "**Salvation** comes from our **God**, who is **seated** on the **throne**,
  and from the **Lamb**."

Revelation = rev-uh-LAY-shuhn

A reading of visionary power and enticing detail. Revelation has inherent drama in its language and imagery. You only need to proclaim the passage with clarity and directness; its power will express itself through your voice.

Note the repetitions: "damage, land, sea."

Even stresses on the words in this line.

Emphasis on "Lamb," which will be repeated at the end of the passage.

READING I The first reading for this feast is taken from the Book of Revelation, specifically from two visions that are inserted between the vision of the opening of the sixth seal of the Book of Life, which the risen Christ holds in his hands (Revelation 6:12–17) and the introduction of the vision of the seventh seal (Revelation 8:1–5). Seals were used by powerful people in the ancient world to mark their property and lend authority to their communications.

These two inserted visions are triumphant in tone, the first being a vision of the sealing of God's elect (Revelation 7:1–8) and the second being the vision of the multitude singing in praise of God's salvation (Revelation 7:9–17). Ancients believed that angels or spirit beings controlled the activities of cosmic phenomena like winds and planets. Thus, the four angels represent the winds at the four corners of the world who stand at the ready to exact God's judgment on the earth. The angel who holds God's seal commands them to wait until God's holy ones are marked with his seal. This seal will not save them from death because, as we learn toward the end of the second vision, they are the martyrs who went through the great ordeal. Having gone through death, the martyrs will be able to participate in the unending heavenly liturgy before God's throne. The author likely has in mind Rome's persecution of Christians under Emperor Domitian (reigned AD 81–96) and might also harken back to the persecutions under Emperor Nero (reigned AD 54–68).

The number who are marked with God's seal is 144,000. However, we should be careful not to take this number literally. Mathematically, it is 12 multiplied by 12 and multiplied again by 1,000, but 12 is symbolic

All the **angels** stood around the **throne**
and around the **elders** and the four living **creatures**.
They **prostrated** themselves before the **throne**,
worshiped **God**, and **exclaimed**:

> "**Amen**. **Blessing** and **glory**, **wisdom** and **thanksgiving**,
> **honor**, **power**, and **might**
> be to our **God** forever and **ever**. **Amen**."

Then one of the **elders** spoke up and **said** to me,
"**Who** are these wearing **white robes**, and **where** did they
come from?"
I said to him, "My **lord**, you are the one who **knows**."
He said to me,
"**These** are the **ones** who have **survived** the time
of great **distress**;
they have **washed** their **robes**
and made them **white** in the **Blood** of the **Lamb**."

Note the heavy emphases on the words in this exclamation.

TO KEEP IN MIND
As you prepare your proclamation, make choices about what emotions need to be expressed. Some choices are evident from the text, but some are harder to discern. Understanding the context of the Scripture passage will help you decide.

Allow this image to expand in your proclamation of it. Emphasis on "Lamb."

For meditation and context:

RESPONSORIAL PSALM   Psalm 24:1bc–2, 3–4ab, 5–6 (6)

R. Lord, this is the people that longs to see your face.

The LORD's are the earth and its fullness;
the world and those who dwell in it.
For he founded it upon the seas
and established it upon the rivers.

Who can ascend the mountain of the LORD?
or who may stand in his holy place?
One whose hands are sinless, whose heart is clean,
who desires not what is vain.

He shall receive a blessing from the LORD,
a reward from God his savior.
Such is the race that seeks him,
that seeks the face of the God of Jacob.

of fulness (and recalls the twelve tribes of Israel) and 1,000 represents an incalculably large number. Hence, John says that he could see, before God's throne, "a great multitude, which no one could count" from everywhere on earth. They are dressed in white, a symbol of victory in the Book of Revelation, because they were washed "in the blood of the Lamb," meaning that these holy ones share in Jesus' suffering to death. Likewise, the palm fronds that they carry are symbols of victory.

And what a beautiful song! It is introduced by the martyrs who cry out, "Salvation comes from our God." The Greek word *sōtēria*, which is translated here as "salvation," can also mean "deliverance or safety," which has led some translators to use "victory" instead of "salvation" in this sentence. Immediately, those stationed around God's throne—the four living creatures that watch over it, the twenty-four elders who sit on thrones surrounding God's throne, and the angels—join the martyrs in singing a victory song to God. Notice that there are exactly seven attributions given to God in this song. Seven is a number symbolizing perfection. Finally, the Hebrew word *amēn* means "truly or so be it." Although Christians use it now to conclude their prayers, it was first used in the synagogue as a way for those in attendance to affirm the words of the leader of prayer.

This reading paints a vivid picture of what the experience of the saints at this moment might look like. All in heaven glorifying God and singing songs of praise. We are invited to rejoice as well, knowing that these holy men and women have reached their reward and the suffering of the saints and martyrs have passed into the glory of God.

A reading proclaiming the mysterious nature of God's revelation.

Emphasis on "know." In the next line, on "him."

Note the interplay between "revealed" and "see."

READING II   1 John 3:1–3

A reading from the first Letter of Saint John

Beloved:
See what love the **Father** has **bestowed** on us
   that we may be **called** the children of **God**.
Yet **so** we **are**.
The **reason** the world does not **know** us
   is that it did not know **him**.
Beloved, we are **God's** children now;
   what we shall be has not yet been **revealed**.
We **do know** that when it is **revealed** we shall be **like** him,
   for we shall see him as he **is**.
Everyone who has this **hope** based on him makes himself **pure**,
   as **he** is pure.

A reading whose expressions are familiar but whose specifics are helpfully reintroduced to your assembly. This Gospel reading is an opportunity to teach the beatitudes anew.

Blessed = BLES-uhd

Note the rhythmical emphases. The first word in each beatitude is stressed, as is the last word in each line. Let that rhythm guide your proclamation.

GOSPEL   Matthew 5:1–12a

A reading from the holy Gospel according to Matthew

When **Jesus** saw the **crowds**, he went up the **mountain**,
   and after he had sat **down**, his disciples **came** to him.
He began to **teach** them, saying:

   "**Blessed** are the poor in **spirit**,
     for **theirs** is the **Kingdom** of **heaven**.
   Blessed are they who **mourn**,
     for **they** will be **comforted**.
   Blessed are the **meek**,
     for they will **inherit** the **land**.
   Blessed are they who **hunger** and **thirst** for **righteousness**,
     for they will be **satisfied**.
   Blessed are the **merciful**,
     for they will be shown **mercy**.

READING II   Our second reading comes from the First Letter of John, which is thought by most scholars to have been written by someone from the Johannine Christian community in a decade or so after the Gospel of John was written. If you know John's Gospel, you will quickly see that the vocabulary of this document is like the vocabulary of the Gospel, though it is not always used in the same way. The author of this document expresses frustration with members of the community who caused harm by separating from his group, even while they claim to love

God and love the brothers and sisters (see 1 John 2:18–23).

With this background in mind, we can understand that the author of this document identifies his community as "children of God," which is an expression of God's love for them. Further, he addresses the problem of the world's refusal to acknowledge them as such by saying that it is because they do not know God. From the tone of this document, we can assume that the author is including the schismatics in this group that he identifies as "the world." A defection from one's own community

hurts much more than rejection by strangers. Perhaps to console his community or at least himself, the author adds "what we shall be has not yet been revealed." What follows is a profound theological teaching. Our author says, "when it is revealed we shall be like him." Grammatically, the pronoun "it" should refer to God, but it is possible that the referent is Christ, since he is God's agent whose identity is one with God. Regardless, our author is saying that, when the divine power is revealed, we will be divinized (not that we will become God, but that "we shall be like him" when he

Blessed are the clean of **heart**,
for they will see **God**.
Blessed are the **peacemakers**,
for they will be called **children** of God.
Blessed are they who are **persecuted** for the sake
of **righteousness**,
for **theirs** is the **Kingdom** of **heaven**.
Blessed are you when they **insult** you and **persecute** you
and utter every kind of evil **against** you falsely
because of me.
Rejoice and be **glad**,
for your **reward** will be **great** in **heaven**."

transforms us at the end of time)! Thus, the author's exhortation is to purify ourselves now so that, when the time comes, we will be worthy to see God as God is, when we join the communion of saints.

GOSPEL Today's Gospel is a familiar one for most of us. The sayings in this reading are called beatitudes because of the Greek word *makarios*, which stands at the beginning of each saying and which means "happy or blessed" as in congratulations. To whom are these beatitudes addressed? They are addressed to the poor in spirit—that is, those who are generous with what they have and care for the poor; to those who mourn—that is, people who go beyond themselves to give proper burial for the dead; to those who are meek—that is, people who are slow to anger and treat others with kindness; those who act justly and mercifully as God is just and merciful; and so on. The last two beatitudes—some describe them as one long beatitude in two parts— are different in style and tone from the others and probably reflect the situation of the early Church where local persecutions of Christians were commonplace. But if you do these things, be glad. God's kingdom is near at hand! C.C.

THE COMMEMORATION OF ALL THE FAITHFUL DEPARTED (ALL SOULS' DAY)

LECTIONARY #668

READING I Wisdom 3:1–9

A reading from the Book of Wisdom

The **souls** of the **just** are in the **hand** of **God**,
  and no **torment** shall **touch** them.
They **seemed**, in the view of the **foolish**, to be **dead**;
  and their passing **away** was thought an **affliction**
  and their going **forth** from us, utter **destruction**.
But they are in **peace**.
For if before **men**, indeed, they be **punished**,
  yet is their **hope** full of **immortality**;
chastised a little, they shall be greatly **blessed**,
  because God **tried** them
  and found them **worthy** of **himself**.
As gold in the furnace, he **proved** them,
  and as sacrificial **offerings** he took them to **himself**.
In the time of their **visitation** they shall **shine**,
  and shall dart **about** as **sparks** through **stubble**;
they shall judge **nations** and rule over **peoples**,
  and the LORD shall be their King **forever**.
Those who **trust** in him shall understand **truth**,
  and the **faithful** shall abide with him in **love**:
because **grace** and **mercy** are with his **holy** ones,
  and his **care** is with his **elect**.

An exhortatory reading, one whose tone is conciliatory and hopeful.

Emphasize "peace."

Emphasize "himself." God gathers all the souls offered to him, transforming them.

Emphasize "grace," "mercy," and "holy."

There are options for today's readings. Contact your parish staff to learn which readings will be used.

READING I The readings for today offer the encouragement of hope and trust in God to those who hear them proclaimed, which is why they are chosen for this celebration of the Commemoration of All the Faithful Departed (All Souls). By digging deep into questions of suffering and salvation, these readings show us how God's overwhelming love draws us to himself and is expressed in the paschal mystery of Christ, which we join in through our sacramental participation.

The Wisdom of Solomon, from which our first reading comes, is one of several books known to Catholics as deuterocanonical or belonging to a second canon of the Bible. However, because of theological debates that arose during the Reformation, Protestant reformers decided to count them as apocryphal, meaning, "of doubtful authenticity." Nevertheless, it is included in the Catholic Bible. Its author (not King Solomon, though the attributions to him in the book lend value to the teachings in the book) writes of many important themes that reveal the nature of God and encourage readers to trust in God.

Today's first reading is part of a longer section of the Book of Wisdom that addresses the question of the vindication of the righteous (Wisdom 3:1—4:19). Briefly, Jewish and Christian theologies express the question this way: if God is sovereign and just, how are the righteous rewarded and the wicked punished? The author of Wisdom addresses the question by commenting on three scenarios in which it might appear that the righteous are being

For meditation and context:

RESPONSORIAL PSALM   Psalm 23:1–3a, 3b–4, 5, 6 (1)

R. The Lord is my shepherd; there is nothing I shall want.
or
R. Though I walk in the valley of darkness, I fear no evil, for you are with me.

The Lord is my shepherd; I shall not want.
  In verdant pastures he gives me repose;
beside restful waters he leads me;
  he refreshes my soul.

He guides me in right paths
  for his name's sake.
Even though I walk in the dark valley
  I fear no evil; for you are at my side
with your rod and your staff
  that give me courage.

You spread the table before me
  in the sight of my foes;
You anoint my head with oil;
  my cup overflows.

Only goodness and kindness follow me
  all the days of my life;
and I shall dwell in the house of the Lord
  for years to come.

READING II   Romans 5:5–11

A reading from the Letter of Saint Paul to the Romans

A reading in which Paul locates the source of hope in Jesus himself.

Emphasize "Christ."

Emphasize "through." This indicates the direction/tendency of our salvation, sparing us from wrath.

Brothers and **sisters**:
Hope does **not** disappoint,
  because the love of **God** has been poured **out** into our **hearts**
  through the Holy **Spirit** that has been **given** to us.
For **Christ**, while we were still **helpless**,
  died at the appointed time for the **ungodly**.
Indeed, only with difficulty does one die for a just **person**,
  though **perhaps** for a **good** person
  one might even find **courage** to die.
But **God** proves his **love** for us
  in that while we were still **sinners** Christ **died** for us.
How much **more** then, since we are now **justified** by his **Blood**,
  will we be saved **through** him from the **wrath**. »

punished: human suffering, childlessness, and early death. This reading focuses on the suffering of the righteous. It begins by asserting that, whatever the foolish might think they perceive, the righteous have immortality or eternal life and peace with God. The beautiful image of being "in the hand of God" is about protection from the forces of evil. Notice, also, the author's belief that suffering can be educative—like a nanny teaching a child to do what is right and good—and that suffering can purify us—like fire can purify and separate precious metal from dross. Suffering can also

be like a sacrificial offering which God accepts to himself. The word "visitation" refers to God's intervention on behalf of the suffering righteous, and their shining and darting around "as sparks through stubble" is a reference to their resurrection or immortality (see Daniel 12:3). Finally, the truth that the faithful ones will come to know is who God is in Godself—something the mystics and saints long to experience!

| READING II | Our second reading is from a long section of Paul's Letter to the Romans on the life of the justi-

fied, that is, those who have been set in right relationship with God through the death and resurrection of Jesus (Romans 5:1—8:39). Immediately prior to our reading, Paul says that those who are justified find their peace in God and their hope is in God's glory (Romans 5:1–2). It is through this peace and hope that Christians can endure the afflictions of this life.

This is where our reading begins. Paul notes that this hope is not simply imagined. Rather, it is sure and can be relied upon, because of God's love for us. Paul goes on to give a particularly poignant explanation

Indeed, if, while we were **enemies**,
    we were **reconciled** to God through the **death** of his Son,
    how much **more**, once **reconciled**,
    will we be **saved** by his **life**.
Not only **that**,
    but we also boast of God through our Lord Jesus **Christ**,
    through whom we have now **received reconciliation**.

GOSPEL   John 6:37–40

A reading from the holy Gospel according to John

Jesus said to the **crowds**:
    "**Everything** that the Father **gives** me will **come** to me,
    and I will not reject **anyone** who **comes** to me,
    because I came **down** from heaven not to do my **own will**
    but the **will** of the **one** who **sent** me.
And this is the **will** of the one who **sent** me,
    that I should not lose **anything** of what he **gave** me,
    but that I should **raise** it on the last **day**.
For this is the **will** of my **Father**,
    that **everyone** who sees the **Son** and **believes** in him
    may have eternal **life**,
    and I shall raise him up on the **last day**."

A powerful and assertive exhortatory reading that expresses one of John's favorite themes, the will of the Father.

"Will" is the operative word in this reading. It is repeated four times (as a noun). Give it weight each time you say it.

For John, will is connected directly to the Father, toward which Jesus, as Son, is utterly obedient and which clearly empowers him. Emphasize "this," "will," and "Father."

of the state of sinful humanity prior to God's gift of justification. In no way did humanity earn this gift of right relationship with God. Rather, in the enormity of divine love, God gave his Son over to death that we might be justified. Paul is so confident in God's love for humanity that he believes that we can also have hope that we can be saved by Christ's life. For Paul, salvation is different from justification. The Greek word "to save" means "to heal, to make well, or to restore to health." Notice, also, the interrelatedness of salvation and reconciliation. When one is reconciled to God, he or she is saved.

GOSPEL   Today's Gospel is part of the Bread of Life discourse, in which Jesus addresses a challenge made by the crowds who were chasing after him in hope of getting more food to eat, after the multiplication of loaves and fishes near the Sea of Galilee (John 6:1–15). When they caught up to him, they asked for a sign, one like the manna that God sent down from heaven during the time of Moses (John 6:30–31). Thus, Jesus declares that he is the bread from heaven, sent from God to give the world life. Coming to today's reading, we see that Jesus is the agent of God, who in complete fidelity receives everything he has from the Father and does only what the Father tells him to do. An integral aspect of his mission as the bread of life is described in this reading; that Jesus receives everyone the Father gives and will not lose any one of them. Not even death will separate Christ from the people; they will be raised up "on the last day." What sweet comfort to all who believe in Jesus' name! They will have everlasting life, that is, the fullness of life now, and be raised up on the last day. C.C.

THIRTY-FIRST SUNDAY IN ORDINARY TIME

LECTIONARY #151

READING I   Malachi 1:14b—2:2b, 8–10

A reading from the Book of the Prophet Malachi

> A **great King** am **I**, says the LORD of **hosts**,
>   and my **name** will be **feared** among the **nations**.
> And **now**, O **priests**, this **commandment** is for **you**:
>   If you **do not listen**,
> if you **do not lay** it to **heart**,
>   to give **glory** to my **name**, says the LORD of **hosts**,
> I will send a **curse** upon you
>   and of your **blessing** I will make a **curse**.
> You have **turned aside** from the **way**,
>   and have caused **many** to **falter** by your **instruction**;
> you have made **void** the **covenant** of **Levi**,
>   says the LORD of **hosts**.
> **I**, **therefore**, have made you **contemptible**
>   and **base** before **all** the **people**,
> since you **do not keep** my **ways**,
>   but show **partiality** in your **decisions**.
> Have we not **all** the **one father**?
>   Has not the **one God created** us?
> **Why then** do we break **faith** with one **another**,
>   **violating** the **covenant** of our **fathers**?

Malachi = MAL-uh-kī

A poetic and heroic-sounding reading, with alluring oratorical overtones.

Emphasis on "curse," which focuses the drama of the reading.

contemptible = kuhn-TEMP-tuh-b*l

Let the forcefulness of the questions that conclude this reading draw you to its end.

READING I Today's first reading is from the Book of Malachi, which is believed to have been written after the Babylonian Exile. In the verses immediately preceding this reading, the prophet describes God as feeling dishonored and suggests that someone should just shut the gates to the Temple so that the priests cannot make defiling or imperfect offerings on the altar. He also casts blame on those who provide the animals for temple sacrifice: they promise with a vow that an animal is appropriate for sacrifice and then, at the time of sacrifice, replace it with a defective one. How disingenuous!

With this context in mind, today's reading begins with the prophet voicing God's assertion that he is a king whose "name will be feared among the nations." Although this statement of universal fear is an exaggeration, the claims of God's universal kingship are valid insofar as God is the creator and sustainer of all life and should be worshipped as such, especially by God's chosen people and by the priests who are charged with carrying out Levi's legacy. Levi was one of the sons of Jacob and founder of the tribe of Levi. The other tribes were allotted land as Moses had promised before they entered the Promised Land (Numbers 33–34), but the tribe of Levi was not given its own land, because "the LORD, the God of Israel, is their heritage, as he had promised them" (Joshua 13:33). Malachi describes Levi as having integrity and as capable of turning people away from the ways of evil with his instruction (Malachi 2:6). By contrast, these temple priests do not give God the honor that is due and use their teaching to advance their own desires. Therefore, God says that he will

For meditation and context:

RESPONSORIAL PSALM   Psalm 131:1, 2, 3

R. In you, Lord, I have found my peace.

O Lord, my heart is not proud,
    nor are my eyes haughty;
I busy not myself with great things,
    nor with things too sublime for me.

Nay rather, I have stilled and quieted
    my soul like a weaned child.
Like a weaned child on its mother's lap,
    so is my soul within me.

O Israel, hope in the Lord,
    both now and forever.

Thessalonians = thes-uh-LOH-nee-uhnz

Paul describes the trouble he has undergone to bring the Gospel to the Thessalonians as a way of praising them for receiving the Good News. In the first half, Paul describes his trouble. In the second half, he turns the description into praise.

READING II   1 Thessalonians 2:7b–9, 13

A reading from the first Letter of Saint Paul to the Thessalonians

Brothers and **sisters:**
We were **gentle among** you, as a **nursing mother cares**
        for her **children.**
With **such affection** for **you,** we were **determined** to **share**
        with you
        not only the **gospel** of **God,** but our **very selves** as **well,**
        so **dearly beloved** had you **become** to us.
You **recall, brothers** and **sisters,** our **toil** and **drudgery.**
Working night and **day** in order not to **burden any** of you,
        we **proclaimed** to you the **gospel** of **God.**

Here the second half begins, and the tone becomes more uplifting.

And for **this reason** we too give **thanks** to God **unceasingly,**
        that, in **receiving** the **word** of **God** from **hearing us,**
        you received not a **human** word but, as it truly **is,**
            the word of **God,**
        which is **now** at **work** in **you** who **believe.**

---

shame them before the people. At the end of the reading, the prophet speaks in his own words, using several rhetorical questions to make the point that Israel is different from other nations, who identify themselves merely by ethnicity or other human factors. In fact, Israel is one family, the children of God, and refusing to uphold the covenant of their ancestors, in essence, makes them "break faith with one another."

READING II In our second reading, Paul presents himself and his fellow missionaries in a way that is quite

different from the priests of Malachi's time. In the sentences that precede this reading, he writes about the indignities they faced in Philippi, which gave them courage to speak the Good News of God to the people of Thessalonica. They did so, Paul says, without deception or delusion or flattery or greed. Moreover, they did not push their weight around by claiming and exploiting their role as apostles (1 Thessalonians 2:1–6a).

Our reading begins with Paul asserting that he and his comrades were gentle and affectionate with the Thessalonian community, acting as wet nurses among them. The

"nutrition" they share with the community is the Good News, of course, but also their very selves. Such is their love (literally, "yearning") for these Christians! By noting the sufferings that Paul and his co-missionaries endured on their behalf and explaining how they worked to avoid being a burden to them, Paul is again asserting that the community was not coerced in any way to receive the Good News. Instead, they knew it to be God's Word, which they allow to work in them. For this reason, he continually gives thanks to God.

GOSPEL   Matthew 23:1–12

A reading from the holy Gospel according to Matthew

A scornful and critical reading that includes challenging imperatives.

Jesus spoke to the **crowds** and to his **disciples**, saying,
    "The **scribes** and the **Pharisees**
        have **taken** their **seat** on the **chair** of **Moses**.
    Therefore, **do** and **observe all things whatsoever** they **tell** you,
        but **do not follow** their **example**.
For they **preach** but they do not **practice**.

Slight pause between "burdens" and "hard."

They **tie up heavy burdens hard** to **carry**
        and **lay** them on **people's shoulders**,
        but they **will not lift** a **finger** to **move** them.
All their **works** are **performed** to be **seen**.

phylacteries = fih-LAK-tuh-reez

They **widen** their **phylacteries** and **lengthen** their **tassels**.
They love **places** of **honor** at **banquets**,
        seats of **honor** in **synagogues**,
        greetings in **marketplaces**, and the salutation '**Rabbi**.'

Consider how strange it is for Jesus to tell the crowd not to call anyone "Rabbi," a commonplace honorific for referring to a teacher.

As for **you**, **do not** be called '**Rabbi**.'
You have but **one teacher**, and you are **all brothers**.

Stranger still to tell the crowd not to call anyone "father." Same goes for "Master."

Call **no one** on **earth** your **father**;
        you have but **one Father** in **heaven**.
Do **not** be called '**Master**';
        you have but **one master**, the **Christ**.
The **greatest among** you must be your **servant**.

The reading concludes with an inversion: exalts–humbles to humbles–exalted.

Whoever **exalts himself** will be **humbled**;
        but whoever **humbles himself** will be **exalted**."

TO KEEP IN MIND
Recognize how important your proclamation of the Word of God is. Prepare well and take joy in your ministry.

GOSPEL   Today's Gospel is the introduction to Matthew's version of the woes that Jesus issues against the scribes and Pharisees. Among prophetic literary forms, a woe is a lamentation or expression of grief followed by charges issued against the persons to whom the woe is directed. Like Malachi's charges against the temple priests in our first reading, Jesus' charges against the scribes and Pharisees highlight the human condition and the potential for people in positions of power to abuse their authority. Thus, in today's Gospel reading, Jesus advises his disciples and the crowd that had gathered around them that they should heed the teachings of the scribes and Pharisees, experts in the Law, because they hold "the chair of Moses," that is, a symbol of Moses' authority, but they should not follow their example. He goes on to name practices that these people employ to bring attention to themselves and impose heavy religious burdens on those who have less power than themselves. Phylacteries, the small leather boxes worn on the forehead and left arm, and tassels are both intended to be reminders to follow covenant law (see Deuteronomy 11:18; Numbers 15:38–39) but making them bigger and longer is a violation of the spirit of the law. No matter a person's station on earth, even if they are in positions of honor or power or instruction, there is only one who deserves the full weight of those titles: God. The Matthean Jesus' message is that the greatest and most exalted should be a humble servant. C.C.

THIRTY-SECOND SUNDAY IN ORDINARY TIME

LECTIONARY #154

READING I   Wisdom 6:12–16

A poetic reading. In Greek and Jewish cultures, Wisdom was traditionally feminized. In this reading, Wisdom is a personified woman who acts and responds and can even be observed.

A reading from the Book of Wisdom

> **Resplendent** and **unfading** is **wisdom**,
> and she is **readily perceived** by **those** who **love** her,
> and **found** by **those** who **seek** her.
> She **hastens** to make herself **known** in **anticipation**
>   of their **desire**;
> whoever **watches** for her at **dawn** shall **not** be **disappointed**,
> for he shall find her **sitting** by his **gate**.
> For taking **thought** of **wisdom** is the **perfection** of **prudence**,
> and **whoever** for her **sake** keeps **vigil**
> shall **quickly** be **free** from **care**;
> because she **makes** her own **rounds**, seeking those **worthy**
>   of her,
> and **graciously appears** to them in the **ways**,
> and **meets** them with all **solicitude**.

READING I | Our first reading comes from the Book of Wisdom. When the author of this book writes about wisdom, he presents her as a personified, feminine power of God, because the Greek word for wisdom is *sophia*, a feminine noun. Today's reading, which focuses on wisdom's accessibility, is part of a longer exhortation to those who wish to be wise. Wisdom is the speaker. She exhorts kings and princes to seek wisdom, because God will punish them harshly if they do not change their ways (Wisdom 6:1–11).

In today's reading, Wisdom's accessibility is described in terms of the theme of seeking and finding, which is also found in Proverbs 1:20–21; 3:13–18; and 8:1–36. Wisdom's unfading radiance is due to her connection to the divine. Elsewhere in Wisdom, she is described as reflecting divine light, as a mirror (Wisdom 7:26). The people who love her learn to be discerning and free from care because she is with them, appearing in their paths and meeting them "with all solicitude." What a beautiful message! If we seek wisdom in discerning love, we will find her and become like her.

For meditation and context:

RESPONSORIAL PSALM Psalm 63:2, 3–4, 5–6, 7–8 (2b)

R. My soul is thirsting for you, O Lord my God.

O God, you are my God whom I seek;
    for you my flesh pines and my soul thirsts
    like the earth, parched, lifeless and
        without water.

Thus have I gazed toward you in
    the sanctuary
to see your power and your glory,
for your kindness is a greater good than life;
    my lips shall glorify you.

Thus will I bless you while I live;
    lifting up my hands, I will call upon
        your name.
As with the riches of a banquet shall my soul
        be satisfied,
    and with exultant lips my mouth shall
        praise you.

I will remember you upon my couch,
    and through the night-watches I will
        meditate on you:
you are my help,
    and in the shadow of your wings I shout
        for joy.

READING II   Thessalonians 4:13–18

Thessalonians = thes-uh-LOH-nee-uhnz

A reading from the first Letter of Saint Paul to the Thessalonians

[We do not want you to be **unaware**, **brothers** and **sisters**,
    about **those** who have **fallen asleep**,
    so that you **may not grieve** like the **rest**, who have **no hope**.
For if we **believe** that **Jesus died** and **rose**,
    so too will **God**, through **Jesus**,
    bring with him those who have **fallen asleep**.]
Indeed, we **tell** you this, on the **word** of the **Lord**,
    that **we** who are **alive**,
    who are **left** until the **coming** of the **Lord**,
    will **surely** not **precede those** who have fallen **asleep**.
For the **Lord himself**, with a **word** of **command**,
    with the **voice** of an **archangel** and with the **trumpet** of **God**,
    will come **down** from **heaven**,
    and the **dead** in **Christ** will rise **first**. »

Emphasis on "not."
Slight pause between "Jesus" and "died."

archangel = AHRK-ayn-jihl

READING II One of the main topics of Paul's First Letter to the Thessalonians is how the community should deal with the delayed parousia, the return of the risen Christ at the end time. Apparently, they understood from Paul that the return of the risen Christ would happen very soon, since resurrection from the dead was thought to be a sign of the end time. Now, some twenty years later, the parousia has not yet happened. This young Christian community is deeply troubled because some of their members are dying. Paul's response is unequivocal! Since we

believe Jesus died and was raised from the dead, God will surely raise your beloved deceased from the dead. Paul continues in the style of a prophet, declaring "on the word of the Lord" how this end time parousia will come about. The imagery is reminiscent of God's appearance to Moses on Sinai or a king's entrance into a heavenly throne room. The line about being "caught up . . . in the clouds" refers to the ancient belief that spiritual beings used clouds as their vehicles to get around heaven. In the midst of this grand imagery, notice that Paul's message is one of consolation and encour-

agement. Their beloved dead are not lost. Indeed, they will be the first to enter into the divine presence!

GOSPEL Today's Gospel reading is about both seeking wisdom and anticipating the end time appearance of the risen Christ. It is the parable of the wise and foolish virgins, which is found only in Matthew's Gospel. Parables are fictional stories that establish a comparison—in this case, "the kingdom of heaven will be like . . ."—and that involve common, everyday images to communi-

Paul's apocalyptic view reveals itself as the reading intensifies toward its conclusion. He's sharing a vision of end times with his fellow believers.

Then **we** who are **alive**, who are **left**,
    will be **caught up together** with them in the **clouds**
    to **meet** the **Lord** in the **air**.
Thus we shall **always be** with the **Lord**.
Therefore, **console** one **another** with these **words**.

[Shorter Form: 1 Thessalonians 4:13–14]

GOSPEL   Matthew 25:1–13

A reading from the holy Gospel according to Matthew

A reading that consists of the telling of a straightforward parable whose message is for believers to be prepared.

Jesus told his **disciples** this **parable**:
   "The **kingdom** of **heaven** will be like **ten virgins**
   who took their **lamps** and went **out** to meet the **bridegroom**.
Five of them were **foolish** and **five** were **wise**.
The **foolish** ones, when **taking** their **lamps**,
    brought **no oil** with them,
    but the **wise** brought **flasks** of **oil** with their **lamps**.
Since the **bridegroom** was **long delayed**,
    they **all** became **drowsy** and **fell asleep**.
At **midnight**, there was a **cry**,
    '**Behold**, the **bridegroom**! **Come out** to **meet** him!'
Then **all those virgins** got **up** and **trimmed** their **lamps**.
The **foolish** ones said to the **wise**,
    '**Give** us some of your **oil**,
    for our **lamps** are going **out**.'
But the **wise** ones **replied**,
    '**No**, for there **may not** be **enough** for **us** and **you**.
Go instead to the **merchants** and **buy** some for **yourselves**.'
While they **went** off to **buy** it,
    the **bridegroom came**
    and **those** who were **ready** went into the **wedding feast**
     with him.

Slight pause between "feast" and "with."

cate their meaning. The phrase "kingdom of heaven" is often misunderstood to refer to heaven. However, it is better understood as the full manifestation of the reign of God and the dissolution of evil and suffering in the land.

Unfortunately, because wedding feasts were a common reality in first-century Jewish communities, the modern reader is given few details about what took place at these celebrations. Yet from other contemporaneous sources we know that marriages were contractual relationships between families for the purposes of estab-

lishing alliances or protecting resources, so the betrothal contract was an important first step in the process. The wedding itself, which could go on for several days or even a week, was focused on the process of transferring the bride from her father's home to her husband's home, which was often somewhere near or even within his father's home. When the procession of the groom to the bride's home and back to his home was complete, the bride and groom would consummate their marriage, with the witnesses waiting outside to confirm the bride's virginity prior to consummation,

after which the witnesses would accompany the bride and groom into the banquet area for lots of feasting!

If we allow ourselves a bit of allegory, we can imagine the ten virgins (the bridesmaids)—young girls not yet eligible for marriage—as the witnesses to the consummation event. Five were not wise and did not prepare sufficiently for the delay of the bridegroom, the parousia of the risen Christ. Because they had to go and purchase more oil for their lamps, they missed the opportunity to accompany the bridal couple when they joined the wedding ban-

Then the **door** was **locked**.
Afterwards the **other virgins came** and **said**,
    '**Lord**, **Lord**, **open** the **door** for us!'
But he **said** in **reply**,
    '**Amen**, I **say** to you, I **do not know** you.'
Therefore, **stay awake**,
    for you **know** neither the **day** nor the **hour**."

quet, and they were not allowed into the feast later, because the bridegroom did not know who they were. Although biblical scholars are divided about the significance of the wedding feast, in this context it likely represents the messianic banquet that is supposed to accompany the end time. The message of the parable is "If you are wise, you will stay alert and ready for the bridegroom's coming!" C.C.

THIRTY-THIRD SUNDAY IN ORDINARY TIME

LECTIONARY #157

READING I   Proverbs 31:10–13, 19–20, 30–31

A reading from the Book of Proverbs

When **one finds** a **worthy wife**,
   her **value** is **far** beyond **pearls**.
Her **husband**, **entrusting** his **heart** to her,
   has an **unfailing prize**.
She brings him **good**, and not **evil**,
   all the **days** of her **life**.
She obtains **wool** and **flax**
   and **works** with **loving hands**.
She puts her **hands** to the **distaff**,
   and her **fingers** ply the **spindle**.
She **reaches out** her **hands** to the **poor**,
   and **extends** her **arms** to the **needy**.
Charm is **deceptive** and **beauty fleeting**;
   the **woman** who **fears** the LORD is to be **praised**.
Give her a **reward** for her **labors**,
   and let her **works praise** her at the **city gates**.

Read this in light of these attributes being descriptive of wisdom. Consider how these everyday tasks take on new meaning when done for the glory of God and describe one who follows God closely. Let that understanding come through in your proclamation.

READING I   On this Thirty-Third Sunday in Ordinary Time, only two weeks before the beginning of a new liturgical year, the First Sunday of Advent, today's readings bring us to thoughts about the fulfillment of the salvation story. We do not know when the time will come, whether it be for ourselves individually or for God's creation in totality, but if we have responded to the grace that is given us in life, we have nothing to fear from a good and gracious God.

On the surface, at least, today's first reading from the Book of Proverbs might be difficult for some modern readers to embrace, because of what we might call gender stereotyping. However, a deeper look might prove beneficial for everyone. First, this entire section, Proverbs 31:10–31, is composed as an acrostic poem. Written in Hebrew, the first verse begins with the first letter of the Hebrew alphabet, *alef*. The second verse begins with *bet*, the second letter of the Hebrew alphabet, and so on until it arrives at the last letter of the Hebrew alphabet, *tav*. Despite the patriarchy of the time in which this masterpiece was created, it outlines the skills and virtues of a strong woman. It also picks up much of the feminine imagery that appears elsewhere in this book, which has led some biblical scholars to describe this woman as the concrete and visible image of Lady Wisdom as she is described in Proverbs 1–9. The wisdom literature of the Bible portrays Lady Wisdom as the power of God who is ever-present and active in the world, a radiant light, the source of insight, the bringer of peace, the breath of God's might, and the pure emanation of God's glory (see Wisdom 7:24–30; Proverbs 8:1–36; Sirach 24:1–33).

For meditation and context:

RESPONSORIAL PSALM   Psalm 128:1–2, 3, 4–5 (1a)

R. Blessed are those who fear the Lord.

Blessed are you who fear the Lord,
   who walk in his ways!
For you shall eat the fruit of your handiwork;
   blessed shall you be, and favored.

Your wife shall be like a fruitful vine
   in the recesses of your home;
your children like olive plants
   around your table.

Behold, thus is the man blessed
   who fears the Lord.
The Lord bless you from Zion:
   may you see the prosperity of Jerusalem
   all the days of your life.

Thessalonians = thes-uh-LOH-nee-uhnz

A reading whose tone is urgent—Paul is imagining what the end of things will be like.

The core of the reading, the "thief in the night."

Emphasis on "not."

Note the contrasts between light and dark, day and night.

READING II   1 Thessalonians 5:1–6

A reading from the first Letter of Saint Paul to the Thessalonians

Concerning times and **seasons**, **brothers** and **sisters**,
   you have **no need** for **anything** to be **written** to you.
For **you yourselves** know **very well** that the **day** of the **Lord**
      will **come**
   like a **thief** at **night**.
When **people** are **saying**, "**Peace** and **security**,"
   then **sudden** disaster comes **upon** them,
   like **labor pains** upon a **pregnant woman**,
   and they **will not escape**.

But **you**, **brothers** and **sisters**, are **not** in **darkness**,
   for **that day** to **overtake** you like a **thief**.
For all of you are **children** of the **light**
   and **children** of the **day**.
We are **not** of the **night** or of **darkness**.
Therefore, let us not **sleep** as the **rest** do,
   but let us stay **alert** and **sober**.

READING II   Our second reading is from Paul's First Letter to the Thessalonians, which is believed to have been written around AD 51 and only a couple years after Paul established this community in Thessalonica. Based on Paul's teaching, they apparently believed that the parousia, the return of the risen Christ, was to take place soon after his resurrection. But now it is twenty-five or more years later, and they are concerned that something is amiss. Some members of the community have died, and they fear that they are forever lost. In the section immediately preceding this reading (1 Thessalonians 4:13–18), Paul gives them strong words of encouragement, saying that their deceased loved ones will actually be the first to join the risen Christ in the heavens, when he comes.

In today's reading, Paul picks up a topic that easily flows from this earlier concern. The heart of their unasked question is: "If we have not missed Christ's second coming, when will it happen?" He begins by reminding the community that they already know the answer to this question, but by repeating his message, he offers further encouragement to the recipients of this letter. The "day of the Lord" is a reference to God's end time judgment of the world borrowed from the prophetic literature of the Hebrew Scriptures (for example, Amos 5:18–20; Joel 2:1–11; Zephaniah 1:7–8). For those who are unaware and unprepared, the day of the Lord will come as if it were a disaster. The images of a nighttime thief and sudden birth pangs are typical of this type of eschatological (i.e., end time) literature. But Paul departs from these themes and asserts, "you are children of the light," so there is no need to fear the things of

GOSPEL　Matthew 25:14–30

A reading from the holy Gospel according to Matthew

[**Jesus** told his **disciples** this **parable**:
　"A **man** going on a **journey**
　　called in his **servants** and **entrusted** his **possessions** to them.
To one he gave **five talents**; to **another, two**; to a **third, one**—
　　to **each** according to his **ability**.
Then he went **away**.]
Immediately the **one** who received **five talents** went and **traded**
　　with them,
　　and **made another five**.
Likewise, the one who received **two made** another **two**.
But the **man** who received **one** went **off** and dug a **hole**
　　in the **ground**
　　and **buried** his master's **money**.

["After a **long time**
　　the **master** of those **servants** came **back**
　　and **settled accounts** with them.
The one who had received **five talents** came **forward**
　　bringing the **additional five**.
He said, '**Master**, you gave me **five talents**.
See, I have made **five more**.'
His master **said** to him, 'Well done, my **good** and
　　faithful servant.
Since you were **faithful** in **small matters**,
　　I will give you **great responsibilities**.
Come, share your **master's joy**.']
Then the one who had received **two talents** also came **forward**
　　and said,
　　'**Master**, you gave me **two talents**.
See, I have made **two more**.'
His master **said** to him, '**Well done**, my **good** and
　　faithful servant.

A reading that consists of the telling of a lengthy parable, one whose meaning appears straightforward but whose content suggests something more ambiguous.

Pacing: It's important to keep the different numbers in mind.

Here, the master uses a formulaic phrase to praise the servant.

Once again, the formulaic phrase.

darkness and the night, as long as you stay awake. Though not included in this reading, Paul ends this section of his letter by urging the Thessalonians to be an encouragement to each other, since all of them are on this journey of hope and expectation as they await Christ's second coming. This is our task as well, as we await the coming of our Lord Jesus Christ.

GOSPEL | Our Gospel reading for today is another parable about the end times. As a reminder, parables are fictional stories that establish a comparison—for example, "the kingdom of heaven is like . . ."—and that involve common, everyday images to communicate their meaning. But parables are also riddles designed to make the reader think deeply about their meaning, and this parable of the talents has several details to make people shake their heads in amazement. For example, the amount of money trading hands in this parable is stupendous! In the ancient world, the value of a talent varied by location and composition, but one example of the estimated value of a talent was 80 pounds of silver, which had an equivalent value of 6,000 denarii, where a denarius was a full day's wages for most workers. Really! Who gives a servant or employee five talents or perhaps the equivalent of eighty-three years' wages to invest, while they go off on a journey to who-knows-where with no indication of when he will return?

One can imagine that the investment activities of the first and second servants were aggressive, even ruthless, because doubling investments as large as these by righteous means is highly unlikely. Why then does the master praise them? Perhaps

Since you were **faithful** in **small matters**,
  I will give you **great responsibilities**.
Come, **share** your **master's joy**.'
Then the **one** who had received the **one talent** came **forward**
    and **said**,
  '**Master**, I **knew** you were a **demanding person**,
  harvesting where you did not **plant**
  and **gathering** where you did not **scatter**;
  so out of **fear** I went **off** and **buried** your **talent** in the **ground**.
Here it is **back**.'
His master **said** to him in **reply**, 'You **wicked, lazy servant**!
So you **knew** that I **harvest** where I did not **plant**
  and **gather** where I did not **scatter**?
Should you not **then** have put my **money** in the **bank**
  so that I could have got it **back** with **interest** on my **return**?
Now then! **Take** the **talent** from him and **give** it to the **one**
    with **ten**.
For to **everyone** who **has**,
  more will be **given** and he will **grow rich**;
  but from the **one** who has **not**,
  even what he **has** will be **taken away**.
And **throw** this **useless servant** into the **darkness outside**,
  where there will be **wailing** and **grinding** of **teeth**.'"

[Shorter: Matthew 25:14–15, 19–21 (see brackets)]

The viciousness of the master, even though we expect it, is shocking.

Emphasis on "useless."

it is because these two servants are like him. The third servant describes the master as "a demanding person, harvesting where you did not plant and gathering where you did not scatter." In other words, the master's wealth comes from taking from others by force. In an honor/shame culture such as the first-century Mediterranean world in which this parable was created, an honorable person would not seek more than what was allotted to him, because it meant taking away what belonged to another. Perhaps this is why the master directed his servants to do his dirty work while he was away.

And what about the third servant? This parable appears among a collection of parables about the end time and how we ought to behave as we await the parousia, the return of the risen Christ. In the context of this story, we can imagine that the third servant did what he thought was prudent, especially given his relatively low status in society. He could not afford to lose the money placed in his care, so he buried it for safekeeping. The master's response is fierce and punishing, but it is not for the servant's unwillingness to take risks. Rather, it is because he considered the servant to be

lazy! Perhaps this is the message of this parable. We live in this in-between time still today, waiting for the master to return, and the worst thing we can do is sit around being lazy. What will you do to help advance the coming reign of God until its full glory will be revealed in the end time? C.C.

OUR LORD JESUS CHRIST, KING OF THE UNIVERSE

LECTIONARY #160

READING I   Ezekiel 34:11–12, 15–17

Ezekiel = ee-ZEE-kee-uhl

An expressive reading that elaborates the powerful metaphor of God as shepherd and believers as the sheep in his flock.

Note the emphatic repetitions of "I myself."

A reading from the Book of the Prophet Ezekiel

Thus says the **Lord G**OD:
  I myself will look **after** and **tend** my **sheep**.
As a **shepherd** tends his **flock**
    when he **finds** himself among his **scattered sheep**,
    so will I **tend** my **sheep**.
I will **rescue** them from **every place** where they were **scattered**
    when it was **cloudy** and **dark**.
I myself will **pasture** my **sheep**;
  I myself will **give** them **rest**, says the **Lord G**OD.

Note the rhythm of each line, beginning with a noun and ending with a verb for what God will do.

The **lost** I will seek **out**,
    the **strayed** I will **bring back**,
    the **injured** I will **bind up**,
    the **sick** I will **heal**,
    but the **sleek** and the **strong** I will **destroy**,
    shepherding them **rightly**.

The reading concludes with a mysterious claim.

As for **you**, my **sheep**, says the **Lord G**OD,
    I will **judge** between **one sheep** and **another**,
    between **rams** and **goats**.

READING I There are many aspects of our culture that attempt to overshadow the sovereignty of Christ in the world, yet today's readings draw our attention to the true power of God that will shine forth in the second coming of Crist and the judgment that will be placed on all peoples. This is an important reminder for us who live in the world: we belong to Christ, not to the ever-changing whims of culture, and must live in a way that reflects our citizenship in his kingdom.

Today's first reading comes from the longer parable of the shepherds (Ezekiel 34:1–31) in the Book of Ezekiel. In the verses that immediately precede this reading, Ezekiel delivers a woe oracle—that is, a warning, against the shepherds of Israel who have been taking advantage of the sheep, ruling harshly against them and not caring for the sick, injured, or lost among them. The metaphor of kings and leaders as shepherds and their constituencies as sheep had long been in use in the Mediterranean world, so people knew well what Ezekiel was talking about. Here, Ezekiel is blaming the king and religious leaders of Judea for the fate of God's peo-ple, scattered about in exile and metaphor-ically eaten by wild animals.

As we pick up today's reading, we hear Ezekiel giving voice to God's word against the shepherds of Israel, who did such great harm to God's people. The imag-ery of God as shepherd is very evocative and can be seen in other Old Testament passages (for example, see Genesis 48:15; Psalm 23; Isaiah 40:11; Jeremiah 31:10). Imagine God collecting his scattered sheep that have been battered and bruised in exile, feeding the hungry ones, tending the sick among them, and providing a place for

For meditation and context:

RESPONSORIAL PSALM   Psalm 23:1–2, 2–3, 5–6 (1)

R. The Lord is my shepherd; there is nothing I shall want.

The Lord is my shepherd; I shall not want.
   In verdant pastures he gives me repose.

Beside restful waters he leads me;
   he refreshes my soul.
He guides me in right paths
   for his name's sake.

You spread the table before me
   in the sight of my foes;
you anoint my head with oil;
   my cup overflows.

Only goodness and kindness follow me
   all the days of my life;
and I shall dwell in the house of the Lord
   for years to come.

READING II   1 Corinthians 15:20–26, 28

A reading from the first Letter of Saint Paul to the Corinthians

Corinthians = kohr-IN-thee-uhnz

An urgent reading from Paul, no less complex for its urgency. Pace your proclamation; there is a lot to absorb here.

Emphasis in these two lines on "man."

Note the sequence of the "proper order" in which death will be defeated.

Brothers and **sisters**:
Christ has been **raised** from the **dead**,
   the **firstfruits** of **those** who have **fallen asleep**.
For since **death** came through **man**,
   the **resurrection** of the **dead** came **also** through **man**.
For just as in **Adam all die**,
   so too in **Christ** shall **all** be brought to **life**,
   but **each one** in **proper order**:
   Christ the **firstfruits**;
   then, at his **coming**, **those** who belong to **Christ**;
   then comes the **end**,
   when he **hands over** the **kingdom** to his **God** and **Father**,
   when he has **destroyed** every **sovereignty**
   and every **authority** and **power**.
For he must **reign** until he has put **all** his **enemies under**
      his **feet**.
The **last enemy** to be **destroyed** is **death**.
When **everything** is **subjected** to him,
   then the **Son himself** will **also** be **subjected**
   to the one who **subjected everything** to him,
   so that **God** may be **all** in **all**.

TO KEEP IN MIND
Use the pitch and volume of your voice to gain the attention of the assembly.

Pause slightly after "death."

Slow your pace slightly at "all in all."

---

them to rest in safety after their long and harrowing ordeal. But not every sheep in a flock is good. The "sleek and the strong" is an allusion to members of the sheepfold who, like the bad shepherds, take advantage of the others for their own benefit. Immediately following this reading is an oracle about separating the bad sheep from the good, the rams from the goats (Ezekiel 34:17–24). Thus, this God who shepherds like a good and great king also judges justly. In summary, God says that he will take the sheep away from the bad shepherds and

take charge of the sheep himself, undoing the damage that the bad shepherds did.

READING II   Our second reading is from Paul's First Letter to the Corinthians, and it is part of his much longer teaching on resurrection of the body (1 Corinthians 15:1–58). Briefly, he argues that Christians who believe in Christ's resurrection must also believe that they will be resurrected bodily. Otherwise, there would be no triumph over death and sin would not be defeated.

In this reading, Paul presents Jesus as the firstfruits of those who are deceased. The term "firstfruits" represents the first and best of the harvest offered to God as a sacrifice in consecration of the entire harvest to God. To further illustrate this theme, Paul uses a method of biblical interpretation called typology, which compares an Old Testament person or event with a New Testament person or event, the former being merely a blueprint of the latter. Here Paul describes Adam as a type of Jesus Christ: Adam brought sin and death into the world for all humankind, while Jesus Christ

---

GOSPEL   Matthew 25:31–46

A reading from the holy Gospel according to Matthew

Jesus said to his **disciples**:
  "When the **Son** of **Man comes** in his **glory**,
  and **all** the **angels with** him,
  he will **sit** upon his **glorious throne**,
  and **all** the **nations** will be **assembled before** him.
And he will **separate** them **one** from **another**,
  as a **shepherd separates** the **sheep** from the **goats**.
He will place the **sheep** on his **right** and the **goats** on his **left**.
Then the **king** will **say** to **those** on his **right**,
  '**Come**, you who are **blessed** by my **Father**.
Inherit the **kingdom prepared** for you from the **foundation**
      of the **world**.
For I was **hungry** and you gave me **food**,
  I was **thirsty** and you gave me **drink**,
  a **stranger** and you **welcomed** me,
  naked and you **clothed** me,
  ill and you **cared** for me,
  in **prison** and you **visited** me.'
Then the **righteous** will **answer** him and **say**,
  '**Lord**, **when** did we **see** you **hungry** and **feed** you,
  or **thirsty** and **give** you **drink**?
When did we **see** you a **stranger** and **welcome** you,
  or **naked** and **clothe** you?
When did we see you **ill** or in **prison**, and **visit** you?'
And the **king** will **say** to them in **reply**,
  '**Amen**, I **say** to you, **whatever** you **did**
  for one of the **least brothers** of **mine**, you **did** for **me**.'

A reading in which, through a kind of visionary parable, Jesus reveals an apocalyptic vision of judgment. It involves repetitions that serve to reinforce the qualities of the vision.

Be attentive to the rhythms here.

These questions are asked in earnest.

---

brought life into the world for all peoples. Paul explains that this sacrifice of firstfruits begins with Jesus' resurrection and comes to its fullness with his return as the exalted Lord. When he comes, all who belong to Christ will also be resurrected. Then, having assumed his role as king, the risen Christ will destroy all other sovereignties and subject competing authorities to his power, until he destroys death itself. Then he will turn over his kingdom to God who is Lord over all, so that "God may be all in all." What a powerful image of God's peaceful kingdom to come!

GOSPEL   The Gospel reading for today gives us important insights into the nature of Christ's kingship and its relevance for our daily lives. This teaching is the last in a series of parables and teachings on the return of the risen Christ in the end time that are found in Matthew 24–25, after which Matthew unfolds for us the story of Jesus' arrest, crucifixion, death, and resurrection.

This teaching, which biblical scholars categorize as an apocalyptic discourse, has no parallel in the other Gospels. The word *apocalypse* means "revelation," and it usu-

ally refers to the revelation of heavenly realities to a human recipient through visions or auditions. The heavenly reality being revealed here is judgment day, when the righteous are separated out for reward and the wicked are separated out for judgment. The phrase "Son of Man" possibly has its origins in Daniel 7 or Zechariah 14, but, in the Gospels, it is spoken only by Jesus and applied to himself. Thus, when Matthew describes Jesus as saying, "when the Son of Man comes in his glory," Jesus is talking about himself and referring to the parousia, his return in glory after his resurrection.

Then he will **say** to those on his **left**,
  '**Depart** from me, you **accursed**,
  into the **eternal fire prepared** for the **devil** and his **angels**.
For I was **hungry** and you gave me **no food**,
  I was **thirsty** and you gave me **no drink**,
  a **stranger** and you gave me **no welcome**,
  naked and you gave me **no clothing**,
  ill and in **prison**, and you **did not care** for me.'
Then they will **answer** and **say**,
  '**Lord, when** did we see you **hungry** or **thirsty**
  or a **stranger** or **naked** or **ill** or in **prison**,
  and not **minister** to your **needs**?'
He will **answer** them, '**Amen, I say** to you,
  what you **did not do** for one of these **least ones**,
  you **did not do** for me.'
And **these** will go **off** to eternal **punishment**,
  but the **righteous** to."

Once again, be attentive to the rhythms.

Once again, the question is asked in earnest.

Note the clear contrast between "eternal punishment" and "eternal life."

The metaphors of the kingly Christ as both shepherd and judge are present in this text. The risen Christ comes to sit on his heavenly throne with all the nations—Jews and Gentiles—gathered around him, representing his universal kingship. Then, as a shepherd, he separates sheep from goats. The Greek word that is translated as "sheep" here can mean any small grazing animal, even small cattle. The Greek word that is translated here as "goat" is the diminutive of *erion*, meaning "wool," as in "little woolly creatures." Perhaps they are less desirable because they are not fully grown or have not reached their full potential. The sheep or the mature grazers are invited into the kingdom that has been prepared for them. The goats or "little wooly creatures" are told to depart from Christ's throne. Jesus even calls them "accursed," because, when it comes time for the final judgment, there are no do-overs; you are either mature and ready to enter God's kingdom or you are not. And what is the measure of readiness? It is that you perform the corporal works of mercy from your heart, with pure motive and without self-flattery or desire to curry favor with someone. Notice the similarities between Jesus' criteria for admission to the kingdom and the seven corporal works of mercy—feeding the hungry, giving drink to the thirsty, sheltering the homeless, visiting the sick and prisoners, burying the dead, and giving alms to the poor. C.C.